Doing Business in Emerging Markets

'This book is the ultimate companion for everyone interested in how to do business in emerging markets. With half of the globe's population living there, emerging economies contribute more to the world GDP than advanced nations and grow at a much faster pace. Having shaped and witnessed Turkey's transformation from import substitution to a liberal, export-oriented economy myself, I am fully conscious of the enormous potential as markets, traders, producers and even investors. Still, foreign companies actively engaging in emerging markets have to be aware of the political, legal, cultural and economic risks which their investments might entail. The attentive reader of this book will, however, be perfectly prepared for a most profitable step into the future of growth.'

Mesut Yilmaz
Former Prime Minister of Turkey

Doing Business in Emerging Markets

S. Tamer Cavusgil, Pervez N. Ghauri & Ayse A. Akcal

Los Angeles | London | New Delhi
Singapore | Washington DC

Los Angeles | London | New Delhi
Singapore | Washington DC

SAGE Publications Ltd
1 Oliver's Yard
55 City Road
London EC1Y 1SP

SAGE Publications Inc.
2455 Teller Road
Thousand Oaks, California 91320

SAGE Publications India Pvt Ltd
B 1/I 1 Mohan Cooperative Industrial Area
Mathura Road
New Delhi 110 044

SAGE Publications Asia-Pacific Pte Ltd
3 Church Street
#10-04 Samsung Hub
Singapore 049483

Editor: Mark Kavanagh
Editorial assistant: Ruth Stitt
Production editor: Rachel Eley
Marketing manager: Alison Borg
Cover design: Francis Kenney
Typeset by: C&M Digitals (P) Ltd, Chennai, India
Printed by: CPI Group (UK) Ltd, Croydon, CR0 4YY

Library of Congress Control Number: 2012935778

British Library Cataloguing in Publication data

A catalogue record for this book is available from
the British Library

MIX
Paper from
responsible sources
FSC FSC® C013604
www.fsc.org

ISBN 978-1-84920-153-7
ISBN 978-1-84920-154-4 (pbk)

Summary of Contents

List of Boxes, Figures and Tables   xiii
About the Authors   xix

1   An Overview of Emerging Markets   1
2   Political, Legal and Cultural Framework
    in Emerging Markets   29
3   Economic Environment in Emerging Markets   62
4   Opportunities and Trends in Emerging Markets   91
5   Companies from Emerging Markets   117
6   Analysis of Selected Emerging Markets   145
7   Entry Modes and Strategies   204
8   The Negotiation Process and Strategies
    in International Business   254
9   Negotiations and Building Relationships in
    Emerging Markets   288
10   Assessing Risks and Opportunities in Emerging Markets   325

Appendix: Information Sources in Emerging Markets   349
References   353
Index   388

Contents

List of Boxes, Figures and Tables   xiii
About the Authors   xix

1 An Overview of Emerging Markets   1

What are Emerging Markets?   3

The Emerging Market Outlook   7

Trade and Foreign Investment in Emerging Markets   10

Common Features of Emerging Markets   14

 Demographic Characteristics   14

 Political and Economic Characteristics   17

 Market Characteristics   20

Emerging Markets and Multinationals' Global Strategy   21

 Emerging Economies as Growing Markets   21

 Emerging Markets as Manufacturing Bases   23

 Emerging Markets as Competitors   25

Factors Effecting International Business   25

**2 Political, Legal and Cultural Framework
in Emerging Markets**   29

Political Systems in Emerging Markets   29

 Types of Political Systems   30

 The Influence of Political Systems   32

Legal Systems   32

 Legal Systems under Islamic Law   33

 Risks Due to Political and Legal Systems   33

 Protectionism   34

 Property Rights   37

Ethical Issues 38

Informal Economy 40

Managing Political and Legal Risks in Emerging Markets 41

Structural Reforms in Emerging Markets 44

Government Involvement in the Financial Sector 45

Trade Reforms 46

Financial Crises and Reforms in Emerging Markets 47

Environmental and Cultural Differences in Emerging Markets 50

Understanding Cultural Differences 50

The Meaning of Culture 50

High and Low Context Cultures 53

Elements of Culture 54

Contemporary Changes Affecting Culture 57

Networks and Emerging Market Culture 58

Managing Cultural Issues 59

3 **The Economic Environment in Emerging Markets** 62

Differences in the Economic Environment
in Emerging Markets 62

Institutional Voids 63

Infrastructure Gaps 66

Income Distribution 68

Business Groups 71

Challenges Facing Emerging Market Economies 84

Integrating the Population into the Workforce 84

Developing Institutions 84

Reducing the Dependency on Advanced Economies 85

4 **Opportunities and Trends in Emerging Markets** 91

The Growth of Middle Income and the Rise in Consumption 92

The Growth of Mid-sized Cities 94

Rural Development 98

Services in Emerging Markets 99

Technology and Telecommunications 100

A Decrease in Gender Inequality 101

Investments in Infrastructure 102

Environmental Responsibility 104
Taking Advantage of Opportunities in Emerging Markets 105
Adapting Business Models to Emerging Markets 110
Business at the Bottom of the Pyramid 111

5 Firms from Emerging Markets **117**
Characteristics of Emerging Market Firms 121
Assets of Emerging Market Firms 121
Challenges to Emerging Market Firms 127
The Internationalization of Emerging Market Firms 131
Motives for Internationalization 132
The Internationalization of State-owned Enterprises 137
The Direction of Emerging Market Firm
Internationalization 137

6 An Analysis of Selected Emerging Markets **145**
Foreign Investment 145
Doing Business in Emerging Markets 147
The Global Financial Crisis of 2008 148
BRIC Economies 150
Brazil 153
Russia 158
India 161
China 164
New Frontier Economies in Latin America 167
Mexico 170
Peru 174
Chile 176
New Frontier Economies in Asia 178
Thailand 182
Indonesia 184
Malaysia 187
The Philippines 189
Pakistan 191
New Frontier Economies in Other Regions 194
South Africa 195
Egypt 199
Turkey 201

7   Entry Modes and Strategies   **204**
   Entry Strategies for Emerging Markets   204
      Market Entry Objectives   205
   An Overview of Entry Strategies   206
   Trade-based Entry Strategies   208
      Exporting   208
      Bidding for Global Tenders   214
      Global Sourcing and Outsourcing   222
   Contract-based Entry Strategies   227
      Licensing   228
      Franchising   229
      Technology Transfer Projects   231
      Management Contracts   231
      Contract Manufacturing or Subcontracting   232
      Turnkey Projects   232
      Infrastructural Projects   233
      Countertrade   233
      Non-equity Collaborative Ventures   235
   Investment Entry Modes   238
      Marketing Subsidiaries   238
      Joint Ventures   238
      Wholly-owned Entry Strategies   240
   Factors Influencing Entry Strategy   244
      Costs in Entry Decisions   246
      Cultural and Institutional Distance   248
      The Liability of Foreignness   248
      Control and Commitment   249
      Timing of Entry   250

8   The Negotiation Process and Strategies
   in International Business   **254**
   Preparing for Success   258
   Self-knowledge   259
   Understanding Your Partner   259
      Political and Social Factors   260
      Cultural Factors   261
      Strategic Factors   264
      Creating Alternatives   265

A Framework for International Business Negotiations   265
  Background Factors   266
  Atmosphere   268
  The Negotiation Process   269
  What is a Good Outcome?   275
Building Bridges: The Negotiating Process   276
  Communication Types   276
  Verbal Versus Nonverbal Communication   277
  It's All in the Tongue   279
  Safety in Numbers   280
Strategies for the Global Negotiator   281
  Understand the Needs of the Other Party   282
  Stick to the Issues   282
  Build up Relative Power   283
  Don't Reduce Your Own Bargaining Position   284
What Makes a Good Negotiator?   285
  Building Relationships   286

**9 Negotiations and Building Relationships in
Emerging Markets**   288
Negotiations in Emerging Markets   288
Negotiating in BRICs   292
  Brazil   292
  Russia   293
  India   294
  China   295
Negotiating in Asia   298
  Thailand   298
  Malaysia   299
  Indonesia   299
  Pakistan   300
  The Philippines   301
Negotiating in Latin America   302
  Mexico   302
  Peru   303
  Chile   303
Negotiating in Africa   304

South Africa   304

Egypt   305

Negotiating in Turkey   305

Developing and Managing Relationships in Emerging Markets 306

Selecting Partners and Distributors in Emerging Markets   307

Selecting a Foreign Partner for a Collaboration/Joint Venture 308

Selecting a Foreign Distributor   313

Managing Relationships in Emerging Markets   318

Managing Relationships with Foreign Partners   318

Managing Relationships with Foreign Customers   319

Managing Relationships with Foreign Governments   320

Managing Relationships with Expatriates   321

Managing Relationships with Foreign Communities   323

**10 Assessing Risks and Opportunities in
Emerging Markets**   **325**

Strategic Alignment for Internationalization   326

Company Capabilities: Finding a Fit   326

Company Competitiveness   331

Evaluating the Potential of Emerging Markets   334

Analysing Data in Emerging Markets   335

The Availability and Interpretation of Information   336

Indices on Emerging Markets   338

Appendix: Information Sources in Emerging Markets   349

References   353

Index   388

List of Boxes,
Figures and Tables

Chapter 1   1

Box 1.1   Who are emerging markets   3
Figure 1.1 Relations between developed and emerging markets   8
Figure 1.2 Emerging market growth   10
Figure 1.3 Trade growth   13
Figure 1.4 Dependency ratio in BRICs   16
Figure 1.5 Education in emerging markets   17
Figure 1.6 Consumption in emerging markets   22
Figure 1.7 The international marketing task   26

Table 1.1   Trends in emerging markets   2
Table 1.2   Who are emerging markets?   4
Table 1.3   BRICs and New Frontier Economies   6
Table 1.4   Top 20 countries ranked by GDP (US$)   9
Table 1.5   World output (top 20 countries)   11
Table 1.6   Population breakdown   15
Table 1.7   Exposure to emerging markets   23
Table 1.8   Global Manufacturing Competitiveness Index   24

Chapter 2   29
Box 2.1   Contexts in emerging markets   35
Box 2.2   Rising protectionism   36
Box 2.3   Government influence on business – an example   42

Box 2.4   State capitalism   49
Box 2.5   Hofstede's dimensions and BRICs   52
Box 2.6   Indian culture   60

Figure 2.1 Worldwide governance indicators   39
Figure 2.2 Hofstede's dimensions and BRICs   53

Table 2.1   The International Property Rights Index 2000–2010   38
Table 2.2   High–Low context cultures   55

Chapter 3   **62**
Box 3.1   GE healthcare in India   65
Box 3.2   Income distribution   70
Box 3.3   Tata's transformation under Ratan
            Tata's leadership   75
Box 3.4   Lessons from Pakistan   77
Box 3.5   National champions – Brazil and China   78
Box 3.6   Business groups in China   80

Table 3.1   The Logistics Performance Index   69
Table 3.2   The income gap in emerging markets, 2005   71
Table 3.3   Largest business groups in EMs, 2007   72
Table 3.4   Summary of privatization transactions
            over US$1 million   77
Table 3.5   World R&D expenditure   88

Chapter 4   **91**
Box 4.1   Income distribution projections in BRICs   93
Box 4.2   Business model adaptation
            to EMs – the Danfoss example   106
Box 4.3   Differences between consumers in China   108
Box 4.4   e-Choupals in India   115

Figure 4.1 Growth in investment and consumption in EMs   92
Figure 4.2 Increased consumption in BRICs   92

Figure 4.3   Income distribution projections in BRICs   93

Figure 4.4   Consumer expenditure in BRICs   96

Figure 4.5   Technology penetration in BRICs   101

Figure 4.6   Urbanization in EMs   103

Table 4.1   Forecast on the growth of middle-income
             ($6,000–30,000) populations   95

Table 4.2   Consumer expenditure in new frontier
             economies (in US$ million)   97

Table 4.3   Spending habits of BoP consumers, 2005   113

Chapter 5   **117**

Figure 5.1   Foreign investment by state-owned
             enterprises   138

Table 5.1   EM brands included
             in the Global 500 in 2011   119

Table 5.2   Strategies of firms from emerging markets   120

Table 5.3   Foreign investment from emerging markets   132

Table 5.4   South-to-South foreign direct investment   141

Table 5.5   South-to-North foreign direct investment   142

Chapter 6   **145**

Box 6.1   The change in economic output in the BRICs   152

Figure 6.1   The change in economic output in the BRICs   152

Figure 6.2   Breakdown of employment in the BRICs   156

Table 6.1   Export and import growth in emerging
             markets and developed countries   146

Table 6.2   Growth indicators in the BRICs   150

Table 6.3   Greenfield FDI projects in BRIC
             economies, 2003–2011   151

Table 6.4   Change in economic output in the BRICs   153

Table 6.5   Major strengths and weaknesses of the BRICs   154

Table 6.6   Average share of exports
in BRIC economies, 2004–2009   155

Table 6.7   Infrastructure and urbanization in the New Frontier
Economies of Latin America   169

Table 6.8   2011–2030 growth forecasts for the
New Frontier Economies of Latin America   170

Table 6.9   Major strengths and weaknesses of the New Frontier
Economies of Latin America   171

Table 6.10   Growth indicators and forecasts for New Frontier
Economies in Asia   179

Table 6.11   Infrastructure and urbanization
in New Frontier Economies in Asia   180

Table 6.12   Major strengths and weaknesses
of New Frontier Economies in Asia   181

Table 6.13   Export performance inNew Frontier Economies in Asia 182

Table 6.14   Major strengths and weaknesses
of New Frontier Economies in other regions   196

Table 6.15   Growth indicators and forecasts
for New Frontier Economies in other regions   197

Chapter 7   **204**

Box 7.1   What is the difference between export management
companies and export trading companies?   210

Box 7.2   The 10 most common mistakes of potential
exporters   211

Box 7.3   Exporters' priorities in selecting intermediaries   212

Box 7.4   Intermediaries' expectations from exporters   213

Box 7.5   Guidelines for marketing to emerging
economies   221

Box 7.6   Motives for global sourcing   223

Box 7.7   Contract based (non-equity) modes – key
advantages and drivers of growth   228

Box 7.8   Advantages and disadvantages of licensing   229

Box 7.9   Advantages and disadvantages of franchising   230

Box 7.10   Motives for entering into strategic alliances   236

Box 7.11   Factors affecting FDI location decisions   241

Figure 7.1   Process of marketing in emerging
              markets: bidding for local tenders   215

Figure 7.2   Strengthening buyer–seller linkages   217

Table 7.1   Summary of advantages and
              disadvantages of different entry strategies 245

Table 7.2   Examples of challenges
              in doing business internationally   247

Table 7.3   Locational determinants
              and relevance for FDI and non-equity modes   252

Chapter 8   **254**

Box 8.1   Potential irritants – words and phrases to avoid   283

Figure 8.1   A framework for international business negotiations 266

Table 8.1   Cultural dimensions in the negotiation process   262

Chapter 9   **288**

Box 9.1   The Chinese 'yes no'   296

Box 9.2   What are the goals of a cross-cultural
              training programme?   322

Figure 9.1   Facilitative relationships in emerging markets   307

Figure 9.2   Selecting a foreign distributor   314

Figure 9.3   Strategic approaches to government relations 321

Table 9.1   Regional differences in the negotiation process   289

Chapter 10   **325**

Box 10.1   Functions and processes that
              can be used in a competitive assessment   333

Box 10.2   Economic freedom scores, 2011   339

Figure 10.1   Key processes and decisions in going international   327

Figure 10.2   How to align company capabilities and
              make internationalization a business strategy 332

Figure 10.3   An example of a company
               doing business in emerging markets   335

Table 10.1   Economic freedom scores, 2011   340
Table 10.2   Investment freedom scores, 2011   342
Table 10.3   The Trade Restrictiveness Index, 2008   343
Table 10.4   The Ease of Doing Business Index, 2009   344
Table 10.5   Dimensions of the Market
               Opportunity Index (MOI) and Data Sources   346
Table 10.6   The Market Potential Index (MPI)
               for Emerging Markets, 2010   347

About the Authors

S. Tamer Cavusgil is Fuller E. Callaway Professorial Chair and Executive Director, CIBER, Georgia State University, Atlanta, GA. Tamer specializes in the internationalization of the firm, global strategy, emerging markets, and buyer-seller relationships in cross-border business. His professional career spans teaching, research, and administrative responsibilities in international business at Michigan State University, Bradley University, the University of Wisconsin, and the Middle East Technical University (Turkey). He has authored more than a dozen books and over 190 refereed journal articles. His work is among the most cited contributions in international business. His books include *International Business: The New Realities*, 2nd edition, co-authored with G. Knight and J. Riesenberger. Tamer holds MBA and PhD degrees in business from the University of Wisconsin.

Professor Pervez N. Ghauri completed his PhD at Uppsala University in Sweden where he also taught for some years. At present he is Professor of International Business at King's College, London. He is also a Fellow of the European International Business Academy. Recently, he was awarded an honorary Doctorate by the Turku School of Economics and Management, Finland. Pervez has published 25 books and numerous articles. He consults and offers training programmes to a number of organisations, such as BP, Airbus Industries and Ericsson. He is Editor in Chief for *International Business Review* and Editor (Europe) for the *Journal of World Business*.

Ayse A. Akcal is a Research Associate at King's College, London. Ayse completed her undergraduate degree at Yale University, USA, as a double major in Economics and Philosophy in 2000. Prior to her academic career, she worked as an auditor in Andersen, Istanbul, a financial analyst in Finansbank (Holland) N.V., and a manager in the risk analysis unit of Citigroup, Istanbul. Ayse has an MBA from Imperial College, UK, and is a PhD candidate at King's College, London. Her research focuses on the determinants of firm performance, firm capabilities, and internationalization, her PhD is centered on the analysis of emerging market firms.

ONE An Overview of Emerging Markets

Introduction

Economic and political developments are rapidly transforming our world and prompting us to consider more global perspectives. Social and cultural changes are helping us renegotiate our identities as well as our values, shaping our vision of the future. Communication and information technologies continue to shrink geographical distances and put more of the world's knowledge at our fingertips. Undoubtedly, the challenges ahead of us will be formidable, but the opportunities in a globalizing world are simply too great to ignore. Our potential to succeed in this exciting environment will depend on our ability to recognize and act on these opportunities.

Over the next two decades, most of the world's growth is expected to occur in today's emerging markets (EM). Many countries which were associated with high levels of volatility and risk have now liberalized and reformed. Once thought of as backward and 'low tech', these countries are now rapidly transforming their economies. By adopting new technologies and production techniques, countries such as China, Brazil and India have become important locations for production. As purchasing power continues to increase with development in these countries they are becoming important consumer markets as well. Parallel to the rapid growth, they are also increasingly becoming competitors. While developed countries are faced with limited growth options and high costs of production, emerging markets are growing rapidly and at a faster pace. Thus, in the 21st century, the focus of international business has shifted towards analysing emerging markets, and identifying opportunities within these markets. Table 1.1 summarizes the changes in the emerging market environment in the past decade.

Table 1.1 Trends in emerging markets

Developing countries (prior to 2000)	Emerging markets (2000 and beyond)
High risk for foreign business	Risks are increasingly manageable
Economically and technologically backward	Technologically competitive
Consumers had poor purchasing power	Increasing purchasing power among consumers
Few opportunities for business	Offer many opportunities, as large untapped markets and low-cost, high-quality sources
Unpredictable growth patterns	Higher income growth than developed nations

For Western managers struggling to sustain growth, cut costs and launch new products and industries, emerging markets can be an ideal answer. With literacy and education levels rising, skilled labour in these countries is relatively inexpensive. Over the next several years, millions of new consumers in these emerging markets will desire and be able to afford Western goods. Western firms can even enhance their capabilities in new markets. The old notion that developing countries are inherently risky for foreign businesses is no longer true. Conditions are continuing to stabilize, and our ability to predict and manage these risks has improved. Many factors have led to an increased focus on emerging markets in international business. The key factors are as follows:

1 Market potential is no longer too small for marketing efforts. Maximum population growth and infrastructure development rates are predicted for emerging economies. The size of the market is huge as over 80% of the world population resides in emerging markets and cannot be ignored.
2 Many emerging economies are investing in infrastructure development, especially in transportation, power and communication. This has helped bring down the costs of selling in emerging markets.
3 Though some emerging markets have highly differentiated structures, the demand forecast has become easier, with professional consulting and advertising organizations established in most of these markets.
4 Many emerging economies have developed or accessed technologies that have made them competitive on a global basis. More and more managers in emerging economies are training themselves with modern management tools and skills, and this has made production planning much simpler.

5 With governments in emerging economies providing full support for foreign investment, reaching business agreements is no longer a cumbersome process. Though intercultural differences remain in some countries, more and more managers have realized the value of creating global 'win–win' relationships and alliances. Many Western managers have started learning foreign languages and have a better understanding of foreign cultures. Also, many local managers have been educated in the West and have gained vast experience in dealing with Western firms and cultures.

6 The information revolution has made more and more information available about emerging economies, and business strategy formulation has become a lot easier.

What are Emerging Markets?

Terms such as 'developing markets', 'emerging markets' and 'rapidly industrializing nations' are often used interchangeably, which often leads to confusion in understanding what emerging markets are. The term 'emerging market' was first used by Antoine van Agtmael, an economist in the World Bank, at the end of 1980s, to refer to rapidly growing economies with rapid industrialization (Van Agtmael, 2007). The lists of emerging markets change rapidly as the markets included are often selected according to growth indicators and projections on an annual basis. The lists also vary between institutions, as they all use a varied range of indicators and different growth projections when creating their emerging market lists. Table 1.2 displays some examples of emerging market lists generated by different institutions.

Box 1.1   Who are Emerging Markets?

The FTSE index breaks down stock market indices according to their development level; accordingly, the advanced emerging countries are Brazil, the Czech Republic, Hungary, Mexico, Malaysia, Poland, South Africa, Turkey and Taiwan. The secondary emerging countries are Chile, China, Columbia, Egypt, India, Indonesia, Malaysia, Morocco, Pakistan, Peru, the Philippines, Russia, Thailand and the UAE (FTSE, 2012).

   MSCI, a global provider of investment decision support tools, classifies the emerging markets of Brazil, Chile, Colombia, Mexico and Peru as part of the

(Continued)

(Continued)

Americas; the Czech Republic, Egypt, Hungary, Morocco, Poland, Russia, South Africa and Turkey as within the Europe, Middle East and Africa region; and China, India, Indonesia, Korea, Malaysia, Taiwan and Thailand within the Asia region. This classification is based on the size of the companies, and market accessibility. With this framework, information such as market capitalization, openness to foreign ownership, efficiency of operational framework and the stability of the institutional framework is considered (MSCI, 2012).

Grant Thornton has created an index called the 'Emerging Markets Opportunity Index', using indicators such as GDP, size, population, international trade and future growth projections (Grant Thornton, 2010), while Goldman Sachs considers BRICs and other emerging markets, referring to the 'Next Eleven' as those economies which will grow rapidly in the 21st century, and their list consists of Bangladesh, Egypt, Indonesia, Iran, Mexico, Nigeria, Pakistan, the Philippines, South Korea, Turkey and Vietnam. This list is based on macroeconomic and political stability and openness to trade, as well as education levels (Wilson and Stupnytska, 2007).

Table 1.2   Who are emerging markets?

	FTSE	MSCI	S&P	Goldman Sachs	Grant Thornton
Algeria					x
Argentina					x
Bangladesh				x	x
Brazil	x	x	x	x	x
Chile	x	x	x		x
China	x	x	x	x	x
Colombia	x	x			x
Czech Republic	x	x	x		
Egypt	x	x	x	x	x
Hungary	x	x	x		x
India	x	x	x	x	x
Indonesia	x	x	x	x	x
Iran				x	x
Korea		x		x	
Malaysia	x	x	x		x
Mexico	x	x	x	x	x
Morocco	x	x	x		
Nigeria				x	x
Pakistan	x			x	x
Peru	x	x	x		x
Philippines	x	x	x	x	x
Poland	x	x	x		x
Romania					x

	FTSE	MSCI	S&P	Goldman Sachs	Grant Thornton
Russia	x	x	x	x	x
South Africa	x	x	x		x
Taiwan	x	x	x		
Thailand	x	x	x		x
Turkey	x	x	x	x	x
UAE	x				
Ukraine					x
Vietnam				x	x
Venezuela					x

Emerging markets are countries which are in a transition phase from developing to developed markets due to rapid growth and industrialization. Hence, markets which have (a) started an economic reform process aimed at alleviating problems, for example of poverty, poor infrastructure and overpopulation, (b) achieved a steady growth in gross national product (GNP) per capita, and (c) increased integration in the global economy, may truly be called EMs.

To differentiate between less developed and emerging markets, growth figures as well as increased levels of improvement in living standards may be considered. Commitment to sustained growth, continuous efforts to catch up with the industrialized nations and an increased presence in world trade distinguish between EMs and developing markets.

In discussions on EMs, the term 'BRIC' is often used. BRIC, as identified by Jim O'Neill of Goldman Sachs in a paper published in 2001 (O'Neill, 2001), stands for Brazil, Russia, India and China. These economies are the fastest growing and may potentially overtake the world's largest economies (Goldman Sachs, 2003). BRIC economies currently constitute 25% of the world's land mass and 42% of the population (Wilson et al., 2011b). The contribution of BRICs and other EMs to the global economy has been increasing rapidly. They are continually investing in education and technology, increasing foreign investments, and focusing on integrating themselves in the global economy as major players. For the purposes of this book, we have identified 11 countries in addition to the BRICs which have been growing steadily, industrializing rapidly, and becoming significant markets, investors, traders and producers within the global economy. These countries, which are shown in Table 1.3, will be referred to as 'New Frontier Economies' throughout this book (the selection criteria for this are summarized in

Table 1.3 BRICs and New Frontier Economies

	GDP ($ billion), 2009	GDP per capita, PPP ($) 2009	GDP growth (%) 2005-2009	Average GDP per capita growth (%) 2005-2009	Population (million), 2009	Investment inflow ($ billion), 2009	Urbanization
WORLD	58,259	10,686	8%		6775	1164	50%
Developed Countries	41,608	36,408	5%		1117	804	76%
Share Held by Developed Countries	71%				16%	69%	
				Developed Countries			
USA	14,119	45,989	5%	2%	307	135	82%
Japan	5,069	32,418	3%	2%	128	12	67%
Germany	3,330	36,338	5%	4%	82	39	74%
France	2,649	33,674	7%	3%	63	60	78%
UK	2,175	35,155	1%	2%	62	73	90%
				BRICs			
Brazil	1,594	10,367	25%	5%	194	26	86%
Russia	1,232	18,932	21%	13%	142	37	73%
India	1,377	3,296	18%	9%	1155	35	30%
China	4,985	6,828	27%	14%	1331	78	44%
Share Held by BRICs	16%				42%	15%	
				New Frontier Economies			
Chile	164	14,311	14%	4%	17	13	88%
Egypt	188	5,673	25%	7%	83	7	43%
Indonesia	540	4,199	21%	7%	230	5	53%
Malaysia	193	14,012	12%	5%	27	1	71%
Mexico	875	14,258	4%	3%	107	14	78%
Pakistan	162	2,609	13%	5%	170	2	37%
Peru	130	8,629	17%	8%	29	5	72%
Phillipines	161	3,542	17%	5%	92	5	66%
South Africa	285	10,278	7%	5%	49	2	72%
Thailand	264	7,995	13%	4%	68	5	34%
Turkey	615	13,668	12%	6%	75	8	69%

Note 1). In the table, average growth rates of these economies within the period 2005–2009 highlight their increased contribution to world growth and further emphasize the potential of these countries in the future. The table also presents important indicators for selected advanced economies to enable comparison. In the table, PPP stands for purchasing power parity.

The Emerging Market Outlook

Recent developments in the global business environment have been unprecedented. Barriers to trade and investment have been reduced over the past decades and this trend is expected to continue as national economies further integrate. Markets have been increasingly liberalizing, especially following the collapse of the Soviet Union's economy, and India's and China's free market reforms. Developments in IT, which can mainly be identified as developments in communications and computing, have undeniably changed the business structure around the globe. Increased globalization of our economies has allowed technology and capital to become very mobile. As the cost of moving a segment of production elsewhere in the world has decreased substantially, production chains have been reconfigured globally. In EMs, market liberalization, together with increased political stability, economic and legal reforms, has led to a more productive business environment and increased foreign investment inflow. In a more productive business landscape, these markets are growing rapidly. Figure 1.1 shows the relationship and trade linkages between developed and emerging economies.

As the economies of the industrialized countries mature, the growth rates of these economies are becoming stagnant. The global financial crisis of 2008 has also affected the economies of industrialized markets adversely. On the other hand, rapid growth can be observed in the economies of EMs. As they grow, economic power and influence is bound to shift towards these countries (Bernanke, 2010). The size of the Indian economy is expected to be larger than those of Japan and the UK within the next two decades, while the size of the economies of Brazil, Mexico and Indonesia is expected to surpass most European countries and Japan by 2050 (Magnus, 2010). Table 1.4 shows the top 20 countries ranked according to their GDP, starting from 1990. BRICs and New Frontier Economies are highlighted in this table.

EMs have been contributing to world GDP more than advanced economies, and their contribution is expected to increase. In fact, IMF estimates reveal that EMs will account for 48% of the world gross domestic production (GDP), which is estimated as US$90,452 billion by

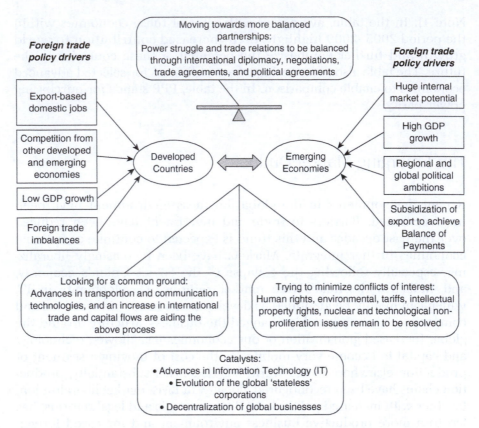

Figure 1.1 Relations between developed and emerging markets

2016, while they accounted for 21% of GDP in 2000, which was around US$32,227 billion at the time (IMF, 2011b). The World Bank estimates a global GDP growth of 2.5% in 2012 and 3.1% in 2013. Within these predictions, growth from EMs and developing countries is expected to be at higher rates, estimated as 5.4% in 2012 and 6.6% in 2011, while the growth rate estimations for developed countries in the same periods are 2.8% and 2.4% respectively (World Bank, 2011c). In terms of GDP, BRICs accounted for more than 50% of the global growth between 2003 and 2007, which shows a significant increase from 2003–2007 where the same figure was approximately 27% (Wilson et al., 2011a). As such, it is clear that EM contribution accounts for more and more of the growth in world production. This difference is more pronounced when GDP figures are considered in terms of PPP. In Figure 1.2, the contribution of EMs and forecasts depicting their performance in the near term can be seen. The weight of EMs in the global economy has increased at higher rates than developed countries, and their contribution is also expected to increase rapidly in the near future, as is also shown in the figure as well.

Table 1.4 The top 20 countries ranked by GDP (US$)

1990	1995	2000	2001	2005	2006	2007	2008	2009	2010
USA	USA	USA	USA	USA	USA	USA	USA	USA	USA
Japan	Japan	Japan	Japan	Japan	Japan	Japan	Japan	Japan	China
Germany	Germany	Germany	Germany	Germany	Germany	China	China	China	Japan
France	France	UK	UK	UK	China	Germany	Germany	Germany	Germany
Italy	UK	France	France	China	UK	UK	France	France	France
UK	Italy	France	China	France	France	France	UK	UK	UK
Canada	Brazil	China	Italy	Italy	Italy	Italy	Italy	Italy	Brazil
Spain	China	Italy	Canada	Canada	Canada	Spain	Russia	Brazil	Italy
Russia	Spain	Canada	Mexico	Spain	Spain	Canada	Brazil	Spain	India
Brazil	Canada	Brazil	Spain	Brazil	Brazil	Brazil	Spain	India	Canada
China	Korea	Mexico	Brazil	Mexico	Russia	Russia	Canada	Canada	Russia
India	Netherlands	Spain	Korea	Korea	Mexico	India	India	Russia	Spain
Australia	Russia	Korea	India	India	Korea	Korea	Mexico	Australia	Mexico
Netherlands	Australia	India	Netherlands	Russia	India	Mexico	Australia	Mexico	Korea
Korea	India	Australia	Australia	Australia	Australia	Australia	Korea	Korea	Australia
Mexico	Switzerland	Netherlands	Russia	Netherlands	Netherlands	Netherlands	Netherlands	Netherlands	Netherlands
Sweden	Mexico	Argentina	Argentina	Turkey	Turkey	Turkey	Turkey	Turkey	Turkey
Switzerland	Belgium	Turkey	Switzerland	Belgium	Belgium	Sweden	Poland	Indonesia	Indonesia
Belgium	Argentina	Switzerland	Belgium	Switzerland	Sweden	Belgium	Indonesia	Switzerland	Switzerland
Austria	Sweden	Sweden	Sweden	Sweden	Switzerland	Switzerland	Belgium	Belgium	Poland
Turkey	Austria	Belgium	Turkey	S. Arabia	Indonesia	Indonesia	Switzerland	Poland	Belgium
Argentina	Indonesia	Austria	Poland	Poland	S. Arabia	Poland	Sweden	Sweden	Sweden
Finland	Denmark	S. Arabia	Austria	Austria	Poland	Norway	S. Arabia	Austria	S. Arabia
Denmark	Turkey	Poland	S. Arabia	Norway	Norway	S. Arabia	Norway	Norway	Norway
Norway	Thailand	Hong Kong	Norway	Indonesia	Austria	Austria	Austria	S. Arabia	Venezuela

Source: World DataBank, 2011.

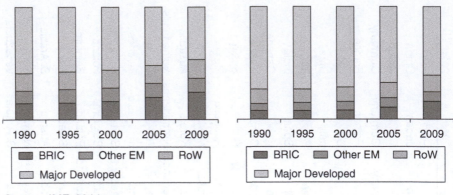

Source: IMF, 2011a.

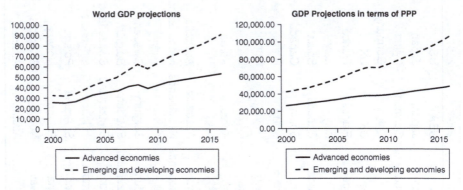

Figure 1.2   Emerging market growth
Source: IMF, 2011a.

As of 2008, China has surpassed the USA in terms of manufacturing output; meanwhile, other EMs such as India, Brazil, Turkey, Mexico, Indonesia and Thailand contribute to world output significantly, as can be seen in Table 1.5.

Trade and Foreign Investment in EMs

Lower trade barriers and global economic integration have led to a dramatic increase in world trade levels since the second half of the 20th century. In parallel to the increased importance of trade in most countries' economies, governments started focusing on easing trade restrictions globally. The General Agreements on Tariffs and Trade (GATT) was signed in 1947 by 23 countries, of which Brazil and India represented EMs. GATT was

Table 1.5   World output (top 20 countries), 2008 (US$ billion)

Largest industrial output		Largest manufacturing output		Largest services output	
USA	3073	China	1850	USA	10562
China	2104	USA	1831	Japan	3036
Japan	1282	Japan	1011	Germany	2517
Germany	1101	Germany	855	France	2215
UK	634	Italy	424	UK	2022
Russia	625	UK	360	China	1734
Italy	622	France	341	Italy	1635
France	584	Russia	293	Spain	1096
Spain	463	Brazil	281	Brazil	1029
Brazil	440	S. Korea	257	Russia	970
Mexico	404	Spain	242	Australia	694
S. Korea	345	Canada	210	Mexico	643
India	334	Mexico	203	Netherlands	635
S. Arabia	329	India	202	India	622
Australia	295	Indonesia	140	S. Korea	560
Indonesia	246	Turkey	132	Turkey	468
Netherlands	222	Netherlands	127	Belgium	383
Norway	209	Australia	110	Poland	341
Turkey	203	Thailand	106	Sweden	338
Poland	163	Switzerland	101	Switzerland	302

Source: *The Economist*, 2011b.

a significant move towards settling trade issues such as tariffs, non-tariff barriers, trade balancing requirements and local content requirements globally, however it did not have any binding power over the member states. Thus, GATT was replaced by the World Trade Organization (WTO), which has the power to settle disputes between members.

The WTO, especially by establishing the Doha Development Agenda, aims to concentrate on the needs of developing countries (Busse, 2009). The issues which developed countries want to focus on in these proceedings can be outlined as trade facilitation, transparency within governments, competition policies, and investment governance. The purpose of the Doha round initially was to enable a fair-trade environment for developing economies. The negotiations agenda was later expanded to include the protection of intellectual property (Gifford and Montemayor, 2008).

Following the initial conference, the Cancun conference – which was designed to agree upon the purpose of the Doha round – failed, as the differences in opinion of members from developed countries and developing countries became more pronounced. At the time of writing, the issues within the Doha round have still not been resolved. The main issues preventing the resolution are: agriculture, compulsory licensing and patent protection, differential treatment for developing countries, and the implementation of the agreements reached in WTO negotiations (Schwab, 2011).

Yet due to the lower tariffs advocated by organizations such as the WTO, many EM countries are also able to fuel growth via increased export levels. In addition to the WTO, over the past few decades, various trade agreements – such as the North American Free Trade Agreement (NAFTA), the Association of South East Asian Nations (ASEAN) and the Latin American free trade regime (MERCOSUR) – have led to trade gains (Ghauri and Cateora, 2010). Recent changes in policy indicate that the trend towards liberalization is likely to continue in the near future, as in 2009, 71 out of 102 policy changes on foreign investments were globally focused on the promotion of foreign investment (WIR, 2010).

At the end of the 20th century, many EMs were faced with financial crises mainly due to reasons such as high deficits, excessive borrowing and an overdependence on foreign capital, which led them to restructure their institutions. Another effect of these crises on some EMs, such as Thailand, Malaysia and Indonesia, was the shift in their development strategy towards export-led growth in order to generate trade surpluses (Magnus, 2010). Asian countries such as China and India, motivated by the economic success of neighbours such as Japan and Korea, started opening up their economies in order to fuel growth. China's entry into the WTO in 2001 has particularly affected the global trade balance. EMs, especially in Asia, focused on export-led growth in a similar way to the Asian Tigers in the 1960s, shifting from import substitution to export promotion. This strategy was successful due to increased efficiencies stemming from globalization and the high consumption levels in developed countries leading to a continuous demand for imports (Magnus, 2010).

Another factor which facilitated the increased involvement of EMs in international trade was the reorganization of production (Buckley and Ghauri, 2004). As companies locate each of their activities in the most suitable location, manufacturing trade grows. For instance, in 2009 over half of the world merchandise trade, excluding oil products, involved intermediate goods (WTO, 2011b). The movement of manufacturing processes to EMs has also led to increased production and increased exports from these markets. As of 2009 China has become the largest exporter of merchandise, while the USA preserved its status as the leading merchandise importer followed by China (Economist, 2011b).

World trends towards increased trade, a shifting of production, and increased EM policy focusing on export revenues have all instigated a rapid growth in exports in EMs. In 1997, exports were US$4,257 billion for advanced economies versus US$1,279 billion in emerging and developing economies. Such a gap has since decreased substantially – as of 2008, the figures were US$9,811 billion and US$6,215 billion respectively (IMF

Statistics Database, 2011). Developing countries including EMs accounted for 45% of the world exports in 2010 (WTO, 2011b). Export volumes of EMs, as well as their involvement in world trade, have been increasing more rapidly than those of developed countries, as can be seen in Figure 1.3.

Growth prospects in EMs, fuelled by increased liberalization, have led to increased investment inflows to EMs (WIR, 2010). In 2008, foreign direct investment (FDI) levels to developed markets decreased by over 30%. On the other hand, foreign investment to EMs increased by 11%. In 2009, the decline in foreign investment to developed countries was much deeper than the decline to EMs, due to the disproportionate effects of the global crisis. In fact, EMs and developing economies attracted more foreign direct investment than developed economies for the first time in 2009 (Sauvant et al., 2011).

Multinational enterprises (MNEs) are increasingly investing in developing and emerging markets in order to generate cost efficiencies. Investment in these economies is also increasing due to the shift in consumption and the emergence of such economies as potential markets (UNCTAD, 2011). Following the global financial crisis, multinationals further increased investments in developing and emerging markets as the growth prospects in their own markets narrowed. Hence, in 2010, 49% of the investment by developed country MNEs was in developing and emerging markets, which showed a radical increase from 32% in 2007 (WIR, 2011). EM attractiveness for foreign direct investment is significantly affected by economic conditions, the regulatory framework, and the promotion of foreign investment. Of these factors, economic growth of the market is regarded as the most important driver for foreign direct investment (Sauvant et al., 2011).

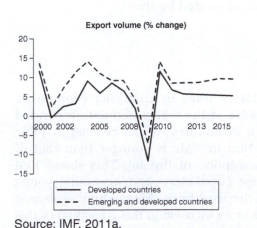

Source: IMF, 2011a.

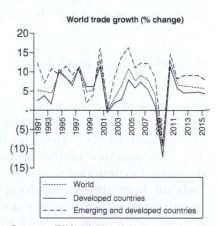

Source: EIU, 2011.

Figure 1.3 Trade growth

In terms of the type of foreign direct investments, non-equity forms of investment are growing rapidly around the globe. In 2009, cross-border, non-equity mode transactions were estimated to be US$2 trillion. Within this total, US$1.1–1.3 trillion is due to contract manufacturing and services outsourcing, US$330–350 billion to franchising, US$340–360 billion to licensing, and US$100 billion to management contracts. Non-equity modes of production employ approximately 18 billion workers, of which 14–16 billion are in developing countries and EMs. Over 50% of global trade in toys, clothing and footwear, and electrical goods is due to contract manufacturing (WIR, 2011). In 2010, global foreign direct investment inflows increased by 5% to reach US$1.24 trillion, from US$1.185 trillion in 2009. FDI to developing countries also increased by 16% (World Bank, 2011c). The recovery was due to a gradual increase in cross-border merger and acquisition activity as the investments in greenfield ventures decreased in 2010. Modest increases in foreign investments are largely due to the cautious approach of MNEs in the aftermath of the global crisis in 2008 (WIR, 2011).

Common Features of Emerging Markets

In defining EMs, large populations, rapid growth in GDP, and an increased contribution to world trade can be identified. Such markets are also characterized by progressive economic reforms and expectations of accelerated economic expansion. Even though EMs are very different from each other in terms of culture, political and economic characteristics, market structures, and demographic structures, some general trends can be identified in order to understand the rise of such markets, as well as the opportunities and challenges presented by them.

Demographic characteristics

Over half of the world's population lives in emerging economies. Figures for 2009 indicated that 42% of the world population resided in BRICs and 14% in new frontier economies, as can be seen in Table 1.3. The structure of the population in EMs is younger than that of developed economies (with the exception of Russia). This shows that EMs all have sizeable working-age populations and upcoming young populations who will soon enter the workforce. Meanwhile, economic growth within these markets leads to an increase in this education of this upcoming labour force, thereby providing a source of human talent.

Another key demographic trend in EMs is the growing rates of urbanization. Urbanization is another result of economic growth and the focus on industrialization. As the weight of agriculture is reduced within EM economies job opportunities are provided with economic growth, urbanization rates have been increasing rapidly. For instance, in 1990 the urbanization rate was 75% for Brazil, 27% for China, 26% India and 31% Indonesia. By 2010, these rates had increased to 87%, 45%, 30% and 54% respectively (World DataBank, 2011). Growth in urbanization indicates the movement of populations from low-income agricultural work to rural-based activities such as higher income industrial jobs. The changing population framework also leads to an increase in the demand for infrastructure, housing, and services in cities (WEO, 2010). As can be seen in Table 1.6, working-age population in EMs is already large. The growth of the urban population results in continuous growth of the workforce in industrial production.

Table 1.6   Population breakdown

	Population growth (annual %)	Population aged 0–14 (% of total)	Population aged 15–64 (% of total)	Population aged 65 and above (% of total)	Urbanization (%)	Growth of urban population (%)
USA	0.86	20	67	13	82	2
UK	0.7	17	66	16	90	1
Brazil	0.91	26	67	7	86	2
Russia	-0.07	15	72	13	73	1
India	1.34	31	64	5	29	2
China	0.51	20	72	8	43	3
Mexico	1.01	28	65	6	77	2
Peru	1.13	30	64	6	71	1
Chile	0.98	23	68	9	88	1
Indonesia	1.15	27	67	6	52	3
Malaysia	1.66	30	66	5	70	3
Thailand	0.56	22	71	8	33	1
Philippines	1.79	34	62	4	65	3
Pakistan	2.14	37	59	4	36	3
Egypt	1.79	32	63	5	43	2
South Africa	1.07	31	65	4	61	
Turkey	1.21	27	67	6	69	2

Source: *The CIA World Factbook*, 2011. Available at: www.cia.gov/factbook/

The old-age dependency ratio shows the ratio of the population not in the labour force to the population in the labour force. The general trend estimated to increase in the long run is due to lower birth rates and higher life expectancy in most of the world. Figure 1.4 shows a comparison of the old-age dependency ratio projections of BRICs with those of Europe and North America. In looking at this figure, the dependency ratios of North America and Europe are consistently higher than the BRIC countries, with the exception of China after 2040. The higher old-age dependency ratios indicate an increased burden on the economy by increased government spending on social security, increased company spending on pensions, and the additional burden on the labour force of supporting higher pensions. Projections indicate that the share of working-age population is not bound to decline in most emerging markets until the 2030s (Magnus, 2008).

The relatively lower old-age dependency ratios of the BRICs then indicate the potential for these markets to be major consumers as well as the potential for continued economic growth. The Chinese trend line is significantly different and shows radical increases in the long run, due to the one-child policy endorsed by the government and the rapid decline in population growth.

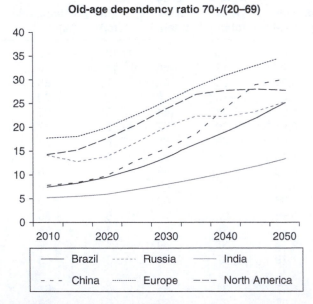

Old-age dependency ratio 70+/(20–69)

Figure 1.4   Dependency ratio in BRICs

Source: United Nations, Department of Economic and Social Affairs, population Division, 2011. World Population Prospects: 2010 revision, CD-ROM edition.

Favourable demographic conditions and increased welfare lead to increased education levels in many EMs. Higher education levels in the working population contribute to productivity (O'Neill, 2011). Figure 1.5 shows changes in spending on education and changes in literacy levels in BRICs over 30 years. As can be seen in the figure, expenditure on education has increased and this is especially so in China and Brazil. Moreover, literacy rates across the BRICs are rapidly growing and are now close to 100% in Brazil, Russia and China.

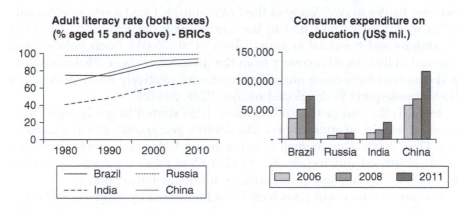

Figure 1.5 Education in emerging markets

Source: Euromonitor, 2012. Data retrieved 22 February 2012 from www.portal.euromonitor.com/(Euromonitor, 2012).

Looking back at Table 1.3, significant differences in GDP per capita between the EMs and industrialized nations can be observed. Even though per capita income shows a rising trend, the level of income in EMs is still significantly lower than that of developed economies. On the other hand, average per capita growth in major industrialized nations between 2005 and 2009 is between 2 and 4%, while this range is between 3 and 14% in EMs (World DataBank, 2011). An unequal distribution of wealth is observed in EMs, meaning a smaller percentage of the population holds the majority of the wealth and economic resources, leading to a large gap between rich and poor.

Political and economic characteristics

Over the past few decades, the fall of socialist economies in markets such as that of Russia and the movement towards more liberalized socialist economies such as exists in China have been cited as major changes in the world. Less pronounced are the similar movements towards more liberal economic policies in other EMs. Traditionally, the EM environment was characterized by protected domestic firms, high tariffs, weak institutions, conglomerates and business groups, and a turbulent climate delaying the entry of the MNE into these countries (Casanova, 2009). In the 1950s, many developing countries – maintaining protectionist policies and low levels of export income – were faced with the burden of subsidizing their economies by increased borrowing. Inefficient state-owned enterprises, as well as the constricted private sectors in these economies, further fuelled their economic downturn and contributed to increased debts which became harder to pay. Many of the EM countries faced a severe economic crisis in the 1990s and had to implement new policies ensuring better conditions and financial systems (Glick et al., 2001). Such policies also assisted in their rapid recovery from the financial crisis of 2008 and many EM countries have come out of the crisis with relatively fewer issues than their counterparts in developed nations (IMF, 2011b).

Towards the end of the 20th century, EMs started to go through structural reforms in an attempt to create stability and growth (Cuervo-Cazurra and Dau, 2008). Due to such reforms, many EMs stabilized their economies and started growing rapidly. As EMs adopt relatively open approaches to world trade, they integrate further with the global economy.

Economic reforms of EMs have been facilitated by external and internal influences. The regulations of trade institutions such as the WTO or credit-providing agencies such as the IMF have significantly contributed to the reforms. Such international institutions recommend and enforce a liberalization of trade, support regulations which contribute to a stable economic environment, and try to ensure that the market system is fair and efficient. Thus, such recommendations lead to the privatization of state-owned enterprises, the deregulation of industries, an opening up of borders to ensure fair competition, the enforcement of laws for the protection of intellectual property, and the implementation of sound fiscal and monetary policies (Aulakh and Kotabe, 2008).

The government's role in the economic development of these countries is substantial. The decision to open up borders and increase the focus on international trade, as well as allocating budgets to the advancement of the economy, has enabled the growth of EMs. In order to sustain this growth, many governments are still trying to ensure that democratic institutions are put in place to shield businesses from economic shocks (Rodrik, 2006), supporting policies towards market-based economies and creating opportunities which can contribute to economic growth. Faced with high budget deficits, governments were also incentivized to privatize state-owned enterprises. State-owned enterprises were mostly a burden on the state budget, and such enterprises – often very large – generally suffered from weak management while also preventing fair competition in their respective industries (Cuervo-Cazurra,

2006). With adequate planning and effective budgeting, successful governments from many EMs were also able to direct their budgets to develop the infrastructure necessary for economic growth.

The active participation of governments in economic activities can often be explained by ambitious developmental goals and historical factors (Magnus, 2010). A government may be involved indirectly through centralized economic planning, or involved directly in the economy through ownership of economic enterprises. The active economic role played by governments in emerging economies is evident in the private sector's ability to accumulate capital required for certain investments, in national and economic security issues, and in subsidizing a sector. The share of state-owned economic enterprises (SOEs) in most emerging economies is quite substantial, although the privatization of government-controlled enterprises is under way in many of them.

Most developed countries often question state control of the economy and advocate market-based economies. However, the effective response of the Chinese authorities in the face of the global financial crisis has challenged this notion and increased the sympathy for government involvement in finance and economic development (Magnus, 2010). A strong performance during the global financial crisis also enabled India to become one of the 10 largest economies in 2010 (Wilson et al., 2011a). China's economic stimulus package – amounting approximately to US$590 billion, emphasizing infrastructure projects and instigating financial institutions to increase loans – enabled the country to avert the effects of the global financial crisis (Magnus, 2010). Hence, especially following the global financial crisis, preheld notions about the superiority of market-based systems and strict beliefs about non-interventionist government policies are being challenged.

The economic growth rates of EMs are higher than those of developed markets. However, growth figures often lead to significant fluctuations as well as high inflation rates. Many multinationals historically avoided EMs due to the volatility associated with such markets. On the other hand, policy reforms in these markets leading to improved fiscal and monetary policies, as well as stronger financial markets, have reduced volatility significantly. Another factor which has decreased volatility is liberalization. As the markets are integrated into the world economy, external earnings decrease external debt. Moreover, output is not significantly affected by rapid changes in policy or in consumer demand within the domestic market, as companies are able to function in an open economy. Efforts at liberalization also give rise to the development of financial institutions (Enderwick, 2007).

Recent policy changes in EMs indicate a growing concern about environmental and social protection, which has resulted in limitations in some industries and a larger involvement by the state in some cases (WIR, 2010). Currently, even though sound investment conditions are emphasized in policies at higher levels, governments are also focusing on regulations which favour specific agreements, ensuring environmental safety as well as appropriate corporate conduct.

Market characteristics

Compared with developed economies, EM business systems are considered as being more relationship-based. First, family businesses are much more common and structures based on multiple firms operating together due to family ties are also frequent. Even when no family connection is present, the business structures are based on long-term relations, which can create entry barriers for multinationals in some cases. Relations with the government also gain precedence in many cases within EMs, as the government's involvement in market operation is greater than that of developed country governments (Khanna and Yafeh, 2007).

Wholesale distribution in many EMs is controlled by manufacturers or importers, thus creating formidable barriers to entry. New entrants soon discover that although their products may be a better buy, there is no way of distributing these through existing channels. Wholesalers tend to control the retail outlets in terms of their product portfolios and financing agreements. These wholesalers can dictate the product mix to retailers in the absence of fair-trade regulations and anti-trust laws. These market imperfections then result in highly controlled markets in which the buyer must purchase whatever is offered. The power of natural monopolies remains unchallenged in many cases because of their traditional ties to the government and each other.

Governments are trying to ensure that adequate infrastructure investments are made in order to support economic activity and also to accommodate growth in major cities. Hence, investments in infrastructure arise as an opportunity for multinationals and also signal the increasing future attractiveness of doing business in such markets (Airoldi et al., 2010). Infrastructure investment in cities with populations over 500,000 in EMs is predicted to be between US$30 trillion and US$40 trillion over the next 20 years (Jin et al., 2010).

MNEs also face problems regarding the availability of information in EMs (Hexter and Woetzel, 2007). Such issues are caused by institutional inefficiencies. Thus, MNEs need to consider and plan for challenges stemming from difficulties in reaching target customers, evaluating the creditworthiness of customers, collaborating with supply chain partners, hiring qualified personnel, raising funding, and finding reliable partners before entering into an EM (Khanna and Palepu, 2010).

Emerging Markets and Multinationals' Global Strategy

Emerging economies as growing markets

EMs have been contributing increasingly to global growth, fuelled by increasing levels of domestic demand. As these countries grow, rising income levels lead to the emergence of a new middle class which will affect the world economy and global demand significantly in the long run (Wilson et al., 2010). Parallel to the economic conditions, the consumption patterns of EM countries are changing with the rise of a new middle class. For instance, demand from the BRICs is expected to rise exponentially – Goldman Sachs estimates that India's GDP per capita will quadruple and the consumption of cars will increase fivefold, while the consumption of oil will increase threefold by 2020 (Wilson and Stupnytska, 2007).

Global players' firms are now fighting each other for resources, talent and capital in order to capture the needs of newly emerging customers. This will depend on their ability to innovate and distinguish the company, create new competitive resources, and defend such capabilities (Nunes and Purdy, 2008). One may imagine the effects of doing business in China for firms such as Coca-Cola, Caterpillar, Carrefour and Ericsson, which have successfully established themselves in this market. China attracts a high level of foreign capital, and investment in factories and manufacturing facilities, which leads to the creation of millions of jobs within the economy. In return, as exports increased fivefold within a decade, currency reserves have also reached record levels, indicating that China can further augment its economic growth by investing in its infrastructure. This rapid growth has led to increased incomes for Chinese consumers and the country has now become the world's largest market for many products such as cars and electronics.

Increased consumption is a major driver of growth in EMs. Long-term forecasts all suggest that BRICs, as well as other large emerging economies, will contribute more to growth, especially via the expanding numbers of the middle classes. The USA doubled its per capita income in 47 years starting in 1839, and the UK doubled its per capita income in 58 years starting in 1780. In contrast, Chinese income doubled in the nine years between 1978 and 1987. After 1987, the per capita income in China doubled again in the following nine years and the same pattern is continuing. India's rate has been somewhat lower, as per capita income doubled first over a 25-year period and then doubled again in the next 15-year period (Enderwick, 2007). Even during the global financial crisis, household spending in EMs increased by 8% in 2009 (IMF, 2011b).

In contrast, in advanced economies, consumer confidence and income declined. As can be observed in Figure 1.6, household expenditure in BRICs, as well as the NFEs, has been growing at higher rates than the world average. The growth of consumption is parallel to the growth of income, and the increased income also leads to a shift in consumption patterns and a greater focus on items such as clothing, which are not basic needs. Figure 1.6 also shows the increased expenditure on clothing and footwear in EMs. Considering that US and UK expenditure on clothing and footwear increased only by 17% and 28% between 2002 and 2010, the significance of the growth in EM spending can be highlighted. The only country which showed decreased expenditure on clothing and footwear in this period was Mexico, and the major reason for the decline can be attributed to the greater effects of the global financial crisis on this country.

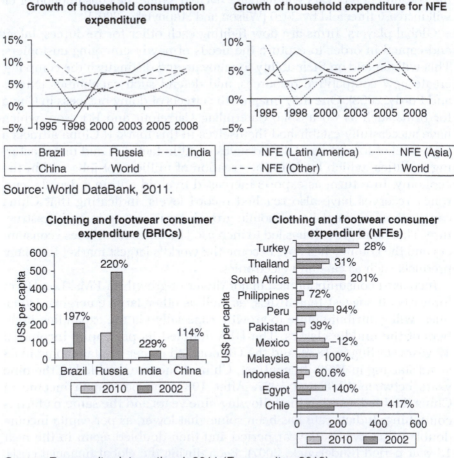

Source: World DataBank, 2011.

Source: Euromonitor International, 2011 (Euromonitor, 2012).

Figure 1.6   Consumption in emerging markets

Multinationals are increasingly focusing on EMs for growth. For instance, in the future, 70% of the income of large pharmaceutical companies is expected to come from EMs (BCG, 2011). Other examples can clearly be observed in Table 1.7. World leaders have already started building their markets in EMs.

Table 1.7   Exposure to emerging markets

Company	Percentage of operating income from EMs
Anglo American	91
Holcim	83
Toyota Motor	68
Barrick Gold	52
Coca-Cola	45
Anheuser-Busch InBev	44
Bayer	41
Unilever	36
British American Tobacco	27
Honda Motor	26
GlaxoSmithKline	25

Source: WIR, 2011.

Emerging markets as manufacturing bases

Increased competition among multinationals resulted in splitting value chain activities internationally at increasing rates during the 20th century. Increased levels of globalization enable today's companies to slice their operations and locate them in the least costly or most advantageous locations (Buckley and Ghauri, 2004). Partially due to lower costs and to more specialized capabilities, multinationals have been locating parts of their operations in EMs. As such, they are able to focus on their core competences, reduce costs, and benefit from the best suppliers of each activity, creating increased levels of efficiency. In this respect, EMs provide opportunities – both as suppliers and customers – to multinationals.

Developments in communication and transportation, along with availability of information, have greatly reduced the costs of procurement from other locations. In outsourcing, a firm can choose to work with independent suppliers or procure from its own subsidiaries. A firm decision to source from its own subsidiary, or from a joint venture that the firm is part of, is referred to as captive sourcing. Offshoring is a type of outsourcing where the vendor is not located in the same country as the company (Gottschalk and Solli-Sæther, 2006).

In choosing a location, the availability of infrastructure and skilled workers, as well as government incentives, play a large role (Farrell, 2007). In order to attract investment, many governments are offering incentives such as tax breaks, cheap land, easy access to energy sources, and duty-free imports (UNCTAD, 2000). Attracting investors who can invest in manufacturing facilities creates jobs in the EM economy and augments the growth of the supplier industries. Moreover, the ability to attract large investors also leads to further investments by suppliers.

The decision to move production facilities to EMs is often accompanied by concerns related to product quality. However, continued presence of multinationals in EMs has enabled them to increase efficiency and raise quality by implementing new technologies and training programmes in the manufacturing facilities. In fact, these manufacturing bases will often surpass the average productivity levels of the manufacturing bases in advanced countries and meet the quality targets of multinationals. Movement of production to EMs has resulted in increased specialization. For instance, Mexico and China are important platforms for manufacturing cars and electronics, Brazil for mining bauxite, Malaysia for semiconductors, and India and Pakistan for textiles (Cavusgil et al., 2008). EMs are also increasingly shifting their production to higher quality services and goods (Magnus, 2010).

Many developed countries experience issues related to diminishing workforces and an aging population, contrary to most EMs. Thus, the growing population within EMs provides not only a prosperous outlet for multinationals but also a potential area for tapping into a new workforce. Table 1.8 shows the drivers for relocating manufacturing to EMs.

Most of the EMs have thus become centres of outsourcing for Western companies. At present, about 40% of the world's software development

Table 1.8   The Global Manufacturing Competitiveness Index

Government forces	Market forces
• Regulations related to trade, finance and taxation • Efficiency of infrastructure • Government's policy on investments • Legal and regulatory systems	• Talent • Cost of labour and materials • Energy costs and relevant policies • Characteristics of the supplier network • Characteristics of the local business landscape

According to the Deloitte study on Global Manufacturing Competitiveness in 2010, conducted by interviewing 400 executives worldwide, the availability of talented labour and the cost of materials and energy were identified as the most important drivers augmenting the competitiveness of a country in manufacturing.

Source: Deloitte Touche Tohmatsu, 2010.

is being done in India. Most multinational companies (MNCs), from Intel to Microsoft, are moving their R&D activities to India. Between 2002 and 2005, 25.6% of all globally offshore R&D projects were based in India and 17.2% in China, while only 6.3% and 4.4% respectively were in the USA and UK (Huggins and Izushi, 2009). Most of the branded clothing companies are now producing in India and Pakistan. Companies such as Motorola, Intel and Philips are producing their semiconductors in Malaysia and Taiwan.

Emerging markets as competitors

Domestic firms in EMs provide intensive competition for multinationals trying to enter these markets. Most of the time, multinationals from developed markets concentrate on high-end markets due to higher competition at lower ends of the market. Local competitors possess a deep knowledge of consumers, and are able to operate at lower costs, and have built strong relations with authorities and have built other players within the value chain. Often, EM firms will have higher production efficiency than MNEs from developed markets, due to their ability to optimize production processes in EM conditions (Ramamurti, 2008). Meanwhile, multinationals from advanced economies are faced with markets dissimilar to their home economies in terms of business processes as well as customer profiles.

Some EM multinationals are catching up with their counterparts from developed economies and becoming global competitors. Such a phenomenon is further fuelled by these companies' efforts to invest in new processes as well as technologies. For instance, China and India have entered another economic arena, investing in innovation and R&D (Sachs, 2008). In parallel, many Chinese enterprises – faced with intensive domestic competition – are no longer relying on cost advantages, rather they are enhancing their technological bases to overcome competitive disadvantages in the domestic market (Yiu et al., 2007). There were approximately 560 companies with sales over US$10 billion headquartered in EMs in 2008, while this number was as low as 20 in 1990 (Magnus, 2010).

Factors Affecting International Business

The concepts of international business and international marketing are universally applicable, but the environments within which firms operate will vary. The environment includes market structure, political and legal forces, economic forces, the level of technology, the structure of distribution channels, and cultural and social characteristics. According to Ghauri and Cateora (2010), international marketing involves managing both controllable and uncontrollable elements, as illustrated in Figure 1.7.

In Figure 1.7, the outer circles show various uncontrollable elements of international markets. Uncontrollable elements are present both in domestic and international business. However, the scope and depth of these elements in international business make international transactions more complicated and comprise the internal decisions and marketing mix of the firm. The elements are very dynamic, involving dramatic social, economic, political and cultural changes with increasing uncertainty. This uncertainty can be reduced significantly by carefully studying the operating environments of each country the firm is planning to enter. Competition, economic restraints, government rules and regulations, infrastructure, and cultural factors are some of the uncontrollables that firms have to manage in foreign markets.

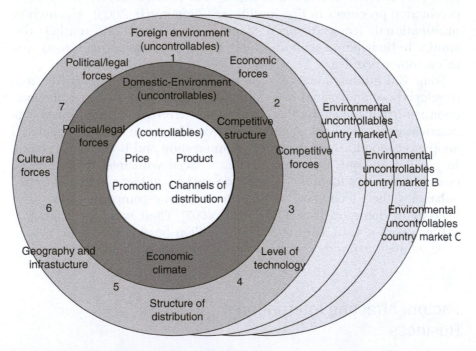

Figure 1.7   The international marketing task

Source: Ghauri and Cateora, 2010, p. 11.

Firms need to adjust and mould the controllable elements to the uncontrollable elements of a particular market. As illustrated by Figure 1.7, these uncontrollable elements differ drastically from market to market, and firms will face a new set of uncontrollables when they enter a new market. Some aspects of the international environment can be directly dealt with using basically identical marketing strategies, and experience in some regions can be helpful in addressing problems in another. Not only do firms need to manage and adapt to these uncontrollables in foreign markets, they also have to handle and adapt to the domestic uncontrollables, the second circle in Figure 1.7. A political decision at home (the domestic market) or an economic recession or boom at home may directly influence a company's international operation. In the same way, if economic conditions at home deteriorate, it may lead to restrictions on purchasing/imports from abroad in order to strengthen the domestic economy, but perhaps will then influence the competitive position of some of the domestic companies.

The economic, political and sociocultural character of the target market can affect the choice of entry mode and strategy. For example, many products can be deemed as luxury items in a market with low levels of economic activity or skewed economic activity, in which most people will live modestly or at a survival level. In many countries, there are dual environmental conditions. These dual economic structures – the coexistence of modern and traditional sectors in the economy – will create additional challenges for foreign firms. China, India and Pakistan are good examples of this idealism, in which people living in cities (some 25–30% of the total population) will demand modern Western-style products, while those in the traditional sector, living in rural areas, will demand more indigenous and simpler products. There are different market segments; each can prove profitable for a foreign company but may require different marketing programmes (Ghauri and Cateora, 2010). Moreover, external or bilateral economic relations will influence the complexity of the environmental impact of a company's entry strategy into a particular market.

The first part of this book analyses uncontrollable elements in an emerging market setting. In the second chapter, political/legal and cultural forces are discussed. The third chapter focuses on the economic environment in emerging markets, discussing technology, infrastructure, distribution, and income levels.

Chapter Questions

1 How do you define emerging markets? What are some of the common characteristics?

2 What are some of the reasons for increased importance of emerging markets in the global economy?
3 What do the current growth and characteristics of emerging markets show in terms of their future potential?
4 What is the role of emerging markets in a multinational's global strategy?

Note

1 In formulating a list of EMs for the purpose of this book, we have first considered the gross domestic product (GDP) figures, both in real terms and adjusted for purchasing power parity (PPP). PPP estimates take into account local living standards and local spending, therefore some economists consider PPP-adjusted measures as a more realistic measure of the comparison between countries. PPP correlates to the pricing in a given country. Especially in EMs, where consumer prices are low, the PPP is a better determinant of lifestyle. For instance, a Big Mac which costs US$3.73 in the USA costs US$2 in China, or US$2.20 in Thailand. In the future, sustained growth in EMs may lead to higher incomes, which will contribute to higher prices, and therefore converging differences in PPP between EMs and developed countries. However, currently price levels are different between EMs and developed countries, hence looking at figures in terms of PPP may give a better indication of the living standards and market growth in these economies (Magnus, 2010).

In categorizing countries as EMs, our first criterion leading to an exhaustive list of countries was based on GDP, PPP levels. From this list, we eliminated developed countries, members of the European Union, and economies intensively based on oil resources.

In narrowing down the list further, we considered market size factors such as five-year average growth in GDP in terms of PPP, and average growth in GDP per capita over a five-year period between 2005 and 2009. The first reason for focusing on averages in our calculations is to avoid biases due to abnormalities in a single year, and identify those countries with the growth potential. Considering that the figures for 2009 present an anomaly due to the effects of the global crisis, looking at the progression of markets over a five-year period is more accurate. In estimating size we also took urbanization levels into account, as urbanization can be an indicator of market potential in terms of consumption and production possibilities. The second reason for using average growth values over a period is due to our focus on the growth attribute of EMs. EMs currently offer many opportunities and their contribution to the global economy in the future is expected to increase continually. To be able to identify markets with continuous growth, we chose a longer-term approach. Another major criterion we used in narrowing down the list of EMs was the trade potential of a country, the growth in exports and imports, and the level of foreign investment attracted. In considering foreign direct investment inflows, we looked at the aggregate figures as well as foreign investment levels with respect to the size of the economy.

TWO The Political, Legal and Cultural Framework in Emerging Markets

Doing business in EMs exposes multinationals to legal and political systems of these markets. Firms need to adhere to laws and regulations in a given market. Country risk or political risk refers to the prevalence of adverse influences which may occur due to changes in a country's political and legal environments. In analysing markets, regulations which may lead to increased risks, as well as the strength of the enforcement mechanisms protecting the interests of the companies, must be considered (Cavusgil et al., 2008).

Political Systems in Emerging Markets

Political systems in a given country consist of a set of formal institutions forming the government and the interactions among these institutions. Thus, political parties, interest groups, trade unions and legislative authorities are parts of the political system (Ghauri and Cateora, 2010). Political systems govern the allocation of resources within a society, and aim to reduce external threats in order to ensure stability (Mühlbacher et al., 2006). In terms of the business landscape, the roles of the political actors are different in each country, ranging from high levels of control in economic activity by methods such as intervention or ownership of enterprises to minimal interference in the economy. The main political systems are totalitarianism, socialism and democracy; however, these are not necessarily mutually exclusive. Many political systems can have elements or be influenced by political systems other than their own (Cavusgil et al., 2008).

Types of political systems

The political system of a country shapes its economic and legislative framework, thereby the term 'political economy' can be used to emphasize the interrelated nature of a country's legislative, economic and political frameworks. Political systems can lean towards collectivism or individualism, and in the modern world each country's political system lies between these two concepts. Another descriptive characteristic of the political system is the position between democracy and totalitarianism (Cavusgil et al., 2008).

Socialism

A country's national culture is founded upon principles of collectivism or individualism. In collectivist systems, the common good is emphasized over the good of the individual. Thus, political systems which emphasize collectivism tend to focus on the wellbeing of the group, even if this means restricting the freedom of individuals within that group. Collectivist cultures emphasize groups and communities, envisioning each individual as an interdependent agent within the collective group (Parker et al., 2009). Nations with collectivist political systems then advocate socialism or communism and emphasize command economies. In a pure command economy, the government owns all businesses and decides on what should be produced, sold and allocated (Welzel, 2009).

Socialism is based on the Marxist ideology advocating that a fair distribution of products and wealth could be achieved by state ownership. This ideology stems from Marx's belief that the wealthy ruling class in a society can take advantage of the workers and oppress them if they have the power over production. This philosophy is strongly advocated in communist regimes, striving to achieve a classless society that has common ownership over the means of production (Magstadt, 2010).

Today, social democracies are prevalent and they uphold the principles of collectivism. Modern social democratic systems maintain a capitalist mode of production while promoting socialist ethics and focusing on a welfare state. Social democracy has influenced Western nations as well as many emerging markets.

Individualism/free market

In contrast to collectivism, individualism stresses the interests of the individual over the group. The tenet of individualism is that the wellbeing of society can be increased if individuals are allowed to act out of their own economic interests. In this system, states emphasize freedom of speech and expression, and equality before the law, independent of the political system. Political systems influenced by individualism lean towards free market economies and democracy (Stanley, 2005). In a market economy, capitalism ensures the private ownership of the means of production. Market forces determine economic activity and government involvement is limited. The main feature of democracy is the ability to own tangible or intangible property, thus accumulating one's own wealth, which is protected by private property rights. Limited government involvement in the economy is also another distinct feature of democracy (Devinney, 2010). Democracy is associated with economic freedom within a given country, and the ease of commercial activity without interference by the regulative authorities.

Totalitarianism

In democratic systems, governments will consist of representatives elected by the people, while in totalitarian systems a person or a party will have absolute control over people without opposition. Totalitarian systems emphasize a group's or an individual's absolute right to power and deny people the right to question their authority. A totalitarian government has authority over economic activities, as well as the ideologies of constituents. Most widespread examples of totalitarian states have been communist totalitarians ruled by communist parties (Hill, 2011). Even though most totalitarian states have shifted their political systems towards democracy, former totalitarian states are still associated with higher levels of government intervention and political control.

The Influence of Political Systems on Economic Systems

In countries which emphasize individualism, the economic system is based on a market economy, while in countries where collectivist systems are prioritized, command economies are prominent. In a market economy, state ownership is minimal and all production is undertaken by private enterprises (Megginson and Netter, 2001). The market functions independent of state interventions on the basis of matching supply with demand. In order for this equilibrium to be achieved, monopolies which can set prices or limit supply are restricted. Governments encourage private ownership and outlaw monopolistic practices (Hill, 2011).

In a command economy, the government allocates resources for the welfare of society, meaning that it plans the production of goods and services as well as the pricing of products. Most command economies have not been successful, due to reduced incentives in the absence of private ownership, in addition to the inefficiencies associated with state ownership of enterprises (Hill, 2006).

Mixed economic systems are observed more often than pure command economies. A mixed economy falls between a command economy and a market economy, as parts of the economy will consist of privately held enterprises while government ownership and planning can be observed in other parts (Aswathappa, 2005). Most EMs will have mixed economies. These have been moving towards market economies since the end of the 20th century by privatizing major state-owned enterprises.

Legal Systems

The legal system of a country is the mechanism which enables the interpretation and enforcement of laws. The legal system includes institutions which maintain order, enforce legal rights, resolve conflicts, and protect property rights. The major legal systems in the world are civil law, common law, and religious law. However, many countries have developed variations of these systems. Civil law (or code law) is based on a written set of rules which are generally divided into commercial, civil, and criminal law. In contrast, common law is based on tradition, past practices, and legal precedents set by the courts. In a religious law system, the law is based on religious teachings (Schaffer et al., 2008).

Contract laws enforce obligations generated by contracts. Differences between common law and civil law are highlighted in disputes stemming from contracts. Under common law, detailed contracts are required in order to account for all contingencies; further, the common law system allows for interpretations in specific situations. In contrast, civil law contracts are brief, as the civil code covers the relevant issues and judges are required to apply the civil code directly without leaving room for individual circumstances. In international trade, disputes will arise due to the trade relations between countries with common and civil law systems. To reduce such issues, the United Nations Commission on International Law developed the United Nations Convention on Contracts for the International Sale of Goods (CIGS) in 1980 (Hill, 2006).

Legal systems under Islamic law

Islamic laws are founded on the holy book of Islam. Although Islamic law is intended to cover moral law, today it has been extended to cover many commercial activities. The main tenets of Islamic economic law are the illegality of interest and the fact that investments in some businesses are considered unethical or immoral. One of the main examples of the practice of Islamic law is the illegality of interest (Riba), which is forbidden by the religion. Today, there are many banks that practise Islamic banking and use a profit-sharing system instead of charging interest (Hassan and Lewis, 2007).

Many Islamic commercial laws are based on practices targeting profit sharing which are referred to as 'Mudharabah', where the investor provides the capital for the business, and collects a portion of the profits in the future. Cost-plus systems can also be used in Islamic finance instead of interest. For instance, in a typical Mudharabah transaction, if a consumer goes to an Islamic bank to obtain a mortgage, the bank may buy the asset in question and resell the asset at a higher price to the consumer (Hesse et al., 2008). In 2009, assets in compliance with Islamic Law increased by 29% and amounted to US$822 billion (Economist, 2009).

Risks due to political and legal systems

Political risk stems from the probability of adverse effects on a multinational's business due to political events in the host country. Factors – such as breach of contract, expropriation, political violence, revolution, sabotage, terrorism and restrictions on currency transfer – are among political risks (Glaeser et al., 2004). Such risks may also arise due to political issues, elections, and changing attitudes within a society. As the political system of a country is closely connected to the legal system, knowledge of the political environment is necessary for an effective legal environment (Djankov et al., 2003). Political risks may relate to seizing a multinational's assets or, more commonly, to explicit or implicit actions by the government against set contractual obligations (Doh et al., 2009). Expropriation is the practice of taking over companies and transferring them to state ownership, or the practice of transferring foreign investments to national controls (also known as domestication). In the current economic climate, expropriation is rarely practised (Ghauri and Cateora, 2010).

Most often, political instability, the weak protection of intellectual property, bureaucracy and a lack of transparency, as well as partner availability, will be cited as challenges when doing business in EMs (Cavusgil et al., 2008). In many cases, even when laws are in place, the enforcement of those laws may not be efficient. As a result, counterfeiting, pirating, violating copyright and a lack of patent protection can be potential issues. Risk in doing business in EMs – ranging from inadequate infrastructure to strenuous legal systems and cumbersome bureaucracies – is declining. Political, legal reforms, along with EM governments' desire to attract foreign investment, reduce such risks.

Protectionism

Though the ideal political government for a multinational is a stable government which welcomes foreign investment, such is often not the case. Even when governments are friendly, adverse changes may occur due to elections or the government response to an emerging pressure. Thus, a company needs to assess the political climate before entering a market and monitor any changes closely after entry as well. Many political risks stem from nationalism, which is based on the preservation of a country's economic independence. Nationalism can lead to a restriction on imports, tariffs and barriers to trade in order to promote the consumption of domestic products. Alternatively, countries may restrict foreign investors' entry and demand that they can only invest in the country as the minority interest partners of joint ventures with locals. Many countries also demand that a percentage of the content of a product should have local content (Ghauri and Cateora, 2010). Examples of other risks stemming from the political environment are: exchange controls when the government restricts the flow of funds; tax controls when taxes are raised without warning; pricing controls when the government sets prices; or labour problems when countries control the labour practices of a firm.

In EMs, government involvement is more than regulatory; however, it is being reduced gradually. The share of state-owned economic enterprises (SOEs) in most emerging economies is quite substantial, although the privatization of government-controlled enterprises is also under way in many of them. Railways, oil production, coal, steel industries, banking, shipping and airlines are controlled by the government in many countries (Kołodko, 2003). Box 2.1 focuses on the importance of analysing the political structure of EMs.

Box 2.1   Contexts in Emerging Markets

Corporations will build knowledge related to a prospective market through available data such as GDP, growth or PPP, and utilize indexes such as the transparency index to assess risks. In many cases, they may be drawn to a certain EM by their customers, suppliers, or other relationships. However, such analysis needs to be more concentrated on the market that the company is trying to assess, and the company needs to focus on the institutional factors which may affect its operations.

In considering EMs, multinationals need to consider institutional contexts such as political and social systems and the openness of markets, labour markets and capital markets as they relate to their own operations. To analyse political and social systems, managers can evaluate bureaucracy levels, levels of centralization, the prominent players in political frameworks, and the country's trust in those political frameworks. In assessing political systems, the company can look at corruption levels, the accountability of political systems, power distribution, and the protection of rights.

A country's restrictions related to investments, as well as the procedures necessary for launching investments, can signify the level of openness. In this way, the company can better identify the structure within the company's power centres such as the regulators, media and civil societies, and ascertaining potential effect of different actors on their future operations. Many countries will regulate the formation of joint ventures with locals as a precondition of entry. Still, openness measures will need to be analysed further in order to estimate the true effects. For instance, investing in China is relatively easier than investing in India, however India is more globally oriented and open to ideas from the West. A deeper analysis of the openness of a country can also shed light on the development of the markets as intermediaries, as markets that are open to investment are more advanced.

Adapted from Khanna et al. (2011).

Active participation by the government in economic activities can often be explained by ambitious developmental goals and historical factors. The government is involved indirectly through centralized economic planning, in addition to being directly involved in the economy through its ownership of economic enterprises. Government intervention increases the concentration in these economies, in the sense that business deals are not made with individual buyers but with bureaucrats in various government agencies (Luo, 2002a). It is common practice for international marketers to start sales calls with civil servants in the capital city instead of with the actual buyer. As in the old adage, 'All roads lead to Rome', all major deals in EMs will go through the government.

In some EMs, the government may be biased in favour of local players in order to protect local industry (Xie and Wu, 2003). Governments may choose to protect the domestic industry, especially if the domestic company is a large employer or a national champion. Protection may also arise due to the local company's networks and connections with the government (Montiel, 2011).

Governments are also able to assist or hinder trade through multiple tools – such as financial assistance, tax refunds, tariffs, non-tariff barriers, tax costs and incentives – in order to promote the preferred type of foreign investment. Such indirect actions can also increase the difficulties in doing business for multinationals (Schaffer et al., 2008). Still, direct or indirect protectionist measures are observed not only in EMs but are also very significant considerations in doing business in developed markets. Box 2.2 provides a recent example of increased protectionism.

Box 2.2   Rising Protectionism

China's growth, and especially its export growth which is twice the rate of economic growth, is creating concern worldwide. The financial crisis of 2008–2009 led to a contraction in global demand, so China's increase in exports and its growth model are alarming many Western economies who would argue for a revision in countries' growth plans. Major Asian economies – which are also increasingly dependent on China's economy – are voicing political and economic concerns.

In contrast, the Chinese government is concerned with job creation in order to maintain domestic stability. As such, the government is not likely to change its growth plan just to respond to the needs of other governments. Elsewhere across the globe, protectionist sentiments are building up as more regulations are demanded for the financial industry, along with greater protection for domestic economies. Those companies which were nationalized during the crisis may as well be kept as they are, in order to maintain their domestic own-ership structure. Even though governments state that they will not be taking protectionist measures in order to support their economies in the aftermath of the financial crisis, they may be forced to do so due to increased political pres-sures from their constituents.

Adapted from Eurasia Group, Top Risks, 2011.

Property rights

Property rights are legal rights over a resource and the income which is generated from that resource. A company's intellectual or industrial property is among its most important assets (Ghauri and Cateora, 2010).

Intellectual property (IP) refers to property created by intellectual activity, and the owners of the intellectual property are granted exclusive rights on that property by obtaining patents, copyrights, or trademarks (Onkvisit and Shaw, 2008). IP includes inventions, literary works and music, as well as designs used in commerce (Hill, 2011).

In EMs, the endorsement of IP laws presents a major issue. However, many EMs are taking measures to increase IP protection in their markets. Table 2.1 shows the International Property Rights Index (IPRI) for selected economies. The index values are derived by a consideration of various factors, such as a country's legal and political environment, the protection of physical and intellectual property rights, the protection of patents and, levels of copyright piracy. Within the IPRI index, legal and political environment factors measure the extent of judicial independence from political and local influence. Rule of law measures the quality of law enforcement, while political stability observes the incentive to obtain property and trust in the rights to the property (IPR, 2010).

Inefficient enforcement of IP laws hurts EM economies in the long run. Multinationals will refrain from transferring know-how in some cases for fear of losing that same know-how. In other cases, they will refrain from investing in the economy altogether, in order to protect their IP. Moreover, limited IP protection in EM economies can also lead to a reduction of investment in intellectual property by nationals. In contrast, strengthening IP protection may benefit EMS. For instance, Mexico increased its focus on IP protection following the emergence of NAFTA, which resulted in an increased investment from developed countries totalling US$217 billion between 1999 and

Table 2.1   The International Property Rights Index 2000–2010

2000	IPRI score	Rank	2010	IPRI score	Rank
Argentina	3.7	95	Argentina	4.4	84
Brazil	4.7	62	Brazil	5.1	64
Chile	6.8	27	Chile	6.4	34
China	4.4	72	China	5.1	64
Colombia	3.8	89	Colombia	5	67
Egypt	4.7	62	Egypt	5	67
India	4.8	60	India	5.5	53
Indonesia	3.7	95	Indonesia	4.1	97
South Korea	6.1	40	South Korea	6.8	24
Malaysia	5.7	45	Malaysia	6.1	41
Mexico	4	83	Mexico	4.7	72
Pakistan	2.5	120	Pakistan	3.9	104
Peru	3.6	100	Peru	4.3	88
Philippines	3.5	104	Philippines	4.5	80
Russia	3.3	107	Russia	4.3	88
South Africa	5.7	45	South Africa	6.8	24
Thailand	4.4	72	Thailand	5.2	59
Turkey	4.7	62	Turkey	5.2	59
Venezuela	1.9	122	Venezuela	3.2	121

Source: International Property Rights
Index, 2000.

Source: International Property Rights
Index, 2010.

2008. Such an amount provided opportunities for technology transfers and led to an increase in the quality of products within the country (IPR, 2010).

Ethical issues

In addition to protection and intervention levels, the efficiency of a government, as well as its effectiveness in regulating the business landscape,
arises as an issue in EMs. Often, high levels of bureaucracy and red tape
will lead to inefficiencies, resulting in a loss of time and funds (Cavusgil
et al., 2008). Figure 2.1 exemplifies the difference between the governance efficiency of developed economies as compared with the BRIC
economies. As clearly observed, control of corruption, enforcement of
regulation, government effectiveness and citizen participation in government selection are very low in BRIC economies, highlighting the
many risks stemming from governance. Still, when looking at these estimates, one must take into account that the comparison is between BRICs

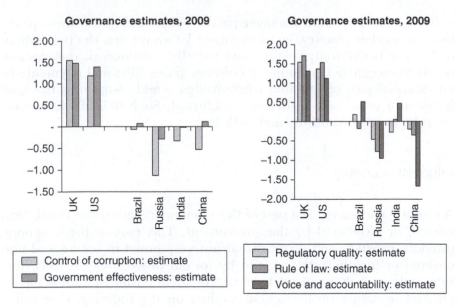

Figure 2.1   **Worldwide governance indicators**

and two of the most developed countries in the world in terms of governance. Lower levels of governance indicators are not solely an EM phenomenon, and even in developed nations examples of inefficient governance can be observed.

The desire to gain entry into an EM may tempt Western managers to offer bribes to government bureaucrats, politicians or corporate buyers making purchasing decisions. Whilst unethical, bribery and corruption can be a reality in many EMs, as well as in many developed markets. In these cases, MNCs from developed markets are equally responsible as they are taking part in an illegal activity. However, EMs are also associated with continuous policy reforms and therefore corruption levels are expected to decrease in the future.

The US government considers bribing foreigners for business deals or contracts to be illegal under the Foreign Corrupt Practices Act (FCPA). The FCPA prohibits American companies or managers from offering bribes of any kind for business to officials in foreign countries (Gillespie et al., 2010). American managers have complained that although the FCPA is good for fostering healthy and ethical practices in international business, it puts them at a competitive disadvantage compared with Japanese and European competitors, who are not restrained by similar laws in their home countries. Clearly, it would be in the best interests of the entire world if no bribes were offered or accepted in business dealings.

But before a Western manager passes judgement on business practices in another country, he or she must be aware that the perception of bribery is culturally relative and socially conditioned: that person needs to recognize that in many cultures giving gifts and payments is an essential part of building relationships – and sometimes the line between a bribe and a gift can be blurred. Such delicate situations must be handled carefully and with tact.

Informal economy

An informal economy is a part of the economy which is not taxed, registered, or monitored by the government. This part of the economy provides products and services that are very broad in nature and not covered or insufficiently covered by formal procedures. In EMs, the informal sector does not solely consist of small businesses but is incorporated by larger businesses, depending on the industry. Generally, construction, apparel and retail are associated with higher levels of informal participation due to the labour-intensive nature of these industries (Montiel, 2011).

Despite improvements in regulations and more entrepreneurial economies, the informal economy still forms a significant part of the economy of EMs. It was estimated that 50% of the agricultural and 30% of the non-agricultural production in Asia was in the informal sector (ADB, 2011).

Main reasons for the existence of the informal economy are strict regulations, high taxes, and excessive procedures which make it difficult for entrepreneurs to register and conduct business. Factors which enable informal sectors to flourish are inefficiencies in law enforcement, weak penalties, and a lack of social pressure advocating compliance with the laws. Government regulations and the high costs of starting up a business can also act as barriers to entry in the formal sector and lead to growth of the informal sector (World Bank, 2009). Moreover, institutional inefficiencies giving rise to low levels of education may prevent many workers from acquiring the skill set that is necessary in formal employment. Rapid economic growth in EMs may also lead to the growth of the informal economy. In many cases economic reforms can lead to the closure of loss-making businesses, as well as a contraction in the public sector. Thus, the informal economy grows due to the increased number of job seekers and the relatively limited job availability within the formal sector.

Companies within the informal economy can avoid income tax, labour market demands such as social security, product regulations such as established quality standards, and obligations due to intellectual property. By evading these obligations, firms can create cost advantages. Such firms are also embedded within this structure and compete by exploiting cost reductions generated by informal practices. Added to this they are immersed in value chains within the informal economic structure which makes joining the formal economy harder (Farrell, 2004). The lower cost burden of the informal sector presents a challenge to formal competitors. Moreover, companies copying innovations threaten the revenue of those firms operating in the formal economy.

Governments can reduce the cost of entering into the formal economy and provide incentives to ensure that businesses formalize their activities. Enhancing the government's audit capabilities and establishing effective jurisdiction for tax evaders may also be helpful in reducing the size of the informal economy.

Managing Political and Legal Risks in Emerging Markets

In considering EMs, political risk is often highlighted. However, it would be inaccurate to write off EMs on the basis of political risk without a thorough analysis. A political risk in a given country may not be relevant to a company's operations at all. Moreover, there are always opportunities which can be accessed despite the political risks, as evidenced by the many American firms licensing their products in Iran despite the US trade sanctions. One of the main distinctions that needs to be made in assessing political risks is whether these will affect sales or physical assets (Pacek and Thorniley, 2007). If the risks are focused on physical assets, then a company may take advantage of sales opportunities.

WTO membership has contributed to the reduction of many risks in emerging markets. EMs are required to decrease the protection of many industries – such as steel, textiles or telecommunications – by WTO regulations. As such, these areas, which were previously dominated by large government-supported conglomerates or state-owned institutions, are opened up for competition. Moreover, WTO regulations can also lead many emerging markets to implement policies protecting property rights or intellectual property.

Today, the probability of expropriation risks has been greatly reduced by the growth of EMs in the international business arena, as well as by stronger international trade laws. Those political risks which remain a concern for investors can be termed as policy risks or political uncertainty, based on risks arising from a government's ability to change the regulations, thereby adversely affecting investment, or a government's failure to enforce contracts (Henisz and Zelner, 2010). For instance, the example in Box 2.3 summarizes a recent political change and its effect on a major company in Egypt. Another major concern is the possibility that contracts may be breeched. Recent figures, such as the 26 regulation changes out of 77 in developing countries introducing restrictions on investment, have contributed to investor concerns.

Box 2.3   Government Influence on Business – An Example

At the beginning of 2011, Ahmed Ezz controlled approximately 40% of Egypt's steel production and was a major influence in the ruling party. One of the main reasons for his success was his friendship with the former President Hosni Mubarak's son and his other political connections. Within a month, Ahmed Ezz's power diminished, his company headquarters (HQ) were ransacked by protestors, his assets were frozen, and he is now under investigation.

Such events are examples of some EM governments' tendency to use business as a tool for asserting state power. Considering that some of the largest firms in these economies are owned by the state or people close to ruling politicians, questions will arise regarding their sustainability through governance shaped by both economic and political considerations.

Companies have employed different techniques such as diversifying operations, employing regulators or forming alliances with government bodies. But, such techniques cannot completely shield these companies from political risk. Companies operating in EMs need to understand the political regimes and relationships within these countries, at the state as well as the local level, always taking into account that stability may be a passing phenomenon in some countries.

Sources: Economist, 2011a; Kirkpatrick and Afify, 2011; Saleh, 2011.

Successful business activities largely depend on the political infrastructure, therefore international marketers need to assess political environments and decide on whether to invest, which adaptations are necessary to their competitive strategy, and which policies can affect them positively or negatively. Political and economic motives are different from each other, however they are usually intertwined. Understanding the political risks before investing in an EM is integral to managing those risks. There are multiple ways of assessing risk, such as Bank of America forecasts, LIBOR rates and the ease of doing business rankings. Yet, solely looking at the figures may not be enough to understand the political system within an EM. Consulting local sources can be of far greater benefit. For instance, a trade association or a lawyer in a market could provide a better insight into the reasons for changes in trade regulations and enable the company to estimate potential risks.

In order to mitigate political risks, companies can invest in personal relations, increase their resource commitments in the host country, stimulate the local economy by purchasing local supplies, employ nationals, or advocate their presence as a responsible corporate citizen, in order to improve their relations with the authorities. Generally, in markets where the political risks are deemed high, multinationals can lower their commitment or focus on increasing firms' importance politically (Jensen, 2009). Another successful approach in dealing with political risk is to manage political relations by assuring the government that the multinational enterprise will contribute to the economic growth of the country by providing technology, employing locals, or investing in public resources. In order to build such a relationship with government, the company must analyse that interests of that particular government, and their attitudes towards the firm's industry.

In most cases, business framework in EMs is dependent on relationships. Local business groups may be in a position to influence the government and harm the multinationals business. In such cases, Multinationals may seek to form ventures with business groups or even state-owned enterprises, in order to reduce the political risks and benefit from their sound relations with government authorities. Employing local managers who know the political structure and have relationships with authorities is another way that multinationals can reduce their exposure to political risk.

Political risk insurance (PRI) is also considered as a tool to mitigate political risk. Such policies cover losses due to the direct and indirect actions of government, compensating the firm if such an action should occur. For instance, PRI can protect the firm by covering losses from a government action which reduces the firm's rights to the investment, or losses to the firm's assets in the event of political turmoil (Sauvant et al., 2011). However, the use of PRI is not currently widespread, mostly because it is relatively new.

A company's production decisions are also affected by legal systems. Governments will differ in the extent to which they deregulate. But when they are forced to agree with international deregulation but do not want any impact on local industry, they can try to find loopholes in the agreements. In order to resolve legal disputes, negotiation is the most efficient way, while arbitration is considered the second best alternative (Onkvisit and Shaw, 2008).

Many multinationals have been trying to reduce their exposure to risks stemming from the lack of protection of intellectual property. Some companies have developed technologies that identify their products, such as three-dimensional markers or different packaging which is hard to obtain by counterfeiters. Another way to deal with such problems is to work with local governments, dedicating company resources to control counterfeit operations (Cavusgil et al., 2008).

Structural Reforms in Emerging Markets

Rapid development of China, India and other EMs is attributed to the global success of the market economy. Another explanation for this rapid growth is that globalization is easier and more efficient in the 20th and 21st centuries, and emerging economies are able to rely on resources in the form of foreign investment for development. Economies which targeted growth through reforms were able to attract resources such as capital, technology, employment opportunities, management skills and market access through foreign investment (Enderwick, 2007).

Host countries benefit from foreign investment due to incoming capital. Another major contribution of foreign investment is the transfer of international know-how and technology to the host country (Busse et al., 2010).

The main factors which attract foreign investment are the size and the growth of the markets, and the availability of local factors of production. Such factors cannot be affected by short-term government policies. However, the government can increase the attractiveness of the country for foreign investors by changing regulations and providing incentives. Some examples of this include opening up industries to foreign investment, reducing restrictions, and offering tax incentives. Governments can also engage in bilateral agreements through which they will commit to binding obligations. Bilateral agreements usually centre on regulations related to the entry of foreign investors, regulations concerning the transfer of capital and profits of the foreign entrant, and the procedures for settling disputes (Busse et al., 2010).

Governments seeking to attract foreign investment also need to ensure economic stability through inflation control, currency fluctuation, and excessive trade deficits. Macroeconomic instability displayed as high inflation rates, overvalued currencies and the inability of financial institutions and governments to pay their debts, can be greatly reduced by efficient fiscal and monetary policies and regulation of the financial sector (Roe and Siegel, 2008). Macroeconomic instability may occur for a variety of reasons. Governments without liquid assets may increase taxes or cut back on expenditure. In order to reduce deficits, governments can rely on taxes or the central bank and this may lead to high inflation. Instability in a country creates uncertainty about the future and thereby hinders investment, considering that investment has high fixed costs. Thus, in an atmosphere of uncertainty, goods are not efficiently allocated and the overall economic productivity is reduced. The fiscal and monetary reforms made in order to increase stability augment the economic growth of the country as well as reduce the risk factors associated with that country.

Government involvement in the financial sector

The financial sector of a country can enable an efficient utilization of capital by allocating it to the most productive uses. Banks increase returns for borrowers by giving them interest and reduce the cost of borrowing for them. Moreover, efficient capital markets provide efficient debt financing options, thereby reducing the risks for firms and enabling efficient investments. Government policies can greatly improve the financial markets and hence augment economic growth. Such policies can reduce the costs associated with contract enforcement to protect creditors and lenders, and also reduce information costs and risks by authorizing efficient disclosure standards.

As an economy grows, the size of the companies within that economy – along with the need for financing – increases. Thus, the need for financial mediation arises. A sound financial system can lead to the efficient allocation of resources, while reducing the risk and increasing the rewards for both borrowers and lenders. Financial intermediaries can then facilitate investment and increase the rewards associated with saving. An efficient system needs to focus on demands on the availability of information through accounting standards, bankruptcy laws and corporate laws – which protect shareholders and creditors while securing a reliable judicial system to enforce contracts. In EMs, financial intermediaries are often burdened with a lack of information about borrowers which highlights the need to monitor their activities. Many institutions have been affected by low-quality loans. On the other hand, many EM countries have gone through an economic crisis due to inefficiencies in the financial systems at the end of the 20th century. Such crises have led to a financial restructuring in most cases, which has also reduced risk and volatility within these economies in the long run.

Trade reforms

In EMs, governments have realized that opening up the economy for competition as opposed to protecting domestic firms can be beneficial for development. They endorse the presence of multinationals to intro-duce competition into the country, and to generate spill-overs and tech-nology transfers. Spill-overs are generated when a MNE introduces superior technology and know-how to its subsidiary and these are then spread to local firms (Marin and Bell, 2003). However, multinationals do not always transfer know-how and technology to EMs, precisely because of the low levels of protection for intellectual property. The government's target of attaining technological know-how is therefore often not realized. Moreover, if the multinational solely uses the host economy as a low-cost producer, it can hinder innovation within the economy.

Effects of brade reforms can be clearly observerd in looking at the dramatic changes in china. Following Mao's death in 1976, Deng Xiaoping introduced multiple reforms in the economy in order to cre-ate a socialist market economy. Agriculture, industry, science, technol-ogy and the military were modernized by means of these reforms. As both agricultural and industrial productivity increased, revenues were used to invest in the economy. Throughout this period, China also shifted from a focus on agriculture to industrial production. Within industrial production, the focus has shifted towards more value-added products. Through industrial production and international trade, economies in the coastal regions as well as the urban areas have grown. Though the rural areas are under development, investment is increasingly being provided for such areas. In 2000 the Chinese gov-ernment also introduced the going-abroad policy, which resulted in increased income from trade and rapid growth in the economy (Bach et al., 2006). Currently, the government's focus is on increasing employment to create equilibrium throughout the country. Another concern is that the population of China is ageing and the working-age population is expected to decrease within the next decade, and therefore the Chinese government is under pressure to establish social security reforms.

Financial crises and reforms in EMs

Historically, EM governments restricted the flow of capital by prohibiting international loans and the acquisition of foreign assets. They have used strategies such as placing high restrictions on the domestic financial sector to limit competition, regulating high reserve ratios which were to be held in the form of government securities, imposing interest-rate restrictions, and interfering with the credit strategy of the institutions.

In the late 1990s, many EMs experienced a financial crisis. Even though country-specific factors were among the causes, there were some common features of EMs which led to these crises. In the 1980s and 1990s many EMs began their liberalization and thus deregulation processes, undertaking ambitious reforms to modernize their economies. Yet foreign entry to domestic markets was still restricted. However, within the more liberalized economies, domestic corporations, and especially financial institutions were able to borrow from foreign corporations and in most cases such borrowing was not monitored closely. Foreign investors, on the other hand, were attracted to higher yields in EMs and trusted the macroeconomic reform policies being undertaken by the EMs (Magnus, 2010). Inflation stabilization programmes – based on fixing the domestic exchange rate against the dollar – further boosted investor confidence and led to an increase in borrowing from EMs to take advantage of the lower interest rates abroad. As a result, these economies gained significant capital inflows but they were also exposed to un-hedged foreign currency debts. Moreover, domestic financial institutions borrowed from foreign investors at low interest rates and provided loans to domestic borrowers at higher interest rates. However, this borrowing was usually on a short-term basis, and lending conditions were long term, thereby creating a mismatch between maturity rates. The exact reasons for the financial crises in different countries are still being debated, but a common feature initiating the crises can be the panic of the foreign investors and their rapid withdrawal from EM economies, followed by inefficient policy responses from the EM countries.

At the end of the 20th century, the governance in EMs was not efficient and investors often did not trust their financial policies. At one point, two researchers from MIT even suggested that countries such as Argentina should give up sovereignty over financial policies and regulations for a period and have an international central banker run their fiscal policy, under a tight set of administrative rules, and an international monitor witness all their transactions in order to build credibility (Caballero and Dornbusch, 2002). Some of the common causes of the financial crises in EMs – such as the 1998 crisis in Russia, the 1994 crisis in Mexico, the 1999 crisis in Brazil, the 2000 crisis in Turkey and the 2001 crisis in Argentina – were the lack of monitoring in lending practices, and the inadequate regulation of domestic institutions (Glick et al., 2001).

Financial reforms of most of the EMs reduced governments' control on the financial sector and ensured that efficient mechanisms were in place to monitor activities. Sound bank regulations monitors the actions of bank owners, limits excessive risk-taking behaviour by instilling adequate evaluation procedures, and regulates entry by setting capital investment limits (Montiel, 2003).

The crises led to the involvement of the IMF in many EMs and risk allocation of rescue funds from the IMF in order to induce stability in these markets and reduce the risk of a financial crises in the future. Governments also increased central bank autonomy, which eventually led to increased investor confidence in these economies. These reforms and the restructuring of the financial system in the 2000s helped shield many EMs from the global crisis of 2008. Most EM economies, except in the case of China and India, had reorganized their economies following the initial financial crises. The global crisis of 2008 affected EMs by putting pressure on exports and imports in a slowing world economy, and restricting capital inflows. The cost of raising funds increased significantly. However, EMs have recovered quickly from the crisis, showing that they have developed into relatively mature, independent economies.

Factors such as trade surpluses, increased in commodity prices and foreign investments boosted the funds available for state-owned corporations in some emerging markets such as China and Russia. Foreign investments by state-owned transnationals from India, Thailand, Indonesia and China have increased rapidly. This form of business is relatively new for advanced economies and had led to debates on political considerations which may potentially arise from government participation in international business (Harris, 2009). Increasing the involvement of governments in managing and directing significant levels of capital and manipulating market outcomes gives rise to a relatively new phenomenon in international business which can be described as state capitalism. State capitalism has been further fuelled by the rise of sovereign wealth funds which can be used as financing tools by the state (Bremmer, 2009). State capitalism is further explained in Box 2.4.

Box 2.4 State Capitalism

State capitalism refers to a society in which the state controls the productive forces in a capitalist manner. The rise of state capitalism is a new phenomenon, which transpires when governments use national and state-owned enterprises as well as private companies for political gain. The state-owned companies are maintained to generate employment while a few privately owned companies are selected and incentivized to become leaders, in certain industries. Income generated by such companies is channelled towards state sovereign funds and their use is determined by the state. In this way, the state aims both to protect the efficiency of the economy and ensure the sustainability of its own power. If left to the market, new companies may emerge as national champions and this may challenge state power. Examples of state capitalism can be observed in Brazil through corporations such as Petrobras, which is the state-owned national champion in oil, or Vale, which is the heavily subsidized private national champion in mining. The state had used both companies to invest in the creation of jobs after the crisis of 2008–2009, which helped the country to mitigate the adverse effects of the recession. Despite the attractiveness of the model, fuelled by the increased needs of regulation highlighted in the financial crisis, as well as successful examples from Brazil and China, in the long run, national champions of state capitalism can experience shortcomings regarding efficiency as well as innovation, as is the case with many state-owned enterprises.

Adapted from Bremmer, 2010.

Sovereign wealth funds (SWF) are investment funds owned by the state which are composed of various financial assets. Such funds are often created when states have budget surpluses, and are used for multiple purposes, such as stabilizing government revenue inflows, increasing savings for the future, diversifying government assets, or generating additional income for development. Many SWFs are formed by countries which export commodities such as the United Arab Emirates or Chile, while others are created to utilize the export income from manufacturing goods and services, as in China. Some EM governments have been using SWFs to acquire strategic assets internationally. For instance, China's SWFs have invested US$3 billion in Blackstone and US$5 billion in Morgan Stanley. Such investments can enable access to networks and know-how (Sen, 2010). As of December 2011, the 50 largest sovereign wealth funds in the world held assets valued at US$4,755 billion, of which US$2,651 were oil and gas related. US$1,867.5 billion of the total assets held by SWFs were held by funds located in BRICs and new frontier economies (SWF, 2011). More recently, many governments in developed and emerging markets have been adopting measures against SWF investments, due to their concerns regarding the usage of SWFs as a tool to exert political influence. These protectionist measures are particularly set in strategic industries related to technology and financial institutions (Chalamish, 2009).

Environmental and Cultural Differences in Emerging Markets

Understanding cultural differences

Consumers differ in terms of their decision-making processes, motivations, and attitudes. Companies in different markets also vary significantly. In international markets, businesspeople need to understand and manage such differences. In doing business efficiently in another country, it is necessary to understand cultural differences in order to be able to offer the right business plan or the right product, and to communicate effectively with all the actors within the business network (Ghemawat, 2007).

In EMs, foreign entrants need to understand the culture in order to be able to compete with local firms, appeal to consumer tastes, and conduct business with local companies successfully. Cultural differences are especially highlighted in the context of EMs due to the dissimilar traits of these markets when compared to developed markets. Hence, understanding these markets is difficult, and firms from developed markets are faced with steep learning curves (De Mooij, 2009).

The meaning of culture

Culture can be briefly defined as a set of values followed by a group (Ghauri and Cateora, 2010).

> Culture is created by the accumulation of knowledge, beliefs, morals, laws, customs which constitute a person's habits and lifestyle as a result of living in a society. In short, culture is everything that people have, think and do as members of their society. (Hall and Hall, 1990, p. 18)

Because culture is learned by people living in the same environment, it is always a collective manifestation; therefore, members of a group can be distinguished from another by their culture which is exhibited through the collective programming of the mind (Hofstede et al., 2010). According to Holden (2002), the characteristics of culture are:

- Culture exhibits itself through shared ideas, beliefs and values.
- Culture is learnt and transferred from one generation to another.
- Culture is shaped by past actions and experiences.
- A person's perception of the world is affected by culture.
- Culture is reinforced by many components such as behaviour, society, nation, and religion.

A group's culture is a combination of many effects or experiences in both the past and the present. Thus, it is very hard to identify, quantify, and change. Culture helps explain a group's lifestyle and behaviour, so understanding a group's or a country's culture is pertinent in forming business relations and in reaching consumers. In the literature on cross-cultural groups and organizations, Geert Hofstede's research is widely acknowledged as a way to analyse the cultural traits which influence behaviour in different societies. Hofstede identifies four dimensions on which national cultures can be scaled (Hofstede and Bond, 1984; Hofstede and Hofstede, 2005). These cultural dimensions are as follows:

- *Masculinity/femininity:* this dimension refers to the acceptance of feminine or masculine values within a society and focuses on the relationship between gender and occupational role. Feminine cultures are associated with less emphasis on the role of gender and a stronger focus on equality, while masculine cultures emphasize gender differences and praise values such as achievement and power.
- *Power distance:* this dimension deals with inequalities within society, and the member's role within their group. High power-distance cultures are associated with authoritarianism, hierarchy, gaps between the classes and an unequal distribution of power.
- *Uncertainty avoidance:* this dimension refers to a society's responses to risk. High uncertainty avoidance cultures value security and refrain from taking risks. In parallel, firms in cultures with high uncertainty avoidance scores focus on minimizing risks in their decision making.
- *Individualism/Collectivism:* this dimension focuses on the individual's interaction with society and their concern for society. Collectivist cultures often focus on values such as sharing, group utility, and looking out for the interests of the group. Such cultures also often display large families that are closely bound to each other. In contrast, in individualistic societies, individuals are more independent and prioritize individual achievement.

Hofstede introduced another dimension to his work, referred to as long-term orientation or Confucian dynamism (Hofstede, 1994). This dimension focuses on a society's time orientation and its focus on the future, present or past. In societies with a long-term orientation, people pursue long-term goals, hence they are focused on actions that affect the future and they are characterized by perseverance and hard work. Another trait of cultures with a long-term orientation is respect for tradition and an emphasis on reciprocation in relationships (Hofstede, 2006). In contrast, short-term oriented cultures emphasize quick results, and members are characterized by high levels of spending and increased levels of leisure. High power-distance and risk avoidance levels can signal the culture's unwillingness to try new products (Yeniyurt and Townsend, 2003). Box 2.5 explains Hofstede's cultural dimensions as they relate to BRICs.

Box 2.5   Hofstede's Dimensions and BRICs

BRIC countries are associated with higher levels of power distance as opposed to the US and many other Western cultures. Hence, companies often have centralized decision-making systems, where the bosses, owners or CEOs make the decisions. In parallel, companies are less open to diffusing the sharing of ideas throughout the organization and only a small percentage of employees are able to participate in decision-making processes. Higher power distance may enable BRIC firms to be more flexible at times, due to the ability to make decisions quickly as only a few individuals are involved in the process. On the other hand, the concentration of decision making and the authoritarian structure can prevent employees from speaking out and contributing to the organization with innovative ideas. High power-distance indices are also associated with structured societies where class differences are well defined. Wealth and power reside in a small percentage such societies.

In terms of individualism, BRIC countries rank lower than the USA. Though the USA is associated with very high individualism scores globally, most Western countries also rank higher then BRICs on this index. China has a very low individualism score, mainly as a result of the emphasis on a collective society due to communism. Low scores indicate close-knit societies in which bonds between members are cherished and strengthened continually. The more collectivist nature of BRIC cultures and many EMs can thus signal the existence of business environments where networks are important and relationships affect business practices. In terms of consumption and preferences, collectivism indicates the propensity of the society members to be influenced by each other in making decisions.

In the masculinity index, BRICs except for Russia are more similar to the USA. Uncertainty avoidance varies greatly among the BRIC countries, with Russia and Brazil scoring very high on the scale. These cultures prefer to eliminate uncertainty and minimize risk, thereby indicating the presence of strict regulations.

High uncertainty avoidance can also show a culture's resistance to change. Companies in high uncertainty avoidance cultures often avoid risky investments and consumers are less willing to try new products. Members of cultures with high uncertainty avoidance are associated with lower tolerance to new ideas and opinions.

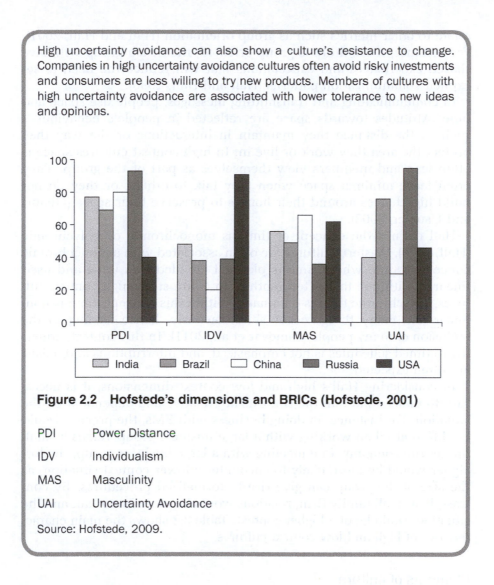

Figure 2.2   Hofstede's dimensions and BRICs (Hofstede, 2001)

PDI   Power Distance

IDV   Individualism

MAS   Masculinity

UAI   Uncertainty Avoidance

Source: Hofstede, 2009.

High and low context cultures

High and low context cultures, as defined by Edward T. Hall (Hall and Hall, 1990), refer to communication styles, and assess a culture's tendency to use high or low context messages. In high context cultures, messages are implicit and less is said. Members are expected to understand the underlying messages. In contrast, in low context cultures, messages are very clear and explicit. Differences between high and low context cultures often lead to problems in communication and information sharing (Rosinski, 2003). High–low context traits within a culture also relate to other metrics such as group orientation (Hall and Hall, 2001). For instance, if a culture is group oriented, then each group will have shared experiences and expectations that will reduce the need to set explicit communication patterns (Hall and Hall, 1990).

In communicating and transmitting messages, people use space and time. Attitudes towards space are reflected in people's behaviour – such as the distance they maintain in interactions or the way they protect the area they work or live in. In high context cultures space is often less, and members view themselves as part of the group. They often leave minimal space when they talk to others, or they do not build high fences around their houses to preserve their space (Ghauri and Usunier, 2003).

Hall defines the concept of time as monochromic or polychromic (Hall, 2000). Western cultures are often associated with a monochromic concept of time where time is planned, divided into units and used linearly, with one task after another. In contrast, in high context cultures, polychromic time is dominant. Within this concept, time is non-linear and many things occur simultaneously, hence leading to the inclusion of many people (Samovar et al., 2011). In this context, adhering to timed schedules is not emphasized, and interruptions and delays are often expected.

In considering Hall's high and low context dimensions, it is necessary to understand that the contexts are relative and dependent on the situation. For instance, in doing business with EMs, the process would be different when working with a large business group versus a small family-run company. In a meeting with a large business group, the foreigner would be more likely to encounter a lower context situation, as the size of the group can give rise to formalized procedures. By contrast, in a small family firm, relations would be more important and the situation would be of a higher context. Table 2.2 shows the main characteristics of high and low context cultures.

Elements of culture

As culture is evolutionary, it is formed by multiple factors and philosophies which influence a society. The main elements of culture are social structure, religion and value systems, language and material culture.

Social structure

The social structure of a society explains how a society is organized by individuals, groups, status and roles (Münch and Smelser, 1992). The main differences in social structure can be explained by an individual's

Table 2.2 High–low context cultures

Higher context	Lower context
• Communication consists of indirect, implicit messages • An emphasis on relationships • Process more important than result • Adherence to group membership; groups with strong relationships • Polychromic time (P-time): relations and general agreement more important than adhering to schedules; time is flexible • Countries: China, Arab countries, India, Brazil, Italy • Examples of situations: party with friends, family gatherings	• Direct communication/explicit messages • An emphasis on tasks • Result more important than process ○ Flexible and open groups with lower commitment and weaker relationships • Monochromic time (M-time): adherence to plans, schedules and sequences in order to complete tasks • Countries: USA, Canada, Germany • Examples of situations: airports, chain supermarkets

degree of autonomy, an emphasis on individual welfare, and the focus on class within a society.

All societies are formed by the interactions of different groups such as families, colleagues, members of unions, political groups, teams, etc. The focus on group welfare as opposed to one's own welfare is influenced by culture. While some societies such as that of the USA focus on individual achievement, others such as that of Japan value group welfare above the individual. In societies where the social structure emphasizes group relations, values such as commitment, loyalty and family will take precedence (Samovar et al., 2009).

Another distinction of social structures between nations is the social strata which determine the individual's or group's social category based on their background, income, or occupation. In many societies, and especially Western ones, social mobility is commonly observed and individuals are able to move easily from one social strata to another. In other societies, such as that of India, class systems are visible. In such societies, a person's strata is pre-determined by their family and changing that strata is very hard. In China, a distinct class separation was observed between the rural farmers and the urban residents, as under Communist rule people were expected to remain in the location in which they were born. Reforms in the government of the 1980s allowed for mobility, leading to greater levels of urbanization and a reduction in class immobility (Hill, 2011).

Religion and value systems

Value systems are influenced significantly by religion and affect a person's habits, outlook on life and lifestyle, as well as their acceptance of new products, procedures and systems (Ghauri and Cateora, 2010). In EMs, the wide scope of religion as well as the intensity of people's religious beliefs can help explain people's norms, values, and approach to business. For instance, Hindu beliefs focus on the 'other world', and therefore Hindus may be less receptive towards capitalist ethics while Christians and Confucians would embrace them.

Language

Language is a combination of spoken and unspoken modes of communication which influence or are influenced by a society's perceptions. In business, an ability to speak the language helps to establish and improve business relations. Even in conditions where the personnel of a company are unfamiliar with the language of the host country, careful attention should be given to language in order to refrain from making blunders and also to understand the nonverbal cues that are used within that culture. For instance, in Latin America, personal space when talking to a person is minimal. By contrast, in North America, people are comfortable with more personal space (Onkvisit and Shaw, 2008). Thus, if businesspeople are unaware of such basic nonverbal cues, a Latin American can feel that a North American is distant and adverse, while a North American can feel that a Latin American party is pushy and aggressive.

Education

Education is another key element that shapes society and culture. Education shapes the norms within a society, influences what is acceptable or not, and affects the society's attitudes towards change (Hill, 2011). Moreover, the level of education is strongly correlated with the competitive advantages of a nation. For instance, within India, the availability of trained engineers helps to build outsourcing facilities within the country. By contrast, the lack of education in many rural areas of India leads companies to focus on creating consumer awareness upon their entering the region.

Material culture

The material culture can be analysed through the economic and technological culture because a technological culture reflects the culture's technological know-how and ability to adapt to technological changes.

The economic culture is focused on patterns of income and consumption. Together, the elements of material culture affect the products demanded, consumption patterns, and the features necessary for a given product (Ghauri and Cateora, 2010). For instance, in a high-technology culture, consumers would demand sophisticated products endowed with enhanced technological features. In such cultures, the sales procedure would be different and may focus on additional technological features or on its image. However, in a society with limited technological capabilities, the basic features of the product would need to be highlighted, and its marketing would focus on educating the customer and its providing detailed material related to usage of the product.

Cultural change

A vital consequence of culture's influence is its impact on acceptance or resistance to change. The focus on change is especially important in international business because such activities often consist of introducing a new product into a new country (Kleijnen et al., 2009). If a particular culture is especially resistant to change, the firm's whole strategy needs to be redesigned to focus on highlighting the compatibility and reliability of its product. In cultures resistant to change, new product adoption takes a long time. A culture's ethnocentrism – which is its identification with the known and tendency to devalue other cultures – will affect the rate at which cultures change (Sharma, 2010).

Cultural borrowing is a way in which a culture can change over time. Many cultures will borrow from others but also adopt and localize the borrowed culture in such a way that it becomes unique to them. For instance, an American might drink coffee and eat pancakes with syrup in the morning. While pancakes were originally derived from a Scandinavian technique, the coffee is Colombian and the syrup is Indian in origin: these borrowed artefacts have been localized to fit with US consumption patterns and this activity has become a reflection of American culture (Ghauri and Cateora, 2010).

Contemporary Changes Affecting Culture

Technology and the internet have affected many cultures profoundly and enabled the dissemination of information, thereby exposing many societies to new cultures. Barriers imposed by distance are lower and different cultures can interact among each other easily. Due to higher interaction levels and the availability of information, subsets of homogenized cultures are now evolving. For instance, young people across the world today share similar tastes in music, and many cultures worldwide are inspired by the same celebrities.

The internet exposes many people to limitless information and helps in the diffusion of culture. Many subcultures are created by technological change and global communication. For instance, in EMs and Western economies, a teen culture or a credit culture can be observed. Such subcultures are more global than cultural on the national level. Targeting and augmenting subcultures creates worldwide business opportunities.

> Critics charge that globalization is harmful to local cultures and their artistic expressions and sensibilities, and is responsible for their replacement by a homogeneous, often Americanized culture. Others argue that increased global communications is positive because it permits the flow of cultural ideas, beliefs and values. In short, globalization is a major factor in the emergence of common culture worldwide. Many products, services, and even holidays are becoming common to world markets. (Cavusgil et al., 2008, p. 147)

The business environment in emerging markets is strongly affected by relationships (Constanza, 2009; Black and Morrison, 2010; Moore and Woodrow, 2010). In collective cultures, indirect confrontation can be a better route to resolving conflicts, as such cultures will often emphasize social harmony. Harmony can be damaged by conflicts and direct confrontation which can often be aggressive and imply blame. With indirect confrontation, negotiators can avoid blaming and disrespecting the other side and resolve issues (Brett and Gelfand, 2005).

Networks and emerging market culture

Many EMs are associated with collectivist cultures which highlight a dependence on the social system and emphasize a person's role within the group. In parallel with the prioritization of collectivist values, the EM social and business environment is affected by relationships. Hence, in such cultures, building long-term relationships based on trust and loyalty is very important (Constanza, 2009; Black and Morrison, 2010).

A focus on collectivist values can be observed in many emerging markets in different ways. For instance, in Confucian societies, individualism is not a desired trait and relationships are key. The emphasis on relations leads to the dominance of family businesses as well as the dominance of networks in the business landscape of Confucian societies. Such networks are referred to as Guanxi in Chinese society, Ningen Kankei in Japanese society and Kwankye in Korean. Similarly, in, Latin American countries, 'compadre' refers to friendship, and friendship arises as a cultural prerequisite for developing effective business relations (Cavusgil et al., 2008).

Guanxi and Confucian societies

Confucianism is an ethical system derived from the work of the Chinese philosopher, Confucius, which influences many cultures in East and Southeast Asia such as those of China, Taiwan, Japan, and Korea. Its teachings emphasize humanity, loyalty, respect and social harmony. 'Guanxi' – which can be described as a network of relationships – influences the business environment.

Guanxi is established by building trust, often through a continuous reciprocation of favours and reinforcement of relations. In China, business strategy is dependent on Guanxi and foreigners often face difficulties doing business there as it is difficult to access information and conduct business without establishing network connections.

The existence and cultivation of the Guanxi spirit also demonstrates the Chinese focus on long-term benefits and commitment. Added to this Guanxi networks are associated with centralized governance due to the emphasis on identifying each member's role in Confucian societies (Abramson and Merchant, 2008).

Business through relations is not a novel concept. However, Guanxi indicates a deeper level:

> In reality, the heavy reliance on relationships means that Western companies need to make themselves known to the Chinese before any business can take place. Furthermore, this relationship is not simply between firms but also between individuals on a personal level. (Fleury and Fleury, 2011, p. 362)

Managing cultural issues

Differences in language, business customs and ethics, lifestyles and values, and other cultural dimensions often cause uncertainty and psychic distance. This type of distance is related to how we perceive a certain market and is different from physical distance. For example, for a US firm, in psychic distance terms, the UK is a closer market than Brazil or even Mexico.

Many authorities contend that Western businesspeople are ill prepared to conduct business in any culture other than their own. They are unfamiliar with the 'hidden dimensions' that frequently play a fundamental role in international business transactions. Different cultures require different behaviour patterns by a firm, because the strategies, structures and technologies that are appropriate in one cultural setting may well fail in another. A foreign firm will be affected by an indigenous culture depending on its level of involvement in that particular market. The greater the involvement, the greater the reliance on cultural growth and survival – and the greater the need to understand the cultural environment.

Knowledge of the business culture, which can be defined as the values and norms that are followed in business activities, as well as a willingness to accept these differences, is essential in an international market, and is especially important in EMs because such markets are often culturally distant. As an example, Box 2.6 shows the different aspects of Indian culture which can be observed in a business environment.

Box 2.6   Indian Culture

Indians appreciate punctuality and keeping to one's commitments. However, many visitors to India find it very disconcerting that Indians are often quite casual in keeping to their time commitments. One of the reasons for this is that in the Indian mind time is generally not considered as a yardstick for planning and scheduling one's activities. Rather, for most Indians, plans and schedules are contingent upon other people and events, and therefore can – and do – get changed. Compared to a business organization, it is normally more difficult to organize an appointment with officials in a government department.

Even in business meetings, it is common to start discussions with 'small talk' on unrelated issues. This is seen as a way of building a rapport and trust. Indians are open and friendly, and compared to many countries in the West, have a lesser sense of privacy.

There are differences between the government-owned public sector companies, which are more often bureaucratic and hierarchical, and many of their private sector counterparts, as well as the 'new economy' service-sector companies (IT, telecoms, insurance, etc.), which are in turn more egalitarian and flexible than the traditional manufacturing-sector firms.

There are also regional differences in business etiquette. For instance, broadly speaking, the southern Indian companies are more conservative when compared to the north or the western part of the country. These sectors are more individualistic and assertive than the eastern portion of India.

Hospitality is a key value in Indian culture, and a guest is considered the equivalent of a god. Indians will normally go out of their way to accommodate guests' requirements. Any breach of etiquette by a guest is normally ignored and never brought to his or her attention.

> It is common practice in India to offer beverages (tea, coffee or soft drinks) with some light snacks/refreshments to a guest, even in business settings. When snacks or beverages are served, it is customary (though not mandatory) to refuse the first offer, but to accept the second or third. It would, however, be a breach of etiquette not to accept anything at all.
>
> Source: www.executiveplanet.com (accessed 11 May 2011).

A country's social, educational, and religious systems will critically influence its business. These cultural variables have a crucial impact on product policy and are considered as major barriers in doing business overseas. Yet many Western managers fail to include these variables in their research. A major reson for this failure is the tendency to view foreign cultures within the same framework as one's own culture.

Understanding social and cultural traits of a country before making decisions, involving employees with foreign country origins in negotiations, and training managers in intercultural differences can minimize the risks and misunderstandings associated with conflicting cultural values.

Managers must make every effort to educate both themselves and their employees in order to have a good understanding of the foreign culture in which their business is done, though it is understandable that not every manager can learn the relevant language. For such cases, we suggest that managers familiarize themselves with some good literature (e.g. short stories) and the history and economic geography of these countries.

Chapter Questions

1 How can governments regulate foreign investment and trade?
2 What are some of the risks that foreign companies face in emerging markets due to the political and legal framework?
3 How can foreign companies manage the political and legal risks in emerging markets?
4 What are property rights and how do they affect foreign firms' strategy in emerging markets?
5 Discuss the main cultural differences between emerging markets and developed economies.
6 Discuss the main traits of culture in emerging markets in terms of Hofstede's dimensions. How do differences in terms of Hofstede's dimensions affect business in emerging markets?

THREE The Economic Environment in Emerging Markets

Differences in the Economic Environment in Emerging Markets

Differences across countries which occur as a result of cultural, administrative, geographic and economic distances can create challenges in international business. Some examples may be different ethnicities, a lack of social networks, different religions, a lack of trust or different values.

> Administrative distances are enforced by governments. They can result in political hostility, closed economies, home biases and reduced membership in international organizations. Administrative distances can also be affected by weak institutions and corruption. Geographic distance may lead to issues in transportation and communication. Economic distances are derived from the size and the strength of the activity and mainly highlight the differences in the richness or the poorness of the economy. Despite the increased levels of global activities, the effects of these distances are still prevailing and directing the economic activity. Especially in considering EMs, these distances need to be analysed as these countries exhibit greater distances economically, administratively, culturally and in most cases geographically. (Ghemawat, 2007, p. 7)

The dissimilarity between emerging and developed markets creates challenges for multinationals and leads to emphasis on risks, even when the risks can be managed and mitigated. In EMs, firms have to deal with an economic landscape which is significantly different from developed markets and are faced with underdeveloped institutional structures and weak infrastructure, and have to deal with consumers whose culture, income and priorities are different. In the previous chapter, the cultural, political and legal forces and challenges arising from these were discussed. This chapter focuses on the economic forces and business environment in EMs. The EM environment is characterized by protected domestic firms, high tariffs, weak institutions, conglomerates and business groups, and a turbulent climate delaying the entry of the MNE into these countries, as well as the emergence of MNEs from such countries (Casanova, 2009). The purpose of this chapter is to describe the business environment within EMs, and EM-specific issues such as institutional voids and structures such as business groups.

Institutional voids

EMs are associated with higher inefficiencies in capital product and labour markets when compared to developed markets which result in institutional voids (Lee and Peng, 2008). Institutions enable markets to function smoothly. They can provide an independent assessment to collect and analyse information or provide consulting services. They can also match customers and suppliers and provide distribution services; platforms for buyers and sellers; help resolve disputes; and regulate business transactions. Limited presence or the absence of intermediary institutions which provide services, weaknesses in the governance systems, weaknesses in legal systems and poor enforcement of regulations are just some of the factors which create institutional voids. The absence or inefficiency of institutions increases the transaction costs of multinationals. In fact, Khanna and Palepu (2010) argue that spotting key institutional voids in a given EM should be the first step when deciding to invest in or manage a business in that market. Managers need to consider the issues arising from institutional voids and determine whether they can reach customers efficiently, evaluate the creditworthiness of those customers, collaborate with supply chain partners, hire qualified personnel, and find reliable partners before entering into an EM (Khanna and Palepu, 2010).

Firms take advantage of institutional incentives and try to avoid institutional constraints such as lack of property rights, and legal frameworks (Deng, 2009). In the internationalization process, institutional actors are essential for firms' success. Many firms fail because they are oblivious to the wants of the various actors in a different environment (Bianchi and Ostale, 2006). Institutional distance also affects companies' internationalization decisions and performance as increasing distances raise the cost of internationalization (Chao and Kumar, 2010).

In developed countries, businesses can rely on specialized intermediaries such as distribution agents, arbitrators and information providers to operate efficiently. Companies are able to distribute information to customers via advertising, marketing and web retail chains. Logistics companies will distribute the product, credit card issuers will facilitate the purchasing, and information agencies will provide information on consumption to firms and information on products to consumers. In EMs, intermediaries either do not exist or their operations are less comprehensive when compared to those of developed markets. Informal institutions exist in order to provide for the gap created by missing intermediaries but access to informal intermediaries is limited (Khanna and Palepu, 2010).

Institutional voids increase costs for foreign firms due to reduced efficiency and higher risks in terms of enforcing contracts, and protecting assets, as well as higher costs in the absence of intermediaries (Chan et al., 2008). The institutional development of EMs affects the entry strategies of foreign firms in these markets. As regards the absence or inefficiency of intermediaries, foreign entrants – especially from developed economies – prefer to gain entry via partnerships with locals (Peng, 2003; Brouthers et al., 2009). Smaller firms are affected by inefficient capital, labour and product markets in the presence of institutional voids and they lack the resources to compensate for such inefficiencies which then put them at a disadvantage (Khanna et al., 2005; Puffer et al., 2010). However, institutional voids can also present an opportunity for entrepreneurs who will be able to fill such gaps.

In EMs, the presence of institutional voids is not always an obstacle to doing business, it can also generate valuable opportunities for entrepreneurs willing to fill such voids (Mair and Marti, 2009). In markets which are growing and rapidly undertaking reforms the need for services which can compensate for institutional voids increases (Khanna and Palepu, 2010). As such voids present a major concern for prospective entrants, the services of firms able to reduce the uncertainties from such voids are highly valued (Tracey and Phillips, 2011).

Many entrepreneurs from EMs have been successful by filling institutional voids and providing intermediary services to other EM firms or to foreign entrants. Companies from advanced economies can also take advantage of such opportunities or unmet needs within emerging markets. For instance, Metro Cash & Carry, a division of Metro AG of Germany, has been successful in many EMs such as China, India and Turkey, by establishing wholesalers that have been designed to facilitate efficient transactions between suppliers and buyers by ensuring quality and ease of buying, and increasing information availability (Khanna and Palepu, 2010).

In EMs, accessing information presents a major challenge for foreign investors. Information regarding consumers or consumption habits is not widely available and may be inconsistent in most EMs (Chiao et al., 2010), while information related to companies may not be available due to a lack of transparency. Increasingly, foreign investors are utilizing the services of third parties with expertise in the relevant areas in order to gather information. Some examples of third parties may be consultants, ex-government officers, researchers, political risk services and market information services. For this purpose, software tools such as information extraction software and data mining tools are also employed. Talking to different sources such as government officials, suppliers, academics, banks and consultants within the market can also mitigate information gaps to a significant extent (Enderwick, 2007). Box 3.1 gives an example of institutional voids.

Box 3.1   GE Healthcare in India

GE Healthcare started to move the production of some of its medical equipment to EMs from 1997 onwards in order to lower its costs. In the process the company was faced with multiple institutional voids, such as difficulty in finding capable suppliers and in protecting its intellectual property.

Within the EMs, it was impossible for GE to identify adequate suppliers because of a lack of information related to companies. Thus, GE Healthcare had to deploy sourcing and quality teams from its facilities to work with suppliers in order to ensure that the components bought met the quality standards of GE. This process, together with a training initiative, was used to select suppliers and ensure the credibility of each of these in the absence of intermediaries providing the information and assessing the companies.

(Continued)

(Continued)

Within this process, GE also encountered issues related to the protection of its intellectual property when one of the suppliers in China started producing the equipment and selling it directly to end users. To reduce the issues related to this loss of intellectual property, GE had to acquire the supplier. The company provides stock options, monitors employees closely, and uses other incentives in order to minimize the loss of intellectual property through employees.

Adapted from Khanna and Palepu, 2010.

Infrastructure gaps

The term 'infrastructure' covers services from public utilities (power, telecommunications, piped water supply, sanitation and sewerage, solid waste collection and disposal, and piped gas) and public works (roads, dams and canals) to other transport sectors (urban and inter-urban railways, urban transport, ports and waterways, and airports). Infrastructure can be analysed in terms of transportation, telecommunications and energy, as well as financial services. In this regard, transportation covers both the means of transportation, such as the availability of roads or airports, and the support services associated with the transportation activities. The telecommunication infrastructure of a country shows the availability of the means to transfer information, and is analysed through coverage of the networks and access to the internet. The financial service infrastructure within a country reflects the availability of financial intermediaries which can facilitate transactions through credits and loans.

The quality of infrastructure directly affects a country's economic growth potential and the ability of an enterprise to engage effectively in business. If infrastructure frameworks of a country cannot support economic growth, the country is bound to lose economic development ground. A country can produce commodities for export but may not be able to sell them because of inadequacies in the infrastructure. Product labour and capital markets cannot function effectively if the physical infrastructure within the country is not developed (Khanna and Palepu, 2010). In emerging markets, increased investments in infrastructure are being made to ensure sustained growth.

Distribution represents a major challenge for multinationals in EMs. Due to a relatively inefficient infrastructures, limited availability of professional logistics intermediaries and the dispersed nature of the population, the logistics processes are inefficient. Many companies try to overcome this problem by establishing joint ventures with locals who have access to distribution networks. However, in many cases, multinationals are faced with the conflicting interests of the local partner and their desire to protect their own turf (Dong et al., 2008). As logistics provides a major challenge in EMs, establishing an efficient distribution network represents a major undertaking. Multinationals such as Palmolive or Hindustan Lever overcame this difficulty in India by establishing their own distribution systems by networking with small-scale suppliers and establishing long-term relations. Many companies have also acquired distributors in order to maintain control over the dissemination of their products.

Distribution and the ability to reach consumers in markets which are more dispersed create a very big opportunity. Nokia has established local R&D centres to provide low-cost products that will meet the demands of the Indian market. In this market, Nokia has established a presence in over 100,000 distribution points that has enabled the company to have a reach that is four times bigger than that of its main competitors. Hence, Nokia has become one of the largest multinationals in India to date, with revenues exceeding US$3 billion. In the Indian market, Nokia is facing competition from locals such as Tianyu, whose business model is focused on meeting local demand by supplying unique features such as an ultraviolet light within the phone which can detect counterfeit currency (Jin et al., 2010).

If a company is not ready to invest in its own distribution network, then building successful relations with local distributors and ensuring effective monitoring of their activities become a necessity. In such cases, companies need to analyse the distributor's operations and make sure that that distributor can fulfil their needs. Effective communication of the brand image as well as continuous monitoring of the activities are essential here. In most cases, training or maintaining personnel from the home office in the host location may be beneficial (Pacek and Thorniley, 2007). Considering the importance of connections in EMs, investing in long-term relations can be a successful strategy.

Another issue which arises is that of establishing a supply chain. The challenge when operating in both EMs and developed markets is to design a supply chain which can be both flexible and able to adopt the products easily. Networking with suppliers' associations enables companies to access the market. In EMs, creating connections with trade associations, political parties or professional associations is often used in order to increase the scope of the network. By utilizing local suppliers, a company may be able to benefit from the lower costs of raw materials or other inputs. In some cases, quality standards may be an issue when choosing local suppliers but many companies will have managed to work with a supplier to achieve the desired quality at a lower cost.

The logistics performance index is expressed as a number between 1 and 5, with higher numbers indicating higher availability and efficiency in logistics. The efficiency of customs clearance, the quality of the transport infrastructure, the ease of arranging and tracking shipments, and the quality of logistics services are all taken into account (WTI, 2010). Countries with low logistics performance index scores face severe constraints in logistics. Logistics covers a number of essential activities such as transportation, warehousing, border clearance and distribution within the country. Countries with weaker logistics performance may be associated with many factors such as unreliable supply chains, longer import and export times, cumbersome border procedures, a low quality infrastructure, low quality logistics services and difficulty in tracking consignments. Generally, logistics performance index scores for high-income countries tend to be higher than those for low-income countries. However, according to 2010 data, China, India, the Philippines, South Africa and Thailand have higher logistics performances than the level their income would predict. In contrast, among EM countries, Russia has a low logistics performance when compared to its income (World Bank, 2010). Table 3.1 shows the LPI ranks and scores of selected EMs, along with the components for such scores.

Income distribution

In developed countries, income distribution is relatively uniform, whereas in EMs, income distribution tends to be shaped like a pyramid, with the majority at the lower end of the pyramid, a small middle class in between, and a very low percentage of high income classes. In developed countries, a company can market a new product to early adopters and then decrease its price and content to offer it to the majority. In EMs, however, the income distribution is not that smooth. Box 3.2 shows the income distribution in BRICs and new frontier economies. Here, the USA is added as a means of comparison. As can be seen from the box, the data on income for EMs show that most of the EM population has an annual income between US$ 2,500 and 15,000.

Table 3.1   The Logistics Performance Index

	LPI rank (2010)	LPI	Customs	Infra-structure	International shipments	Logistics competence	Tracking & tracing	Timeliness
China	27	3.49	3.16	3.54	3.31	3.49	3.55	3.91
South Africa	28	3.46	3.22	3.42	3.26	3.59	3.73	3.57
Malaysia	29	3.44	3.11	3.5	3.5	3.34	3.32	3.86
Thailand	35	3.29	3.02	3.16	3.27	3.16	3.41	3.73
Turkey	39	3.22	2.82	3.08	3.15	3.23	3.09	3.94
Brazil	41	3.2	2.37	3.1	2.91	3.3	3.42	4.14
Philippines	44	3.14	2.67	2.57	3.4	2.95	3.29	3.83
India	47	3.12	2.7	2.91	3.13	3.16	3.14	3.61
Chile	49	3.09	2.93	2.86	2.74	2.94	3.33	3.8
Mexico	50	3.05	2.55	2.95	2.83	3.04	3.28	3.66
Peru	67	2.8	2.5	2.66	2.75	2.61	2.89	3.38
Indonesia	75	2.76	2.43	2.54	2.82	2.47	2.77	3.46
Egypt	92	2.61	2.11	2.22	2.56	2.87	2.56	3.31
Russia	94	2.61	2.15	2.38	2.72	2.51	2.6	3.23
Pakistan	110	2.53	2.05	2.08	2.91	2.28	2.64	3.08

Source: WorldBank, 2010.

Box 3.2   Income Distribution

Households by annual disposable income band as a percentage of total households in 2010:

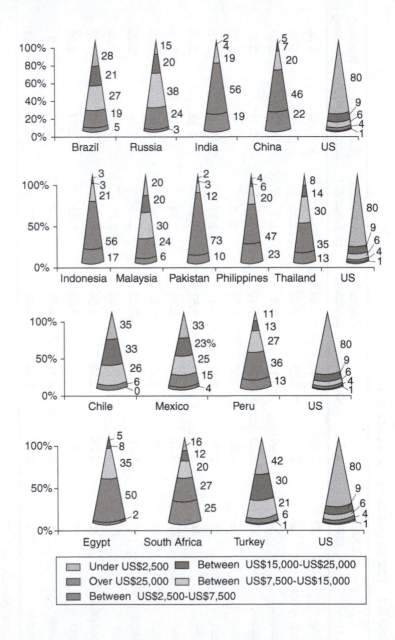

Source: Euromonitor International, 2011(Euromonitor, 2012).

Table 3.2 The income gap in emerging markets, 2005

	GINI index (%)	Poverty gap at $2 a day (PPP)	Income share held by highest 10%	Income share held by lowest 20%
Pakistan	31	19	26	9
Egypt	32	3	28	9
India	37	30	31	8
Russia	38	1	28	6
Indonesia	39	17	32	7
China	42	12	31	6
Turkey	43	3	33	5
Peru	52	6	41	4
Brazil	56	6	44	3

Source: World Bank Database, 2011.

EMs are associated with populations where a small percentage has the highest income. The GINI index measures inequality in wealth, assigning a value between 0 and 1, with 0 corresponding to perfect equality and 1 to maximum inequality. The index is calculated by looking at the ratios between total income earned by the poorest and richest segments in the population. Table 3.2 shows the GINI index and a measurement for income inequality in selected EMs.

Business groups

Business groups are legally independent firms connected by formal and informal ties that often operate in multiple industries. As they grow, business groups will expand into related and unrelated areas, often acquiring or establishing financial institutions to meet their capital demands. Business groups can be 'network-type' or 'hierarchy-type'. There are no dominant control agents in network-type business groups, rather these groups function like business clusters or networks such as the Japanese keiretsu. In contrast, in hierarchy-type business groups, a holding company controls the independent units that are often subsidiaries of each other. They are often united via family ties or by equity ownership among each other (Colphan et al., 2010).

> Diversified business (or corporate) groups are ubiquitous in EMs (e.g. India and Pakistan, Brazil and Chile, Indonesia and Thailand, Korea, and many more) and even in some developed economies (e.g. Italy, Sweden). These groups typically consist of legally independent firms, operating in multiple (often unrelated) industries, which are bound together by persistent formal (e.g. equity) and informal (e.g. family) ties; varying degrees of participation by outside investors characterize many business groups around the world. (Khanna and Yafeh, 2007, p. 335)

Table 3.3 shows the largest business groups in EMs and their ownership structures.

Table 3.3 The largest business groups in EMs, 2007

Name	Country	Revenue (US$ million)	Control	Industry
China Petrochemical Co. (Sinopeg)	China	159,260	Government	Petroleum, petro chemicals
State Grid Co. of China	China	132,885	Government	Electric power
Petrobras	Brazil	112,046	Government	Petroleum, petro chemicals
Lukoil	Russia	67,205	Family	Petroleum, petro chemicals
Tata Group	India	62,500	Family	Diversified
Carso	Mexico	51.199	Family	Diversified
PTT	Thailand	51,193	Government	Petroleum, petro chemicals
China Mobile Telecommunications Co.	China	47,055	Government	Telecommunications
Koc Holding	Turkey	36,392	Family	Diversified
BHP Billiton Plc	South Africa/ Australia	39,210	Institutional	Mining, petroleum and natural gas
Bradesco	Brazil	38,264	Family	Diversified
Reliance Group	India	35,915	Family	Diversified
Vale (CVRD)	Brazil	34,080	Pension funds	Diversified
Old Mutual	South Africa/UK	33,917	Policy holders	Insurance, banking
China Southern Power Grid	China	33,861	Government	Electric power
Sinochem	China	30,204	Government	Diversified
Baosteel Group	China	29,939	Government	Diversified
Anglo American	South Africa/UK	29,532	Institutional	Diversified
Aditya Birla Group	India	29,200	Family	Diversified
Itausa	Brazil	28,729	Institutional	Banking, insurance
Banco di Brazil	Brazil	28,449	Government	Banking
China Telecommunications	China	27,856	Government	Telecommunications
Base Element	Russia	26,800	Family	Diversified
China FAW Group	China	26,391	Government	Automobiles
China Railway Group	China	23,732	Government	General construction
Surgutneftegas	Russia	23,302	Family	Petroleum, petro chemicals
Shangai Automotive (SAIC Group)	China	22,607	Government	Automobiles
State Bank of India	India	22,402	Government	Commercial banking

Name	Country	Revenue (US$ million)	Control	Industry
China State Construction	China	22,128	Government	General construction
Techint	Argentina	22,000	Family	Diversified
Cemex	Mexico	21,658	Family	Cement
China Ocean Shipping	China	20,480	Government	Shipping
China National Offshore Oil	China	20,637	Government	Petroleum and petro chemicals
China Minmetals	China	20,517	Government	Diversified

Source: Colphan et al., 2010.

Business groups emerge as key players in their respective industries due to advantages such as relations with the government, extensive networks, strong brand names, and superior access to knowledge and resources. They often have a loyal customer base and a group name associated with high quality and trust. Moreover, they will have built extensive distribution networks. Collaborating with business groups presents an opportunity to multinationals who wish to enter EMs.

> By collaborating with a family conglomerate (business group), the foreign firm can: (1) reduce the risks, time, and capital requirements of entering target markets; (2) develop helpful relationships with governments and other key, local players; (3) target market opportunities more rapidly and effectively; (4) overcome infrastructure-related hurdles; and leverage the family conglomerate (or business group's) resources and local contracts. (Cavusgil et al., 2008: 273)

Some examples of collaboration between multinationals and business groups are the partnership of Ford and Kia in South Korea and the joint venture between Sabanci and Danone in Turkey.

In entering multiple industries and continually engaging in unrelated diversification, business groups may have formed a competitive advantage which enables them to undertake such operations efficiently.

> The main argument is that business groups appear in developing and newly industrialized countries because entrepreneurs and firms learn the capability to combine the necessary domestic and foreign resources for repeated industry entry. Combining domestic and foreign resources requires entrepreneurs to establish networks of relationships with relevant actors. Such a capability, however, can be developed and maintained as a valuable and rare skill only under asymmetric foreign trade and investment conditions with the rest of the world. (Guillen, 2010, p. 743)

However, a lack of specialization may impede business groups from competing effectively in the international arena (Globerman and Shapiro, 2008). In different circumstances, importance and success of business groups may decline due to increased competition in deregulated economies and the increased specialization necessary to generate competitive efficiencies (Khanna and Palepu, 2000). In parallel, high levels of diversification in business groups may lead to cost inefficiencies (Singh et al., 2007).

Business groups and their influences on innovation in EMs are often debated. Business groups may create entry barriers for new companies and hinder competition or they may engage in predatory price cutting to drive out new entrants. Moreover, they may also engage in preferential agreements between themselves, further creating the barriers to entry. If an industry is populated by groups that are similar in nature, the idea flow within industry among groups may be limited in nature (Mahmood and Mitchell, 2004). Business groups are large and characterized by rigidities. In such organizations, innovative ideas cannot easily flow throughout and innovators cannot easily reach management and foster their ideas. In contrast, the size and resources of groups can foster innovation if groups can act as venture capitalists (Hobday and Colpan, 2010).

In most cases, business groups' ongoing collaboration with the government will lead them to enter into diversified businesses as they gain favours from governments (Amsdem, 1989; Evans, 1995). Political connections can result in favourable treatment in privatization, access to government investment projects, and the ability to influence government policies. Research in Latin America shows that government ministers rely on business groups for information who then enjoy preferential access to government officers (Schneider, 2010). In some cases, close ties with the government can also become a burden for the business group, especially when that government changes. An opposing party may also target groups who were close to the prior government, in order to reduce the original group's power in the economy and strengthen their own.

For multinationals from developed markets, entering EMs through partnering with business groups or conglomerates appears to be a sound strategy, especially in the presence of institutional voids (Khanna and Palepu, 2000). Through partnership with business groups, multinationals from developed markets can overcome institutional inefficiencies (Wan, 2005; Lee and Peng, 2008).

Ownership in business groups

Business groups can be characterized as family-owned, state-owned and widely held. In widely held business groups, professional managers undertake the business activities and there are no distinct shareholders. Within this construct, family groups will usually have the highest performance due to a reduction in ownership-management conflicts; widely held groups would be expected to be in the middle since they will face agency problems but are also endowed with skilled management. State-owned business groups are expected to be the least successful groups since they suffer from conflicting goals, poor management and a lack of incentives and investment (Cuervo-Cazurra, 2006). Box 3.3 provides an example of the evolution of Tata, one of the largest business groups in the world.

> Known as chaebols in Korea, business houses in India, holding companies in Turkey and grupos in Latin America, huge family companies represent a unique business enterprise. Because family companies play a significant role in many EMs, it is critical for Western companies that aspire to enter these markets to develop a comprehensive understanding of their nature and impact. (Kim et al., 2008, p. 211)

The founding families of business groups are usually dominant in the groups' boards. For instance, in the largest 10 business groups in Turkey, the chairperson of the board is from the founding family and almost all of the 30 affiliates of the largest Mexican groups have family members as chairperson (Usdiken, 2010). Initially, firms founded by family members can be more flexible. Due to a long-term commitment and trust between members, monitoring costs are lower. However, the transferability of such advantages across generations will present as a bottleneck (Bhaumik et al., 2009). Even in cases where the management group is professionalized, family interference in business group management can be an issue, especially in an era when advanced management skills are becoming increasingly necessary.

Box 3.3   Tata's Transformation under Ratan Tata's Leadership

Ratan Tata is about as different from the popular image of a business titan as can be: he is a natural gentleman who lives austerely, and is happiest when talking about his pet dogs. He owns less than 1% of the group that bears his family name. But he is a titan nonetheless – the most powerful businessman in India and one of the most influential in the world.

The Tata group is a giant too. This family of companies covers cars and consulting, software and steel, tea and coffee, chemicals and hotels. Tata Consultancy Services (TCS) is Asia's largest software company. Tata Steel is India's largest steelmaker and number 10 in the world. Taj Hotels Resorts and Palaces is India's biggest luxury hotel group by far. Tata Power is the country's largest private electricity company. Tata Global Beverages is the

(Continued)

(Continued)

world's second-largest maker of branded tea. Overall, the group earned 3.2 trillion rupees, or US $67.4 billion, in revenues in 2009–10 and 82 billion rupees in profits.

Mr Tata has transformed the group. When he became chairman in 1991, India was groaning under the License Raj and Tata seldom ventured outside its home market. As he prepares to step down and the search for a successor speeds up, India is one of the world's most dynamic economies and Tata operates in over 80 countries. Mr Tata's enthronement in Bombay House, the group's HQ, took place just before the liberalization of India's economy. He spotted that liberalization was both an opportunity and a threat. It was an opportunity because it set Tata free: the economy had been so tightly regulated that you could be fined or even imprisoned for exceeding your output quotas. It was a threat because Tata was vulnerable: its companies were uncoordinated, over-manned, and under-managed.

Mr Tata focused the group on six industries that have provided most of its revenue since 2000 – steel, motor vehicles, power, telecoms, information technology (IT) and hotels – and increased its often paltry shareholding in these core businesses. The pace of foreign acquisitions has grown dramatically: in 1995–2003, Tata companies made, on average, one purchase a year; in 2004, they made six; and in 2005–06, they made more than 20. Tata Tea's takeover of the Tetley Group, a British company, for US$450m in 2000, was the first of several bold purchases of well-known brands that announced the group's arrival in the global big league. In 2007, Tata Steel bought Corus, Europe's second-largest steelmaker, for US$12.1 billion. A year later, Tata Motors paid US$2.3 billion for Jaguar Land Rover (JLR).

In late 2011, Cyrus Mistry, a director in the group and a distant relative of the Tata family, was appointed as the future CEO, and will be taking over as the chairman of the group after Ratan Tata's retirement.

Source: The Tata Group: Out of India, *The Economist*, 3 March 2011.

State-owned enterprises are created and managed by governments in order to serve commercial purposes. Failing enterprises may also be nationalized in order to prevent bankruptcy. Governments can pursue social goals and political agendas through state-owned enterprises (Luo and Tung, 2007).

Governments are now trying to take measures to increase the productivity of state-owned enterprises (Park et al., 2006). In the last decade, the internationalization of state-owned enterprises has increased rapidly (WIR, 2011). Many governments have been privatizing inefficient state-owned enterprises in order to obtain funds and then direct these funds to more efficient channels. Privatization also contributes indirectly to economic growth by attracting foreign investment. Table 3.4 shows the

Table 3.4   Summary of privatization transactions over US$1 million

$ millions	2000	2001	2002	2003	2004	2005	2006	2007	2008
Brazil	10,790	3,867	275		649	74	594	871	1,246
Russia	313	1,103	120	288	4,633	165	10,844	28,949	6,077
India	33	460	1,717	837	3,853	63	458	119	1,831
China	10,281	958	1,599	6,066	4,122	14,088	50,355	71,536	11,738
Argentina	11	11							
Chile	282	235			781		27		
Colombia	483			70		462	1,282	3,136	
Indonesia	115		188	691	841	448	270	1,622	
Malaysia			16	347	1,871				
Mexico	189					351	1,376	4,030	331
Pakistan		20	563	399	812	3,647	1,129	975	17
Peru	190	450	262		398		23		
Thailand	239	631		1,025	1,065				
Egypt	308	207			52	2,173	7,583	311	926
Turkey	2,603		218	10	1,086	11,518	8,099	4,257	6,673

Source: World Bank Privatization Database, 2011.

largest privatizations in EMs between 2001 and 2008, while Box 3.4 highlights the process of privatization in Pakistan.

Box 3.4   Lessons from Pakistan

Pakistan has been especially successful in privatizing state-owned financial institutions, reducing state ownership in the sector from 92% of assets in 1990 to 18.6% in 2004.

Influenced by socialist trends, Pakistan nationalized most of the country's industries in the 1970s, resulting in an economic setback and low levels of growth. By the 1990s, 92% of assets in the country's financial sector were owned by state-owned institutions, which were characterized as overstaffed, inefficient, under-capitalized, and poorly managed. Such banks provided credit to large corporations and other state-owned enterprises while options were limited for the housing sector, as well as for small- and medium-sized enterprises. Political interference in bank operations, as well as political agendas in staffing the institutions, contributed to such policies.

The Pakistan government started to liberalize its economy in the 1990s. It was necessary to privatize the state-owned financial institutions in order to reduce the fiscal deficit, as these institutions were a great burden on the state

(Continued)

(Continued)

due to continuous losses and lack of efficiency. In order to facilitate a successful privatization, the government set out a policy which outlined the methods of privatization, including partial and total disinvestment strategies and a focus on transparency issues.

During the privatization, many issues were encountered. First of all, policies were amended in order to restructure the national banks before privatization as investors would not be interested in the banks considering their profile at the time. Excess staff were reduced and unprofitable branches closed. The management of the banks also changed, as the number of political appointees was reduced and professional managers were employed. The government also had to recapitalize the institutions as they were burdened with accumulated losses, and increase the transparency of institutions via new laws requiring more detailed information.

The State Bank of Pakistan (SBP) was assigned to the privatization of national financial institutions. In order to minimize the risks and burdens on the government following the privatization, the SBP undertook the restructuring of the banks, ensured that the documents for privatization were clear, and evaluated potential investors. As a result of this process, 80% of the state's banking assets had been sold by 2004, leading to increased competition in the sector, lower lending rates and lower intermediation costs.

Pakistan's experience in privatizing state-owned financial institutions highlights the importance of establishing a clear and comprehensive framework, and the government role in ensuring that inefficient institutions are restructured in order to attract major investors.

Adapted from Caprio, 2005.

Governments can also choose which industries and enterprises to support, providing them with access to funding under favourable conditions, as well as subsidies.

For instance, in China, two of the largest high-technology companies, China Telecom and Lenovo, are state-backed. The main objectives of supporting selected industries and enterprises include creating national champions, creating a successful industry, and creating avenues in the economy which may be utilized for political and economic purposes. Box 3.5 gives an example of the major national champions in Brazil and China.

Box 3.5   National Champions – Brazil and China

Petrobras (Brazil) was founded by the state in 1953 to have a monopoly of all aspects of the oil sector. Together with many other state enterprises, Petrobras was founded in an effort to reduce the country's dependence on basic inputs in line with import substitution industrial policies. During the oil crisis of the 1970s, Brazil's dependence on external oil sources became noticeable, leading to a change in the state's policy on Petrobras as well as an increase in the technological capabilities of the company, shifting its focus to the extraction of deep sea oil and alternative energy sources. During this time, the company also started internationalizing in order to secure the supply of resources. Its investments were mainly focused on other developing countries such as Argentina, Mexico and Africa. In 1997, the domestic market was opened up to investment, and the government, in an effort to increase investment and fuel innovation, allowed entry into the oil sector as well.

Chinese oil and gas enterprises were set up in the 1980s by the state and restructured into the vertically integrated firms China National Petroleum Corporation (CNPC), China Petroleum and Chemical Corporation (Sinopec) in 1998. Chinese oil companies are among the most international companies in the country and to date they can be compared in size to the largest global players. Yet their growth and internationalization followed a different path from that of Brazil, as Chinese expansion was based on utilizing existing facilities or refining in countries where global competitors were not present. Thus, Chinese oil companies were less technologically advanced than Brazil and focused on conventional oil production in the domestic market. The initial strategy of Chinese oil companies therefore focused on securing resources. At the end of the 20th century, the government's motives in creating global players had led to a different strategy of forming joint ventures and making acquisitions in order to access strategic assets.

Both Petrobras and the Chinese oil giant's success can be attributed to the government support they received. The Brazilian government encouraged technological development as the country's oil reserves were mainly deep-water and a higher technological capacity was necessary in order to utilize these. With this strategy, the Brazilian government aimed to protect the country's economy from international oil crises. The internationalization of Petrobras increased development of the technological as well as management capabilities of the company, thereby leading the government to increase the international activities of the company further. The Chinese government focused on the internationalization of Chinese firms to secure resources and is currently occupied with the development of strategic capabilities in line with the government's plans to see China as a major player in the global economy. Through this process, government subsidies motivating investment and government funding have enabled the oil company's growth.

Adapted from Carvalho and Goldstein, 2009.

State-owned enterprises may limit competition. Inefficient management and a focus on social wellbeing, such as the preservation of jobs, can lead to losses. These then lead to increased financial burdens and an inefficient allocation of funds. For instance, most loans in China are provided by state-owned banks and, as of 2005, over 70% of bank loans were given to state-owned enterprises (Morck et al., 2008). Box 3.6 further explains the relationship between the state and business groups in China.

Box 3.6 Business Groups in China

In China, firms with loose associations filled the gaps generated by inefficiencies and generated economies by sharing production facilities or marketing resources before business groups emerged in the late 1980s. The state aimed to generate efficiencies by advocating centralized ownership among the loosely held associations and thereby endorsed the creation of business groups. Another target was to increase specialization and generate economies of scale.

Business groups in China were formed by creating spin-offs from the core parts of a company, by establishing new firms by joint ventures, or by mergers and acquisitions.

As the state decided to create a socialist market economy, strategies were directed towards improving the competitiveness of the formation of business groups, which eventually led to establishing the State-Owned Asset Supervision and Administration Commission of the State Council (SASAC) in 2003. The state supports business groups and views them as vehicles which can enable China to catch up with industrialized nations and strengthen the competitiveness of domestic firms. In this effect, government also supported mergers and acquisitions through an initiative referred to as the 'strong–strong combination'.

Within the country, local governments also own multiple business groups, and try to promote their own business groups. In some cases, local governments, facing shortages in terms of skilled labour and talent, will unite companies into business groups and allocate management posts accordingly. Local governments also force mergers between a profitable and a non-profitable enterprise in order to keep unprofitable enterprises from bankruptcy. This is often referred to as a 'forced marriage'.

Most business groups in China will have a large enterprise focused on the core business of the group, which will manage several specialized affiliates and research and development companies. These groups will mostly have an affiliate focused on finance, set on raising capital and arranging capital flows between its members. Cross-shareholding between business group members is common. This shareholding structure is especially endorsed because it enables group members to pursue the same objectives and be involved in joint products.

Chinese business groups pursue unrelated diversification strategies less than groups in other EMs and are concentrated on energy, utility and service industries, while the share of business groups in manufacturing industries is also increasing. State involvement in these groups is higher than in other EM groups, for instance the government had controlling power in approximately 45% of business groups in China in 2007. Still, non-government ownership is growing.

Adapted from Colphan et al., 2010.

State-owned financial institutions are still prevalent in emerging economies as well as in some developed nations, mainly due to the government's
political and economic motivations. Governments can maintain power
within an economy, which has major players such as large private banks
and conglomerates, through state-owned financial institutions. It can also
redistribute power and support industries, as well as its own enterprises,
by controlling the lending policies of state-owned financial institutions
(Caprio et al., 2005).

In EMs, highly diversified conglomerates have been successful due
to the support of the government and monopolistic advantages (Luo,
2002). However, they may also create entry barriers for new entrants
and hinder competition in the economy. Business groups are often very
large and constrained by bureaucracy and institutional rigidities which
can hinder their own innovation. The benefits and costs of belonging
to a business group, especially in the context of EMs, have been widely
discussed with ambiguous conclusions (Cuervo-Cazurra, 2006; Estrin
et al., 2009).

Business groups as a response to institutional inefficiencies

EMs are associated with market imperfections and inefficient supporting
institutions. Business groups can be analysed as organizations formed
in response to costs arising from imperfections in product, capital and
labour markets. Group members can access the technological, human
capital and financial capital of the groups and meanwhile learn from
the group's network. The group name enables the companies within the
group to attract talent, raise capital efficiently in the domestic market,
and build customer confidence quickly.

> When entering a new line of business, group organizations often can bypass
> the voids faced by another start-up by using the capital, talent or reputation
> built by another business in the group. The business group can thus serve as
> a private equity firm, executive search firm and branding consultant in a mar-
> ket that lacks a sophisticated network of these intermediaries. (Khanna and
> Palepu, 2010, p. 157)

For instance, the Tata Group in India has formed a large training pool
in order to have access to highly skilled employees. Meanwhile, the
group can also create economies of scope through joint promotion and
the utilization of a corporate brand. Another group in India, the Hero
Group, pursues a related diversification strategy unlike the Tata Group,
but is able to leverage the distribution network to provide their products (bicycles, mopeds and scooters) through rural areas efficiently.

EM companies can be faced with difficulties in raising capital as they are often not transparent, and countries are considered risky. Financial intermediaries, mutual funds and venture capitalists may not be prominent. On the other hand, business groups can transfer funds between themselves, and many have acquired or invested in financial institutions. As groups are often associated with strong track records as well as with large resources, investor relations and access to capital are easier, and capital costs are often lower since institutions and investors associate groups with a lower risk of default.

Failures in labour markets can occur due to the difficulties in obtaining information about prospective employees, a lack of trained employees and high costs in recruiting high-level management. Managerial training is often not widespread. In order to deal with such inefficiencies, many business groups such as Tata (India) and Koc Holding (Turkey) run training programmes. Groups can lower the cost of training by spreading the fixed cost among group companies. Such training and development of an internal talent pool also enables the group to shift talent where it is needed and to access talent easily. The advantages of working in a high-quality institution, the prospects and challenges offered by a structure with multiple businesses, and financial security also attracts well-trained personnel to business groups.

In product markets, some issues in EMs are weak contract enforcements, the opportunistic behaviour of suppliers, or limited availability of suppliers. When a business group invests in the supply chain, it can overcome these difficulties. A group name can also become a brand which signifies quality and enhances trust. As such, advertising and the focus of the media in EMs can concentrate on group identity. Once built into a brand, a group's name can be very valuable, helping the group to enter into new businesses, even in unrelated areas. Consumers trust group brands and thus the group is able to accumulate sales in new areas with lower costs in terms of advertising.

Business groups engage in diversification, leveraging relationships and resources, however in the presence of continuous liberalization this diversification may become a liability (Hoskisson et al., 2005; Lee and Peng, 2008). In the long run, as institutional inefficiencies decrease, the positive effects of the business group – stemming from responding to institutional inefficiencies – may decline (Lee and Peng, 2008). As governments liberalize the economy and reduce their role in the economy, firm dependence on the government decreases. As regulatory policies are more stable, the need to maintain strong relations with the government lessens. In parallel, as the legal system is strengthened, the application of commercial and corporate law becomes stable, and firms need to rely less and less on strong ties in order to compensate for legal inefficiencies and shield themselves from legal risks (Peng and Zhou, 2005). Hence, the importance of relations and personal connections in business may decline as institutions develop and economies move towards more market-based systems (Peng et al., 2005). All the factors indicate that the advantages of business groups, stemming from relationships with the authorities and compensating for institutional inefficiencies, may decline in the future, parallel to the development of the EM business environments.

Family-owned small and medium sized enterprises (SMEs)

Many EM firms are family firms or firms with concentrated shareholdings. Family firms are usually embedded in local culture, and prefer high levels of control (Bhaumik et al., 2009). They are often more centralized, risk averse, and informal. While such characteristics enable the firm to be flexible, they can also impede growth due to risk averseness and a lack of professional management. Family firms can face conflicting interests due to the co-existence of managers and family members who are not involved in management. Employee productivity may be affected due to the propensity to employ family members. Such issues could lead to counterproductive growth strategies, which will impede the firm from maintaining its competitive position (Fernandez and Nieto, 2006). Governance based on relationships, family ownership and minimal use of professional management is characteristic of many EM companies. Internationalization based on relations may lead to suboptimal choices in such companies (Globerman and Shapiro, 2008).

On the other hand, family members will often exhibit a long-term commitment to the firm (Gallo and Sveen, 1991). Many family firms will acquire corporate shareholders to tackle management issues which then encourages the development of both the management process and the internationalization process (Fernandez and Nieto, 2006). Another advantage of family firms is that they tend to form closer ties with suppliers, customers and those external parties who provide financing or advice. In EMs, such connections may be used to overcome institutional voids. In fact, in a Korean analysis of high-technology family and non-family owned firms, connections and community are used by family firms more frequently and improve performance (Miller et al., 2009).

Challenges Facing EM Economies

Integrating the population into the workforce

A challenge pertaining to the growth of the population and the increase in productivity is the ability to direct the proceeds of growth into productive activity. The rapid expansion of the working-age population contributes to EM growth. This increase also means that countries are challenged with ensuring gainful opportunities for new entrants to the labour force. Countries such as Turkey and India have a young population, and the working population within these countries is bound to increase. Thus, the capacity to create employment and the ability of institutions to meet the demands of the growing population will gain importance in these economies (EIU, 2011).

The structure of the population creates different challenges for China and Russia, which are faced with lower population growth rates. China is facing issues in integrating the working-age population into the labour force. Looking forward, different challenges will arise in the Chinese economy as working-age population gets older. Due to the one-child policy of the government, population growth has decreased substantially, and the younger generation will have to bear the burden of a very large retired population in the long term. Similarly, Russian population growth has been very low, thereby indicating the country may have issues related to a limited availability of working age population.

Economic growth leads to a rise in income, enabling people to move out of poverty and join the middle class. Thus, economic growth is often associated with a reduction in poverty and inequality and the rise of the middle class. Emerging economies such as China and Brazil display high levels of income disparities between classes, and they are faced with the challenge of reducing such disparities and creating a consumption-led economy. The creation and sustainability of the middle classes are largely driven by stable employment and higher education levels. On the other hand, the new middle-class population largely consists of new entrants and its sustainability is a concern (Kharas, 2010).

Developing institutions

High savings rates have enabled many EMs to invest in infrastructure to an extent, however their infrastructure needs are rapidly increasing.

EMs need to preserve high savings rates in order to invest in the development of their economies. In order to channel savings within the economy efficiently, institutions need to be improved. These improvements would require the development of property rights, financial intermediaries, and efficient market systems.

EMs need to allocate savings efficiently in order to catch up with developed countries. In this, the development of intermediaries which can enable a sufficient allocation of savings will prove to be a challenge. Therefore financial institutions in EMs need to be strengthened further in order to meet the demands of economic growth.

Despite optimistic figures for growth in emerging economies, the latter are very different from advanced economies and their catching up may take time due to various constraints such as institutional voids. The necessary institutional infrastructure to support a capital economy takes time to develop and in most cases emerging economies are behind in this infrastructural development.

Institutional deficiencies stemming from inefficiencies in legal systems, and in the enforcement of policies, bureaucracy and underdeveloped intermediaries, increase firm costs and risks, thereby hindering growth in EMs (LiPuma et al., 2011).

Reducing the dependency on advanced economies

Sustained development is dependent on political stability, efficient institutions, and good governance. Increased support for investment, as well as the influences of international institutions on economic policies, enable the development of EM economies. However, an increased focus on trade by itself is not enough to sustain growth in the long run. To do so, EMs need to focus on inward investments in developing institutions, infrastructure, and technological and managerial know-how within the economy. Inward investment can enable the country's economic actors to function effectively, contribute to know-how, and maximize the benefits of foreign investment. For instance, by ensuring an acceptable level of local content or by insisting on a level of local partnership, government can encourage the transfer of know-how. However, investments in the technological capabilities of the country is necessary to ensure that the knowledge transfer actually takes place.

Investing in technological capabilities comes about as a condition for the sustained development in EMs. Innovation is generally explained as the creation of new technology and its introduction in a market.

The growth level of developed markets is attributed to innovation in the markets while EMs are considered backwards in terms of innovation. Thus, for EMs developing technological capabilities is integral to catching up with developed markets. EMs have focused on copying technologies, but in order to sustain growth they need to build their capabilities for innovation. Inward investments in technology are necessary for building these capabilities.

Governments endorse the presence of multinationals in EMs to introduce competition into the country, and generate spill-overs and technology transfers. (Marin and Bell, 2003). Multinationals which were once considered as tools for economic control by industrialized economies are now considered as tools for the development of emerging economies (Narula, 2009). Foreign firms entering into an EM can act as a source of information for local firms, thereby reducing the cost of exports for such firms (Aitken et al., 1997).

On the other hand, traditional arguments on the beneficial effects of MNCs in developing markets due to spill-over effects are fading due to concerns related to agency costs, a reduced investment in technology facilitated by transfers, and the prevalence of global suppliers. Agency costs arise if the motivations of the parties entering into an alliance are contradictory. EM firms typically seek access to MNE resources while the MNE's try to access local know-how. In this respect, providing the EM firm with new technology and know-how may reduce the incentive for the EM firm to collaborate. Thus, MNEs may be unwilling to transfer knowledge to their international joint venture (IJV) partners in the presence of agency costs, especially if the MNE does not hold the controlling stake (Rui and Yip, 2007; Li et al., 2009; Saebi and Dong, 2009). Similarly, MNEs also tend to acquire control or form wholly owned subsidiaries (WOS) in R&D-intensive industries, impeding knowledge transfer to local firms in developing countries (Demirbag et al., 2007). Sole transfer of such technology may hinder the developing country's development if it is not accompanied by generating know-how within the developing country (Bell and Pavitt, 1993). The crowding-out effect indicates that FDI may lead to less innovation by increasing technology imports. An analysis of spill-over effects indicates that at a certain point crowding out and market-seeking activities dominate, thereby exerting negative effects on low-technology industries where technology orientation of firms are also significant in determining the level of spill-over effects (Buckley et al., 2007). An EM firm may reduce its investment in R&D and transfer technology fromits MNE partner, thereby failing to acquire innovation skills or even a deep understanding of the technology (Hatani, 2009). Due to technology gaps, low IP protection and underdeveloped supply chains in EMs, the MNE often chooses to cooperate with its own partners or other MNEs globally, using the host country as a means to access cheap resources. In such cases, spill-overs are impeded (Hatani, 2009) as the average MNC evolves into a corporate umbrella global supplier (Ghauri and Yamin, 2009). Pure acquisition of new technologies or gaining access to technologies by outsourcing can have negative consequences on performance if the firm fails to invest in its integrative capabilities and internal processes, through which the firm would understand and deploy the new technology (Weigelt, 2009).

EMs have been associated with a limited investment in technology. Traditionally, economies within these markets are based on non-value added production, which is labour intensive. Thereby, many EMs are dependent on developed economies for a technology transfer (Lall, 2001). EM growth has mainly been facilitated by economic and political reforms and the adoption of existing know-how and technologies. However, improvements in policies in terms of the protection of property rights and macroeconomic stability, as well as increased exposure to new technologies, have contributed to an increased rate in technological advancement (World Bank, 2011b). Competition from MNEs from developed countries has also accelerated the growth of innovative capabilities of EM firms (Gorodnichenko et al., 2008). Even though firms from developed markets are still the creators of new technologies, firms from EMs have been absorbing new technologies more rapidly as their exposure to such technologies increases (World Bank, 2011b).

The technological bases of many EMs are weaker than those of developed nations, however governments and firms have realized the importance of investing in technological capabilities for global competition and are increasing their investment to this effect. China, India, and many other countries have increased their investment in technology (Grueber and Studt, 2010). In 2010, 114 firms from EMs were included in the top 1,000 firms worldwide in terms of R&D spending. While the number of patents obtained by EM residents was approximately 2% of the number of patents obtained globally in 1995, this ratio had increased to over 10% by 2008 (World Bank, 2011b). As seen in Table 3.5, the share of EMs and developing countries in world research expenditure increased from 30% in 2002 to 37% in 2007, and spending per researcher has increased significantly in BRIC economies. Yet in order to sustain growth, EM firms need to reduce their dependency on advanced economies for technology and improve their own technological capabilities substantially.

Table 3.5 World R&D expenditure

	Researchers (thousands)		World share of researchers (%)		Researchers per million inhabitants		GERD per researcher (PPP, $ thousands)	
	2002	2007	2002	2007	2002	2007	2002	2007
World	5810	7209	100	100	926	1080	136	159
Developed countries	4047	4478	70	62	3363	3655	161	195
Developing countries and EMs	1734	2696	30	37	398	580	79	101
Brazil	72	125	1	2	401	657	181	162
Russia	492	469	9	7	3385	3304	32	50
India	116	155	2	2	111	137	103	127
China	811	1423	14	20	630	1071	48	72

Source: UNESCO, 2011.

There is evidence that some EM countries are making efforts to develop their technological capabilities. In EMs, people are now empowered by universities, research centres and access to information via improved communication technologies, which should transfer into developments in innovation (Sachs, 2008). Meanwhile, many MNEs from developed economies are also trying to spread R&D efforts globally and are also investing in R&D centres in both EMs and developed countries (UNESCO, 2011).

The formation of globally distributed R&D networks has been accelerated over the past two decades. Due to the increasing availability of technical personnel in EMs, many multinationals have been shifting their R&D investments to such countries, and especially to China and India (Ghemawat, 2010). The global R&D shift is mostly to India and China, and China is preferred due to market size and a need to access the market. Hence, new product development R&D centres are increasingly located in China. Investments into R&D centres in India are mostly asset-seeking and designed to exploit access, thus growing the intellectual infrastructure within the country (Sauvant et al., 2011). Currently, MNEs such as Microsoft, GE and Intel have research centres in India. Coca-Cola and Nokia have also been investing in product development centres in China in order to be able to utilize the large pool of engineers and scientists in the country (Tse, 2011). Russia, Brazil, and Eastern Europe are also becoming increasingly competitive in attracting R&D investment, due to escalating wages and also because quality personnel in China and India have already been employed (Sauvant et al., 2011).

There is some evidence that, traditionally, China and India would import a technology, and then assemble and re-export products, which is a model still in existence today. However, the strategies of many Chinese and Indian firms are shifting through a growth model based on investment in R&D and innovation (Sachs, 2008). For instance, the behaviour of the Indian pharmaceutical industry suggests that they first imitate the product and then invest in R&D development, with resources generated by the generic business (Athreye and Godley, 2009). Similarly, Chinese enterprises, faced with intensive domestic competition, are no longer relying on cost advantages and are instead enhancing their technological bases to overcome competitive disadvantages in the domestic market (Yiu et al., 2007). Though the shift in R&D is predominantly focused on adapting designs or contributions to existing products (Sauvant et al., 2011), some firms have also been focusing on building innovative structures and becoming global leaders. For instance, Huawei has invested 10% of its sales in R&D since its inception, has established 12 R&D centres around the world, and has formed technical alliances to improve its offerings. The company has developed new products to penetrate different segments within the country's market and successfully built brands that have enabled the company to compete globally. Huawei first internationalized into EMs and then moved towards developed countries. Some of the factors which have augmented its growth have been the ability to take advantage of low-cost manufacturing and low-cost R&D in China, as well as a continued focus on marketing (Gadiesh et al., 2008).

The Chinese government is planning to increase R&D funding from 1.7% of GDP in 2011 to 2.5% of GDP by 2020. Current levels in the USA sit at around 2.7% of GDP. One of the reasons for the increased focus on technology is the domination of foreign firms in high-tech industries. For instance, 85% of high-tech exports from China were from foreign-owned firms in 2008, and within these products the share of Chinese content was very low. Thus, new policies aim at increasing the technological competence of local firms and boosting the production of value-added products by domestic firms. In this way, the government hopes to provide jobs for increasingly skilled workers and maintain the growth rates of the country, especially considering that competition from other EMs, such as Malaysia, Thailand and Vietnam, as bases for low-technology manufacturing, is increasing. In order to increase the competitiveness of national firms, domestic manufacturers have been consolidated into national champions, such as CSR and

AVIC, in an effort to create economies of scale. Foreign investment policies are also changing as the transfer of technology has become a precondition of operating in China in some sectors (Hout and Ghemawat, 2011).

Chapter Questions

1 In emerging markets, why do institutional voids occur and what can companies do to operate successfully in the presence of institutional voids?
2 What are business groups and how do they develop? Discuss the advantages and disadvantages of business groups.
3 How do technological capabilities affect emerging markets? What are the future indications?
4 How does infrastructure availability and efficiency affect multinationals' decisions when entering emerging markets?

FOUR Opportunities and Trends in Emerging Markets

Economic growth in EMs has led to higher urbanization levels, as discussed previously. Increased urbanization has multiple indications in the economic structure of EMs, some of which have been mentioned. As cities develop, the need for infrastructure and investment increases. Moreover, as populations migrate to cities, they often join the formal workforce, and the size of the population employed in jobs which offer higher incomes increases. In parallel, urbanization leads to a change in customer lifestyles and preferences, and such changes are different in each market (Chu-Weininger and Weininger, 2009). The consumption of higher-end goods increases with higher income (Budhwar and Varma, 2011). As consumption increases, parallel to income, demand shifts towards the consumption of durables and away from the consumption of staple goods. Thus, accelerated growth in a middle-class population indicates a rise in the demand of value-added products such as cars and technological goods. Population growth in cities also provides opportunities as regards infrastructure as cities are faced with the need to accommodate a rising population (Wilson et al., 2010). This phenomenon can clearly be observed in Figure 4.1, which shows that growth rates in investment and consumption for EMs are higher than those of advanced economies.

Figure 4.2 shows the forecasted increase in car penetration levels within BRICs, which can indicate the level of growth in spending that is expected from these countries. Figure 4.2 also shows the predicted changes in household consumption expenditure within five years. While the share of consumption by developed economies decreases, the share held by developing economies increases, thereby reducing the gap between these.

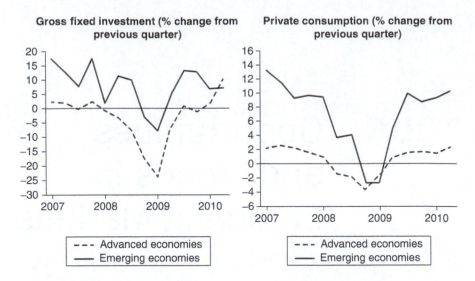

Figure 4.1 Growth in investment and consumption in EMs
Source: UNCTAD, 2011.

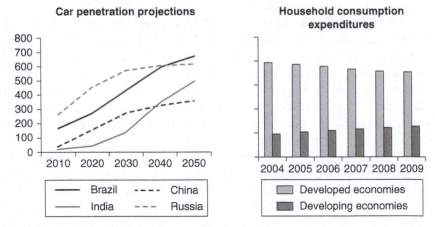

Figure 4.2 Increased consumption in BRICs
Source: Global Economics Paper No. 192, The Long-Term Outlook for the BRICs and N-11 Post Crisis (car penetration calculated as number of cars for 1000 people)(O'Neill and Stupnytska, 2009).

The Growth of Middle Income and the Rise in Consumption

The growth in consumption in EMs is due to economic growth, which increases income levels within these countries. Higher income levels are then translated into the economy as increased demand and a growing middle class (Kharas, 2010). For instance, growth in the BRIC economy is mainly attributed to the rise of a new middle class, defined as a population with an annual income between US$6,000 and US$30,000 in PPP terms by Goldman Sachs. According to their forecasts, the middle class,

Box 4.1 Income Distribution Projections in BRICs

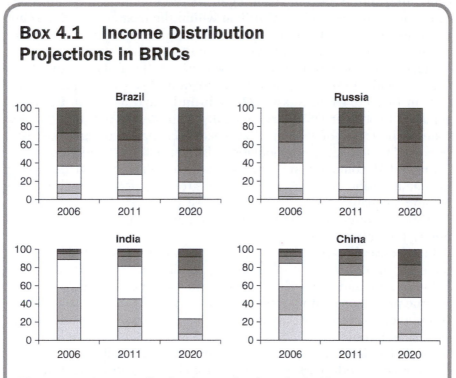

Figure 4.3 Income distribution projections in BRICs

- Households (% of Total) with an Annual Disposable Income Over US$25,000
- Households (% of Total) with an Annual Disposable Income Between US$15,000 and US$25,000
- Households (% of Total) with an Annual Disposable Income Between US$10,000 and US$15,000
- ☐ Households (% of Total) with an Annual Disposable Income Between US$5,000 and US$10,000
- Households (% of Total) with an Annual Disposable Income Between US$2,500 and US$5,000
- Households (% of Total) with an Annual Disposable Income Under US$2,500

Data source: Euromonitor, 2012. Data retrieved 22 February 2012, from www.portal.euromonitor.com/

which is approximately 1.7 billion people in 2009, is expected to increase to 3.6 billion by 2030; 85% of this increase is expected to be from EMs (Lawson and Gilman, 2009). Table 4.1 shows forecasts of the percentage of the population considered as middle class in selected EMs.

Currently, the middle classes within BRIC economies consist of 2 billion people, whose spending totals are $6.9 trillion per year. If growth in these economies continues, the spending of the middle classes within these economies could reach US$20 trillion within the next decade (Court and Narasimhan, 2010). In contrast, the domestic demand in industrialized countries continues to shrink (O'Neill and Stupnytska, 2009).

Income distribution in BRICs, as well as in other EMs, is expected to change rapidly in the near future. As shown in Box 4.1, income levels of 68% in Brazil, 64% in Russia, 22.7% in India and 34.3% in China are expected to be over US$15,000 annually. Considering that Box 4.1 illustrates a short span of 15 years, the speed of change in the income distribution of these countries' population also needs to be highlighted.

Many EM countries are now increasing their focus on decreasing income inequality. For instance, China has recently declared that reducing income inequality is a priority in its latest five-year plan. Such policies in EMs are bound to affect consumption patterns and forecasts considerably (Accenture, 2012).

In a research report by Accenture, it was stated that the income increase in EMs will correspond approximately to US$8.5 trillion between 2010 and 2020. This increase also corresponds to 60% of global income projections within this period (Accenture, 2012). In parallel, consumption patterns in EMs are bound to change as members consume the additional income.

Parallel to the increase in income, consumer expenditure on a variety of goods across industries is changing across EMs. Figure 4.4 and Table 4.2 provide examples of increased spending across BRICs and New Frontier Economies over a five-year period. As can be seen from the data, spending on clothing, housing, household goods and health has increased rapidly throughout these countries.

The growth of mid-sized cities

Many multinationals have traditionally focused on the largest cities in EMs with populations above 10 million. Such markets offer feasible entry points, and provide firms with the opportunity to establish a presence and brand in areas with adequate infrastructure. Moreover, mega cities have relatively high-end consumption habits, due to a vibrant population

Table 4.1 Forecasts on the growth of middle-income ($6,000–30,000) populations

Percentage per year	Brazil	Russia	India	China	Egypt	Indonesia	Mexico	Pakistan	Philippines	Turkey
2009	46	71	6	37	39	16	61	9	15	79
2015	52	71	16	59	57	29	65	13	23	81
2025	59	56	46	75	84	57	65	22	22	70
2040	57	29	89	53	82	82	49	42	49	35

Source: Goldman Sachs: The power of the purse, Lawson & Gilman, 2009.

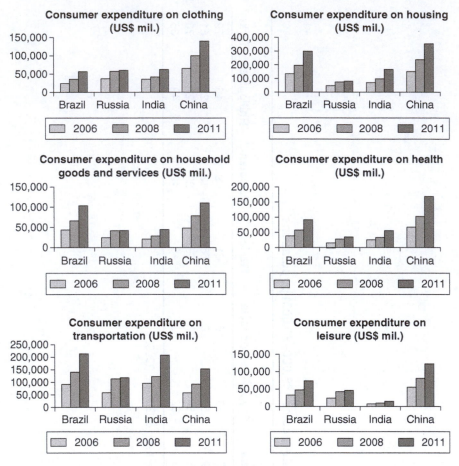

Figure 4.4   Consumer expenditure in BRICs

Source: Euromonitor, 2012. Data retrieved 22 February 2012 from www.portal. euromonitor.com/

with high income and education levels. Meanwhile, according to research by the Boston Consulting Group, 60% of the GDP growth in the world is due to the growth of EM cities, and by 2015, 67% of the growth will be from mid-sized cities. Meanwhile, by 2030, 371 new EM cities with a population over 500,000 will be added to the 717 emerging cities of a similar population which exist as of 2010 (Jin et al., 2010).

Within the next 15 years, mid-sized cities in EMs may account for 40% of global growth (Dobbs et al., 2011). Growth in relatively smaller cities leads to increased demand in household goods, consumer products, education, healthcare and financial services. In parallel, multinationals can take advantage of this growth and enter these relatively unsaturated markets (Marr and Reynard, 2010). Major opportunities in such areas are also associated with various challenges. In order to take advantage of the rapid

Table 4.2 Consumer expenditure in new frontier economies (in US$ million)

Consumer expenditure, clothing				Consumer expenditure, housing		
	2006	2008	2011	2006	2008	2011
Indonesia	8,392	8,607	10,998	38,511	46,464	64,761
Malaysia	1,864	2,302	2,587	13,721	18,053	22,016
Pakistan	4,243	4,680	6,750	21,070	25,243	38,346
Philippines	1,959	2,630	3,019	19,594	27,776	3,488
Thailand	8,527	10,304	10,763	9,253	11,226	14,960
Chile	4,218	4,499	7,029	11,494	15,145	20,942
Mexico	11,695	11,766	10,403	137,715	159,713	169,710
Peru	1,424	2,308	3,274	1,109	14,362	18,992
Egypt	4,964	6,507	8,359	13,490	21,991	32,627
South Africa	7,578	7,767	11,127	20,942	21,616	30,617
Turkey	20,238	23,508	20,894	69,781	108,247	116,952

Consumer expenditure, household goods and services				Consumer expenditure, health goods and medical services		
	2006	2008	2011	2006	2008	2011
Indonesia	13,108	16,521	24,420	8,886	13,231	19,764
Malaysia	3,941	6,092	8,785	1,553	2,155	2,782
Pakistan	2,570	3,017	4,572	3,315	4,203	6,554
Philippines	4,817	6,905	8,356	2,686	4,145	5,476
Thailand	7,592	9,992	11,557	7,871	9,830	12,378
Chile	6,808	8,363	11,467	6,093	7,616	11,528
Mexico	29,961	33,376	34,998	27,032	30,995	32,465
Peru	1,794	2,790	3,927	4,571	7,304	9,881
Egypt	3,386	4,740	6,223	3,804	7,396	11,265
South Africa	12,398	12,167	16,310	14,803	15,966	24,191
Turkey	31,824	38,203	41,936	15,961	21,827	21,122

Consumer expenditure, transport				Consumer expenditure, leisure and recreation		
	2006	2008	2011	2006	2008	2011
Indonesia	14,257	21,393	31,149	3,087	4,558	6,446
Malaysia	10,265	15,877	21,305	3,746	5,364	7,222
Pakistan	5,407	6,652	10,502	1,593	1,913	2,970
Philippines	7,035	10,408	13,093	463	656	779
Thailand	19,989	24,659	31,348	7,355	8,404	10,422
Chile	12,670	17,096	21,091	4,747	5,881	8,195
Mexico	97,323	109,221	118,035	29,694	34,458	36,553
Peru	5,632	7,219	9,519	1,204	1,426	1,839
Egypt	3,466	5,563	7,986	2,047	2,863	3,462
South Africa	22,228	23,408	33,648	6,500	6,395	8,546
Turkey	57,136	75,272	74,669	18,319	21,014	22,534

Source: Euromonitor, 2012. Available at: www.portal.euromonitor.com/

growth in mid-sized cities, firms may have to invest in infrastructure, warehousing or distribution centres. In most cases, they will also need to form relations with distributors in these regions.

A major task when considering entry into different areas in EMs is defining customer segments and identifying those areas which are likely to have the largest number of consumers within the segment (Egan and Ovanessoff, 2011). Clustering EMs can prove to be a cost-effective strategy to encourage in EMs. A company can both try to achieve economies of scale and minimize the costs related to customization and marketing if accurate clusters are formulated (Pacek and Thorniley, 2007). Moreover, a cluster management system may enable the flow of management ideas in similar markets and thereby enable the company to meet the needs of consumers more effectively, increasing the innovation of the company both on the product and the process side. The middle classes will also have sub clusters, such as more traditional clusters focused on savings and less open to innovation and foreign products. Such clusters may be attached to local customs and resist the change offered by multinationals. In contrast, there will be sub clusters consisting of the younger and more affluent consumers who like to experiment and are more often the target of many consumer product companies.

Rural development

In EMs, rural segments are growing in parallel to overall growth within their economies. Even though rural areas may have low income levels, their aggregate spending is considerable. Hence, many multinationals have identified rural areas as a future opportunity and are working to create markets in such areas. For instance, Procter and Gamble sends out researchers to rural areas and has recently come up with a purification system called PUR which has been designed to provide clean drinking water in poor countries (INSEAD, 2011). Procter & Gamble in China has allocated 30% of its product development budget in the country to products for rural consumers (Walters et al., 2010). Likewise Essilor International established rural branches because they discovered that in rural areas most consumers didn't wear spectacles because they didn't have access to them. Like Essilor, many companies are focusing on distribution system innovations in order to overcome issues with access. Yet, in these segments, companies still need to make sure that they have conducted adequate research as rural consumers will differ greatly between areas in a given market. For instance, in China the highest income rural consumers have incomes almost 30 times that of the lowest income consumers. Thus, what is acceptable in one rural area may not be so in another (INSEAD, 2011).

Services in EMs

As markets develop, new opportunities are created for multinationals, especially in the services area. Local firms in EMs which are trying to be on a par with their competitors from developed countries are increasingly seeking services such as consulting. In parallel to rising incomes, the demand for personal services such as real estate, personal banking and private healthcare is also increasing. Considering that the demand for services is associated mostly with middle and higher income segments of the population, the demand in EMs is due to increase continually. In parallel, the professional services industry is rapidly growing in EMs (Freeman and Sandwell, 2008).

Many financial service providers have started to provide microfinance services in EMs. Microfinance is the provision of financial services to poor segments of the population who generally do not have access to such services. Microfinance represents as a significant opportunity by which firms can generate financial returns and also contribute to social development (Dieckmann et al., 2007). The major providers of microfinance used to be NGOs, however the share of private firms in this industry is rapidly increasing. A major contribution of microfinance services is providing capital for a populations poor for small businesses, which can then have positive effects in reducing poverty in the long run (Morduch et al., 2009).

In 2007, the size of the microfinance industry was estimated at US$40 billion (Constantinou and Ashta, 2011). Firms utilize different strategies in microfinance to ensure credit repayment. A common strategy is to undertake group lending practices which ask for joint liability for repayment. Hence, if a member does not pay the loan, the other members of the group are obliged to repay that member's share as well. As a result borrowers will form groups, after carefully ensuring that each member is trustworthy (Hermes and Lensink, 2007). In this manner, firms can reduce the risks associated with repayment by using social capital as collateral (Lerpold, 2012). Other strategies in microfinance can be insisting on monthly savings and demanding small repayments on a monthly basis.

Major categories that poor households use loans for include care and household needs, health expenses, investments, and education. Such households can obtain loans through multiple sources, such as well-known providers, pawnbrokers, family and friends, and small shops providing credit, which are mostly informal institutions (Guérin et al., 2011).

Technology and telecommunications

Internet penetration has been increasing at higher rates in EMs when compared to developed nations and this trend is expected to continue (Persinger et al., 2011). Across the BRICS, the mobile penetration rates for China and India remain at around 91% and 41%, while the penetration rates for Brazil and Russia are 48% and 96% respectively. Currently, the internet penetration rate of the BRIC countries is approximately 20% while the same rates are around 70% and 74% in Japan and the USA respectively. BRIC countries present a great opportunity for internet and communication services (Aguilar et al., 2010). For instance, cellular phone penetration in Latin America increased from 25% in 2003 to 80% in 2008. Higher penetration of new technologies in the area also indicates improved access to global markets and information (Aguilar et al., 2009). This trend and also the relatively lower consumption of the internet across EMs together highlight a growth potential.

Increasing productivity levels is crucial for sustaining economic growth in EMs. Such an increase is dependent on multiple variables such as government policies, the investment environment, increased education, and the diffusion of technology. Technological progress can increase productivity across many economic activities. Such progress can even increase the efficiency of low-tech industries such as agriculture. In parallel, EMs can increase productivity levels at accelerated rates and thereby reduce the gap between themselves and developed markets through the increased use of technology (O'Neill, 2011). For instance, according to the World Bank, a 10% increase in broadband service penetration corresponds to an average of 1.3% growth in a study of 120 countries, and this effect is stronger in developing markets when compared to developed ones (World Bank, 2009). The usage of technology in EMs can be measured by the usage of telephones, mobile phones, computers, and the internet (O'Neill, 2011). Figure 4.5 shows the penetration of technology across BRICs, measured as telephone, mobile phone, personal computer usage, and number of internet users over five years. As can be observed the levels are relatively low, however they are increasing rapidly in BRICs.

Globally, younger populations are associated with a tendency to try new things, and this is especially visible in the technology field. For instance, there are similarities in the consumption of technology-related goods and the internet among the BRICs, however more pronounced similarities exist within consumer segments, and especially that of the younger population. Younger customers across the BRICs are changing their lifestyles continually as their income rises (Gupta, 2011). In fact, younger populations constitute the majority of online

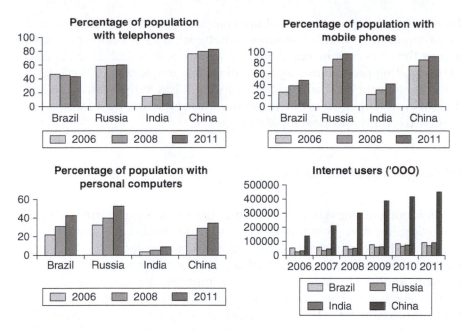

Figure 4.5 Technology penetration in BRICs

Source: Euromonitor, 2012. Data retrieved 22 February 2012 from www.portal.euromonitor.com

customers (Aguilar et al., 2010). Many companies, especially in telecommunications, are investing rapidly in EMs in order to have the resources to meet the demand as consumption rises. For instance, in Latin America, America Movil and Telefonica are continuously engaging in investments and undertaking acquisitions in order to build infrastructure and establish their presence. As a result, these two companies accounted for 90% of new connections in the region (Accenture, 2012).

A decrease in gender inequality

In general, gender equality leads to economic growth as women are introduced to the labour force and the overall level of human capital in the economy increases. (Lawson and Gilman, 2009). The increased presence of female participation in consumption affects consumption patterns, creating even bigger opportunities for the consumption of household goods in EMs.

In many EMs, education levels of women are increasing rapidly. However, family- or work-related issues cause a significant number of them to leave the workforce. Many companies are developing mentoring programmes, enabling women to network and develop relations to ensure their success in business. For instance, General Electric has a talent-spotting programme, open to all female employees in the UAE, in order to cultivate networking. Similarly, Intel has WIN (women at Intel Network) in China, in order to promote professional development for women (Hewlett and Rashid, 2011).

Investments in infrastructure

In considering business in EMs, the limitations of infrastructure will create challenges, however growth rates in the improvement of the infrastructure as well as the commitment of EM governments, as indicated by budget allocations, also show that this challenge will be mitigated considerably in the near future. The increased need to improve infrastructure also provides business opportunities as governments work with the private sector in commissioning infrastructure investment projects or fund raising.

In countries with accelerated growth patterns, the demand for infrastructure and housing increases rapidly. Multinationals can work with EM governments in undertaking construction activities. Moreover, in order to finance infrastructure governments need funding, which highlights significant opportunities for financial service providers. As governments invest in the development of a country's infrastructure in an attempt to facilitate an efficient business landscape, their need for products and services such as machinery, transportation equipment and technology products increases, which creates a major opportunity for multinationals in the relevant industries. In most technology-transfer projects, Western machinery and equipment are being bought by EMs. Even other developing economies that cannot be considered as emerging are striving hard to build up their infrastructures and basic industry sectors, for which they are importing Western technologies and components.

Many emerging economies have yet to extend their basic facilities such as telephone lines, roads and electricity beyond their capital city. The growth rate of EMs has accentuated the importance of investing in infrastructure because its current state in many EMs is not sufficient to support high growth rates. For instance, in India 40% of the traffic is on 2% of the roads. Thus, investments in infrastructure, and mainly on transportation, are expected to rise 10% annually until 2030 (Airoldi et al., 2010).

EM growth is associated with rapid urbanization. Figure 4.6 shows urbanization forecasts for BRICs and new frontier economies. This pattern especially highlights the infrastructure development that cities will need in order to support an increased population as well as rapid

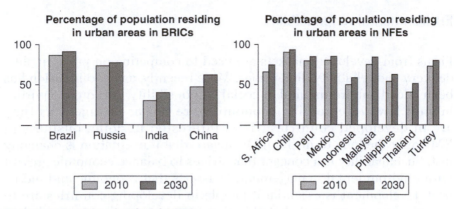

Figure 4.6 Urbanization in EMs

Source: United Nations, Department of Economic and Social Affairs, Population Division, 2011. World Population Prospects: 2009 revision, CD-ROM edition.

growth. For instance, according to the estimates of the Boston Consulting Group, EMs will need approximately US$13.8 trillion of investment in housing between 2010 and 2030. This need for housing also highlights the opportunities in all construction-related industries. As an example, 70% of the demand for elevators in 2010 was from EMs and China alone made up 50% of this demand (Jin et al., 2010). Similarly, the demand for transportation and electricity is expected to grow rapidly in EMs, particularly because of urbanization.

Countries such as China, where rates of urban population growth are high, need especially to focus on the development of infrastructure, on improving their electricity systems, housing and water supply, and on increasing transportation links. While growth increases the demand for infrastructure, investing in infrastructure is necessary to sustain that growth. As such, the Indian government has tripled its spending on its logistics infrastructure from US$10 billion in 2003 to US$30 billion in 2010 (Gupta et al., 2010). Infrastructure investment in cities with populations over 500,000 in EMs is predicted to be US$30–40 trillion over the next 20 years (Jin et al., 2010). Such figures and budget allocations indicate that the infrastructure of EMs is bound to improve considerably in the near future.

Another opportunity arising from investments in infrastructure is the need for financial services. While some countries with surplus funds such as China can meet their infrastructure needs, other economies with less liquid budgets such as Brazil, India and Turkey (as well as developed countries such as the USA or UK) will need funding from investors (Airoldi et al., 2010). Such a need will create opportunities for private investors who are willing to help governments, leading to increased levels of public–private partnerships.

Environmental responsibility

Firms from developed markets are used to competing on price, quality, delivery and reliability dimensions. More recently, a new dimension has been added: environmental or social responsibility. Although environmental laws in emerging economies are not as stringent as they are in developed countries, firms interested in doing business in EMs over the long term should be aware that the situation is changing fast. Sustainability is a concept that strives to balance economic growth with environmental management. It asserts that economic and industrial development is essential if people in developing countries are to rise above poverty, and that this development can be accomplished without destroying the environment: long-term economic growth ultimately depends on the integrity of the ecosystem. For instance, Mexico is an important emerging economy that is developing environmental regulations as stringent as those in the USA or Canada. Environmental awareness is also rising in other emerging economies, and governments may have to pass laws under public pressure to protect the environment. By being involved in environmental preservation attempts, corporations can build goodwill with the public and attract more customers.

All economies are confronted with the need to take action towards reducing carbon emission levels. As such, the role of multinationals in investing in low-carbon economies is highlighted. Investing in low-carbon projects presents an opportunity for multinationals, and as such investment, requiring technology transfers and an upgrading of facilities in EMs, can contribute to the growth of these economies considerably. However, increasing low-carbon investment requires policies supporting and promoting low-carbon investments in EMs. Through favourable policies, EM governments can attract low-carbon investments and support networks between multinationals from developed and developing countries, enabling technology transfers (WIR, 2010).

Increased concerns about climate change and the need to shift to low-carbon economies have generated a new trend in foreign investment. In many EMs, younger generations especially are environment-conscious (O'Connell, 2009). EMs and developing countries need to move towards a low-carbon economy to be able to cope with climate change; in order to do so, they must attract investment and sources of finance, as well as disseminate the necessary technology. These needs generate opportunities for investors. Approximately 40% of the low-carbon projects between 2003 and 2009 were directed at EMs and developing countries. Such projects are generally undertaken by major multinationals from developed markets and about 10% of these investments are from multinationals in EMs (WIR, 2010).

The direction of low-carbon investments is affected by policies focused on establishing technological capabilities, investment promotion measures, and stakeholder pressures. In this respect, EMs are faced with the challenge of generating increased investment in low-carbon projects, as well as disseminating the required technology. This movement may improve EM production as well as technological capabilities, enabling domestic players to catch up as regards technology. However, increased investment in low-carbon projects by multinationals may also create technological dependencies and higher costs in EM economies. Thus, the balance between economic growth and environmental health needs to be considered when making decisions on low-carbon investments, and policies targeted at attracting investment and acquiring technology need to be emphasized. In this case, government support and increased regulation of required environmental clauses may become a necessity. For example, faced with such concerns, countries such as Malaysia and Korea have taken action to attract foreign investors in low-carbon projects to selected industries which have higher levels of absorptive capacity, in order to ensure the transfer and dissemination of technology.

Taking Advantage of Opportunities in EMs

Rapid growth in the middle-income markets in EMs offers both growth opportunities and challenges for multinationals from advanced economies. These markets are a relatively untapped area, however firms in advanced economies are offering products designed for consumers in their own markets based on superior technology, high quality and design features (Chen, 2004; Bhattacharya and Michael, 2011). Traditionally in EMs, local companies offered affordable products while foreign companies focused on high-end markets (Chen, 2004). Targeting middle-income consumers is a relatively new challenge for multinationals from developed markets. Box 4.2 briefly discusses Danfoss's experience in China of market penetration.

In many EMs, a very limited percentage of the population has tastes similar to consumers in developed markets and can afford the products offered by firms in these markets. Meanwhile, the majority of the population has a low income (Jain, 2003). In developed countries, a firm can market a new product to early adopters and then decrease its price, content to offer it to the majority. In EMs, the income distribution is not smooth (Montiel, 2003). Hence, by simplifying an offering, the company cannot reach the middle-income segment because the gap between the middle-income segment and the high-income segment is very large (Dawar and Chattopadhyay, 2002). Even though middle-income consumers in EMs have a higher income than they did in the past decade, there is still a wealth gap between the middle-income levels of the West and EM consumers.

Box 4.2   Business Model Adaptation to EMs – the Danfoss Example

When the CEO of Danfoss, a global manufacturer of components and solutions for refrigeration, heating, water and motion controls, visited China, he realized that their products were concentrated on the affluent market alone and could not appeal to the low end. The company's products were over-engineered and fit for other markets but too costly for Chinese consumers. Despite rapid growth in the Chinese market with such products, the company realized they were losing market share due to their inability to customize their offerings to meet the demands of a large market there. For instance, the company offered products which appealed to high-end Chinese appliance manufacturers but could not serve the needs of manufacturers producing mid-priced units designed to meet the needs of Chinese end-users.

Acknowledging that the company could increase market penetration and profits significantly by appealing to lower-end markets, the company changed its strategy in China. In doing so, Danfoss had to re-evaluate its assumptions about the market and its products, recognizing that its product portfolio needed amending if the company was to be successful there. As the company targeted China to become its second biggest market, those targets were revised. Hence, Danfoss adopted market share growth targets as opposed to sales growth targets.

Danfoss generated growth in the Chinese market by increasing its coverage in China, beyond the first- and second-tier cities that they were already in. The company also developed variations of existing products which would appeal to more cost-conscious segments. Hence, the company added new products designed solely for the Chinese market, taking into consideration the specific needs of Chinese appliance manufacturers.

Adapted from Hexter and Woetzel, 2007.

When multinationals enter these markets with their products designed for middle-income consumers in the West, they can only appeal to high-income EM customers who constitute only a small percentage of the population. Moreover, middle-income populations in EMs do not necessarily have the same preferences as middle-income populations in developed economies. Therefore, business models designed for developed economy customers may fail to meet the needs of EM customers both in terms of cost and functionality.

Although consumer tastes in advanced economies are converging to an extent, such is not the case in EMs (Matusitz and Reyers, 2010). In many EMs, even consumers with a high income are mostly associated with different spending habits when compared to developed markets (Chavan et al., 2009). Many multinationals from developed markets have been unsuccessful in EMs, mainly due to a limited understanding of those markets. A major error that such firms make is to offer standard products that have been slightly modified for the market. Meanwhile in EMs, understanding the consumer and their needs and offering products customized for the market can arise as a necessity (Chandra and Nelankavil, 2008). For instance, a Chinese kitchen is more likely to contain a rice cooker, soy milk machine and a water purifier than a cappuccino maker or a dishwasher (Jin et al., 2010). When foreign entrants do not consider the tastes and conditions of EMs, they risk losing markets to the local competition which in general understands the needs of the domestic customer better. For instance, in China, Dell lost a considerable amount of its market share when Lenovo introduced a low-cost computer for lower income levels and rural areas. Through efficient marketing of the budget computer as an educational tool, Lenovo has enjoyed rapid market growth and its budget computers account for 70% of sales (Enderwick, 2007).

In formulating a strategy, firms need to make sure that their product suits the consumer culture (Johnson, 2011) and create value propositions which focus on providing benefits valued by EM consumers at the right price (Chavan et al., 2009). Many consumers in EMs prefer products with an acceptable quality at relatively low prices (D'Andrea et al., 2010). However, price is often not the most important determinant in purchasing decisions. EM consumers are often more cautious than their counterparts in advanced economies, hence they may focus their purchasing decisions on quality as opposed to searching for the lowest price (Chavan et al., 2009). Another factor which influences purchasing decisions is product availability. In EMs, targeted segments may reside in dispersed locations or their shopping habits in terms of retail locations may be different. Firms need to make sure that they are able to reach their target consumer base (Johnson, 2011).

In entering different markets, firms need to think about the differences between EMs (Prahalad and Lieberthal, 2003). Treating all EMs in a uniform manner can be a mistake. For instance, Fiat introduced Palio in Brazil which was very successful. Later on Fiat introduced Palio in India. However, the car was not received well there. Some of the reasons for its failure were the high price of fuel in India, and a lack of after-sales and maintenance services available (BCG, 2011).

Firms also need to consider differences within an EM country. Differences between regions in China are discussed in Box 4.3.

Box 4.3   Differences between Consumers in China

In China, the sole challenge in creating a marketing strategy is not the difficulties associated with segmentation. Rather, executives need to consider regional differences as well. While in developed countries the same marketing mix can be used across countries, in China regional differences make this kind of strategy very hard. One of the main problems is the inadequacy of distribution channels which change distribution costs between regions. In parallel, the availability of distributors and retailers differs between regions as well. Another problem is the different tastes and perceptions between regions. Companies have often observed significant differences in their product's acceptance in various regions. For instance, while consumers in first-tier cities like to experiment, consumers in third-tier cities prefer brands they know, and flashy advertising is more effective in first-tier cities then in those in the third or fourth tier. Northern cities prefer colourful cosmetics while in southern cities, skincare is more important. Such differences arise due to many factors, including local cultural differences, the local government approach, and the level of diversification of the local economy. As a result of multiple levels of changes within the country, pursuing the same strategies as those for developed markets becomes an inefficient and unprofitable strategy for multinationals.

Except for younger, affluent segments in large cities, a trend in China in the late 2000s was the preference for local products in the general population. A focus on domestic brands may be the result of national pride, or the rise of traditional sentiments in response to rapid changes in the country. Chinese consumers are more prone to focus on quality as opposed to image and are less willing to pay a premium for brands than consumers in developed nations. They are also more price-resistant.

In some cases, foreign companies will try to appeal to Chinese consumers by focusing on the local aspect. For instance, Voltaren and Novartis only use the Chinese language on their packaging. Similarly, P&G has introduced products appealing to Chinese tastes by using green tea and jasmine extracts.

In China, word of mouth is a very effective sales tool, which is more effective than advertising. Most Chinese consumers will trust their friends' or family's opinion and will seek this out as regards their purchases, unlike consumers in developed markets. Hence, many companies, when they advertise, will use celebrity endorsements to reach the customer via their recommendations.

Building relations at the point of sale arises is an important sales tool in China. Many companies will employ promoters within stores to educate customers about their products or to answer their product questions. This occurs partly because, in many cases, consumers are first-time users, as evidenced in the motor industry. Hence, auto dealers in China spend more time talking with and explaining things to the customer than anywhere else.

Adapted from Hexter and Woetzel, 2007.

Significant cultural and environmental differences can exist within many EMs. For instance, in a given EM some cities can have populations enjoying purchases from 'mom-and-pop' stores (small local stores often run by families) and shopping for necessities on a daily basis, while other cities will have higher shopping rates in large retail centres. Moreover, different areas within EMs will grow at varying speeds and it is difficult to predict the future consumption patterns of consumers in growth areas. As an example, in China, SUV sales are expected to grow by 20% annually, however in some cities the growth rate is expected to be around 50%, while other cities are not expected to contribute to this growth at all. Such differences are bound to multiply when considering the different lifestyles and infrastructure among regions (Atsmon et al., 2011). MNEs in EMs also need to adapt to an environment which is continually changing. Rapid growth corresponds to changing consumer needs (D'Andrea et al., 2010). In some emerging economies, the dynamism of the market can create an issue in allocating customer tastes as consumers develop and change their preferences rapidly (Kahn, 2002).

Some multinationals have been very successful in EMs as they were able to meet customer demands effectively. For instance, American Yum, which owns brands such as KFC and Pizza Hut, has a widespread presence in China due to its ability to offer customized menus and its introduction of many new varieties annually. The company also reformatted its stores according to customer needs, and refined its marketing strategy to emphasize nutrition and educational content. Its network, consisting of 16 distribution and two processing centres, its commitment to ensuring high quality by using strict supplier selection processes, and its work with the Chinese government in influencing food safety and supply chain regulations, have also supported the company's growth and acceptance within China. As of 2007, the company had 2,000 KFC restaurants in China compared to 800 McDonald's outlets (Pacek and Thorniley, 2007).

In order to determine what consumers want and design a business plan to this effect, firms need to focus on research. They also need to consider customer habits and plan their marketing strategy accordingly. For instance, when L'Oreal entered the Indian market, it offered a range of products similar to what it offered in other countries. Products were adapted by using smaller packaging and taking out some ingredients, and hence lowering the cost. The products failed as the company was unable to reach and appeal to Indian consumers in the absence of market research and consumer information providers, as well as having inefficiencies in penetrating retail agents. Following this, the company repositioned itself as a luxury brand, trying to understand the newly emerging middle class in India with the help of information analysts and advertising executives. Their research showed that hair dye was a promising area as it offered better results than henna which was traditionally used by Indian women. The company was able to reach target consumers through salons and training programmes for hairdressers. As the hair dyes (introduced under the name Excellence Crème) and salon products became successful, the company increased its presence in India, targeting higher income consumers via a positive brand image and localized products (Khanna and Palepu, 2010). Likewise Nokia in India has developed a mobile phone which has a flashlight due to frequent power shortages in the country. The company also offers phones which can be shared by multiple users (Ghemawat, 2010).

Adapting business models to EMs

Many companies have encountered problems in EMs because they set up the same manufacturing facilities and systems as those used to serve developed economies. However, in EMs, multinationals need to compete with local companies who emphasize low costs and are able to achieve operations at such cost levels due to their efficiency in production, with high labour-intensive systems and their ability to serve the product which meets the needs of the local customer. In addition, the multinationals are also then faced with the pressure of creating efficient production processes which can compete with local margins while also meeting customer need (BCG, 2011). For instance, a company can replace a process with a more labour-intensive one and cut the costs stemming from equipment and machinery. To maintain low costs, a company can also dispense with processes that are necessary in Western markets such as invoicing systems.

Doing business in EMs offers major learning opportunities for firms as they learn to operate in environments which change and evolve rapidly. In this structure, firms are met with multiple forces such as rapid urbanization, industrialization and liberalization (Enderwick, 2009). Moreover, they are also faced with various consumer cultures and needs. The EM structure often necessitates high levels of customization, through which many multinationals are confronted with a need to rethink their business models in order to create valuable consumer propositions for EM consumers. Through this process, doing business in such environments can lead to product and process innovation in EMs (Ghemawat, 2010).

Multinationals in developed countries focus on maintaining a loyal customer base and on increasing their market share. In contrast, in EMs in many cases, market creation presents as a profitable opportunity. New opportunities may arise from identifying those areas where consumer needs are poorly met and designing a solution to offer better alternatives. For instance, Tata in India – which created Nano, a car sold at US$2,500 – started out with the premise of improving options for consumers who had to use scooters for transportation. The business model and processes in creating the car were completely new. Similarly, in Kenya, Vodafone introduced a mobile money transfer service after identifying the inefficiency and scarcity of banking services throughout the country (Eyring et al., 2011).

The increased importance of EMs and the need to create or adapt products for these markets have also led to discussions on reverse innovation (Alcácer and Chung, 2011). Reverse innovation occurs when an innovative product is designed for EMs and less developed economies and is transferred to advanced economies afterwards. Though examples of such cases are rare, the prospect of operating under different conditions in EMs can lead to further advancements in terms of innovation which can then be exploited in advanced economies as well (Govindarajan and Ramamurti, 2011).

An example of reverse innovation is Galanz of China which created energy-efficient, affordable microwaves that could also be used for other functions by the Chinese consumer such as stir frying or steaming, and then started marketing this product in developed countries as well. Multinationals doing business in EMs can develop new products for consumers in these markets, and as they re-think their value propositions to appeal to a different consumer base and redesign their business model to operate in a new environment, they may be able to innovate new products and services which can then be exported to their home economies (Hang et al., 2010).

Business at the Bottom of the Pyramid

The Bottom of the Pyramid (BoP) constitutes the largest share of the world population at 65% and this is also the poorest group globally. Discussion of business at the BoP has been gaining attention in parallel with an increased focus on EMs and less developed economies. This discussion is mainly due to arguments which highlight that the aggregate spending of this population can be considerable and also generate new growth opportunities for firms (Prahalad, 2010).

> The base of the pyramid is the socioeconomic segment that primarily lives and operates their local enterprises in the informal economy and often has annual per capita income of less than $3,000 in PPP. The key characteristics of the BoP segment is that: BoP is heterogeneous across multiple dimensions; includes the portion of the world's population with the least amount of income; contains local enterprises that generally are not well integrated with the formal capitalist economy; lives primarily in the informal economy and constitutes the majority of humanity. (London and Hart, 2011, p. 212)

A major tenant in BoP discussions is that consumers' unmet needs can create business opportunities for MNEs and also support successful businesses focusing on meeting the needs of the poor which can in turn improve living conditions (London, 2008). The continued involvement of MNEs and long-term relations between BoP consumers and MNEs can help reduce poverty. However, many researchers would argue that this tenant is unclear and not supported by empirical evidence (Jenkins, 2005; Karnani, 2006; Landrum, 2007). Some critics consider an MNE presence in the BoP markets an exploitation of such economies (Singer, 2006). Such worries exist because MNEs can replace local players and increase their own power without contributing to economic growth in such markets (Davidson, 2009). In contrast, other researchers would argue that MNEs can increase the welfare of BoP markets by providing resources that will increase the rate of economic growth (Kolk and Van Tulder, 2006).

Most firms will assume consumers at the BoP are too poor to purchase their products and services and that it is impossible to enter such markets due to bureaucracy. Both these assumptions are inaccurate as barriers to entry in many poor economies are lower and their consumers, who are not able to save large amounts, prefer to spend the majority of their income on goods that may enhance their quality of life in the present, such as television sets, telephones and dishwashers. As seen in Table 4.3, BoP consumers' spending habits range across multiple industries. Due to a lack of infrastructure and low income levels, only a few products are able to enter these markets. BoP customers are often confronted with higher prices for the products and services they need (Kacou, 2010).

Contrary to popular assumptions, price is not the only determinant in consumer purchase decisions in EMs and BoP markets. For instance, one piece of research on BoP customers identifies availability, awareness, affordability and acceptability as pillars for selling to BOP customers (Anderson and Billou, 2007). Many companies have been successful at the BoP through a series of changes that have improved the affordability and accessibility of their products. Companies which present their products in single servings will provide monthly instalment or pay-per-use models, in addition to companies who introduce

Table 4.3 The spending habits of BoP consumers, 2005

Percentage by country	Food	Household goods	Info. and communication	Housing	Health	Energy	Education	Other
Bangladesh	54.7	10.2	0.4	9		7.2	2.7	10.5
Brazil	30.4	14.3	3	5.2		6.7	1.3	20.9
Columbia	41.3	8.6	1.8	21.3		5.2	1.4	11.2
India	70.5	1.7	1	2.5	2.9	11.8	1.2	6.6
Indonesia	52.5	7.7	1.1	9.8	2	6.2	1.8	14.4
Jamaica	32.5	7.1	1.4	3.2	2	7.8		36.5
Mexico	32.6	9.7	1.5	15.6	3.2	5.5	4.6	15.4
Nigeria	52	9.4	1.1	11.2	5.7	7.1	2	5.3
Pakistan	50.1	12.1	2.6	8.8	3.7	8.1	2.1	9.7
Paraguay	45.4	8.2	1.7	18.5	3.9	3	0.4	11.5
Peru	49.6	10.3	1	14.6	5.3	6	1.3	6.8
Russia Federation	41.7	9.7	0.2	24	6.8	4.8	0.9	7.7
South Africa	43	11.2	1.3	11	1.4	6.4	2.2	15.9
Sri Lanka	58.4	6.3	0.3	12	2.5	4.7	1.1	8.5
Thailand	37	5.5	2.8	15.9	1.8	4.3	1	21.9

Note: BoP refers to those earning less than $3,000 annually.

Source: World Resources Institute (WRI) (Hammond et al., 2007)

http://pdf.wri.org/n4b_appendixb.pdf

new distribution models, make their products accessible and affordable to consumers who did not have access to those products before (London and Hart, 2011). For instance, Singer has been successful in low-income markets by creating buying power and allowing consumers to pay for their sewing machines in installments (Osterwalder, 2005).

BoP consumers value products which can meet their specific needs, and products that they can purchase in the areas they reside in. Any brand at the BoP needs to be associated with functionality and with functions that appeal to BoP customers; these are usually different from the functions that appeal to customers in developed economies. Serving their needs and providing value at affordable prices often requires process or product innovations. As a result, the risks inherent in doing business at the BoP are higher, considering the possibility of failed business models and failed experiments. Even when the business process is successful and fills an unmet need in the BoP segment, the business may not generate enough capital to be self-sustaining (Karamchandani et al., 2011).

Areas where the BoP population reside often have a very poor infrastructure, thereby the basic needs of a firm such as roads, electricity, power and water cannot be directly assumed. At the BoP, most companies have found that – in order to maximize profits from the large customer base – the equation of price–product–quality needs to be revisited (Prahalad and Hammond, 2002). This entails reorganizing the whole production process as well as the product in many cases. At the BoP, affordability and accessibility are highlighted. Moreover, many companies highlight the education of customers as their main marketing procedure.

At the BoP, businesses are often faced with the need to create the market and generate awareness in the first place (Anderson and Markides, 2007). There may be inefficient processes or products and replacing them with better versions can provide major business opportunities, however consumers are often unaware of the existing inefficiency in what they are offered. The firm is then faced with the challenge of establishing the product or service, as well as creating the market by generating awareness. In doing so, companies will often seek the help of non-profit organizations (Prahalad and Hammond, 2002). In creating products and marketing them for BoP consumers, companies need to create awareness, enable access to the product, make sure that the product is affordable, and facilitate a continuous supply. The process of creating value propositions with such considerations can lead to increased innovation, resulting in the creation of new business processes, services and products (Prahalad, 2011). For instance, Box 4.4 shows how ITC changed the structure of agriculture by organizing an efficient collection system, as well as educating farmers through seminars and e-Choupals.

Box 4.4   e-Choupals in India

The Indian agricultural system was an inefficient process. After 1966, the Indian market was opened up to international competition and domestic farmers were unable to compete with foreigners, due to the high costs arising from intermediaries and inefficient sales processes. The farmers were unable to see price trends in the markets, and they would just bring their produce to government-authorized locations for auctions among agents. After these the payments were spread over time and entering an auction was also costly in terms of transportation and time. The payments were made following delivery of the produce, thereby burdening farmers even more.

As ITC entered the industry, the company recognized issues arising from the demographically dispersed locations of the farmers, the inconsistencies arising due to the auction system, and the empowerment of the agents. ITC deployed the 'e-Choupal' network, designed to provide customized technology applications and integrate farmers within the sales framework. The e-choupals consisted of a computer kiosk and an internet connection distributed to villages. In addition each village was assigned an administrator who was also a farmer. With this system, the farmers could establish a continuous communication with ITC despite the geographic dispersion. Moreover, prices could be communicated and benchmarks could be set. In this manner, the farmer could obtain better information and save time and money, thereby foregoing the need to travel to auctions, and benefitting from rapid transaction processes and professionalism.

The e-Choupal initiative started in 2000 with soya farmers. Today, the network extends to over 4 million farmers.

Adapted from: Prahalad, 2010.

Successful companies at the BoP have analysed their value propositions and the needs of the customer, redefining products by focusing on those attributes valued by the customer. For instance, HLL (Hindustan Lever) realized that Indian consumers suffered from a lack of iodine in their diets, as environmental factors such as impurities and poor quality reduced the iodine level of the salt, and furthermore in Indian cooking, salt was added before cooking the food, thereby leading to a further loss of iodine. HLL created its Annapurna brand, competing at the lowest price point, educating retailers on brand differentiation, and educating the customer on the necessity of iodine in their diet. HLL distributed educational material via Pracharani's, who were communicators hired by the company to travel through districts and educate the customer. HLL also realized that the media did not reach half of the population in India and that the population was dispersed among rural villages. Thus, the company initiated Project Shaki, which was targeted at developing an entrepreneurial sales force that would be able to stimulate the demand for the company's products as well as generate income for many participants (Prahalad, 2010). Hindustan Lever also created a detergent business with Wheel, a low-cost detergent with different oil and water levels, resulting in a different cost structure. The detergent was created on the basis that the poor would wash their clothes in rivers and the product was formulated accordingly. Distribution of the product is mainly through small local shops (Wisse, 2011).

Due to a weak infrastructure, businesses operating at the BoP will often collaborate between each other and cross traditional industry boundaries to generate creative solutions and meet the needs of customers (London et al., 2010; Rivera-Santos and Rufín, 2010). Partnerships can often lead to success. For instance, in Bangladesh, Grameen Phone obtained a license from Telenor and partnered with Grameen bank, initiating a sales system based on providing women in villages with credit to buy mobile phones. In return the women sold phone calls to the villagers, while paying off their debts, and they also earned a daily income (Yunus et al., 2010).

Chapter Questions

1 Discuss the implications of changing the income distribution in EMs for foreign entrants.
2 Discuss the issues foreign investors need to consider when trying to capture EM customers. Suggest ways to capture opportunities in EMs for new entrants.
3 What are some new business opportunities arising from changes in EMs?
4 Define the bottom of the pyramid. How can the bottom of the pyramid offer business opportunities?
5 What do you think managers need to consider when making the decision to adopt their business models for EMs?

FIVE Companies from Emerging Markets

EMs have been going through liberalization processes which have resulted in the entry of MNE's enterprises (MNE) and increased the competition for domestic firms (Read, 2008). Within their markets, many EM firms defended their position, some contracted out or sold their businesses, and others have managed to create new opportunities, restructure their processes, and emerge as strong competitors.

Many MNEs assume that the EM structure will resemble that of developed markets in the long run and will thereby operate using similar strategies to their home base. In doing so, foreign MNEs in EMs will often not meet the prices of local competitors and will restrict their appeal to a small segment by ignoring local preferences in the product offering. On the other hand, in many industries, local leaders are more successful than the MNEs because they are able to customize products according to local demand, and also customize business models, utilizing local competitive advantages such as low-cost labour. As such, in many cases, home-grown firms in EMs are able to generate a greater market share than MNEs. For instance, Grupo Positivo in Brazil has a higher market share than Dell or Hewlett Packard, Baidu has a higher share in China than Google, and Grupo Elektra in Mexico has a higher market share than Wal-Mart (Bhattacharya and Michael, 2011). Firms such as China's Wahaha and Turkey's Koc, Sabanci and Dogus have been competing successfully in their domestic markets. Others such as Chile's S.A.C.I, China's Lenovo, India's Infosys, Tata and Wipro, Mexico's CEMEX, and the Philippine's Jollibee foods have emerged as international or, in some cases, global players (Khanna and Palepu, 2008). In fact, in 2010, the list of Forbes 2000 contained 398 EM firms. Today, Jaguar and Land Rover are owned by Tata of India; the largest bread maker in the world is Mexico's Grupo Bimbo; and the largest aluminium producer is Russia's United Company Russia (Bhattacharya and Michael, 2011). Multiple firms from EMs are now considered leaders in their industry and their brands are recognized globally. Table 5.1 shows the BRIC and NFE brands which are considered to be among the top 500 brands globally.

Governments can promote the growth of selected industries or selected firms by imposing restrictions on entry, providing raw materials at reduced rates, enabling easy access to capital, adjusting tariffs and providing tax breaks. Such efforts by EM governments have sometimes been inefficient and have resulted in industries or local companies which did not evolve due to excessive advantages and a lack of competition. In other cases, government support has led to the creation of national champions and industries with competitive advantages. In following export-led growth strategies, governments can support firms or industries which are exporters by offering various incentives, such as lower prices on raw materials and energy, and lower costs on importing equipment or cash rebates. In most EMs, the availability of a larger market in the presence of export opportunities has enabled exporters to specialize in products that they had a comparative advantage in. As these companies were not constrained by local demand, they could also invest in their own capabilities and move up the technological ladder (Rajan, 2010).

EM firms have been growing rapidly and also internationalizing into both similar countries and developed countries (Dunning et al., 2008). Many local players have grown by consolidating and generating their economic scale and scope. Improvements in the economy, government support and rising consumption levels have also augmented the growth of EM firms, and enabled these firms to start investing in building capabilities. EM firms can expand at home, build capabilities, and internationalize. Hence, they can emerge as competitors with MNEs from developed countries in other markets, as well as in the EM domestic markets (Gadiesh et al., 2008). Upon the entry of MNEs, there are multiple strategies being used by EM firms. Table 5.2 discusses such strategies broadly.

As MNEs start to internationalize into emerging markets, issues related to the different structures of business, different customer tastes and priorities in these countries and their unique institutional framework, have gained attention in the literature (London and Hart, 2004). Faced with increased competition, local firms in EMs followed multiple strategies, such as concentrating on local adaptation and protecting their market share, venturing into similar markets in order to sustain growth, focusing on niche products to create a competitive advantage,

Table 5.1   EM brands included in the Global 500 in 2011

Brazil		
Rank	**Name**	**Brand value (US$ million)**
28	Bradesco	18,678
41	Itaú	16,655
95	Banco do Brasil	9,526
106	Petrobras	8,697
191	Oi	5,046
241	Vivo (Brazil)	4,286
278	Vale	3,749
403	Pao de Açucar	2,723
440	Eletrobras	2,519
497	Natura	2,274

India		
Rank	**Name**	**Brand value (US$ million)**
50	Tata	15,087
133	Reliance	6,994
171	State Bank of India	5,670
234	Indian Oil Corp.	4,351
284	Airtel	3,686
348	Bharat Petroleum	3,090
381	Infosys	2,908
444	ICICI Bank	2,501
476	Wipro	2,352

Russia		
Rank	**Name**	**Brand value (US$ million)**
306	MTS	3,458
349	Lukoil	3,089
65	Sberbank	12,012
246	Beeline	4,189
372	Rosneft	2,943

China		
Rank	**Name**	**Brand value (US$ million)**
99	Agricultural Bank of China	9,283
129	China Telecom	7,261
130	Sinopec	7,135
183	Bank of Communication	5,476
193	China State Construction	5,018
273	Ping An	3,827
436	China Southern Airlines	2,533
449	COSCO	2,468
457	PICC	2,441
480	China CITIC Bank	2,342

New Frontier Economies			
Rank	**Name**	**Country**	**Brand value ($ million)**
188	Petronas	Malaysia	5,352
200	MTN	South Africa	4,920
307	Claro	Mexico	3,447
376	Telcel	Mexico	2,930
402	EmpresasCopec	Chile	2,740
404	Genting	Malaysia	2,721
471	Astra International	Indonesia	2,360
495	Isbank	Turkey	2,280

Source: The BrandFinance® Global 500 http://brandirectory.com/league_tables/table/global_500, 2011 (BrandFinance, 2011).

or investing in their capabilities to be able to compete with MNEs. As foreign firms focus more on their businesses in EMs, the need to

Table 5.2 Strategies of firms from emerging markets

Summarized below are some common strategies that firms from EMs have used to compete with MNEs.

DODGERS: If the pressure to globalize is high and the company's competitive advantages are very local, the company may have to sell out to MNEs, enter a joint venture, or focus on a different area within the value chain, where local advantages can be utilized.
Examples:
Vist (PC producer in Russia): when MNEs entered the market, the company changed its focus to downstream activities, such as providing service and warranties, where the company's local know-how emerged as a competitive advantage.

DEFENDERS: firms operating in industries where the pressure to globalize is relatively low, and where the company's competitive assets are customized for the home market can leverage a local advantage and focus on aspects where MNEs are weak.
Examples:
Group Bimbo (largest bread producer in Mexico): invested in an extensive sales and distribution network and used this network as a competitive advantage.
Shanghai Jahwa (cosmetics company in China): concentrated on meeting the needs of those consumers loyal to traditional products, developing low-cost offers and appealing to local beliefs and culture.

CONTENDERS: In some cases, where an industry is globalizing rapidly and the company's competitive advantages can be transferred abroad, firms can upgrade their capabilities and resources and compete with MNEs globally.
Examples:
Indah Kiat Pulp &Paper (Indonesia): invested in machinery to increase efficiency in production, and utilized its advantage of being located in a country with a good supply of logs and low labour costs. The company competes aggressively in export markets due to cost advantages stemming from the low cost of resources and efficient production systems.

CEMEX (cement producer from Mexico): The company shed its diversified businesses focusing on cement production, upgraded its systems, invested heavily in training and information systems, and obtained capital at lower costs from international markets.

EXTENDERS: firms with a competitive advantage which can be transferred to similar markets can internationalize even when the pressure to globalize in the industry is low.
Examples:
Jollibee Foods (fast-food chain from the Philippines): following the entry of MNEs such as McDonald's, the company upgraded its operations and services while creating menus customized to local tastes. Localized offerings enabled the company to venture into other countries with high expatriate populations.
Televiso Mexico (media company from Mexico): the company internationalized in areas with large Spanish-speaking populations, forming alliances to facilitate distribution and marketing.
Asian paint (paint producer in India): recognizing that their product formulation and packaging gave the company a cost advantage, the company internationalized into other emerging and less developed markets.

Source: Dawar and Frost, 1999

analyse the competition from local industries becomes more important, as the MNEs' greater presence as well as the increased desire to permeate different segments within EMs are challenged by local competitors in many cases.

Characteristics of Emerging Market Firms

Assets of emerging market firms

In analysing how local EM firms maintain and increase their market share in EMs, Bhattacharya and Michael (2011) have identified some common strategies. According to their research, local firms are able to be successful through employing six strategies:

1 Unlike global firms, local leaders are not constrained by existing products or preconceived notions about consumer needs. They customize products and services to meet different consumer requirements and they initially go after economies of scope.

2 Their business models overcome roadblocks and yield competitive advantages in the process.

3 They turn globalization to their advantage, deploying the latest technologies by developing and buying them.

4 Many of the home-grown champions find innovative ways to benefit from low cost labour pools and overcome shortages in skilled talent.

5 They go national as soon as possible to prevent regional rivals from challenging them.

6 The domestic dynamos possess management skills and talent that MNE firms often underestimate. (Bhattacharya and Michael, 2011, p. 17)

Firms from developed countries are advantaged in terms of technological and marketing capabilities (Dhanaraj and Beamish, 2003). In contrast, EM firms often do not have firm-specific assets defined within the context of firms from developed markets. However, EM firms are still able to utilize various assets when competing with MNEs from developed economies in their domestic markets and internationalization (Athreye and Godley, 2009). Often, EM firms are able to exploit country-specific advantages that are defined as the country's resource base and can be accessed by all firms. Firms can benefit from country-specific advantages by drawing on the resources of their home base, such as the availability of labour or resources. Many EM firms will utilize such advantages in internationalization. For instance, many Russian, South African and Brazilian firms utilize their respective country's natural resources, while many Chinese, Indian and Thai firms take advantage of the availability of labour and networks in the internationalization process (Ramamurti, 2008).

Many EM firms have generated firm-specific assets through their experience in the environment. For instance, Chinese construction firms have been growing rapidly and internationalizing. In fact, overseas contracts for such firms are estimated to have been increasing by 29% annually for the past decade. This success is due to several factors. Chinese construction firms have labour-cost advantages and they are mostly vertically integrated which enables firms to buy supplies from their own subsidiaries. Moreover, Chinese firms have domestic experience due to increased infrastructure efforts within their home base. Contractors also benefit from state support financially and in terms of diplomacy (Verma et al., 2011a). Similarly, Indian firms have become the telephone and internet service providers with the lowest cost and Indian banks have the lowest cost per transaction in the world (Kant, 2008). Another reason for the development of such capabilities is that EM firms will often choose a business model and organizational innovation in order to avoid direct competition with incumbent MNEs (Mathews, 2002).

Knowledge of the market

A major advantage of EM firms, both in their domestic markets and in similar international markets, is their local know-how and deep understanding of the consumer. In fact, the ability of EM firms to meet the demands of the local customer more efficiently than MNEs from developed markets has often been cited as a reason for the limited success of MNEs in EMs (Chandra and Nelankavil, 2008).

Many MNEs from developed countries face difficulties in adapting their products to EM tastes as they are not familiar with consumer preferences, and many MNEs are reluctant to take on board the risks and costs associated with creating products for EMs. Local firms can both meet the demands of larger markets by offering customized products which better suit local requirements, and maintain a leaner cost structure due to their knowledge of the market as well as their flexibility stemming from operating in fewer markets (Khanna and Palepu, 2008).

Local firms can also take advantage of new opportunities as they are often the first to identify the features required. For instance, Haier developed a washing machine for consumers in rural areas which could also clean vegetables; for those in areas with humid weather, the company created a small washing machine designed to clean a small load of clothes with minimum energy, recognizing that consumers needed to change their clothes frequently. Deep knowledge of the market enabled Haier to realize such needs and meet them effectively (Dawar and Frost, 1999).

Knowledge of the business environment

EM firms will often have higher production efficiency than MNEs from developed markets, due to their ability to optimize the production process in EM conditions (Ramamurti, 2008). Firms from EMs will also often use the availability of low-cost labour as an advantage and rely less on automation (Bhattacharya and Michael, 2011). In contrast, when MNEs try to operate under systems developed for their home base, they lose efficiency due to capital-intensive processes. Hence, manufacturing in EMs – especially by domestic firms – is often leaner than that of developed economies. EM firms can also generate further savings through lower levels of customer service, R&D, quality control and marketing (BCG, 2011). For instance, Indian firms have developed a competitive advantage in skill-intensive products and services (Ramamurti et al., 2009). Locals can cut prices due to the advantages of localization, such as using local resources, management and advertising channels, as well as utilizing local sales networks, which all give rise to lower costs.

A distinct difference between developed and emerging economies is the presence of infrastructural inefficiencies in the latter, and EM firms have adapted their operations to function efficiently in areas where logistics and distribution systems are not yet developed (Cuervo-Cazurro and Genc, 2008). Logistics also arise as a major challenge for MNEs in EMs. Low-income customers offer major opportunities for MNEs as they are a very large part of the population, however, low-income customers often live in dispersed locations and it is difficult for firms to reach them. For instance, the Chinese firm Hangzhou Wahaha became a major competitor to Coca Cola and PepsiCo by targeting rural areas. As such, the company was better able to meet the needs of local customers. The development of a wide distribution and service network is also a major advantage for Haier, as the company can meet the needs of consumers in such areas, while others find it very hard to penetrate these areas due to the challenges associated with distribution (Khanna and Palepu, 2008). EM firms are accustomed to working under local conditions and can easily adapt products to suit such conditions as a poor infrastructure, dispersed consumers, and difficulties with implementing an after-sales service. Many firms will adapt imported technology to the conditions in their countries, combining technical skills with their knowledge of the local customer. Such abilities have enabled them to internationalize to other EMs as well as developing countries (Ramamurti, 2008). In similar countries, EM firms will rely on cost, efficiency, responsiveness and knowledge of the culture as advantages in their home economies, unlike firms in developed markets which rely on intangible assets (Hennart, 2009).

Deep knowledge of the business environment has also enabled EM firms to make significant process innovations. Moreover, knowledge of the market and a novel approach can lead EM firms to appeal to the customer and increase efficiency at the same time. For instance, Bharti Airtel of India has become the world's fifth largest mobile operator by means of a business model innovation which involves outsourcing a major part of its network and thereby achieving flexibility and the ability to meet increased demand effectively. By outsourcing, the company is able to have less capital-intensive operations and has thereby increased its financial liquidity. The company has also benefited from profitable deals with vendors as a first mover in many markets. By relying on the distribution networks of consumer goods, the company was also able to generate a standardized model to expand into new areas and overcome the logistical challenges of India. Bharti Airtel has an operating profit margin of 40% and is considered to be one of the most successful firms in India (Verma et al., 2011b).

Anand Milk created a process innovation in India by integrating local skills and activities. Instead of importing milk powder as was the procedure in the country, Anand Milk built an industry with local farmers, becoming the country's largest milk producer. Narayana Hrudayalaya, a hospital chain in India, has reduced the cost of cardiac surgery to US$5,000–7,000 compared with US$50,000 in the USA. The chain has even started to attract international customers due to its lower price at a similar quality. The reduction in price is mainly achieved by process improvements, the bulk purchase of equipment from vendors, and lower construction costs (BCG, 2011). Aravind in India, an eye-care system, has also been able to reduce costs significantly by process improvements, slicing the process of examination as well as eye surgery. Parts of the operation which can be conducted by healthcare personnel have been transferred and thus the doctors are able to perform more surgeries (BCG, 2011).

Experience of working in the presence of institutional voids

Institutional voids or the ability to work around institutional voids can become an advantage for EM firms. Institutional intermediaries in developed markets offer a large range of services, such as providing funds, analysing information and giving access to facilities during transactions. Such services often require local know-how such as culture, language or regulations. In contrast, in EMs, intermediaries which provide information, capital and supporting activities within the value chain are either non-existent or at the growth stage. EM firms, then, have established their operations in ways which minimize the issues stemming from institutional inefficiencies (Cuervo-Cazurra and Genc, 2008). For instance, firms in EMs cannot access capital easily compared to corporations in developed countries. Such capital shortages can make it difficult for them to invest in capabilities such as marketing or technology. On the other hand, local business groups build strong reputations, and can utilize local stock markets to raise capital. As EMs open up, many foreign investors are also willing to provide capital for reputable EM firms (World Bank, 2011a).

Local firms can also access local talent easily and select highly skilled personnel, while foreign MNEs often experience problems in finding and employing the right talent. Moreover, large EM firms and business groups often have established in-house training programmes to build a talent pool and can overcome the challenges associated with finding skilled labour (Khanna and Palepu, 2008). For instance, Apollo Hospitals of India has formed a joint venture to offer online medical classes, and finances new educational institutes in addition to introducing programmes to further train medical personnel (Bhattacharya and Michael, 2011).

Firms from EMs functioning as intermediaries can often meet local needs better, due to their local knowledge and ability to access local information. For instance, in Turkey banks such as Garanti or Akbank have been more successful in catering to the needs of small and medium-sized firms, as well as larger domestic enterprises, since their customer knowledge enables them to assess risks efficiently. In China, Emerge

Logistics, has become one of the main logistic services providers by specializing in providing assistance for import and distribution services (Khanna and Palepu, 2008). Local firms have also developed their business models so as to overcome legal or regulatory challenges. For instance, the Chinese Shanda, a pioneer in video games, developed online multi-player games in China, thereby reducing piracy issues to a great extent. The company also enabled users to purchase prepaid game cards from local facilities and thus diminished customers' concerns related to online purchases (Bhattacharya and Michael, 2011).

Networks

A network consists of actual or future customers, suppliers and distributors, whether directly or indirectly related. Moreover, governments, institutions, competitors, or the suppliers of complementary products which create the environment of the firm are all parts of its business network (Wilkinson and Young, 2002). In EMs, networks can provide access to resources in the presence of market imperfections (DeClercq et al., 2009). Networks can also constitute advantages for EM firms, both in the domestic economy and in internationalization.

The business environment in EMs is often based on building relationships and leveraging such relationships. Local firms can utilize their relations throughout the value chain as they already possess connections with network members. Such relations can enable local firms to access markets more efficiently, obtain information easily, and carry out their operations efficiently. Moreover, relations with regulatory bodies and government present a major advantage in EMs. Local firms can gain advantages by reaching authoritative figures and utilizing their relations in surpassing regulatory hurdles, benefiting from incentives or from participating in government deals (Constanza, 2009).

Networks are also highlighted in EM firm internationalization as they can be a motive for internationalization (Filatotchev et al., 2007; Yiu et al., 2007), provide access to resources (Stuart, 2000), and give access to market know-how, thereby decreasing the liability of being a foreigner in that market (Bausch et al., 2007; Gubbi et al., 2009). Many firms from EMs are pulled into internationalization as suppliers or contractors of foreign firms (Mathews, 2002a). When EM firms enter the same countries as their suppliers or customers, they can establish legitimacy relatively easily and obtain knowledge more efficiently through the network (Yiu et al., 2007) since external relations provide access to information (Lorenzoni and Lipparini, 1999).

Latecomer advantages

Many firms from EMs are latecomers. Latecomer advantages can be exploited via several strategies, such as taking advantage of changing consumer preferences, benchmarking against established industry parameters, investing in new technology, and utilizing improved information dissemination channels to buffer demand (Cho et al., 1998). Latecomers can also move through the learning curve more efficiently, benefiting from an incumbent's prior experience as well as taking advantage of the available networks in the value chain. As such, latecomer advantages may help EM firms to catch up with incumbents (Mathews, 2002c).

EM firms can surpass incumbents' new superior technologies as they are not constrained by sunk costs and are able to construct the new managerial, marketing competencies required by new technology (Luo and Tung, 2007; Athreye and Godley, 2009). Technological advances can increase the efficiency of domestic players in emerging economies and enable them to catch up with competitors from developed markets rapidly. First, technology enables the transfer of know-how. Second, firms can benefit from the experience of predecessors and apply best practice. Alternatively, they can invest in the newest technologies and forego major investments which act as sunk costs for the dominant players. Many local firms can also employ new technologies and create consumer value propositions with high quality at lower-end prices. In fact, following the liberalization of their economies, many successful EM firms invested in the newest technologies in an effort to gain an upper hand on increasing competition. In most cases, MNEs' assumption that EMs can be served with old technologies is thus contradicted. For instance, the Brazilian airline, GOL, invested in new models with a 30% higher capacity and maintains a younger fleet with lower maintenance costs. Additional steps such as e-ticketing and internet sales have also helped GOL to lower costs further. Today, GOL is considered the world's second most profitable airline after Ryanair (Bhattacharya and Michael, 2011). Similarly, CEMEX from Mexico improved its services considerably by increased usage of technology such as tracing systems, and became one of the global leaders in its industry. By adopting new technologies, EM firms can also create a niche position for themselves (Bonaglia et al., 2007; Yiu et al., 2007).

Challenges to emerging market firms

Local firms in EMs competed with each other until relatively recently and they have relatively little experience in competing with internationals

(Black and Morrison, 2010). Firms in developed markets possess knowledge assets such as managerial capabilities, marketing capabilities and technological know-how which enable them to internationalize into other countries and compete. They are also active in multiple countries and thus have developed the skills and capabilities that can enable them to establish and manage operations in multiple markets. In contrast, EM firms have operated in closed markets for a long time and been protected from external competition. The internationalization process has come late for them. Moreover, protection from competition has also limited many EM firms' stock of the knowledge-based capabilities that are necessary to compete with international firms.

EM firm capabilities are mostly based on local knowledge of the market or business processes and utilizing local inputs effectively. Despite the flourishing position of EM firms in the current economy, with increased liberalization, the significance of firm-specific assets such as local know-how and cost efficiency could decrease because the MNE presence in EMs gives these firms access to similar assets (Khanna and Palepu, 2004). Then, as MNEs learn to operate effectively in developing countries, their dependence on locals' as well as EM firms' advantages due to the effective deployment of home-based advantages could decrease (Khanna and Yafeh, 2007).

Managerial capabilities

Managing an international company, whether it is regional or global, requires additional capabilities, such as the managerial skill needed to manage a dispersed production network. In a world which is becoming global, a company needs to align multiple aspects, and introduce changes to transform its organization. Here, the role of management and the capacity to execute a long-term strategic plan are of major importance (Hult et al., 2006). A lack of managerial capability, which can also confound a firm's absorptive capacity, will act as a bottleneck for EM MNEs. As such, managing regional or global networks becomes another challenge (Buckley et al., 2008). In addition, in mergers and acquisitions (M&A), integrating firms with established operations with the acquirer's value chain is another managerial challenge. Such managerial capabilities that are necessary for international business are often lacking in EM MNEs (Sauvant, 2008).

Managing international competition can require various capabilities that local firms from EMs will not necessarily be accustomed to.

For instance, locals in EMs will often have a uniform workforce, and managing a diverse workforce internationally can be a challenge. In parallel, the top management of EM firms is homogeneous, while MNEs from developed nations will have international top management teams who can undertake the difficulties associated with the management of international organizations (Black and Morrison, 2010).

Governance based on relationships, family ownership and minimal use of professional management is also characteristic of EM firms. Internationalization based on relations may lead to suboptimal choices in such firms. EM firms are faced with the challenge of moving away from relationship-based governance to rule-based governance. Such a shift may necessitate the involvement of outside managers with expertise, as well as a reduction of family involvement in management (Globerman and Shapiro, 2008). For example, in Latin America, upon the entrance of MNEs, successful domestic firms were identified by the clarity of their strategic perspectives, willingness to review their business scope, efficient governance, and high-quality management. Such firms pursued strategies ranging from international expansion, entering new businesses and forming strategic alliances to gaining brand equity, improving management as a priority and engaging in cost reduction and quality improvement processes. However, unsuccessful firms were often characterized by unprofessional governance and a lack of strategic perspective (Anand et al., 2006).

Corporate governance measures in emerging countries are changing slowly, however they are still not on a par with Western standards. Improving such measures by means of transparency, board responsibility, shareholder protection and international reporting would enable EM firms to compete more effectively in the international arena and facilitate acceptance of mergers while lowering political pressures (Bhattacharya and Michael, 2011).

Many firms or groups in EMs have built business models based on their own countries' structures, such as the Chinese focus on Guanxi or the Russian focus on government relations for success. Relying extensively on such strategies, which are more national in nature, can hinder such firms from internationalizing, as local advantages can no longer provide a competitive edge in global markets (Black and Morrison, 2010). Moreover, acquisitions or joint ventures by EM firms can lead to cultural issues, first due to the foreign perception of EM firms, and second to the intensive local culture of the EM firm which is often restricted by local experience. In most cases, EM firms are faced with the challenge of adapting their products to international markets, as well as increasing the quality level of their products. In fact, many EM firms face the challenge of complying with the strict product standards required in developed countries (Kant, 2008).

Technological and marketing capabilities

A major challenge for EM MNEs is their lack of experience of global competition and managing a global operation. For instance, Chinese firms 'long used to competing solely on price, have little experience in understanding and addressing segment-specific needs, linking those needs to R&D and brand-building efforts, and creating the required infrastructure in sales and distribution' (Gadiesh et al., 2008, p. 23).

A shortage of marketing skills has negatively affected EM MNEs, especially in international operations (Wells, 2009). A firm can differentiate its products and develop its brands (Denekamp, 1995), and communicate its value proposition effectively through marketing (Bahadir et al., 2009; Liao and Rice, 2009). Marketing capabilities enhance a firm's ability to acquire new knowledge, and to meet customer need effectively by utilizing the acquired knowledge (Hsu and Pereira, 2008). In fact, one of the main reasons for government efforts to attract foreign investment is to develop capabilities within the economy by enabling a technological transfer (Marinov and Marinova, 2000). Foreign direct investment, whether it is inward or outward, can increase the efficiency and capabilities of firms due to their exposure to different know-how. However, the lower levels of technological capabilities and managerial skills in EM firms can hinder their development, as they may be unable to access and utilize the know-how that has been introduced into their markets (Globerman and Shapiro, 2008).

Many EM firms have copied technologies or accessed new technologies by outsourcing. However, the pure acquisition of new technology or gaining access to technology by outsourcing can have negative consequences on performance if a firm fails to invest in its integrative capabilities and internal processes through which it understands and deploys the new technology (Vega-Jurado et al., 2008). While many EM firms will focus on less technologically intensive processes and products, some of them have caught up with technology or developed capabilities on a par with MNEs from advanced markets. For instance, in Brazil, Embraer – which is one of the top aircraft manufacturers in the world – and Petrobras – which is one of the leaders in oil and energy – are also leaders in their respective industries in terms of technological capability (Ramamurti, 2008). Other examples are GOL (Brazil), Huewai (China) and Lenovo (China). Yet EM technological capabilities are significantly lower than those of developed nations overall and EMs may not be able to boost innovation solely by copying and adopting technologies (Magnus, 2010).

The Internationalization of Emerging Market Firms

The share of developing countries as investors in cross-border transactions increased from 27% in 2007 to 31% in 2009 (WIR, 2010). Despite the increased levels of investment outflows from EMs, the aggregate foreign investment outflow level in such markets still remains below the levels of foreign investment inflows. For instance, the world's largest MNEs have approximately 70% of their affiliates abroad, while the largest MNEs from developing countries have 51% of their affiliates abroad as of 2007 (WIR, 2011). Growth prospects in EMs, fuelled by increased regionalization and liberalization, have also enabled the increased participation of MNEs from these countries as providers of foreign investment (WIR, 2010). Table 5.3 contains graphs analysing the aggregate outward foreign investment from BRICs and New Frontier Economies divided into regions. Graphs show that most EMs have increased foreign investment, and the ratio of outward investment with respect to the GDP of emerging markets such as Russia, Chile and Malaysia is growing rapidly.

Following liberalization and deregulation in most EMs, foreign economic policies in such markets have increased their focus on facilitating and promoting outward foreign investment in an effort to stimulate the competitiveness of domestic firms (World Bank, 2011a). In many EMs, governments are providing incentives such as tax breaks to promote internationalization. Thus, the relatively low cost of foreign investment is motivating EM firms of all sizes to invest abroad (Dunning et al., 2008). The number of transnational firms from EMs is increasing rapidly, accounting for 8% of the world's transnational firms in 1992, 21% in 2000, and 28% in 2008 (WIR, 2010).

Most EMs are still associated with increased volatility. As such, when firms from these countries internationalize, they are able to reduce their exposure to country risk. Thus, in the case of a crisis in the domestic economy or an unfavourable development affecting domestic sales, an international EM company can direct its efforts at its international markets. During a period of crisis, international

Table 5.3   Foreign investment from emerging markets

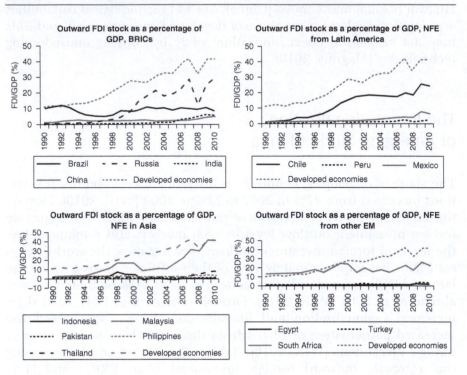

involvement provides a firm with greater strategic flexibility because the firm is able to shift and adapt its resources (Lee and Makhija, 2009). For example, Indian firms mostly internationalize in order to increase their global share and to overcome constraints within the domestic market, especially those which are due to the cyclicality of the domestic market (Kant, 2008).

Motives for internationalization

In explaining the internationalization of EM firms, motives as well as the incentives for internationalization have often been discussed. EM firms can diversify risks by spreading their operations into multiple locations, and benefit from government incentives, grow their markets, increase efficiency, and access resources by internationalizing. Generally, EM multinationals – like their developed country counterparts – expand by means of resource-seeking, efficiency-seeking, and market-seeking behaviour. Another feature of EM firms is expansion based on asset-seeking motives, particularly for established brands.

Market-seeking motives

Market-seeking EM firms will try to increase their customer base primarily in similar environments. In some cases, a company's target market within the domestic economy may not be sufficient for the company to achieve economies of scale, and thus EM firms can internationalize into similar countries to access larger markets. In other cases, increased competition at home and a declining market share can motivate EM firms to grow their markets by investing in similar or less developed economies (Casanova, 2009). Another reason for investing similar economies is the decreasing attractiveness of developed countries for investment, mainly due to financial stress and ageing populations (Magnus, 2010). Investment by EMs in similar markets is also due to the significant prospects offered in these markets (WIR, 2011).

In similar environments, firms from EMs can utilize their experience and know-how. As such, operations are bound to be similar to operations in the home base. For instance, the Chinese electronic producer TNC has been very successful in India and in Vietnam, especially due to their ability to manufacture television sets for approximately US$50. Yet while pursuing market growth opportunities in similar markets, EM MNEs can also increase their know-how in terms of managing an international operation and often access new knowledge or spot new opportunities. As a result, internationalizing with similar economies can enhance an EM firm's competitiveness in the domestic market as well (Yiu et al., 2007). There is also some evidence that EM outward investment can increase with risks in the host countries. One of the reasons for seeking investments in risky environments is the search for less crowded markets where firms can utilize their home-grown advantages (Buckley et al., 2006).

Resource-seeking motives

Many EM firms will expand abroad to access raw materials (Kant, 2008). Those which operate in resource-intensive industries are faced with increased demand due to global growth. Thereby, firms in fuel and energy such as Gazprom, Petrobras and China Petroleum are internationalizing mainly to secure resources (Accenture, 2008). China has also taken steps to build its ties with countries in the Middle East, Africa and Latin America in order to secure access to resources (Magnus, 2010).

Generally, firms from countries with a high consumption of natural resources will internationalize in order to secure downstream markets, while firms from countries with high reserves of natural resources will do so in order to secure upstream resources. For instance, firms such as Gazprom and Lukoil from Russia and Vale from Brazil have engaged in downstream internationalization to secure markets, while firms such as Bharat of India and CNOOC of China have engaged in upstream internationalization to secure resources (Ramamurti, 2008). In 2010, firms such as CITIC (China) and Reliance Group (India) invested in extractive industries, while metal firms in the region focused on investing in mineral assets. Asian transnationals from EMs also accounted for 60% of foreign direct investment in Latin America and the Caribbean in 2010, and such investments have mainly been motivated by resource seeking (WIR, 2011).

In markets such as Brazil and China, firms focusing on providing resource-based products are prominent players. Firms such as China Oil and Petrobras (Brazil) have been internationalizing rapidly to secure resources. Government support and a focus on developing such countries into national champions have led to rapid internationalization (Cantwell and Barnard, 2008). Major firms in EMs associated with high growth announced 154 cross-border M&A deals between 2006 and 2010, which is significantly higher than the 86 M&A deals announced in the previous five years. These M&A deals are concentrated on accessing resources to meet the demands of the local market and also on accessing the markets of other EMs which are growing rapidly (Verma et al., 2011a).

Efficiency-seeking motives

Efficiency-seeking firms will try to vertically integrate or take advantage of lower costs in other countries. Rapid growth in EMs often corresponds to rising input costs in terms of labour as well as raw materials, thus EM firms can reduce their costs by moving parts of the production chain to less costly locations and increasing efficiency. For instance, in China the cost advantages of labour decreased between 2004 and 2008, thereby compelling many Chinese firms to access markets with lower labour costs (Laudicina, 2010). Moreover, government incentives offered by other countries, as well as the reduced costs of relocating production closer to customers, may enable firms to lower their cost base (Cavusgil et al., 2008).

Asset-seeking motives

In foreign markets, firms are faced with risks and additional costs due to a lack of experience in the market. However, they can compensate for the disadvantages of operating in a foreign environment if the value derived by exploiting firm-specific assets exceeds the costs of internationalization (Goerzen and Asmussen, 2007). Hence, knowledge-based intangible assets and capabilities can enable the firm-specific assets which are to create value in multiple markets (Rugman and Oh, 2010). However, EM MNEs often lack those firm-specific advantages which are mainly intangible in nature, such as managerial, marketing and technological capabilities, yet are considered to be the basis for international expansion in international business theories. Thus, the internationalization of EM firms to developed countries has led to a discussion of the asset-seeking motive (Miller et al., 2009b).

Firms from EMs may internationalize in order to acquire strategic assets, which will enable them to compete with MNEs from developed countries. Such strategies are designed to gain access to resources such as technology, brand and managerial capabilities, which EMs need (Aykut and Goldstein, 2007; Luo and Tung, 2007; Athreye and Kapur, 2009; Casanova, 2009). In venturing abroad, such EM firms are motivated by the need to acquire assets which may generate a competitive advantage (Athreye and Godley, 2009). China, in its quest to create global champions, encouraged the national oil and gas leader Petro China to acquire strategic assets through acquisitions and alliances (McKinsey, 2010). Likewise, in the food and beverage sector, firms from EMs are acquiring brands in other markets. For instance, JBS acquired Bertin in Brazil, Pilgrim Pride and Swift in the USA; Thai Union Frozen Products acquired Chicken of the Sea in the USA; and similarly, Mabe from Mexico acquired Bosch's Brazilian subsidiary in an effort to invest in branding. In a different assert-seeking pattern, Haier established R&D centres in developed markets in order to understand the needs of consumers, build the brand, and also develop relationships with retailers (Verma et al., 2011a). In the white goods industry, Haier, Mage and Arcelik used alliances with MNEs to upgrade their operations, thus treating global competition as an opportunity to build upon their capabilities (Bonaglia et al., 2007).

An advantage for EM firms is that the complementary assets they need – such as R&D capabilities – are available in the form of smaller enterprises, as larger MNEs are becoming more integrated and focused (Hennart, 2009). Many MNEs are willing to sell business units in order to dilute slow businesses and align their strategy with competencies, and as a result EM MNE acquisitions are possible (Luo and Tung, 2007). Firms are increasingly restructuring in order to concentrate on their core activities, and this trend towards concentration creates many merger and acquisition opportunities for EM MNEs.

However, even when firms acquire resources, the efficiency of the acquired information or resource is dependent upon the firm's internal efforts. For instance, in a study which analysed external technology acquisitions, it was observed that the acquired firm could increase its performance in parallel with its internal R&D efforts (Tsai and Wang, 2007). EM firms with technological advantages show a propensity to invest in developed countries in order to grow their markets and augment their technological capabilities, exhibiting both asset-seeking and asset-exploitation patterns (Makino et al., 2002).

Organizational learning opportunities – especially learning which can augment firm innovation – motivate many EM firms to invest in developed economies (Dunning, 2004). Firms can gradually build their technological capabilities and create products good enough for other EMs, and then focus later on producing world-class products and engaging in innovation activities – however this process is dependent on the firm's ability to learn, disseminate, and internalize knowledge (Teagarden and Cai, 2009).

There is evidence that some EM firms will start to internationalize by exporting low-price/low-content goods and will then move on to exporting higher priced goods of a higher quality, indicating increased learning facilitated by internationalization (Domingues and Brenes, 1997). Recently, the internationalization processes of Latin American firms – especially those from Brazil, Chile and Venezuela – have accelerated. Latin America's continuous growth rates, increases in productivity, improved capabilities, and increased access to credit are some of the reasons for this (Sauvant et al., 2011).

The internationalization of state-owned enterprises

In the last decade, the internationalization of state-owned enterprises from EMs has been increasing rapidly. Approximately 56% of state-owned transnationals, which constitute a significant source of foreign direct investment, are located in EMs. State-owned enterprises are mostly active in capital-intensive industries such as financial services or in industries which require economies of scale or are of interest to the country strategically. Overall, 9% of state-owned enterprises are in primary industries, and 22% in manufacturing, which includes chemicals, metals, motor vehicles, fuel and food. The remaining 69% of state-owned enterprises are in services, of which 16% are in transport and communications, 19% are in finance, and 9.6% are in utilities. State-owned enterprises from EMs accounted for over 70% of the cross-border M&A flows between 2005 and 2010. In the last decade, while cross-border investments by state-owned enterprises from developed nations have focused on utilities, the investments of state-owned enterprises from EMs have focused on extractive industries and telecommunications. This is in parallel with the goal of state-owned enterprises in many EMs, which is to secure access to natural resources (WIR, 2011). Figure 5.1 shows the outward investment by state-owned MNEs. Here, we can observe the increased levels of internationalization by state-owned firms, and especially by Chinese firms.

Governments in EMs also support the internationalization of selected firms in an effort to create national champions. National champions enjoy state protection which results in preferential access to resources and low-cost capital. The expansion of such firms into other countries has been considered unfair and on some occasions their expansion was prevented by the host economies. For instance, Haier could not acquire Maytag in the USA and CNOOG of China was unable to acquire Unocal in the USA (Enderwick, 2007). In Brazil, the knowledge that the country had oil in deep sea areas motivated the government to increase the technological advancement of Petrobras, the national oil company that has become one of the major global players. Similarly, China, in its quest to create global champions, encouraged the national oil and gas leader Petro China to acquire strategic assets through acquisitions and alliances (Carvalho and Goldstein, 2009).

The direction of emerging market firm internationalization

EM firms internationalizing on the basis of their home-grown capabilities will mostly focus on entering similar markets where they can exploit such advantages, which may be termed as 'south-to-south foreign direct investment'. Internationalization into developed markets is

Outward FDI projects by state-owned MNEs from emerging markets

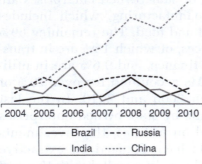

2004 2005 2006 2007 2008 2009 2010

—— Brazil ---- Russia
—— India ······ China

Source: UNCTAD, 2011.

Outward FDI projects by state-owned MNEs, by home region/economy, 2003–2010

(Number of TNCs and value in millions of dollars)

	Number of TNCs	2007	2008	2009	2010
World	653	187,393	221,034	169,106	145,691
Developed countries	285	85,881	98,137	84,937	56,051
Developing countries	345	91,100	111,606	74,254	85,698
Brazil	9	2,501	9,592	2,381	5,808
Russia	14	8,968	10,718	9,898	3,809
India	20	1,096	4,529	5,174	487
China	50	21,267	32,492	28,613	38,899
Chile	4	800	1	-	58
Mexico	1	-	-	-	-
Peru	1	-	-	-	-
Indonesia	7	-		46	44
Malaysia	45	4,288	4,813	2,854	19,811
Pakistan	3	-	14	-	15
Philippines	1	11	-	-	-
Thailand	7	1,290	2,242	830	47
Egypt	6	-	-		18
South Africa	54	1,358	2,166	2,323	2,225
Turkey	2	-	-	-	-

Source: UNCTAD, 2011

Note: The data include major SOE investors. FDI projects include both cross-border M&As and greenfield FDI projects.

Figure 5.1 Foreign investment by state-owned enterprises

mostly associated with building assets and accessing know-how. EM firms have taken advantage of internationalization strategies for multiple reasons and successful internationalizers have often engaged in asset-seeking and asset-exploiting strategies at the same time. EM firms can also focus on niches, by exploiting either latecomer advantages or cultural similarities.

Firms from EMs will often choose greenfield investment methods when investing in similar economies, while prioritizing M&A transactions when investing in developed economies. Investments motivated by market seeking in similar economies are mostly based on extending home activities and tighter controls are necessary to coordinate such extension. As greenfield investments offer more control, and protect firms' know-how and enable the company to design processes specifically for their purposes, this entry mode is often a preferred method. In fact, in other EMs, 72% of the EM company investment was through greenfield investments between 2003 and 2009. In the same period, 85% of the investments from EM firms to developed economies were M&A transactions. EM firms investing in developed economies are faced with challenges, such as the need to access the market rapidly, and the need to obtain local expertise and access customer base environments which are significantly different from the home base (World Bank, 2011a). Before the 1990s, FDI from India was mainly to other developing and emerging countries (approximately 80%), based on manufacturing (80%) and mostly in the form of greenfield investments or joint ventures with minority interests. In the internationalization period that followed, Indian firms' FDI shifted towards developed countries, and focused on services (62%), and entry methods were predominantly through acquisitions or majority-owned subsidiaries. Changes in FDI patterns and entry methods over time will stem from changes in government policies, leading to reduced government protection and increased openness towards international business. In a more open business environment, Indian firms were able to seize new opportunities and were also encouraged to grow by building their own capabilities (Ramamurti et al., 2009).

South-to-South FDI

Over one third of FDI to EMs were from other EMs, as of 2010 (World Bank, 2011a). South-to-South trade accounted for approximately 10% of the world trade as of 2009, however this is expected to increase (Magnus, 2010).

South-to-South FDI, especially from Asia, increased considerably in 2010, reaching US$210 billion. A total of 60% of the investment outflow from developing nations was due to the investments of Brazil, Russia, India and China (World Bank, 2011b). M&A transactions by EM firms are mostly on a regional basis except for deals originating in South Asia. Regional expansion enables EM firms to communicate more effectively with the acquired company as well as rapidly accumulate information related to the new market. Moreover, the company can transfer its business model relatively easily and is also met with fewer requirements in terms of product adaptation. However, such investments can also expose firms to impacts stemming from regional business cycles (World Bank, 2011a).

Table 5.4 shows the largest cross-border merger and acquisition deals among EM firms in other EM markets between 2009 and October 2011. The table was prepared by identifying completed M&A transactions over US$1 billion between 2009 and October 2011 and by using Thomson One Banker analytics and selecting transactions where the acquirer company was from the BRICs or NFEs. Within this period, state-owned enterprises engaged in major transactions that were mainly motivated by access to resources. In general, the largest EM firms are in the oil and gas sector (Magnus, 2010). The transactions of privately held EM enterprises are also motivated by access to resources but also access to markets as well. In the table, the highlighted firms denote those which are state owned or controlled. As can be seen, state-owned firms – especially in industries pertaining to resources such as oil and gas – are still predominant in EMs. However, such firms are also accessing assets and resources globally and building their capabilities.

South-to-North FDI

EM firms' investment into developed economies can be motivated by access to assets as well as markets. In some cases, EM firms are able to utilize their local knowledge and create a niche market of similar customers internationally. In other cases, EM firms can invest in developed economies in order to access strategic assets and know-how. In doing so, while many firms from EMs have engaged in acquisitions, others have chosen to internationalize gradually, increasing their commitment level alongside accumulating their experience and know-how in the developed economy.

EM firms will internationalize to serve similar clusters of consumers by globally customizing their products (Kant, 2008) to serve an ethnically similar population, and by carving out a niche where they can leverage their knowledge of the customer and reduce the liability of being a foreigner in the market (Miller et al., 2009b). For instance, common traits within successful firms from EMs, such as Haier (China), Conchay Toro (Chile), Group Modelo (Mexico) and Group Televisa (Mexico), are focusing on niches and understanding the customer better (Van Agtmael, 2007). In some product groups, 'ethno brands', which are defined by the ethnic origins of the company – thereby promoting cultural values – can lead to SME internationalization, and leverage the brand over its counterparts (Poulis and Yamin, 2009).

Many EM MNEs are concentrating on undertaking value-chain activities and specializing in these areas, and thereby investing in developed markets by following their MNE customers (Khanna and Palepu, 2008). Investment in developed countries in the form of acquisitions intensified, especially following the global financial crisis, as firms in developed nations contracted their operations. For instance, in 2010 continued economic growth in their markets enabled Latin American firms from Brazil, Chile, Colombia and Mexico to invest in developed markets mainly through acquisitions due to increased investment opportunities (WIR, 2011).

Table 5.5 shows South-to-North M&A transactions over US$1 billion in BRIC economies. The firms highlighted represent those which are either state-owned or state-controlled. As the table shows, resource

Table 5.4 South-to-South foreign direct investment

Date	Target Name	Target Nation	Acquiror Name	Industry	Acquiror Nation	% of Shares Acq.	% Owned After Transaction	Value of Transaction ($ mil)
2009	Aracruz Cellulose SA- Guaiba	Brazil	Empresas CMPC SA	pulp mills	Chile	100	100	1,430
2011	Occidental Argentina Expl	Argentina	Sinopec Group	Crude petroleum and natural gas	China	100	100	2,450
2010	Bridas Crop	Argentina	CNOOC Ltd	Crude petroleum and natural gas	China	50	50	3,100
2011	CBMM	Brazil	China Niobium Investment	Investment offices	China	15	15	1,950
2010	Repsol YPF Brasil SA	Brazil	Sinopec Group	Crude petroleum and natural gas	China	40	40	7,111
2011	Peregrino Project, Campos Basin	Brazil	Sinochem Group	Crude petroleum and natural gas	China	40	40	3,070
2011	BorsodChem Zrt	Hungary	Yantai Wanhua Polyurethanes Co	Chemicals and chemical preparations	China	58	96	1,701
2009	OAO MangistauMunaiGaz	Kazakhstan	Investor Group	Investors	China	100	100	2,604
2010	Zain Africa BV	Nigeria	Bharati Airtel Ltd	Telephone communications	India	100	100	10,700
2010	Republic of Venezuela- Carabobo	Venezuela	Investor Group	Investors	India	40	40	4,848
2011	Beijing Jingdong Century	China	Investor group	Investors	Russia	15	15	1,531
2011	Petroperija SA	Venezuela	TNK-BP Holding	Crude petroleum and natural gas	Russia	40	40	1,800
2010	Kyivstar GSM	Ukraine	Vimpelkom	Radiotelephone communications	Russia	100	100	5,516
2009	MOL Group	Hungary	surgutneftegaz	Crude petroleum and natural gas	Russia	21	21	1,852
2010	BSG Resources Guinea	Guernsey	Vale SA	Iron ores	Brazil	51	51	2,500

Source: Thomson ONE Banker Analytics, 2011 (ThomsonOneBanker, 2011)

Table 5.5 South-to-North foreign direct investment

Year	Target Name	Target Nation	Acquiror Name	Industry	Acquiror Nation	% of Shares Acq	Owned After Trans-action	Value of Trans-Transaction ($mil)
2010	Keystone Foods LLC	US	Marfrig Aliment os SA	Sausages and other prepared meat products	Brazil	100	100	1,260
2010	Uranium One Inc	Canada	ARMZ	Uranium-radium-vanadium ores	Russia	37	52	1,055
2011	Ruhr Oel GmbH	Germany	NK Rosneft'	Crude petroleum and natural gas	Russia	50	50	1,600
2009	Lukarco BV	Netherlands	NK LUKOIL	Crude petroleum and natural gas	Russia	46	100	1,599
2009	Sibir Energy PLC	UK	OAO Gazprom Neft	Oil and gas field exploration services	Russia	33	60	1,001
2011	Abbot Point Coal Terminal	Australia	Mundra Port& Special Eco Zone	Marine cargo handling	India	100	100	1,951
2011	Australia Pacific LNG Pty Ltd	Australia	Sinopec Group	Crude petroleum and natural gas	China	15	15	1,765
2009	Felix Resources Ltd	Australia	Yanzhou Coal Mining Co Ltd	Bituminous coal and natural gas	China	100	100	2,807
2009	OZ Minerals Ltd-Certain Assets	Australia	China Minmetals	Primary nonferrous metals	China	100	100	1,386
2010	Syncrude Canada Ltd	Canada	Sinopec Intl	Crude petroleum and natural gas	China	9	9	4,650
2010	Athabasca Oil Sands-Assets	Canada	PetroChina Intl Invest Co Ltd	Crude petroleum and natural gas	China	60	60	1,737
2009	Teck Resources Ltd	Canada	Fullbloom Investment Corp	Investors, nec	China	17	17	1,502
2011	Elkem AS	Norway	China Bluestar(Group)Co Ltd	Chemicals and chemical preparations	China	100	100	2,179
2010	Volvo Personvagnar AB	Sweden	Zhejiang Geely Hldg Grp Co Ltd	Motor vehicles and passenger car bodies	China	100	100	1,500

Year	Target Name	Target Nation	Acquiror Name	Industry	Acquiror Nation	% of Shares Acq	Owned After Transaction	Value of Trans-Transaction ($mil)
2011	INEOS Group Ltd-Eurpean	UK	Petro China Co Ltd	Crude petroleum and natural gas	China	50	50	1,015
2011	InterGen	US	China Huaneng Group	Electric services	China	50	50	1,232
2010	Chesapeake-Oil,Gas Asts,TX	US	CNOOC International Ltd	Crude petroleum and natural gas	China	33	33	1,080
2010	AES Corp	US	China Investment Corp {CIC}	Management investment offices	China	16	16	1,581
2011	Progress Energy-Altares,Lily	Canada	Petronas Int Corp Ltd	Crude petroleum and	Malaysia	50	50	1,097
2010	Parkway Holdings Ltd	Singapore	Integrated Healthcare Holdings	Health and allied services, nec	Malaysia	70	93	2,380
2009	PowerSeraya Ltd	Singapore	YTL Power International Bhd	Electric services	Malaysia	100	100	2,357
2010	Univision Communications Inc	US	Grupo Televisa SAB	Radio broadcasting stations	Mexico	35	35	1,200
2009	ASARCOLLC	US	Grupo Industrial Minera Mexico	Copper ores	Mexico	100	100	2,200
2009	Dunedin Hldg-US Bread Making	US	Grupo Bimbo SAB de CV	Bread and other bakery products	Mexico	100	100	2,500
2011	Talisman Energy Inc-Cypress A	Canada	Sasol Ltd	Petroleum refining	South Africa	50	50	1,063
2011	Talisman Energy Inc-Farrell	Canada	Sasol Ltd	Petroleum refining	South Africa	50	50	1,037
2011	Conforama SA	France	Steinhoff Intl Hldg Ltd	Wood household furniture	South Africa	100	100	1,653
2010	Centennial Coal Co Ltd	Australia	Banpu PCL	Bituminous coal and lignite surface mining	Thailand	80	100	1,646

Source: Thomson ONE Banker Analytics, 2011 (ThomsonOneBanker, 2011).

seeking, as well as building the capabilities of firms in the resources industry, shows a strong motivation for internationalization. EM governments will also focus on enhancing the resources as well as the capabilities of the national champions in resource-based industries in internationalization. Other major transactions indicate market access motives, as well as taking advantage of opportunities in accessing brands and marketing capabilities in developed markets.

Chapter Questions

1 Discuss the strategies of emerging market firms in the face of increased competition in their markets.
2 Discuss asset-seeking motives as they relate to multinationals from emerging markets.
3 What are some of the advantages of multinationals from emerging markets when compared to companies from developed economies?
4 How can multinationals from emerging markets compete globally?

SIX An Analysis of Selected Emerging Markets

Foreign Investment

In the past decade, production as well as consumption has been shifting towards emerging markets (EMs). This trend is likely to continue at increased rates, considering that industrialized nations were affected by the global financial crisis of 2008 more severely than EMs, and thus such nations are experiencing a contraction in their economies. Continued improvement in these markets also leads to increased income levels, that will further augment their growth and emphasize their presence as consumers. Most EMs can be considered to be diverse economies that are also focused on increasing their know-how and capabilities in order to shift towards more value-added economic structures.

EMs have also been contributing to global trade at growing rates as they increasingly integrate with the world economy. In fact, when compared to developed countries, the trade volumes of emerging market countries are growing at significantly faster levels. As such, the gap between the trade volumes of emerging markets and developed countries is bound to decrease further in the near future. For example, Table 6.1 shows that export growth averaged 15% between 2004 and 2008 globally, while export growth in developed countries was 13% in the same period. The same observation also holds for the change in import levels. Another observation which is less clear in the table stems from the difference in averages between the calculations of 2004–2008 and 2004–2009. The growth rates, when 2009 figures are considered, are significantly lower due to the effects of the global financial crisis.

Table 6.1 Export and import growth in emerging markets and developed countries

	Export growth 2004-2008 average	Export growth 2004-2009 average	Import growth 2004-2008 average	Import growth 2004-2009 average
World	15%	8%	14%	7%
Developed countries	13%	6%	12%	6%
UK	9%	3%	8%	2%
USA	12%	7%	9%	3%
BRICs				
Brazil	20%	12%	28%	18%
Russia	27%	14%	29%	17%
India	23%	17%	26%	20%
China	25%	17%	19%	14%
New frontier economies				
Colombia	22%	15%	22%	15%
Egypt	25%	17%	28%	22%
Indonesia	16%	10%	20%	12%
Malaysia	12%	6%	11%	5%
Mexico	11%	5%	11%	5%
Pakistan	8%	6%	17%	22%
Peru	24%	17%	29%	18%
Philippines	9%	4%	8%	2%
South Africa	14%	7%	16%	8%
Thailand	16%	10%	18%	9%
Turkey	17%	10%	19%	10%

Source: World Data Bank, 2011.

In 2010, developing economies and emerging markets accounted for over 50% of foreign direct investment inflows globally, while the outflows from such economies also increased significantly. Foreign direct investment – in the form of M&As and greenfield projects – from developed countries to emerging markets increased rapidly as companies in developed markets challenged the contraction in their own markets. As a result, foreign direct investment in emerging markets increased from 32% of global investment in 2007 to 50% of global investment in 2010. Within this figure, emerging markets and developing economies attracted two-thirds of the global greenfield investments and a quarter of the M&A transactions (WIR, 2011). On the other hand, EMs are attracting higher levels of private equity-based M&As due to the stabilization of their economies. Moreover, global restructuring has been creating opportunities for emerging market multinationals, who tend to prefer M&A strategies to greenfield entry. The majority of the investment from emerging markets is in similar economies, although there are also increased levels of investment in developed economies. Yet, despite increased levels of investment outflows from emerging markets, the aggregate foreign investment outflow level remains below the level of foreign investment inflows.

Regional trade still accounts for most of the world trade. For instance, 52% of Asian exports are within the Asian region, while 48% of North American exports are within the continent. Increased regionalization allows countries to expand their markets easily due to a reduction in trade barriers within the region, and to achieve economies of scale. Companies have easier access to suppliers within the region and are able to increase efficiency levels. Another factor which contributes to the growth in trade is the growth in regional production networks. Within a region, production processes can be divided up and each country may specialize in parts of the process. For instance, East Asian countries specialize in producing parts and components, while China assembles them into final products. The regional network of production constitutes a major part of China's trade volume (BCG, 2011).

Doing Business in Emerging Markets

In doing business in EMs, multinationals must utilize multiple strategies. The main differences between the markets, and hence the strategies involved, stem from the unfamiliarity of the multinationals from developed markets with the cultural, institutional and regulation framework of these economies and the difficulties stemming from the limited availability of infrastructure or support networks (Ghauri and Cateora, 2010). Multinationals are faced with the need to build relations with all the actors within a business network in an emerging market in order to operate efficiently (Elg et al., 2008). Relations in EMs can compensate for information deficiencies and strengthen the multinational's position against the local competition, as well as reducing the risks posed by government intervention. Many multinationals from developed nations have chosen to partner with conglomerates or business groups, or to work with governments (Cavusgil et al., 2008).

In partnering with business groups, multinationals can benefit from a group reputation as well as connections. Moreover, conglomerates will have already established distribution and retail networks, thereby providing easy and efficient access to the market (Lu and Ma, 2008). Local companies are knowledgeable about the customer and market trends and therefore a multinational may be able to spot opportunities efficiently while working with a local partner. Among numerous others, Ford's joint venture with the Koc Holding in Turkey in automotive, Rakuten's (Japan) with Baidu (China) in e-commerce, or Danone's (France) with Sabanci Holding (Turkey) in consumer goods has enabled these multinationals to gain information about consumers as well as the business environment, access partners' distribution networks and build a presence rapidly (Khanna and Yafeh, 2007).

Another successful way of doing business in EMs has been in working with governments. As discussed throughout this book, countries considered to be EMs have infrastructural deficiencies. Most emerging market governments have prioritized the development of infrastructure which creates a bottleneck in attracting foreign investment or in boosting the economy in many cases. Governments will often buy large quantities of products and services from foreign companies, ranging from vehicles and computers to architectural or consulting services (Luo, 2001). Bidding in tenders which governments regularly announce or working with state-owned enterprises can prove to be a successful form of entry for multinationals (Cavusgil et al., 2008).

Despite the positive outlook towards emerging markets and their increased contribution to the global economy, companies doing business in such countries are often faced with difficult conditions. Some examples of challenges within the business environment are a weak infrastructure, a lack of availability financing options, mishaps within the regulatory framework, and issues arising from the protection of contract and property rights. Sustained growth in many emerging markets depends on the removal of all such obstacles.

The global financial crisis of 2008

The financial crisis has affected emerging economies less than the developed nations, and their recovery has been more rapid, while industrialized nations are still struggling with higher taxes and persistent unemployment. Most of the emerging market countries faced a severe economic crisis in the 1990s and, in response, have implemented new policies to ensure better conditions and a sound financial system. Such policies assisted in their recovery from the financial crisis of 2008 as many emerging market countries have come out of the crisis with relatively fewer issues than their counterparts in industrialized nations. The rapid diffusion of the financial crisis of 2008 has highlighted the interdependence of economies around the globe (World Bank, 2011c).

Mainly due to export-led growth policies, many emerging markets generated current account surpluses which in turn helped to reduce risk ratings and the perceptions of such countries globally and propelled further foreign investment (Griffith-Jones et al., 2010). Globally, emerging markets have been increasing their contribution to foreign direct investment both as sources and destinations, and this contribution is expected to increase. This trend towards a further internationalization of production is continuing. The focus of foreign investment activity has been shifting from manufacturing to services and primary sectors (WIR, 2010). The global liberalization of financial markets and increased usage of financial intermediaries and instruments have increased the interconnectedness between countries globally. A reliance on international funding has enabled the growth of many EMs but this also exposes such countries to shocks in advanced economies, as experienced in the global financial crisis of 2008 (Claessens et al., 2010). Among the emerging markets, the largest Asian countries such as China and India have intensified trade relations with developed countries, although business cycles within the countries are not strongly correlated. However, with increased trade and integration in the world economy, the interdependence that exists between emerging markets and developed countries has been increasing (Fidrmuc and Korhonen, 2010).

EM economies were affected by the global crisis of 2008 in various ways. The decline in demand in advanced economies affected the trade performance of EMs as export demand declined. The rapid decline of foreign capital inflows from advanced economies also affected many EMs adversely (Llaudes et al., 2010). A major impact of the global financial crisis has been the decline in lending which has also meant a decline in cross-border lending. Since the financial crisis of 2008, financial institutions in advanced economies have been faced with reduced liquidity and a credit crunch, hence the amount of credit available for cross-border trade and investment is restricted. In parallel, the amount of credit available for investing in emerging markets or that available for emerging markets from institutions in developed markets is also restricted (Griffith-Jones et al., 2010). Financial institutions and corporations in EMs which rely on lending from institutions in advanced economies are facing major challenges. Meanwhile, countries whose financial systems had relied more on domestic deposits have been able to better shield themselves against the crisis (Llaudes et al., 2010).

Among EMs, countries which relied on domestic demand for growth fared better during the crisis. For instance, domestic demand in Indonesia, which amounted to 90% of the GDP as of 2007, enabled the country to rebound from the crisis rapidly, despite decreased demand among its major trading partners (Llaudes et al., 2010). The global crisis of 2008 particularly highlighted the necessity of reducing the dependence on advanced economies. Many EMs are faced with the challenge of boosting consumption within their economies and reducing their dependence on foreign capital inflows (Rajan, 2010).

The crisis also highlights the dangers stemming from volatility in the capital flows in emerging economies. A significant factor which contributed to the growth of many emerging markets was increased foreign investment.

The volatility of such investment has created problems for some EMs in the past. For instance, one of the reasons for the financial crisis in Turkey in 2001 was a rapid withdrawal of foreign investment. More recently, the global financial crisis has highlighted potential risks due to the volatility of foreign capital flows (Griffith-Jones et al., 2010).

The BRIC Economies

In the past decade, the BRICs have grown at consistently higher rates than the rest of the world, and the preservation of these growth rates indicates that the gap between emerging markets and developed economies is converging. GDP per capita clearly shows this trend. Table 6.2 shows

Table 6.2   Growth indicators in the BRICs

2009	GDP ($ bill.)	GDP per capita, PPP ($)	GDP growth 5-yr average	Ave. GDP per capita growth (5 yrs)	Population (mill.)	FDI inflow ($ bill.)	Urbanization
World	58,259	10,686	8%	5%	6,775	1,164	50%
Developed countries	41,608	36,408	5%	3%	1,117	804	76%
Brazil	1,594	10,367	25%	5%	194	26	86%
Russia	1,232	18,932	21%	13%	142	37	73%
India	1,377	3,296	18%	9%	1,155	35	30%
China	4,985	6,828	27%	14%	1,331	78	44%
Share held by BRICs	16%				42%	15%	

Source: World DataBank, 2011.

2011–2030 forecasts		
Growth of real GDP per head	Growth of real GDP	Labour productivity growth
Brazil	3.5	4.1	2.9
Russia	3.6	3.3	3.3
India	5.1	6.5	4.3
China	5.2	5.7	5.6
USA	1.9	2.7	2
UK	1.2	1.9	1.4

Source: EIU, 2011.

Table 6.3 Greenfield FDI projects in BRIC economies, 2003–2011 (in US$ million)

	2003	2004	2005	2006	2007	2008	2009	2010	2011 (Jan–Apr)
Brazil	25,927	26,299	20,487	10,578	16,720	35,952	36,866	43,184	28,714
Russia	32,124	44,006	40,819	37,031	46,459	58,453	30,198	33,355	9,224
India	19,658	34,227	27,224	86,738	51,564	74,335	50,022	45,358	28,538
China	144,906	124,792	83,691	114,024	95,115	111,582	94,555	84,579	31,561
World	761,918	708,720	709,764	884,087	940,100	1,461,783	952,200	806,969	295,867

As % of World	2003	2004	2005	2006	2007	2008	2009	2010	2011 (Jan–Apr)
Brazil	3%	4%	3%	1%	2%	2%	4%	5%	10%
Russia	4%	6%	6%	4%	5%	4%	3%	4%	3%
India	3%	5%	4%	10%	5%	5%	5%	6%	10%
China	19%	18%	12%	13%	10%	8%	10%	10%	11%
Developed countries	29%	33%	32%	32%	32%	32%	32%	33%	25%

Source: fDIMarkets, based on information from the Financial Times Ltd, FDi Markets (www.fDimarkets.com) (fDIMarkets, 2012).

the GDP and the GDP growth rates for BRICs. While developed countries grew by an average of 5% between 2004 and 2009, BRICs' growth rates were 18–27%. Table 6.2 also shows the forecasts for growth in BRICs, compared to the USA and UK. As clearly observed, in the coming decades, the BRICs are expected to continue growing at higher rates than developed countries.

Liberalization, rapid economic growth, and increased improvements in the business environment have attracted significant levels of foreign investment in the BRIC economies. In fact, as seen in Table 6.3, these economies have attracted 25% of the world's greenfield FDI in 2010 and 34% in the first quarter of 2011, while the developed countries combined attracted 25% and 33% in the same period (UNCTAD, 2011).

Box 6.1 shows the breakdown of production in the BRIC economies compared to world output. Economic output increased considerably among the BRIC economies. Within the last five years, the share of services in the output of all the BRIC economies has increased, though the change is less pronounced in Russia and India. One of the main reasons for this shift has been the reallocation of resources, leading to increased investment and a focus on value-added activities. More importantly, while the world industry and manufacturing output increased by an average of 35% and 30% respectively, the same rates for BRIC countries are twice the growth rates of the global averages.

Box 6.1 The Change in Economic Output in the BRICs

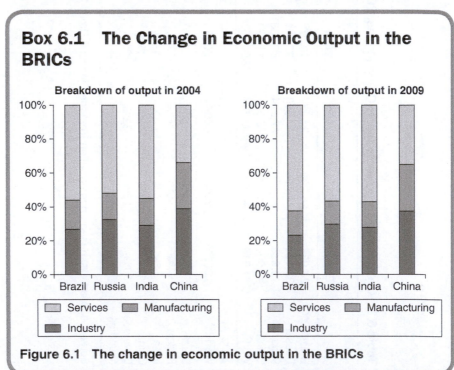

Figure 6.1   The change in economic output in the BRICs

Table 6.4   The change in economic output in the BRICs

	Industry ($ mill.)	Growth 2004– 2009	Manufacturing ($ mill.)	Growth 2004– 2009	Services ($ mill.)	Growth 2004– 2009
Brazil	348,726	103%	216,924	98%	939,845	162%
Russia	353,551	89%	161,878	80%	673,270	125%
India	347,744	88%	190,333	89%	712,797	103%
China	2,308,038	158%	1,691,153	170%	2,161,669	177%
World	15,044,154	35%	9,103,814	30%		

Source: World Data Bank, 2011.

BRIC economies, as with other emerging markets, need to invest in infrastructure in order to sustain growth. However, compared with the overconsumption patterns of industrialized countries, the largest emerging markets, have higher reserves of foreign exchange and higher savings rates which indicate that they can undertake those investments, especially in infrastructure. The growth patterns of the various BRICs are significantly different from each other. China's growth can mostly be attributed to a growth in exports, India's to an increase in consumption, and Russia's to natural resources (Accenture, 2012). Table 6.5 summarizes some of the strengths and weaknesses associated with individual countries.

In many emerging markets, exports have been a significant driver of growth. Table 6.6 shows export level for the BRICs.

Though employment patterns vary greatly among the BRIC economies, the share of agriculture has decreased within these countries over the past 10 years. As seen in Figure 6.2, employment in construction has increased rapidly across the BRIC economies, in parallel with rapid growth and the increased need for infrastructure.

Brazil

Brazil gained its independence from Portuguese rule at the end of the 20th century and became a republic. The country was governed by a populist military government for 20 years until a military governance was abolished in favour of civil rule. Brazil had a closed economy and followed import substitution policies until the 1990s. Afterwards, the country adopted a more liberal regime, focusing on the reduction of trade barriers, which resulted in increased macro stability and financial credibility (Green and Dickerson Jorge, 2001).

Table 6.5 Major strengths and weaknesses in the BRICs

Brazil	Russia	India	China
		Strengths	
• Abundant and varied natural resources • Significant proportion of manufactured products in total exports • Increased capacity to cope with exogenous shocks and international financial market volatility • Policy of maintaining fundamental macroeconomic equilibrium	• Abundant natural resources, including oil, gas and metals • Skilled labour force • World's largest exchange reserves • Reasserted regional and energy power • Political stability	• Diversified growth engines • Solid fundamentals: high savings and investment rates • Good private sector performance in industry and service • Moderate foreign debt and large foreign currency reserves	• External accounts buoyed by industrial competitiveness and diversification • Gradual move upmarket • Infrastructure development spurred by the economic stimulus programme • Very high corporate savings rate that funds most investment • China's growing influence on the international scene
		Weaknesses	
• Sociopolitical obstacles to necessary structural reforms • Lack of investment in energy, rail, road, port and airport infrastructure • Exposure to fluctuations in world prices for certain stable commodities • High public debt exposed to domestic interest rate trends and maturity that is still too short	• Limited economic diversification • High dependence of the economy on raw material prices • Excessive private sector foreign debt • Weak banking sector • Persistent deficiencies in the business environment	• Lack of infrastructure • Rise in wages for skilled labour; susceptible to eroding the competitive advantage • Increase in private corporate debt • Fragile public finances • Persistent uncertainty over the Kashmir question	• Increasing social tensions associated with the growth of inequality • Industrial and commercial overcapacity • Weakness of Chinese banks, considering the dynamism of credit and the uncertainties • Environmental problems • Uncertainty around the Taiwan issue

Source: globalEDGE, 2011.

Table 6.6   The average share of exports in BRIC economies, 2004–2009

Export of goods and services (% of GDP)		Change in exports as a % of GDP over 5 yrs
Brazil	11%	-7%
Russia	28%	-4%
India	20%	3%
China	27%	-4%

Source: World DataBank, 2011.

In reforms undertaken in 1999 as a result of 'Plano Real', banks were restructured and several state-owned businesses were privatized. Brazil's development policy shifted towards export promotion and an increased reliance on the private sector (Shaffer et al., 2008). Between 2002 and 2010, President Lula of the left-wing party became the president of the country. Governance under President Lula focused on creating macroeconomic stability and alleviating poverty. During his term, redistributive social policies enabled approximately 30 million people to be lifted out of poverty and join the middle class (de Souza, 2011). In this period the government tried to promote export by trade negotiations and by providing incentives to exporters (Jansson, 2008).

The economic outlook

Brazil has the fifth largest population in the world, and is the 10th largest economy in terms of GDP. The country is rich in natural resources and a major supplier of iron ore and petrochemicals globally. If Brazil can maintain its macroeconomic stability, abundant natural resources can generate a long-term economic advantage. The industrial sector is also advanced and diverse, ranging from automobiles, machinery and equipment, textiles and cement to aircraft and durables (Franco et al., 2011).

Despite a slowdown in economic growth due to the global financial crisis of 2008, the effects of the crisis on the economy were relatively minor. Reforms undertaken prior to the crisis enabled Brazil to rebound from the crisis relatively quickly (Da Rocha et al., 2008); 60% of economic output was directed at meeting domestic demand, hence firms did not need to downsize during the crisis (Mendonca, 2011).

Exports increased by 27.5% in 2010, totalling US$89.2 billion. Oil and derivatives as well as soybeans constituted a significant portion of

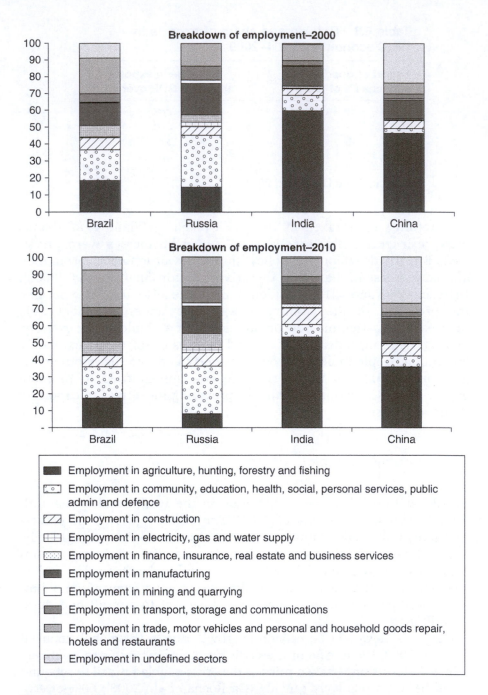

Figure 6.2 Breakdown of employment in the BRICs

Source: Euromonitor, 2012. Data retrieved 22 February 2012 from www.portal.
euromonitor.com/(Euromonitor, 2012).

these exports. GDP growth continued in 2011, driven mainly by increases in domestic investment and consumption. Forecasts suggest that annual growth in GDP will average 4.1% between 2011 and 2030. These forecasts are dependent on improvements in infrastructure, the development of deep water oil reserves, and an increased international presence. Challenges to growth are slow growth in the labour force and in labour productivity (EIU, 2011). The economy may also be adversely affected by changing prices for Brazilian commodities (Mendonca, 2011).

Doing business in Brazil

Foreign direct investment to and from Brazil is concentrated in extractive industries, resource-based manufacturing industries, infrastructure and telecommunications. Recently, investments in key sectors such as the automotive industry, sugar refining and steel have increased (OECD, 2008a). Some of the leading sectors for investment are agriculture, aircraft, telecom equipment and services, oil and gas, computer software, drugs and pharmaceuticals. Of these, aircraft, air transportation and telecoms are expected to maintain high growth levels (US Commerce, 2011a).

In Brazil, the middle class is growing rapidly, hence the demand for consumer goods and services is increasing (Kharas, 2010). As such, many opportunities in the country in terms of consumer products and services can be observed. For instance, internet usage and the need for telecommunications services are growing, as evidenced by the increase in e-commerce consumers from 13.2 million in 2008 to 20 million in 2010 (EIU, 2011).

The Brazilian government has been reducing its role in the economy. As a result, many new opportunities in the private sector have opened up. Currently, the focus of the government is on improving public health, safety, and education (Doctor, 2009). Planned infrastructure privatizations in the near future will generate further opportunities for investors. The country needs to improve its infrastructure and the Brazilian National Development Bank estimates that an investment of approximately US$145 billion needs to be made between 2011 and 2014. In order to achieve this, Brazil must attract private investors, and as a result tax incentives are being offered to investors within the transportation, energy and construction sectors (Mendonca, 2011).

Foreign investors prefer entry via joint ventures, especially in heavily regulated industries and in bidding for foreign contracts. Local partners in joint ventures are mostly family firms, as half of the country's GDP is generated by family businesses. Partnerships with such firms may prove to be lucrative for foreign entrants, as family firms are often associated with less bureaucracy, quick decision making, and increased flexibility. In forming joint ventures, firms need to consider the difficulties in solving disputes within the country's judicial system, as court procedures can take up to seven years. Careful selection of partners and agreeing on detailed contracts beforehand become necessities in forming a joint venture (Mendonca, 2011).

The fragmented nature of distribution channels increases the costs for companies doing business in Brazil. Economic disparities throughout the country also lead to different levels of infrastructure availability among the regions within the country (US Commerce, 2011a).

Brazil has become South America's economic leader as the first country to initiate economic recovery. It is still burdened with issues such as unequal income distribution, crime, unemployment and an informal economy (Fan et al., 2008). Foreign investment is welcome in most industries, apart from media, telecommunications, transportation and mining, where foreign entry is limited by ownership requirements (Franco et al., 2011; US Commerce, 2011a). Domestic regulatory barriers are a bigger concern in doing business as opposed to border restrictions. A burdensome tax regime and infrastructural constraints also increase the cost of doing business (OECD, 2008a).

Russia

Russia, with a population of more than 200 million, is the most important market which has emerged from the former Soviet Union. In Russia, upon the collapse of the Soviet Union and the downfall of the Communist Party, a new constitution was adopted by referendum in December 1993.

Russia has become a semi-authoritarian state. Poor monetary and fiscal policies have instigated high budget deficits and macroeconomic instability. Such instability – combined with the effects of the Asian crisis, falling crude oil prices and the weakness of its institutions – caused a major financial crisis in 1998. This crisis resulted in the collapse of the ruble and a partial default on government debts (Hanson, 2009).

Russia joined institutions such as the IMF and the World Bank in an effort to increase its integration into the global economy and receive support for macroeconomic stabilization (Miroshnikov, 2009). Under the governance of President Putin between 2000 and 2008, one of the major changes in the country was the move towards a centralized system. Economic reforms in banking, tax, labour and land, as well as increasing commodity prices, enabled the country to break out of the recession.

During this period, productivity rates increased as unused capacity was utilized. Resources were also reallocated away from uncompetitive industries and placed in the services sector (Hanson, 2009). Industrial growth and increasing commodity prices led to higher revenues which were directed towards the economy to boost domestic consumption. Exports in natural resource-based sectors also became a major driver of growth in the 2000s (Ahrend, 2005).

As the economy began to recover at the beginning of the 21st century, foreign investment inflows increased (Miroshnikov, 2009). Since then, prices have been liberalized, large and medium-sized manufacturers are increasingly being privatized, and lavish government subsidies for inefficient producers have been decreasing. All these changes are forcing a massive restructuring of Russian industry. After the crisis of 1998, structural reforms also gave rise to an industrial structure where large industrial groups, which had mainly started out as commodity exporters, came to dominate the business environment (Ahrend, 2005). Such groups are often led by powerful oligarchs who have strong relations with the government.

The economic outlook

Russia has the highest income per capita among the BRIC economies (O'Neill and Stupnytska, 2009). However, economic development is concentrated in the larger urban areas and income inequality has increased following the fall of the communist regime (Aidis and Adachi, 2007).

The Russian economy was severely affected by the global financial crisis of 2008, due to the withdrawal of foreign capital and a rapid decline in commodity prices and demand (Miroshnikov, 2009). The government injected capital into the economy and prevented the collapse of the financial system, however, in doing so, the country's reserves declined considerably. As such, the funds available for infrastructure investments and public services declined. Russia's GDP fell by 7.9% in 2009 (EIU, 2011), but is now rebounding due to global recovery and an increase in commodity prices.

The country is a leading producer and exporter of minerals and fuels. The economy is dependent on resource-based industries and has developed capabilities in manufacturing, mainly for metals and transport equipment. A dependence on commodities exposes the Russian economy to external shocks from fluctuations in commodity prices (Mankoff, 2009) and hinders diversification and innovation (Åslund et al., 2010). Hence, currently, the government's focus is directed towards the promotion of innovation as a driver of sustained growth and the reduction of its dependence on oil and gas revenues. The agriculture, forestry and automotive industries, which traditionally lagged behind, are evolving rapidly. In parallel, the share of oil and gas in exports has decreased from 90% in the 1980s to 60% in 2008, indicating that the economy is relatively less dependent on revenue from oil and gas (Åslund and Kuchins, 2009). However, Russian trade performance is still dependent on world commodity prices as the majority of its exports are commodity based. In 2009, 67.4% of its exports were oil and gas, 12.9% metals, 6.2% chemicals, and 5.9% machinery and equipment (EIU, 2011).

In Russia, lower birth rates and high mortality rates have led to an ageing population structure, and the population has been declining since 1992 (Heleniak, 2009). In order to improve the demographic outlook, the government launched a programme in 2007 in order to provide capital to women who have a second or third child, and increased benefits to families with children (Miroshnikov, 2009).

In Russia, reforms aimed at increasing the productivity and transparency of corporations, along with reforms in tax and banking, increased macro stability and resulted in a rise in disposable income. Tax evasion continues to be a major problem for the government (Aidis and Adachi, 2007). The economy needs further investment in infrastructure and raising production capacity. Such investments are difficult in the presence of inflation, limited levels of long-term resources within the financial system, and corruption (Åslund et al., 2010). Another issue stems from the banking system which is dominated by government-owned institutions, leading to an inefficient allocation of finances (Åslund and Kuchins, 2009).

Doing business in Russia

The investment environment of the country is characterized by movement towards a market economy in some respects and high levels of state intervention in others (Donaldson and Nogee, 2009). Relatively high per capita income, a sophisticated consumer base, and the presence of natural resources have increased the attractiveness of the country for multinationals. Foreign investment in Russia is predominantly from partner countries and concentrated in the primary sector and manufacturing (OECD, 2008c). The government's current focus in its foreign investments policy is on prioritizing investments that can bring new technologies (Marchick and Slaughter, 2008).

Russian consumers continue to admire Western, and especially American, products, and well-recognized brand names do well. Smaller foreign investors can be at a relative disadvantage due to the cost of market entry, uncertainties in trade financing, general difficulties in conducting business, severe infrastructure problems, and mounting crime and corruption (Aidis and Adachi, 2007).

Currently, Russia is increasing its protectionist measures, and recent policies have focused on the renationalization of banking and energy (Åslund and Kuchins, 2009). There has also been an increase in sovereign wealth funds undertaking foreign investment. And like many other countries, Russia is planning to restrict acquisitions via such funds. Russian authorities are also planning to adopt new foreign direct investment review procedures in order to protect selected industries that are deemed strategic for the country (Marchick and Slaughter, 2008).

Since 1995, Russia has been trying to gain entry to the WTO (Donaldson and Nogee, 2009) and has gained access in 2011. Accession to the WTO could increase foreign investment and lead to improvements in the legal system. WTO membership could also produce significant gains for the Russian economy due to a more optimal resource allocation, as a result of a reduction in tariffs and increased access to Russian products in foreign markets (Åslund and Kuchins, 2009).

India

After centuries of British colonial rule India gained its independence in 1947 and has been a democracy ever since. After 1991, the economy shifted from a mixed economy between capitalism and socialism towards a more market-based system (Bose, 2009). The Indian government started to liberalize its economy after 1991, followed by a US$1.8 billion loan from the IMF. Both government and local businesspeople were convinced that the Indian economy must be integrated into the rest of the world and undertook major reforms to this effect (Franco et al., 2011).

Currently, the fragmented nature of the governance system with over 40 political parties affects the economic reform process adversely. There have been instances where the political stability within the country was influenced by allegations regarding corruption. Further concerns have arisen due to ongoing conflicts with neighbours in particular, and with groups operating in the central and eastern parts of the country (Kretzberg, 2008).

The economic outlook

India lags behind China and other emerging markets in several measures of performance such as GDP per capita, percentage of the population below the extreme poverty line, life expectancy, and foreign direct investment. Yet among the emerging markets, India holds a relatively good stance in terms of business development and innovation. Its economy is diverse, ranging from traditional farming to modern industries, and the country has a highly developed service industry. Even though almost half of the working population is in agriculture, the driver of the Indian economy is services (Bose, 2009).

India is one of the fastest growing economies globally. Real GDP growth increased from 8% in 2009 to 8.6% in 2010. Recently, the contribution of the agricultural sector to the GDP has been increasing as the sector is growing by approximately 6% annually, while manufacturing sector growth remains relatively stable. Forecasts suggest an average GDP growth of 6.5% between 2011 and 2030 in India. Such high forecasts are dependent on increasing the value-added nature of the information technology industry, which is the highest growth industry in the nation, and increasing the efficiency of the agricultural sector, which employs the highest number of people (EIU, 2011).

India has a young population and high urbanization rates, which have led to a positive outlook in terms of economic growth through a rise in consumption and production (Bose, 2009). In rural areas, employment is shifting away from agriculture towards small and medium-sized businesses, which has meant higher wages for rural citizens. As such, the market potential in these areas is becoming more pronounced (Krishna, 2011).

Indian companies enjoy comparative advantages in services sectors such as information technology and outsourcing. Industrial sectors such as pharmaceuticals, automobiles and textiles are also very strong in the country. The service sector has been a main driver of growth in India and, currently, the manufacturing industry is also growing (Bensidoun et al., 2009). A focus on knowledge and technology, which resulted in large investments in training, has led to the emergence of a large, skilled workforce. The country is especially prominent in outsourcing multinationals and has become the main provider of services, especially in IT and software, due to the availability of a large, educated, English-speaking, working population (Nelson and Forsans, 2008; Franco et al., 2011). India also offers a workforce with engineering capabilities and technical expertise, and therefore 40% of the manufacturing base of the country is in high-skill sectors (Kumar and Annushkina, 2010). Companies such as ABB, Honeywell (electric and electronic products), Toyota Motor (auto components), and Degussa (specialty chemicals) have invested in manufacturing facilities in India, as they operate in industries which require an advanced technological skills set (WIR, 2011). Rapid development of the computer and software service industries in India has also led to increased growth in supplier industries, such as telecommunications or computer hardware (Aggarwal, 2009).

The country remained relatively resilient throughout the global financial crisis, partially due to expansionary monetary and fiscal policies propelling investment (Subbarao, 2009). However, its fiscal deficit increased, especially with the government's decision to implement fuel and fertiliser subsidies and increase protection for farmers by waiving a portion of their debts in 2008. Further efforts by the government to support the rural areas also contributed to the deficit in 2008. Since then, it has focused on reducing the fiscal deficit, mainly by increasing the rate of privatization (Raju and Mukherjee, 2010).

Indian exports increased by 34% in 2010, while imports increased by 30.7%. China is its largest trading partner, followed by the USA. Intraregional trade with China has been growing (Nelson and Forsans, 2008), and FDI flow to the country also increased from US$35.18 billion in 2009 to US$37.18 billion in 2010, despite the prevailing global crisis (EIU, 2011).

Population growth and increased urbanization levels are intensifying the need to build infrastructure within the country. In the long term, alleviating poverty and overcoming infrastructural weaknesses remain as major obstacles for India. Increased wages, together with the rise of input and commodity prices, have led to price increases in produce, especially in agricultural output, which in turn has contributed to increased inflation (Fan et al., 2008).

Doing business in India

India has been an attractive destination for foreign investors, due to the availability of a large English-speaking population, continuous economic growth and a stable government (Aggarwal, 2009). Rapid economic growth has allowed the emergence of a young middle-income population with disposable income (Kumar and Annushkina, 2010). The market for consumer products and services is enormous, and Western firms must not ignore rural markets since three quarters of the Indian population live in rural areas. As income levels in rural areas are also rising, companies can find significant opportunities which are relatively untapped (Krishna, 2011).

Airport and ground handling, education, electric power generation and distribution, food processing, industrial textiles, machinery, and mining and telecommunications equipment have been highlighted as some of the areas with significant growth prospects in India (US Commerce, 2011c). India is attractive not only as a market but also as a sourcing country (Marr and Reynard, 2010).

India has been very active in establishing business relationships with major industrial countries, including the USA, Germany, the UK, Japan and Canada. The government has signed a number of bilateral agreements, exchanged ministerial visits, and sent combined government and business delegations to these countries. The country has over 50 bilateral investment treaties which have allowed it to attract capital from developed countries (Sachdeva, 2007).

Poor infrastructure and high tariffs remain a challenge to foreign investors (Bensidoun et al., 2009). India is currently focusing on increased investment in infrastructure, as well as the implementation of internet-based technologies, which will increase the attractiveness of the country for foreign investment and ease difficulties in doing business (Aggarwal, 2009). Lack of urbanization in India also poses a challenge for multinationals as the country is dispersed, and reaching the urban population creates financial and human capital challenges. Many companies have met this challenge by identifying clusters which can be served efficiently by a sound supply chain with acceptable costs (Gupta et al., 2010).

When compared to BRICs, India's tariff structure still remains high and more protectionist (OECD, 2008a). Domestic protection is strong, especially in agriculture, however in many industries the government has restructured the tariffs significantly. It is relatively easy to set up companies in India, except for a few industries such as banking, real estate and wireless communications, where government restrictions apply (Franco et al., 2011). Despite high domestic public debt, government borrowing from international markets remains limited. In order to reduce the deficit, the government needs to induce investment in the economy which can be accomplished by decreasing the entry barriers in some sectors, improving infrastructure, and increasing the investment in human capital (Kumar, 2009).

China

The People's Republic of China was formed in 1949. The country was ruled by the Chinese Communist Party under the leadership of Mao Zedong until 1978, when China's economic reforms began and the country started to open up its borders. The authoritarian governance system enabled the country to implement policies rapidly and effectively. International trade has played a substantial role in China's economic growth (Ambler et al., 2008). The Chinese constitution, created in 1954, by the Chinese People's Political Consultative Conference, has been amended several times, and the most recent adjustment to the constitution in 2004 recognized private property and propelled the growth of the private economy. Economic controls have gradually been reduced and the country is moving towards a market economy though political controls remain rigorous (Kretzberg, 2008).

China is still a communist regime but the government's economic reforms have propelled growth. Over the past few decades, the state has reduced its control of economic activity and has been moving towards a market economy. The government has attracted foreign investment by liberalizing trade rights and providing incentives for investors. Such policies led to a major reduction in poverty and a rapid rise in income, resulting in an average growth rate of 9.5% over two decades. Another factor which has contributed to the growth of per capita income in China is the one-child policy, which has limited population growth.

China's government faces challenges regarding environmental issues, as well as a high burden of state-owned enterprises. Other issues include the government's struggle to collect revenues, reduce corruption and illegal economic practices, and tackle excess labour in rural areas (Kretzberg, 2008).

The economic outlook

China has become a global low-cost manufacturing base, and many multinationals have facilities within the country. Approximately half of its GDP is generated by industry and construction, among which the major industries are mining, iron, steel, aluminium, machinery, textiles, petroleum, consumer products, electronics, automobiles and telecommunications equipment (World Bank, 2011a). Its fastest growing cities are mostly located inland, which indicates a shift in growth from coastal regions to those inland (EIU, 2011).

In China, savings rates are high due to the relatively weak social security system, people's desire to save for their retirement, and the high costs of healthcare (Chamon and Prasad, 2008). Investment rates by households and the government are high in comparison to other countries but remain steady. Investment in the enterprise sector is also rising. This investment is facilitated by the funds available to enterprises generated by the banking system and the government (Kuijs, 2005).

China launched a US$586 billion package in 2008 to support economic growth and counter the effects of the global economic crisis. Higher savings rates in the country, and the rapid influx of FDI, has enabled such investments. The package was designed to increase spending on infrastructure, such as the construction of housing, roads, power systems and transportation networks. Another purpose of the package has been to increase spending on medical services, education and innovation, and to boost the financial system by removing the lending restrictions of commercial banks (Naughton, 2009). The global financial crisis outlined a need to focus on domestic consumption as a driver of economic growth. Hence, the government has increased its efforts in boosting consumption. It is also increasing the availability of capital for small businesses to boost entrepreneurship within the country (Choi, 2011). In China, the state-owned sector still accounted for 40% as of 2008 (globalEDGE, 2011). However, reforms in state-owned enterprises are leading to higher performance and improved management (Ralston et al., 2006).

High levels of growth are straining the financial system within the country, as well as increasing inflation (IMF, 2011a). Rapid economic growth has also led to a greater demand for energy, and China has become the world's largest energy consumer and the third biggest importer of oil as of 2010 (Economist, 2011b). Due to continued economic growth, its energy needs are expected to further increase, highlighting the need to invest heavily in clean energy.

Doing business in China

Low-cost labour in China has traditionally been a major advantage in locating manufacturing facilities in the region. However, as more workers are immersed into the economy wages are rising, generating increased costs for manufacturers. More recently, rising wages and production costs have reduced investment in low-cost manufacturing and led to the divestment of coastal areas (WIR, 2011). First-tier cities in China are competitive and factor costs are rising. On the other hand, smaller/regional cities are associated with rapid growth, lower costs, developing markets and strong local government support, hence they provide multiple opportunities for investment (UKTI, 2010a).

Even though the government seeks to attract further foreign investment, the regulatory framework can sometimes pose a challenge for investors in China (Ambler et al., 2008). The Ministry of Foreign Commerce publishes a guide for foreign investors, in which businesses are classified as encouraged projects, restricted projects, and prohibited projects. Investments which are not in these categories are permitted projects. It is easier to set up an enterprise in a permitted or encouraged investment category (Ching, 2008). Industries which offer significant prospects for foreign investment are marine industries, education, industries focused on the prevention of pollution, renewable energy, safety, aviation, automotive components, healthcare, travel tourism and agriculture. China has also been attracting companies in the steel industry due to its vast iron ore resources. The country has also become the third largest market for luxury goods, following the USA and Japan, as of 2010 (US Commerce, 2011b).

In China, economic goals are set in a five-year programme. The latest plan was released in 2006 and focuses on increasing the technological and managerial capabilities within local companies, increasing energy efficiency, strengthening intellectual property rights protection, and protecting local firms by controlling foreign dominance in some sectors. Parallel to the objectives of the five-year plan, investment incentives and policies focus on increasing technological know-how within the country. Investors are faced with the dilemma of investing in a high-growth economy which offers significant incentives in value-added sectors, though intellectual property rights may not always be protected (US Commerce, 2011b). In some cases, the government may discourage investment in industries where it prioritizes developing local firms, or in industries dominated by state-owned enterprises. Investments which are not consistent with the goals of the five-year plan may also be regulated. Currently, the government is imposing restrictions in sectors such as petroleum and minerals, as well as selected areas within the high-tech industry (Choi, 2011).

The legal environment is characterized by inconsistencies and IP protection is limited, therefore many investors have faced difficulties with stolen IP (Newberry, 2008). On the other hand, the Chinese government is adamant about strengthening IP protection and improving the application of IP regulations, hence such concerns may mitigate in the near future. Companies which focus on the protection of their IP have focused on equity investments, either as wholly owned or joint ventures, in order to maintain control. Increasingly, foreign companies are establishing greenfield operations inland for manufacturing, which is a slight shift in investment trends as foreign entrants have traditionally focused on establishing joint ventures in China (Choi, 2011).

New Frontier Economies in Latin America

Latin American economies have a history of successful reforms followed by occasional relapses. Over the last two decades, most Latin American economies have tackled inflation, freed markets, and reduced state controls in major enterprises. Furthermore, apetura, or the liberalization of markets, has taken place in most of these countries. As a result of tariff cuts and the elimination of import/export licenses, intraregional trade has doubled. Moreover, restrictions on capital flows have been removed, and new sectors have been opened up to foreign investment. Foreign banks and insurance companies are now allowed to enter many Latin American markets. Numerous state-owned enterprises, ranging from oil firms to telecommunications and electricity companies, have been sold into private hands.

Latin America is relatively more culturally uniform when compared to Asia or even Europe. Its countries are similar in terms of language and also enjoy low trade barriers between each other. The region is also home to many emerging companies that are growing and internationalizing (Casanova, 2009). Latin American companies operate within a diversified range of industries, from aerospace, defence and telecommunications to automotive and even software design. The education levels of the growing young population increase continually, tendering the region as a hub of talent; 57% of the Latin American population is under 30 years old and the literacy rate among the young population is increasing. Another factor contributing to the growth of Latin America is its abundance of natural resources, as it has 30% of the world's fresh water, 48% of its copper, 23% of its forests, 19% of its iron ore, and 13% of its petroleum (Aguilar et al., 2009). Table 6.7 shows internet users, mobile cellular subscriptions and telephone lines as an indicator of infrastructure in selected Latin American economies, and the changes in these figures between 2000 and 2009. As clearly observed, the infrastructure and the adoption of technology in these economies have improved considerably. With mobile penetration reaching 89% as of 2012, Latin America is expected to be one of the fastest growing markets for telecommunications within the next five years (Accenture, 2012).

The urbanization forecasts, also shown in Table 6.7, highlight growth in the urban population, which in turn affect income and consumption patterns as well as the infrastructure needs within these economies.

GDP in the Latin American region contracted slightly by 2.2% in 2009, however this bounced back from the effects of the global crisis rapidly, and aggregate GDP expanded by 5.7% in 2010. Latin American countries were able to sustain performance and resume growth following the crisis, as they enjoy low levels of credit penetration as well as sound financial systems. In 2010, increased commodity prices and growing demand from China contributed to high capital flows in the region (IMF, 2011a). Other factors which currently contribute to growth within the region stem from sound monetary policies and a diversification of trade towards an emerging Asia (World Bank, 2011b).

Within the Latin American region, Brazil, Chile, Colombia and Uruguay are the major commodity exporters. An increase in commodity prices

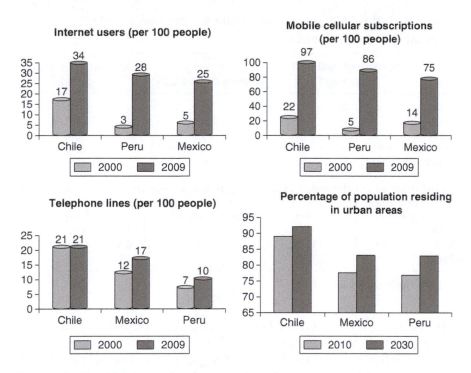

Table 6.7   Infrastructure and urbanization in the new frontier economies of Latin America

Source: World DataBank, 2011.

after the global financial crisis played a significant role in the growth of these economies (IMF, 2011a). In fact, 70% of exports to China from Latin America are commodity exports from Brazil, Chile and Peru. However, these Latin American economies' exposure to commodity prices may create a potential risk in the future because the demand for and price of commodities can be volatile.

Firms entering these emerging markets should be aware of regional and bilateral agreements. A successful bilateral trade pact between Argentina and Brazil led to the creation of Mercosur in 1991. At present, there are four members: Argentina, Brazil, Paraguay, Uruguay, and two associate members, Chile and Bolivia. Mercosur seeks to achieve the free movement of goods and services, establish a common regional tariff for third-country imports, and harmonize macroeconomic trade and exchange rate policies. Although Mercosur had a slow start, its members had cut tariffs for most of each other's imports. This reduction led to a 200% jump in intraregional trade in five years (Ghauri and Cateora, 2010).

Table 6.8   2011–2030 growth forecasts for the new frontier economies of Latin America

	Growth of real GDP per head	Growth of real GDP	Labour productivity growth
Mexico	2	3	1.6
Peru	2.4	3.3	2.3
Chile	3.4	4.1	3.4

Source: EIU, 2011.

Export of goods and services (% of GDP), 2004–2009 average	Change in exports as a % of GDP over 5 yrs
Chile	38%	-1%
Peru	24%	3%
Mexico	28%	1%

Source: World DataBank, 2011.

In the short term, GDP in Latin America is expected to grow by an average of 3.6% in 2012 and 4.2% in 2013. Though continued growth is expected in the region in the long run, the growth rates of individual countries are forecast to be around 3–4%, as shown in Table 6.8. Relatively conservative forecasts are affected by factors such as slower growth in the USA, high unemployment rates in some of the Latin American countries, and overall capacity utilization within the region (World Bank, 2011b).

Table 6.9 provides a brief summary of the challenges of selected Latin American economies, along with their strengths.

Mexico

Although Mexico's progress has been hampered by several financial, political and economic crises, it remains a promising market. Its economy consists primarily of private manufacturing and services, although it also has several large and traditional agriculture-based enterprises. At the beginning of the 1990s, the government implemented wide-ranging economic reforms, adopted a stricter fiscal policy, reduced the external debt, and brought inflation under control. As a result, the country was able to produce budgetary surpluses in 1992 and 1993. In 1994, peasants in the state of Chiapas briefly took up arms against the government, claiming governmental indifference to poverty and oppression, and this movement led to political instability. Consequently, Mexico experienced a monetary crisis, often referred to as the Tequila Crisis, which resulted

Table 6.9   Major strengths and weaknesses of the new frontier economies of Latin America

Mexico	Chile	Peru
Strengths		
• A manufacturing power notably capitalizing on its membership in NAFTA • Relatively good macroeconomic fundamentals • Moderation of foreign debt reassuring to international investors • Relatively healthy banking sector • Young and growing working population	• Abundant mining resources (world leader for copper), extensive agriculture, fishing and forestry • Multiple trade agreements • Regional platform for investors attracted by the country's political stability, the quality of its institutions, and a sound financial system • International standing boosted by membership of OECD since the end of 2009	• Abundant natural resources in mining, energy, agriculture and fishing • Tourism attracted by exceptional cultural heritage • External financial position in satisfactory state • Increasing number of free trade agreements signed
Weaknesses		
• Excessive concentration of exports to the USA • Dependence of public sector finances on oil revenue • Sociopolitical obstacles to structural reforms • Lack of investment and skilled labour • Extensive social inequality and poverty	• Small size economy, heavily exposed to world economic fluctuations due to its openness • Excessive dependence on copper exports • Dependence on foreign sources for energy • Disparities of income among the greatest in the world, notably due to deficiencies in education	• Economic contrasts following ethnic lines, with a relatively modern sector in the coastal plains and mining areas and a subsistence sector in the interior • Insufficient infrastructure reinforcing social and geographical inequalities • Poverty affecting more than half the population

Source: globalEDGE, 2011.

in the devaluation of its currency. Its economic activity therefore contracted by 7% in 1995 (Glick et al., 2001).

An international bailout effort, led by the USA, has helped to stabilize the economy and allowed Mexico to repay loans to the USA more than three years ahead of schedule. Recovering much more quickly than anticipated, Mexico's economy grew by more than 5% in 1996, and by 2000, it was fully recovered (US Department of State, 2001).

NAFTA has played a strong role in strengthening ties between Mexico and the USA. Both countries continue to benefit from the free trade agreement, which hopes to eliminate all trade restrictions in the future (Casanova, 2009).

The economic outlook

The macroeconomic environment of the country has improved significantly due to the reduction in public sector debts and inflation. Mexico has privileged access to the US market and is integrated with US manufacturing chains. Moreover, the country has a large portfolio of free trade agreements and a sizeable domestic market. Such factors highlight Mexico's potential as an important market for foreign investment. In 2009, its largest investor was the USA (56%), followed by Spain, the Netherlands, Canada, and the UK (IMF, 2009).

The country's GDP increased by 3.3% in 2007, 1.3% in 2008, and contracted by 6.5% in 2009. Approximately 75.1% of Mexican exports are manufactured goods. The rest of the exports are divided between fuel/mining products and agriculture, which accounted for 15.8% and 36.1% respectively in 2009 (WTO, 2011). More than a quarter of Mexico's GDP is from exports, and 80% of these are to the USA. The main reason for Mexico's contraction during the global financial crisis of 2008 was the poor state of the US economy during the crisis. Foreign direct investment also decreased to US$15.3 billion in 2009 from US$26.2 billion in the previous year, mostly due to the economic downturn. However, other elements which may have contributed to this decline are security concerns and frequent changes in regulations. However, foreign direct investment in the country slightly rebounded in 2010, increasing to US$18.6 billion (WIR, 2011).

In 2010 Mexico's GDP increased by 5.5%, reflecting its recovery from the recession. The Economist Intelligence Unit's forecasts suggest that economic growth will average 2.4% between 2011 and 2020, and decrease to 1.7% in the following decade. Such forecasts are influenced by the development needs of the country (EIU, 2011). Multiple trade agreements with other countries such as China, Turkey and Korea may shield Mexico's economy against other potential shocks to the US economy in the future (Macotela, 2011).

In 2009, Mexico was the world's seventh largest oil producer. Both oil production and sales are undertaken by the state-owned enterprise, Pemex, which has a constitutional monopoly. Oil is the largest source of foreign currency, followed by remittances which average US$21 billion annually. Manufacturing is also a significant contributor to the economy, constituting 30% of economic output (globalEDGE, 2011). Mexico is dependent on oil revenues, however 23 out of 32 of the largest oil fields report declining levels of oil, and the country may become an oil importer by 2017 (Marr and Reynard, 2010). Government revenues are highly prone to changes in oil prices and demand, thus the government is trying to reduce the dependency on oil income by introducing changes in tax regulations in order to increase earnings from non-oil-based collections.

Doing business in Mexico

In 2010, Mexico had 11 free trade agreements involving 41 countries in the Western Hemisphere, and also negotiated trade agreements with Israel, the EU, and Japan (Villarreal, 2010). Multiple trade agreements, decreasing regulations in doing business, the growth of the market, and the country's ability to offer low-cost manufacturing services render Mexico an attractive location for foreign investment. However, cumbersome tax regulations which change frequently, and security concerns related to relatively high crime rates, may pose challenges for foreign investors (Macotela, 2011).

Some of the significant industries within the economy are automobile, aerospace, processed foods, tourism and mining. Aerospace, automobile manufacturing, renewable energy, life sciences, and professional services are today attractive industries for growth (HSBC, 2010). Increased growth rates within the past decade have led to the emergence of a large middle class in Mexico which in turn has resulted in increased consumption. For instance, in 2010, the average salary in the country doubled when compared to the previous year and over 730,000 jobs were created. Hence, Mexico provides significant opportunities for firms producing consumer goods or services (Macotela, 2011). The country has also often been a preferred location for setting up manufacturing facilities. Companies are then able to provide a just-in-time delivery to Latin America and the USA and enjoy lower transportation costs to regional markets. The country is currently trying to increase its capabilities in value-added production, as well as in engineering and IT (UKTI, 2010h).

Export assembly plants (*maquiladora*) are a major source of income for the country. Such operations are factories or assembly plants established by the government under preferential tariff programmes. Materials can enter duty free, and the finished product is generally exported (UKTI, 2010h). In fact, over 5,100 plants are located throughout the Mexican–American border, creating a continuous trade in inputs as well as services. Such areas may present opportunities for new investors due to their intensive activity (US Commerce, 2011f).

For international investors, the main challenges within the business environment of Mexico are the high costs of utility, the complex tax system, and demanding labour legislation. Improvements in the business climate, such as regulations simplifying the tax system and a reduction in bureaucracy, could increase economic growth. In fact, in 2010, business procedures have been further simplified in order to keep Mexico an attractive location for foreign investment (EIU, 2011). Though the transportation network in Mexico is ample, further efforts are in progress to improve it. Such efforts are due to intensified trade relations which have increased the need to update and improve the network. Logistic services represent a significant cost in the country, however such costs may decrease in the long term due to improvements in infrastructure (Arias et al., 2010).

Peru

Peru was ruled by the military for 12 years until 1980. The change in the ruling system led to a decade of economic instability, which was reduced by the government of Alberto Fujimoro between 1990 and 2000 through reforms resulting in increased liberalization and the prevention of hyperinflation. However, the country's institutional development needs were largely overlooked and eventually led to the downfall of the government after a major corruption scandal in 2000. Since then, successive governments have been successful in creating macroeconomic stability (Taft-Morales, 2009). The poverty rate declined from 50% in 2003 to 36% in 2009 (World Bank, 2011c) though inequality still remains a major issue (Parnell, 2008). Reforms which began in the 1990s and continued into the 2000s focused on opening up and diversifying the economy and increasing access to social services.

At the beginning of the 21st century, large privatizations in the country contributed to economic growth. The economy was adversely affected by financial turmoil, as well as by the climate generated by El Nino, and political instability between 1998 and 2001. Since then, the government has managed to maintain political stability and improve the macro environment by lowering the budget deficit and unemployment rates (World Bank, 2011c).

The economic outlook

In Peru, approximately 65% of economic output relates to services. The manufacturing industry is also diverse and includes sectors such as food, metals, steel, textiles and petroleum refining (Parnell, 2008). The country's GDP decreased by 1% in 2009, largely owing to the global financial crisis which led to a decline in international trade. Despite the contraction in economic output, consumer confidence in the country remained strong. In 2010 the country's GDP grew by 8.8%, signalling a rapid recovery. In the near future, average growth in 2011 and 2012 is expected to be around 6.2% mainly due to increased consumption and investment (US Commerce, 2011h).

Average GDP growth between 2011 and 2030 is forecasted to be 2.4%. Such conservative forecasts are mainly because of income disparities and institutional deficiencies. The business environment is also adversely affected by strong labour legislation and low levels of education (EIU, 2011).

In Peru, 40% of the population is below the poverty line, however economic growth is above average Latin American growth rates (Heritage, 2011); 30% of the population resides in the capital Lima and approximately half of the country's GNP is generated via the capital. Approximately half of its economic output comes from services while the remainder is mostly from manufacturing and mining. Fishing is an important industry in Peru and accounts for 10% of the world's fishing industry. The country also has significant natural resources such as gold, copper, silver, oil and gas deposits, and fisheries (World Bank, 2011c).

Peru sustains a trade surplus which was preserved in 2010 with exports increasing by 30% to US$35.1 billion. Exports in 2010 consisted of fuels and mining products (49.5%), agricultural products (16.7%), and manufacturing (10.7%) (WTO, 2011). The country is dependent on commodity imports and thus remains vulnerable to changes in commodity prices (globalEDGE, 2011). The economy is dependent on export income which is necessary for import financing as well as for the payment of external debts. The dependence of export revenues on fuels and mining products, especially on minerals, creates exposure to external shocks, and the country is faced with the challenge of diversifying its export base (Hausmann et al., 2008; Colburn, 2009). FDI inflows were measured at US$19.4 billion in 2009 and increased to US$17.6 billion in 2010 (World DataBank, 2011).

Civil unrest exists due to clashes between the urban and rural populations over income disparities. There are also multiple conflicts over mining resources concerning their allocation. Extractive mining does not contribute to job creation significantly, hence the government's efficiency in transferring mining revenues to alleviate poverty gains importance. Conflicts arise due to concerns with the reallocation of mining revenues and concerns related to mining companies' compliance with environmental standards (Arellano-Yanguas, 2008).

Doing business in Peru

Huge natural resources, stable macroeconomic policies, favourable legal frameworks, favourable foreign investment policies, and trade agreements with multiple countries increase the attractiveness of Peru for foreign investors (UKTI, 2010f). However, weak contract enforcement mechanisms and intensive regulatory procedures in starting up businesses or employing workers remain a challenge.

Significant opportunities in the market are in the mining industry, which is the main export sector in the country. Other opportunities are in telecommunications, construction, air conditioning equipment, plastics, industrial chemicals, and computers (US Commerce, 2011h). The infrastructure deficit amounts to approximately US$37 million and there are major projects which will be undertaken in energy transmission, roads, and railways. In such projects, public–private partnerships are becoming more frequent. Many companies will choose joint ventures or acquisitions as an entry strategy in order to access the networks of local partners (UKTI, 2010f).

Its foreign investment policy is open and the country has taken measures to ensure transparency in regulations (OECD, 2008b). In the 2000s, the government changed the regulations for mining and transferred a significant level of revenue to the government. More measures were imposed to increase the local contribution of mining companies, however such measures have not been very effective in decreasing local political conflicts (Arellano-Yanguas, 2011).

Chile

Chile was governed by a military dictatorship between 1973 and 1990. Since 1980, the country has consistently followed sound economic policies; in that decade the government introduced market-oriented reforms which resulted in increased foreign investment and rapid economic growth. Military governance ended in 1990 and democracy was established (Marr and Reynard, 2010). Between 1990 and 2005, the GDP per capita increased from 4,800 to 12,250, resulting in a transformed socioeconomic structure (Aninat et al., 2010).

The economic outlook

Growth in exports, and especially of copper, has been a driver of the Chilean economy (Marr and Reynard, 2010). One third of the government's revenue in 2010 was due to copper. However, the government needs to diversify its revenue base to generate further growth (Hughes, 2010). The state's involvement in the economy is limited, although it still owns the copper giant CODELCO. Currently, the country is trying to increase its exports in other areas, such as forestry and wood products, agricultural produce, seafood, and wine (globalEDGE, 2011).

Chile is a major producer of copper, minerals, wood, fruit, seafood, and wine (Heritage, 2011); 65.9% of the GDP is due to services, 17.6% to mining, and 12.8% to manufacturing. Though services constitute a major proportion of the GDP, the value created through them is lower when compared to that of other OECD countries (Hughes, 2010).

In 2010, a major earthquake resulted in massive loss, and reconstruction and rebuilding costs are estimated at US$15–30 billion (Beittel and Margesson, 2010). During the global financial crisis of 2008, a fall in the price of copper, which provides 40% of government revenue, led to a 23% decrease in government revenue. The government launched a stimulus package amounting to 2.9% of GDP (approximately US$4 billion) in order to offset the effects of the global financial crisis (Heritage, 2011). The plan focused on infrastructure projects, and providing support for the low-income population (Meyer, 2010). The Chilean economy remained relatively stable despite the adverse effects of the 2010 earthquake and the global financial crisis, due to sound monetary and fiscal policies which gave rise to a rapid recovery in consumption and investment (De Gregorio, 2011).

Between 2010 and 2012, GDP growth is expected to be around 5.4%. Within this period, reconstruction due to the massive earthquake in 2010 is expected to contribute to the growth of economic output significantly (World Bank, 2011a). Demographic statistics indicate that the working-age population will increase by 1.6 million by 2020, and the country is challenged with increasing employment for this population. Income inequality in the country also remains an issue despite reduced poverty (Hughes, 2010).

Doing business in Chile

Chile is more open and developed when compared to the other markets of Latin America (UKTI, 2010b). Having signed trade agreements with 59 countries, it is committed to promoting international trade and welcomes investment. Foreign investment law in Chile ensures the same treatment of local and foreign investors. Favourable investment policies and the transparency of regulations in the country increase its attractiveness for foreign investors (Arroyo and Edmunds, 2010; Pueyo et al., 2011).

In Chile, opportunities in small equipment and consulting services in the mining industry are abundant. The country is now trying to diversify its energy supply and increase its capacity for power generation, hence there are opportunities in power generation and distribution. Due to damage by the 2010 earthquake, the government has announced plans for 38 mega infrastructure projects amounting to US$5 billion. There are significant opportunities in training and educational tools as well. Many investors also regard Chile as a point of entry for South America (UKTI, 2010b). The market is competitive and associated with price-sensitive consumers.

In the long run, Chile is faced with the challenge of diversifying its exports and increasing the capabilities of companies to generate growth from value-added activities (Arroyo and Edmunds, 2010). Investor concerns relate to Chile's poor protection of intellectual property, restrictive labour laws, unemployment rates, and inequality. Further reforms can increase the transparency and efficiency of the state (Aninat et al., 2010), and greater clarification in the legal policies for doing business can also help improve the business environment (Khemani and Carrasco-Martin, 2008). Job creation is critical as unemployment rates are bound to increase due to the country's demographic profile, indicating growth in the workforce after 2011 (Hughes, 2010).

New Frontier Economies in Asia

One of the largest economic shifts in history is occurring as Asian emerging markets come on-line. Although the industrialized countries have dominated the world for the past 150 years, many of these may be outpaced in the next 20 to 25 years by the remarkable growth and progress of Asian emerging economies. In the long run, the new frontier markets of Asia are expected to sustain high growth levels, as shown in Table 6.10.

A number of Asian economies have transformed their countries from agrarian societies to high-tech centres. The Asian crisis of 1996/1997, which affected the region severely, led to increased deregulation and forced companies to be more competitive. It also forced some of the region's conglomerates, leading family companies, and financial institutions to restructure. Indonesia, Thailand, Malaysia, the Philippines and Vietnam, which are referred to as ASEAN-5 by the International Monetary Fund, are expected to grow approximately by an average of 5.5% in 2011 and 5.75% in 2012. Of these countries, growth in Indonesia is expected to be slightly higher at 6.75% in 2011 and 6.5% in 2012. Higher growth rates in Indonesia are mostly due to the growth

Table 6.10 Growth indicators and forecasts for new frontier economies in Asia

2009	GDP ($ bill.)	GDP per capita, PPP ($)	GDP growth 5-yr average	Ave. GDP per capita growth (5 yrs)	Population (mill.)	FDI inflow ($ bill.)	Urbanization
Indonesia	540	4,199	21%	7%	230	4.9	53%
Malaysia	193	14,012	12%	5%	27	1.4	71%
Thailand	264	7,995	13%	4%	68	5.0	34%
Philippines	161	3,542	17%	5%	92	1.9	66%
Pakistan	162	2.609	13%	5%	170	2.4	37%

Source: World DataBank, 2011

2011–2030 forecasts

	Growth of real GDP per head	Growth of real GDP	Labour productivity growth
Malaysia	2.8	4.4	2.4
Indonesia	4.5	5.4	3.4
Thailand	3.9	4.3	4
Philippines	3.8	5.4	2.9
Pakistan	2.7	4.4	1.7

Source: EIU, 2011

in consumption and increased foreign investment (IMF, 2011a). In 2010, growth in the East Asia region (excluding China) was as a result of robust domestic demand and increased fixed investments (World Bank, 2011a). Table 6.11 shows internet users, mobile cellular subscriptions and telephone lines as an indicator of infrastructure in selected Asian economies, and the changes in figures between 2000 and 2009. As can be observed, infrastructure has improved considerably. Overall, the availability and adoption of technology have increased significantly in most of these markets. The urbanization forecasts, also shown in Table 6.11, highlight growth in the urban population which in turn affects income and consumption patterns, as well as infrastructure needs within these economies.

Table 6.12 highlights the main strengths and weaknesses of selected emerging markets in Asia. Major challenges highlighted in the table are the dependence of many Asian markets on exports and the need for further reforms. Another challenge for selected markets in Asia is that of increased competition. Providers of low-cost manufacturing and services are faced with increased competition from other emerging markets and developing economies.

In many emerging markets, exports have been a significant driver of growth. Table 6.13 shows the export levels of selected Asian economies.

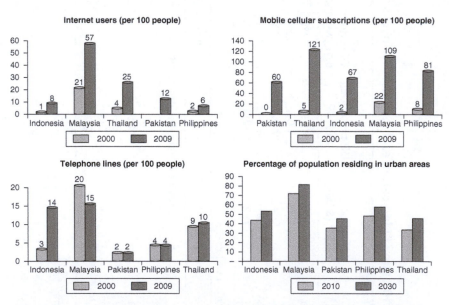

Table 6.11 Infrastructure and urbanization in new frontier economies in Asia

Source: World Databank, 2011.

Table 6.12   Major strengths and weaknesses of new frontier economies in Asia

	Malaysia	Thailand	Philippines	Indonesia	Pakistan

Strengths	• Diversified exports
	• Dynamic services sector
	• Effective education system, good infrastructure, high R&D
	• Support for investment via development of the financial market and broader access to FDI
		• Diversified, high performance production in agriculture and industry
		• Move upmarket in manufactured products
		• Regional hub open to dynamic neighbours
		• Strengthened banking system
			• Stronger banking sector
			• High levels of education and training
			• Highly productive and adaptable workforce
			• Significant inflows of expatriate worker remittances providing support for consumption and external accounts
				• Banking sector strengthened
				• Natural resource diversity (agriculture, energy, mining)
				• High competitiveness thanks to low-cost labour
				• Entrenched political stability
				• Dynamic tourism
				• Large population and domestic market
					• International community backing
					  ○ Transfers from expatriates as an important source of foreign exchange earnings
					  ○ Liberal rules for foreign trade
					• Comparative advantage in textile
					• Large population and domestic market

Weaknesses	• Economic dependence on foreign demand • Dependent on the performance of the gas and oil sectors • Very high stock of bank credit to the private sector • Erosion of the competitiveness associated with high labour costs • Persistent regional disparities	• Thai foreign trade subject to Chinese competition • Excessively weak investment rate • Lack of structural reform • Persistent ties between the private sector and political circles • Recurrent political instability since 2006	• GDP growth limited by low savings and investment rates • Persistent shortcomings concerning the business environment • Insecurity linked to rebellion in the south of the archipelago	• Low investment rate • Limited bank intermediation • Infrastructure deficiencies • Persistent corruption and lack of transparency • Inter-ethnic tensions stoked by high unemployment and poverty	• Reforms deterred by regional geopolitical tensions and domestic political instability • Dependence on imports and foreign capital • Deficient infrastructure and education system

Source: globalEDGE, 2011.

Table 6.13 Export performance in new frontier economies in Asia

Export of goods and services (% of GDP), 2004–2009 average		Change in exports as a % of GDP over 5 yrs
Indonesia	24%	–5%
Malaysia	96%	–3%
Thailand	68%	–1%
Philippines	32%	–9%
Pakistan	13%	–4%

Source: World DataBank, 2011.

As can be seen, exports, especially in Malaysia and Thailand, are integral to the economy. Asian emerging economies are perhaps the most receptive to foreign firms and investment. The gaps between the West and Asian emerging markets with respect to marketing, technology, capital, management, and motivation are not as big as those between the West and Eastern and Central Europe, or the West and Africa. Companies and consumers are both very familiar with Western-style marketing activities. These countries, excluding China, are technologically quite close to Western levels, and they have extensive experience with technologically advanced products. Also, English is widely used in government and business.

In Asia, the higher the need for control, the more a firm should establish a wholly owned subsidiary, especially if the technology or know-how to be transferred is of a sensitive nature and the firm is concerned about copyright and patents. Joint ventures are also common entry modes in these markets. Selecting the right partner/agent is an important element. Asians have a problem saying 'no', which can lead to a risk that they will promise more than they can deliver. A foreign firm should systematically investigate whether a prospective agent or partner can actually fulfil the terms of an agreement.

Thailand

The Thai kingdom was established in the 14th century and was referred to as Siam until the mid-20th century. A constitutional monarchy was formed in 1932. Despite frequent government changes, political and economic stability is ensured by a balance between the king, the military, bureaucrats, and the business sector. There is also close cooperation between the public and private sectors.

In 1997, Thailand devalued its currency, leading to an economic collapse which in turn affected other Asian countries. Following the Asian financial crisis, Thailand implemented an economic reform programme parallel to conditions set by the IMF, which targeted increasing the attractiveness of the country for investment (Glick et al., 2001). The country was able to exploit its natural resources successfully and generate capabilities in primary processing. Rapid industrialization also generated competencies in labour-intensive assembly activities. As a result, the country has a diverse production base which is utilized by export-led growth policies (Intarakumnerd and Lecler, 2010).

The economic outlook

Thailand's economy is in transition from an agricultural based economy to an industry and trading based economy. Although the majority of the workforce is employed. still depend on agriculture, manufacturing, trading and service sectors are expanding (Lawn, 2008). Exports are concentrated in the automotive, petrochemical and electronics sectors, while the income from tourism is also an influential factor in the economy. The share of high-technology exports, such as integrated circuits, hard-disk drives or vehicle parts, is also significant. Exports from Thailand accounted for approximately 60% of its GDP in 2009 (US Commerce, 2011k) and an average of 68% of the country's GDP between 2004 and 2009, highlighting the economy's dependence on export income. Its main export markets are the EU, China and Japan (WTO, 2011a).

In Thailand, a shortage of skilled personnel and environmental degradation has increased over the years (Warr, 2007). In the past, only low-wage, labour-intensive industries were expanding, and a poorly educated workforce was adequate, but now such industries face competition from China and Vietnam (Marr and Reynard, 2010). Thailand needs to attract high-technology industries, and needs to increase education levels in order to compete (Warr, 2007).

Thailand was significantly affected by the global financial crisis. In 2010, the economy recovered and GDP increased by 8%. The main reasons for Thailand's rapid recovery following the crisis were increased government spending and growth in exports. However, political unrest in the spring of 2010 reduced investor confidence in the country (IMF, 2011a).

One challenge facing the Thai government is the dispersed growth patterns within the country. While Bangkok and its nearby regions are prosperous and economically advanced, the northeast part of the country remains very poor. The government is currently trying to reduce the income disparity between regions by promoting investment and providing economic stimulus programmes for poorer regions. Other issues in the country stem from political uncertainty, civil unrest, and violence in the provinces (Marr and Reynard, 2010).

Doing business in Thailand

Thailand has been one of the fastest growing and most attractive markets for foreign exporters and investors for the past couple of decades. Currently, it is associated with market-based policies, and openness to investment (Kretzberg, 2008). Thailand has signed numerous trade agreements in order to promote trade (Lawn, 2008). The size of the market increases its attractiveness to foreign investors. Meanwhile, natural resources and manufacturing capabilities provide excellent export opportunities (Intarakumnerd and Lecler, 2010).

Rapid growth in Thailand has led to an increased demand for infrastructure. Meanwhile, government stimulus packages focus on long-term competitiveness, and the government is expected to spend approximately £27 billion between 2010 and 2012 in sectors such as transportation, public health, housing, and education (UKTI, 2011). Other opportunities are created by growth in consumption in areas such as automotive accessories, cosmetics, food supplements, and medical products. In Thailand, consumers are highly price-conscious, therefore price competitiveness is a major challenge for potential investors (US Commerce, 2011k).

Indonesia

Indonesia, with its 3,000 islands, became independent from the Netherlands on 27 December 1949, although it proclaimed independence on 17 August 1945. Following this, the economic collapse of the country allowed the army to seize power and General Suharto became the president. His presidency, which began in 1967, ended in 1998 as he was forced to resign. Under his leadership, the country demonstrated great potential, averaging 6.8% growth annually for 20 years.

Indonesia is now the world's third largest democracy and is home to the world's fourth largest population. Following decades of authoritarianism, the country has been focusing on economic and financial reforms. Since 1998 significant political reforms have been undertaken, and a more democratic governance system based on presidential elections has been implemented. In 2004, the president and vice president of the country were democratically elected for the first time. The current president, Mr Yudhoyono, was elected in 2009 for a second term, and the next election will be held in 2013. Presidents have traditionally held high powers within the political structure, though recent changes within the constitution have increased the power of the legislature (EIU, 2011).

The economic outlook

In 2011, President Yudhoyono launched a 15-year economic growth plan. The plan is designed to facilitate economic growth and enable the country to become one of the 10 largest economies in the world by 2025. Within this plan, investments in education, infrastructure and the need to promote development across regions are highlighted. The plan also emphasizes the need to shift the focus of exports from primary commodities to value-added products. The government intends to invest in infrastructure and improve connectivity between separate regions, and improve the business environment in less-developed areas. The economic growth plan requires an investment of over US$470 billion and the strategy for fund raising is unclear. In fact, without reducing its bureaucracy, the country may face problems in attracting foreign capital (Kretzberg, 2008). In 2010, the government increased privatization in order to increase funds. The major privatizations were those of Krakatau Steel and Bank Negara Indonesia.

Consumption is expected to grow rapidly owing to a 237.5 million population, of which approximately 50% is below 30 years of age. The share of the middle-income population of Indonesia with an annual income between US$5,000 and US$15,000 was 36% of the total population as of 2011, and this share is expected to increase to 58% by 2020 (US Commerce, 2011e). The increase corresponds approximately to 60 million workers joining the middle class. The EIU forecasts a GDP growth of 5.4% annually between 2011 and 2030. A young population structure, a government commitment to improving the business environment and a reduction in corruption are the main factors affecting this forecast (EIU, 2011). Poverty and the need to absorb a rapidly growing working-age population into the economy present major challenges (Murphy, 2009).

Foreign direct investment in Indonesia decreased to US$4.8 billion in 2009 from US$9.3 billion in 2008, mainly due to the effects of the global financial crisis. However, the gross national income grew by 3.3% in the same period, owing to the strength of the economy and its financial institutions. Foreign investment inflows also increased above 2008 levels in 2010, reaching US$13.3 billion (WIR, 2011). Due to a relatively low share of exports, strong domestic demand and appropriate policy responses from the government, Indonesia recovered quickly from the crisis (Basri and Rahardja, 2010). In 2010, 22.8% of merchandise exports were due to agricultural produce, 39.4% to fuels and mining, and 37% to manufacturing (World DataBank, 2011).

Foreign investment in the economy is focused on property, transportation, telecommunications, and plantations. Investment in Indonesia comes particularly from neighbouring countries, possibly due to Asian countries' familiarity with the environment (Headifen, 2011).

Doing business in Indonesia

Indonesia offers significant opportunities for companies involved in airport construction and expansion, railroad development and investment, healthcare equipment and services. Other opportunities can be observed in infrastructure, financial services, oil and gas, power generation, renewable energies, mining, the environment, media, information communications technology, and consumer products (UKTI, 2010d). The Indonesian government intends to create over 10 million jobs, reducing the poverty rate by a third by 2025. As such, consumption is expected to grow rapidly, highlighting the country's importance as a potential market for foreign investors (Headifen, 2011). Local companies in Indonesia are often small and cannot compete with multinationals in terms of resources. Hence, the Indonesian market offers huge opportunities in terms of a customer base developing a taste for foreign products (Marr and Reynard, 2010). The need for investment in infrastructure also presents large opportunities for foreign investors. For instance, Japanese investors have been especially active in working with the government in building power plants to meet the increasing electricity needs which are growing by 8% annually (Headifen, 2011).

Overall, Indonesia is receptive to foreign investment. On the other hand, the country is enforcing limits on some of the industries available for foreign investment, while undertaking reforms in liberalization through decentralization and a reduction in bureaucracy. Increased restrictions in employment laws have increased labour costs and led to a reduction in foreign investment and a rise in unemployment (OECD, 2008a).

Distribution and sales channels are well organized and available throughout the country. However, the infrastructure of the country is inefficient and may lead to high costs for transportation. Warehousing may also be costly for local suppliers. Thus, some foreign companies prefer offshore warehouses, especially in Singapore. Similar to exporters who are advised to retain local agents or distributors upon entry, firms interested in joint ventures are recommended to work with local partners. Local partners' knowledge of the conditions in Indonesia, their networks and their approach to local customers provides significant advantages for foreign entrants. In forming a partnership, the partner selection process in Indonesia needs to be especially highlighted because of the difficulties in dissolving partnerships in the country (US Commerce, 2011d).

Political stability is a concern for investors, especially because of the apparent lack of unity within the coalition government which was elected in 2009 (Marr and Reynard, 2010). However, the president's commitment to continue reforms despite issues within the coalition government has improved investor sentiment. The government is also committed to increasing liberalization levels in the economy despite strong opposition. International investors are challenged by the regulatory framework on entering the market (Headifen, 2011). Major difficulties in investing in Indonesia stem from legal uncertainties, nationalist sentiments in economic decisions, and the prevalence of local interest groups in matters of national policy (EIU, 2011).

Malaysia

Great Britain established colonies in the area which is now Malaysia in the 18th and 19th centuries. These colonies, which were occupied by Japan between 1942 and 1945, formed the Federation of Malaya in 1948 and became independent in 1957. Malaysia, as we know it, was formed in 1963. The Malaysian economy prospered particularly during the reign of Prime Minister Mahathir between 1981 and 2003, through which the government emphasized economic reforms that were focused on a diversification of the economy to reduce the country's dependence on exports and supported the growth of the manufacturing and service sectors. In the late 1980s, the government realized that the public sector had grown too large, and started an ambitious privatization programme. The Malaysian economy was significantly affected by the Asian financial crisis of 1997–1998 in which GDP contracted by more than 7%. Following the Asian financial crisis at the end of the 20th century, Malaysia implemented reforms aimed at strengthening the financial sector (Glick et al., 2001). Economic policy is influenced by the government's efforts to reduce poverty among the ethnic Malays and decrease economic disparity.

The economic outlook

The Malaysian economy today is based on services and manufacturing, whereas the country was heavily dependent on the trade of primary products for most of the 20th century. The government's progress towards engaging in reforms to establish a knowledge-based economy has led to improvements in the business environment. In 2010, it announced the New Economic Model which focuses on measures to induce investment in value-added sectors designed to generate economic growth and enable the country to become a high-income nation by 2020 (EIU, 2011).

Average growth between 2005 and 2009 was approximately 12%. In 2009, economic growth was halted by the decline in manufacturing output which constitutes 63% of the industrial production of the country. Such a decline meant a decrease in disposable income as well as an increase in unemployment (EIU, 2011). The Malaysian economy recovered quickly from the crisis due to the government's stimulus plan, and also recovered its domestic demand and exports.

Malaysia is a major producer of five key commodities: rubber, palm oil, tin, timber, and pepper globally. The country has the 24th largest oil reserves and 13th largest gas reserves. In the Malaysian economy, services and manufacturing accounted for 85% of the GDP in 2010, with a distribution of 57% in services and 28% in manufacturing. The country has a large consumer market with per capita rates higher than many of the emerging markets. In 2010, income per capita was approximately US$7,000 and this figure is expected to increase to US$15,000 by 2020 (US Commerce, 2011e). Growth has led to better living standards and reduced inequalities in the distribution of income. Low trade and investment barriers have been a significant factor sustaining growth of the economy and have enabled the country to take advantage of opportunities in world trade and the internationalization of production (Athukorala, 2011).

The country is one of the most trade-dependent economies in the world, and exports amount to 96% of GDP, as observed in Table 6.12. Malaysia is a major exporter of electronics and a provider of services such as financial services, insurance and tourism. It is also Asia's largest net exporter of fuel and the world's second largest exporter of palm oil (globalEDGE, 2011). The export growth of Malaysia was affected by a shift in global tastes and the global consumer's preference for unbranded goods at lower prices produced in China or Vietnam, as opposed to the more sophisticated products that Malaysia produces (Marr and Reynard, 2010).

Doing business in Malaysia

Investors are attracted to Malaysia due to its openness to trade, its increased investment in infrastructure, its size, and the growth rates of its economy (Ang, 2008). Increased liberalization in the service sector, the growing middle class, and continued reforms in the banking system have also increased the country's attractiveness. Aside from being one of the main producers of timber, Malaysia is also the largest producer of rubber and computer disk drives (UKTI, 2010g).

Malaysia is one of the founding members of the Association of Southeast Asian Nations (ASEAN) which focuses on regional cooperation, a member of Asia Pacific Economic Cooperation (APEC), and an active participant in the United Nations. The country is increasing its commitment to liberalization as evidenced by the free trade agreement with India in 2011, with Chile in 2010, and ongoing negotiations with the EU which are expected to be finalized in 2012. Major investors in Malaysia come from the USA and Japan, followed by Germany, Singapore and Hong Kong (Marr and Reynard, 2010). Significant foreign investments are in manufacturing, financial services and mining, with manufacturing accounting for approximately half of all foreign investments between 2003 and 2007 (Masud et al., 2008).

Malaysia has one of the region's strongest legal structures for intellectual property protection, and the country has accepted both the Berne Convention and the Paris Convention, as well as being a member of the World Intellectual Property Organization (Athukorala, 2011).

Government debt, mainly caused by high levels of government subsidies and inefficiency in managing public services, presents a major concern. To sustain growth, the country needs to increase investment in technological capabilities and shift to value-added production (Tanggapan et al., 2011).

The Philippines

The Philippine Islands were first ruled by Spain, then the USA and then declared independence in 1946. A democratic system was established afterwards, however it suffered from mismanagement and political instability which resulted in a military coup in 2001. Since 2001, the governance of the country has been more stable.

The Philippines was not affected by the Asian financial crisis at the end of the 20th century as much as other countries within the region. However, GDP shrank and was followed by bank failures in 2000 and political instability in 2001. Recovery was quick and the economy grew consistently in the 2000s (Skinner, 2011).

Political turbulence in some regions is an issue, but the new administration, under the presidency of Benigno S. Aquino – elected in 2010 – aims to negotiate with the groups creating political turmoil. In 2010, the country received assistance from the USA for development (US$128 million) as well as military assistance (US$67 million), relief efforts

(US$1.4 million), and logistical support for the delivery of supplies. The Philippines and the USA also signed a five-year contract amounting to US$434 million, in order to reduce poverty and enable further economic growth (US Commerce, 2011i). The government announced a six-year development plan in 2011, which focuses on macroeconomic stability, reducing poverty, and stimulating economic growth. The government also plans to invest in infrastructure and human resources by improving public finances through introducing administrative reforms.

The economic outlook

The Philippines has made the transition from an agriculture-based economy to an industrialized economy over the last three decades via reforms targeting the development of labour-intensive services and industries which contribute to exports. The service sector became a major driver in the economy partially due to supporting policies, such as creating special economic zones for exports, focusing on developing medical tourism, creating information technology parks, and developing business-process outsourcing capabilities (Clausen, 2010). The Philippines has become a particularly attractive location for business-process outsourcing and the outsourcing of support functions.

In 2010, GDP grew by 7.3% owing to increased consumption, export and import levels as well as increased government spending as a result of elections. A 40% increase in revenue from electronics manufacture contributed to export growth. In the Philippines, food processing, textiles and electronic assembly are key sectors, however services dominate the economy (US Commerce, 2011i). Remittances are another important source of revenue contributing to growth (Kumar, 2010). The Philippines also has one of the largest gold nickel and copper reserves globally.

Imports are mainly from Japan and the USA, followed by Singapore, China and Thailand. China is a major market for exports from the Philippines. In 2009, approximately 70% of exports were value-added electronics and components for China (Marr and Reynard, 2010). Though China and the Philippines are in conflict over ownership of the Spartly Islands, the Philippines is trying to take a diplomatic approach to settling the dispute, given China's importance for the country's economy.

Doing business in the Philippines

In the Philippines, significant opportunities exist within the IT, telecommunications, electronics, automotive, construction, medical equipment and electric power industries. Within these, the government is actively seeking foreign investment through public and private partnership programmes. Ford, Toyota, Mitsubishi, Nissan, and Honda are some of the major car manufacturers in the country. Intel has been a major producer there for over three decades, as have been Texas Instruments (DSP chips for Nokia and Eriksson), Lexmark (printers), and Toshiba (hard-disk drives).

Foreign investors are attracted to the Philippines due to the growth of the middle class and the availability of a skilled English-speaking workforce. Sectors which exhibit high growth are business-process outsourcing, infrastructure, and the power industry. In 2010, the government also established a public–private partnership centre to oversee infrastructure projects (UKTI, 2010i). The government requires 60% local ownership for state-funded projects in goods and consulting services. In infrastructure projects, the required local ownership is 75% (US Commerce, 2011i).

Economic growth in the Philippines is hindered by institutional inefficiencies which can prevent the effective implementation of economic policies. Inefficient management of public finances instilled by poor tax administration, as well as high burdens generated by state-owned public institutions, remain a major challenge for the government. Such inefficiencies need to be addressed in order to increase public finances and enable investments in infrastructure and education, which are necessary for promoting economic growth. Corruption is a major issue in the business environment in the country, as are an ineffective judicial system and weak IP protection.

Pakistan

In 1947, Pakistan separated from India and the state of Pakistan declared its independence as East and West Pakistan. Ongoing conflicts within the two sections led to the separation of East Pakistan and the foundation of the nation of Bangladesh in 1971. Disputes over the region of Kashmir still prevail with India, though the countries have begun discussions to work through the dispute. Since Pakistan's independence, there have been several military coups in the country which were halted under the presidency of Pervez Musharraf between 2001 and 2008. After Mr Musharraf stepped down from the presidency in 2008, a new coalition government between the Pakistan People's Party and Pakistan Muslim Leagues was formed, though this was disbursed due to the withdrawal of the latter party towards the end of 2008. The presence of the military is pronounced within the country's political structure, as it has been in power several times.

Pakistan has taken positive steps in boosting its economy and liberalizing trade, especially through commitments made to the WTO, IMF and World Bank. In parallel, the government has been introducing significant reforms, strengthening financial institutions, and establishing a firmer legal framework which focuses on the protection of IP, effective conflict resolution and stronger governance mechanisms, all of which are designed to prevent illegal economic activity (Butt and Bandara, 2009).

The economic outlook

The country's economy is dependent on support, particularly from the IMF. Loans obtained from the IMF, especially in the 2008 agreement, are directed towards improving the economy's stability. In 2009, the IMF raised its support to US$11.3 billion and one of the conditions of the loan was for the Pakistani government to address its shortage of tax revenue. In 2009, the USA also signed the Enhanced Partnership with Pakistan Act of 2009, which aims to provide the country with US$5 billion assistance over a five-year period that will be directed at the development of infrastructure.

Over the past 10 years, average growth rates have been influenced by ongoing political disputes in the region, internal political conflicts, and low levels of foreign investment. Inflation averaged 13.6% in 2009, driven by increases in food and utility prices and the depreciation of the rupee against the dollar. In 2010, severe flooding affected the country significantly and the GDP growth of the country is expected to be 4% in 2012, which is higher than the 3% growth that it experienced in 2011. Liberal investment policies should lead to an improved business environment within this period. However, investors are still concerned about high levels of political instability and the risk of terrorist attack (EIU, 2011). Ongoing poverty, especially considering Pakistan's high population growth rates, is a major concern.

The country is endowed with natural resources which are not yet fully capitalized due to the shortage of capital. Manufacturing is significant in the economy and half of all exports are in textile and apparel manufacturing. Economic growth is mostly generated by the growth in textiles and expansion of low-end manufacturing (EIU, 2011). Pakistan has been reducing the share of agriculture and forestry in the economy and has focused on industry and services for the past three decades (Iqbal et al., 2010).

The Pakistani population is relatively young and the middle-income class is estimated at around 30 million people. Future growth in the country can be accelerated by an increase in the working population, however this demographic change also indicates that unemployment may prove to be a challenge. In order to sustain growth, Pakistan needs to ensure macroeconomic stability and decrease its reliance on foreign loans. As such, the country needs to undertake structural reforms to boost economic growth (Ahmed and Wahab, 2011).

Foreign investment and a growth in trade have been major drivers in the economy (Iqbal et al., 2010). Increased privatization between 2002 and 2007, especially in financial services and telecommunications, helped increase foreign investment levels in Pakistan. However, since 2008 privatizations have declined and this, coupled with the contraction of global investment due to the global financial crisis of 2008, gave rise to foreign investment in the country decreasing from US$5.15 billion in 2008 to US$2.15 billion in 2010. Weak infrastructure and political instability also contributed to this decline. The government is faced with challenges such as the subsidy burden, inflation, concentrated export structures, an insufficient infrastructure, and an unskilled labour force (US Commerce, 2011g). Inflation and macroeconomic instability remain as obstacles to continued growth. The government needs to focus on bringing inflation down and reducing poverty, as well as controlling the fiscal deficit. Furthermore, to sustain growth, technological improvements and structural reforms to enhance factor productivity are necessary (Lodhi, 2011).

Doing business in Pakistan

Pakistan has always been open to foreign investment and most multinationals are present in the country. Other features which increase its attractiveness for investors are the prevalence of English in the business community, a legal system similar to that of industrialized nations, and an evolved service sector which contributes 60% to the country's GDP. In 2010, the government created a board to attract international investors in infrastructure and to engage in public–private partnerships in infrastructure projects on a build–operate–transfer basis. Other sectors which offer opportunities for foreign investors are airport and ground support equipment, computers, construction equipment and services, electrical power systems, oil and gas equipment, telecommunications equipment and services, and transportation services (US Commerce, 2011g).

Foreign investment policies which allow equity ownership of 100%, and treat local and foreign investors equally, increase the attractiveness of the country for investors. The government provides incentives such as a 100% repatriation of profits, duty free imports, and a relaxation in taxes to attract foreign investment. Export opportunities in Pakistan are in specialized industrial machinery, power generation equipment, and medical products. Meanwhile, investment in the automotive, telecommunications, information technology, oil and gas, and infrastructure industries has been increasing (UKTI, 2010e).

The business environment is dominated by family structures, which creates an emphasis on the importance of relationships. Hence, working with a local partner or a representative is highly advisable. The availability of local firms seeking foreign capital and technological know-how increases the attractiveness of joint ventures as an entry method for Pakistan (US Commerce, 2011g).

Though the previous government emphasized economic liberalization, political instability and threats of violence, due to the country's proximity to Afghanistan, affect investors' confidence, and the government needs to further increase stability to boost foreign investor confidence. In Pakistan, the tax system is cumbersome and inefficient. However, the country has undertaken reforms in order to increase the efficiency and transparency of the tax system. Though Pakistan has privatized some of its state-owned enterprises, state involvement has created challenges for foreign entrants in some cases (Heritage, 2011).

New Frontier Economies in Other Regions

Sub-Saharan Africa is growing rapidly, mainly due to domestic demand, commodity prices, and sound economic policies. In fact, economic growth in sub-Saharan Africa is expected to be around 4.2% in 2012 and 5% in 2013. Low-income countries within the region are increasingly contributing to such growth as their economies are boosted by infrastructure investments and improved production in agriculture (IMF, 2011a).

Economies within the Middle East and North African region are very diverse, partially owing to the possession of and dependence on natural resources. Parts of the Middle East and North African region are affected by social unrest and political discontent, which are bound to affect the economy adversely. Meanwhile, oil-exporting countries are benefiting from high commodity prices. Europe is a major trading partner for most of the African countries focused on non-oil exports, thus a contraction in the European economy may pose risks for such countries, and especially for manufacturing exporters like South Africa. Another potential risk may be an increase in fuel or food prices which could affect importing countries (IMF, 2011a).

In looking at emerging markets in other regions, we have included two economies from Africa – South Africa and Egypt. The other emerging market which we have included in our focus is Turkey. Table 6.14 highlights major strengths and weaknesses in these economies, and Table 6.15 shows growth performance and forecasts for these.

South Africa

South Africa is faced with ongoing challenges stemming from apartheid, such as reducing inequality among the population by providing education, housing, and healthcare to the majority of the population. The unrest caused by continued fighting, even after the multi-racial elections of 1994, was settled with the resignation of President Mbeki in 2008 and the succession of Kgalema Mothalnthe. In 2009, Jacob Zuma, the president of the African National Congress, was elected as president.

In 2003, The Black Economic Empowerment (BEE) Act was launched. The BEE act reflects the government's strategy of empowering the black population and reducing inequality in the country which can further increase economic growth in the long run. One of the main goals of the BEE is to generate changes in the composition of management structures and the skilled workforce throughout the country, mainly by enabling more black people to own and manage enterprises, assisting in the development of black-owned enterprises, and increasing, the access of the disadvantaged population to economic activities, education, and infrastructure (Hamann et al., 2010). In 2011, a new platform to facilitate trading in line with the BEE was also launched.

The economic outlook

It is said that South Africa has two parallel First and Third World economies existing side by side. To succeed, it must merge these economies together and create a middle-income, emerging-level country. This being the case, while a part of the economy is productive and industrialized, the other part is burdened with challenges related to developing economies, such as an uneven distribution of income and the prevalence of a large informal sector. South Africa has many advantages as an emerging market. It is the largest producer of platinum and also has rich resources such as gold, manganese, chrome and titanium. The country also has large coal reserves which contribute to its exports considerably. A growing area in the economy is the value-added processing of minerals. The country is becoming a significant producer of ferro alloys

Table 6.14 Major strengths and weaknesses of new frontier economies in other regions

South Africa	Turkey	Egypt
Strengths		
• South Africa has 33% of sub-Saharan GDP • Extensive mining resources • Diversified industry, efficient tertiary sector (banks, telecommunications) • Public sector finances under control • Business environment among the most efficient in emerging countries	• Private sector dynamism and labour quality • Potential for tourism • Public sector finances partly consolidated • Restructured banking sector • Economic convergence with Europe • Demographic dynamism	• Strong development potential, thanks to oil and gas reserves • Potential for tourist industry due to archaeological heritage sites • Large domestic market
Weaknesses		
• Significant social risk: degree of income inequality among the highest in the world • Human capital deficit (26% of unemployment and 11% AIDS prevalence rates) • Dependence on inflows of volatile capital • Vulnerable to a crisis of confidence in the markets	• High external financing needs making Turkey dependent on foreign capital • Sharp rise in corporate foreign debt which increases the exposure to exchange rate risk • Antagonism between the government and Kemalist groups • Poor prospects for progress on negotiations with the EU	• Economy lacks diversification and is dependent on hydrocarbon • Underdeveloped banking system • Difficult business environment • Political instability

Source: global EDGE, 2011.

Table 6.15 Growth indicators and forecasts for new frontier economies in other regions

2009	GDP ($ bill.)	GDP per capita, PPP ($)	GDP growth 5-yr average	Ave. GDP per capita growth (5 yrs)	Population (mill.)	FDI inflow ($ bill.)	Urbanization
South Africa	285	10,278	7%	5%	49	5.4	61%
Egypt	188	5,673	5%	7%	83	6.7	43%
Turkey	615	13,668	12%	6%	75	8.4	69%

Source: World DataBank, 2011.

2011–2030 forecasts		
Growth of real GDP per head	Growth of real GDP	Labour productivity growth
S. Africa — 4	4	3
Egypt — 3.8	5.3	2.6
Turkey — 3.6	4.3	3.2

Source: EIU, 2011.

and stainless steel. The manufacturing industry is very advanced in several sectors such as those for motor vehicles, railway rolling stock, and mining equipment (globalEDGE, 2011).

The South African economy is mixed, with 7% based on agriculture, fishing and mining, 20% on manufacturing construction and utilities, and 73% on trade, transport and services. A diversified export range and the well-developed financial system are strengths within the country's economy. South Africa's exports, which are mainly to China, Germany, the USA and Japan, were approximately 35% of its GDP in 2008. As the country is also a member of the Southern African Customs Union (SACU) and Southern African Development Community (SADC), trade within the African region is also growing (US Commerce, 2011j).

The growth of FDI in South Africa is mainly due to its extensive mineral wealth, and the size, stability, and advanced conditions of its market. Due to conservative consumption levels, and the conservative approach of business during and after the recession, as well as changes in commodity prices, the FDI inflows to the country fell from US$9.6 billion in 2008 to US$5.4 billion in 2009. Weakening commodity and food prices leading to higher inflation and high interest rates resulted in the contraction of GDP growth, and South Africa went into a recession in 2009. A decline in domestic consumption and lower tax revenues also troubled the economy in 2009. Its financial institutions are well established and these were not affected by the global crisis significantly. South African GDP grew by 2.8% in 2010. This relatively low increase in GDP growth can be mostly attributed to consumer caution. However, household spending increased by 5.1% in the first quarter of 2011. Household debt decreased to 76.8% of the GDP in the first quarter of 2011 but this figure is still high. Such high levels of household debt in the country may impede consumer spending in the long run (EIU, 2011). At the same time though, the rapidly growing black middle class is giving a boost to consumer spending (Van Aardt, 2011).

Even though the South African government was able to increase its commitment to democracy and augment public finances, it failed to increase the investment in infrastructure sufficiently in rural areas in 2010. For the future growth of the country, problems related to years of apartheid, such as the unemployment of the black population, education levels and delayed infrastructure investments, pose challenges. The main issue that the government is faced with is high levels of unemployment, which stood at around 25.3% in September 2010. The government is trying to improve labour laws, as well as regulate the informal sector, in order to deal with high unemployment rates (EIU, 2011). Increased investments are necessary, especially in education, in order to reduce income gaps in the population (Van der Berg, 2010).

Doing business in South Africa

South Africa is the largest economy in Africa, and the country's commitment to a market economy has established its position as a vital business centre. It is expected to draw more business due to its fiscal stability, and the emergence of a black middle class. An abundance of natural resources, the soundness of its financial system, investment in infrastructure, and a relatively stable political climate have increased South Africa's attractiveness for foreign investors (UKTI, 2010j). On the other hand, increased crime rates and skill shortages are impediments to economic growth.

Infrastructure in areas associated with high levels of economic activity, is comparable to most countries of the developed world, and offers enormous opportunities in a number of sectors, such as consumer products, financial services, construction, mining, and project management. The market has opened up to a strong demand from industry for aerospace and aircraft parts, chemicals, machinery, computers, electronics, and pharmaceutical equipment (US Commerce, 2011l). In order to attract investment, the government has also been introducing reforms such as the change of ownership threshold – South African ownership, required for operating in the country, dropped from 50% to 25% in 2007 (globalEDGE, 2011).

The government applies the same rights and rules to foreign investors as it does to domestic investors. Some sectors considered important to national security are reserved as domestic sectors. All others are open to foreign firms, which can own up to 100% of the subsidiaries. Although government involvement in the economy has been quite high, South Africa remains a relatively open economy from an emerging-market perspective (Fan et al., 2008). For market entry, firms need to consider income distribution patterns as 10% of the population earns 45% of the income, which results in price-sensitive consumers. Business areas are also faced with the high costs of security and big telecommunications expenses (OECD, 2008a).

Egypt

Egypt was governed by a British-backed monarchy until 1952 when the regime changed via an army coup. Until 1970, the country pursued nationalist policies. After that date, the new president, Anwar Sadat, introduced more liberal policies and focused on integrating Egypt into the world's economy. The presidency of Hosni Mubarak focused on increasing the size of the private sector in the 1990s. In the 2000s, the government focused on reducing tariffs and quotas while implementing economic regulations to boost the economy. Increased levels of privatization were observed in this period. Economic growth in Egypt averaged 7% between 2000 and 2008 (US Commerce, 2010).

In 2011, civil resistance against the government began in the face of issues such as corruption, police brutality, limited freedom in elections, and concerns regarding the economy centring on inflation and low wages. As such, the government of Hosni Mubarak was forced to resign and a temporary military rule was established. In February 2011, the supreme council of the armed forces appointed Essam Sharaf as president. Youth groups are active in Egyptian politics, having played a major role in the fall of President Mubarak. Currently, Egypt is in a transition period and this is expected to move towards a more democratic structure.

The economic outlook

Egypt has a large population and an economy that is dependent on commodities and agriculture. One third of the population was employed in agriculture in 2010. The government is trying to control debt levels while trying to create jobs for the increasing working population. Egypt is rich in natural resources such as petroleum, natural gas, and iron ore. The economy is dependent on oil and gas exports. Tourism income and income from the Suez Canal are other major sources of revenue. As such, the economy is exposed to risks stemming from the changes in global demand and trade, as evidenced by the contraction of the Egyptian economy due to the global financial crisis (globalEDGE, 2011).

The government offers high levels of subsidies for food, housing and energy, thereby contributing to large fiscal deficits which present a major issue. Government interventions are also a risk factor for foreign investors (globalEDGE, 2011). The government aims to decrease the budget deficit by reducing fuel subsidies, both by increasing the use of natural gas as opposed to diesel in government-owned enterprises, and by charging market prices for butane and diesel for all enterprises (US Commerce, 2010).

Doing business in Egypt

Egypt has long been attractive for foreign investors due to its proximity to Asia, Africa, and Europe. Investors can ideally use Egypt as a base to coordinate their export activities in the region. Moreover, the country is home to the largest population in Africa, and has a young and growing workforce. Since 2003, the government has been decreasing tariffs and corporate taxes in order to boost the economy. Foreign investment in Egypt declined from US$9.5 billion in 2008 to US$6.7 billion in 2009. Political risk is a main concern for investors (EIU, 2011), but Egypt offers various opportunities in construction, education and training, energy, engineering, communication technologies, and retail (UKTI, 2010c).

Due to increased investment needs in infrastructure, the government is implementing public–private partnership projects aimed at building schools, hospitals, and a transportation network. Moreover, the need for housing is significant, and the government signed a US$250 million agreement with the US Overseas Private Investment Corporation in order to finance mortgages for housing. Apart from infrastructure-related industries, Egypt also offers significant prospects for companies in petroleum-related industries, telecommunications, and IT. The country is also very strong in tourism, as evidenced by 10% of the workforce being employed in tourism-related activities (US Commerce, 2010).

Egypt started a reform programme prioritizing its openness to investment in 2004. Foreign investment is liberalized and 100% of ownership is permitted in financial services and telecommunications. There are some sectors however where foreign investment is restricted, such as construction, maritime and air transport, and courier services (OECD, 2007).

Egypt is very active in negotiating international agreements, such as bilateral investment treaties that were signed with all EU members except for Estonia, Ireland, and the USA. The country has bilateral trade agreements in the region as well (OECD, 2007). Foreign investment regulations are generally favourable and do not impose stringent restrictions on investors. For instance, the government has liberalized exchange regulations and allowed the transfer of funds abroad; it does not impose ownership restrictions on ventures and permits the transfer of profit in ventures. However, having a local partner is advisable because local partners may be able to deal with bureaucracy more effectively, provide an after-sales services, and enable foreign investors to bid for government tenders (UKTI, 2010c).

Turkey

Turkey's history as a nation state began after the First World War, when the Treaty of Sevres dismantled the Ottoman Empire in 1920. In 1923, the present boundaries of Turkey (with the exception of Alexandretta) were established, and the country was formally proclaimed a republic. Despite the liberalization of the economy from the 1980s onwards, its economy suffered from weak economic policies and volatility, partially due to coalition governments unable to implement sound economic policies. Such policies resulted in an economic crisis in 2001. Sound monetary and fiscal reforms were undertaken after this crisis.

Turkey has been a member of NATO since 1952 and has allowed the establishment of several US military bases. Despite its official standing as a parliamentary democracy, the country's political history has been plagued with numerous military interventions. Although liberalization efforts have been taking place since the early 1950s, Turkey's efforts to shift from a state-run economy to a market-driven system began in earnest during the 1980s. In 1986, the privatization law was enacted. Freed from the burden of state-owned enterprises, the government has now shifted its investment toward improving the country's infrastructure.

Political stability is affected by the Kurdish issue, as well as by tensions between the ruling government and the opposing parties, which remain more secularist in nature. In the future, the slow progress of negotiations with the EU may reduce investor positivity towards Turkey. EU negotiations are mainly hindered by the Kurdish issue, the Cyprus issue, and resistance towards improving the judicial system (EIU, 2011).

The economic outlook

The business landscape in Turkey has improved due to the country's willingness to adopt EU standards and regulations. After the economic crisis in 2000, GDP growth averaged 6% annually until 2007, and the macroeconomic environment stabilized considerably. The government focused on privatization in order to generate funds for investment and reduce the burden on state-owned enterprises. Still, privatization levels have been reduced from US$6.3 billion in 2008 to US$2.27 billion in 2009. Due to reforms in the financial sector following the national banking crisis in 2000, the financial system of the country has become relatively efficient when compared to other emerging markets and many industrialized nations.

The Turkish economy is highly dependent on foreign investment. However, this foreign investment is characterized as being relatively volatile and short term. Between 2002 and 2009, the Netherlands was the largest investor in Turkey, followed by Austria, France, Luxembourg and Germany. The main investment attractions are electricity, manufacturing, and property (EIU, 2011). FDI to Turkey decreased from US$22.2 billion in 2007 to US$18 billion in 2008, and to US$7.6 billion in 2009 (US Commerce, 2011l). In 2010, over 21,000 firms were operating in Turkey, and EU countries accounted for approximately 69% of FDI inflow. FDI predominantly consisted of financial brokerage services (35.9%), electricity, gas and water (15.2%), manufacturing (13.6%), and construction (8%) (WIR, 2011).

Doing business in Turkey

Structural reforms, a strong financial sector, increased efforts to reduce the informal economy, and a growing focus on improving the skills of the working population have enabled the country to become a very attractive environment for investors. Despite the adverse effects of high taxes and debates on intellectual property clauses, the investment climate of the country has improved significantly due to stability, growth, and reforms in the banking, retail, and telecommunications sectors.

The leading sectors for investment are identified as oil and gas, construction machinery, defence equipment, health and medical technologies, ICT technologies, and plastics materials and processing machinery. As the country is surrounded by 75% of the world's oil reserves, and energy remains a major import, the demand for exploring oil and gas resources is very high. Turkey is therefore focusing on expanding energy production to meet the demands generated by economic growth.

Hence, opportunities here are significant for investors in oil gas distribution, power generation, and renewable energies (US Commerce, 2011l).

In 2010, Turkey had the 12th highest number of internet users globally; 70% of internet transactions are within financial services and banks are increasingly relying on ecommerce in customer service. The government aims to increase computer ownership to 51% by 2013 from 15% in 2009. In ICT, the Turkish market is already very large and main players such as Turkcell Vodafone Turk Telecom and AVEA are continually investing in telecommunications services and equipment. The increasing attractiveness of telecommunications equipment and consumer electronics has led to the entry of international electronic supermarkets, such as the German Mediamarkt and the British Electroworld.

The Turkish government has made a firm effort to create a friendly environment for international investors. Foreign capital and domestic capital are treated equally. Foreign investment is restricted only in a few sectors. Foreign investors however are still challenged by excessive bureaucracy, and frequent changes in regulations. Turkey has adopted the common external tariffs for the EU, though there are some non-tariff restrictions such as non-transparent and arbitrary regulations, import licensing requirements for agriculture, and service market access barriers (Heritage, 2011).

Chapter Questions

1　What are the main drivers of growth in different emerging markets?
2　Discuss those factors which could impede sustained growth for emerging markets in the long run.
3　Discuss the effects of the global financial crisis of 2008 on different emerging markets.
4　What are the advantages of having a local representative/agent in emerging markets? Discuss some of the issues that a firm may encounter with local agents/representatives and suggest ways to minimize these.
5　Discuss the main features of emerging markets which increase their attractiveness for foreign investors. Suggest some strategies for emerging markets in increasing their countries' attractiveness to foreign investors.

SEVEN Entry Modes and Strategies: An Overview of Factors Affecting Entry Strategies

Entry Strategies for Emerging Markets

This chapter describes various strategies a manager can consider for entry into a foreign market. Dissimilarities in the economic environment, infrastructure, the level of technology, and the political, legal and cultural environment can create obstacles to successful entry into EMs. Western companies have to deal with these dissimilarities at different levels: the *global level*, in which firms should investigate international (multilateral) agreements, communication and relationships; the *macro level*, in which bilateral agreements and relationships between the two countries could support business operations in a certain market; and the *micro level*, in which firms need to take concrete steps for its realization of a successful market entry (Ghauri and Holstius, 1996). Selecting an entry strategy may depend on various factors, such as the promise and size of the market, its business environment, managerial understanding of the market, internationalization objectives, the product–market fit, the level of asset commitment for the target market, and the nature of competition in the target market.

Market entry objectives

In contemplating entry strategies, a firm has to be clear about its objectives, and why it wants to enter a particular market. The literature suggests that firms normally follow one of the following three strategies when investing in a market: (a) market seeking, in which a firm is attracted to a market due to its size and potential; (b) efficiency seeking, in which a firm wants to enter a market because the market has special capabilities in a certain industry; and (c) resource seeking, in which a firm invests in a market to obtain access to a crucial resource (Buckley and Ghauri, 1999).

Market-seeking motives

By growing their markets, firms can attain economies of scale and scope. Moreover, market growth and dissemination of the consumer base in multiple countries can shield firms from country-specific risks (Makino et al., 2002).

Market size or the availability of a target customer base in a different market can motivate a firm to invest abroad. The availability of a substantial market can also motivate that firm to move its production facilities nearby in order to reduce costs and generate efficiencies (Buckley et al., 2007). For instance, Intel has invested considerably in China in anticipation of a substantial future market, as the income level in the country is rising rapidly. Companies can also grow their markets by following their customers in an effort to preserve their status as the main supplier. Moreover, market growth can be a competitive strategy if the firm invests in a competitor's market and can force that competitor to focus its efforts and resources on defending the home market and limit their involvement in the firm's home base.

Efficiency-seeking motives

Efficiency-seeking investments are motivated by maximizing benefits and lowering costs through allocating operations within the value chain in the most efficient or most cost-effective locations. Foreign investments of this kind are usually associated with distributing value-chain activities in specialized locations or sourcing inputs from regions with cost advantages. By spreading activities across multiple markets, a firm can generate increased efficiencies. In some cases, a firm may lower costs by moving production in a market to take advantage of the incentives offered to attract further investment (Dunning, 1994).

Location choices based on efficiency-seeking objectives depend largely on the entrant's production process. For instance, if the production process is knowledge-intensive, then the company would need to direct the foreign investment to locations associated with technological capabilities, whereas if the product or the process is labour-intensive, wages and the availability of low-cost labour would be the priority in choosing the location (Dunning, 2009).

Resource-seeking motives

Firms with resource-seeking objectives prioritize accessing and securing of natural resources, raw materials and low-cost inputs in foreign investments (Dunning, 1994). Investments in markets where inputs or raw materials are less costly are mostly motivated by resource-seeking motives. For instance, Chinese firms have increased investments in Africa in order to secure raw materials.

An Overview of Entry Strategies

A Western firm that wants to internationalize should align its capabilities to meet the needs of internationalization and then decide on the most appropriate foreign market entry strategy.

The internationalization process can be explained as a progression shaped by the resources a firm has and the commitment that it wants to make. Resources devoted to international activities show its level of commitment to the market. In the international business literature, stage theory, which explains the gradual progression of firms in internationalization, has been widely accepted. This theory explains the internationalization process through a gradual progression, where the major steps are not exporting, exporting, creating a subsidiary, and investing in production (Johanson and Vahlne, 1990).

Firms will face additional costs in internationalization due to their limited knowledge in the host market. This limited knowledge represents a cost and a risk; hence firms will prefer low commitment entry strategies initially (Johanson and Vahlne, 1993). Perceived risk stems from psychic distances, which are differences between a company's perception of the host country risk and the actual risk. The level of difference between the host country and home economy in terms of culture, consumers, and the business environment contributes to this psychic distance. Managers perceive countries with high psychic distances to be risky and are reluctant to commit significant resources initially. The psychic distance is reduced through increased knowledge of the business environment within a country, which can be formed by building relations, gaining experience, and acquiring information (Johanson and Wiedersheim-Paul, 1975).

A firm's continuous exposure to multiple experiences abroad leads to experiential knowledge which lowers the perceived costs of internationalization, thereby increasing that firm's commitment. Experiential knowledge consists of business, market, and institutional knowledge. Movement across the stages is then generated by increased experience, resulting in experiential knowledge which reduces the psychic distance and enables the firm to increase its commitment (Johanson and Vahlne, 1977). International expansion helps companies to acquire market knowledge, and adapt to the differences between markets (Bianchi, 2009). That firm's journey to internationalization does not have to follow in an evolutionary, step-by-step manner, which means that one with no experience in international business does not have to start by exporting, then get into licensing, followed by a joint venture. Though the internationalization of firms in the past has been evolutionary, more often than not these days a firm can internationalize by choosing any one or more strategies directly. Firms with limited exposure to a market will often choose to start with trade-based entry strategies in an effort to minimize the risks stemming from unfamiliarity.

The main entry strategies can be grouped into three categories: (a) trade-based entry modes, including indirect and direct exporting; (b) contractual entry modes, including licensing, franchising, technology transfer, countertrade, counter purchase, buyback, offset, clearing, management contracts, contract manufacturing or subcontracting, turnkey projects, and infrastructural projects; and (c) investment entry modes, including a marketing subsidiaries (which include company-owned sales, service and distribution networks), joint ventures, and foreign direct investments (which include mergers, acquisitions, and holding companies).

Trade-based entry activities focus on purchasing of resources internationally or exporting products. Thus, companies whose strategy is to maintain operations in their own country may engage in international trade through global sourcing, which refers to buying products or services from foreign suppliers. Alternatively, they can produce in their own country and export to customers in other countries.

Contractual entry modes in international bu3siness refer to activities such as licensing and franchising, where the firm engages in agreements with international partners, enabling the partner to use their intellectual property in exchange for fees.

Investment entry modes or equity-based business activities involve direct investment abroad. The investment may result in joint ventures, wholly-owned subsidiaries, mergers and acquisitions, depending on the type of deal. However, all of these strategies involve the ownership of equity and investment of capital.

In choosing an entry form, control has been regarded as a critical factor because by holding control a firm ensures that it retains the responsibility for decision making, coordinating actions determining or changing strategies, and assuming a larger share of the profits. However, control has a high price in the form of resource commitment and creates additional responsibilities for the firm as well as switching costs (Anderson and Gatignon, 1986). In parallel, higher degrees of control demand higher levels of commitment. Risk and flexibility are also dominant considerations in choosing an entry mode (Mascarenhas, 1982). Entry modes which require substantial commitment are more risky. As it is harder to cease operations after high levels of resources are committed and further commitments are made in operating in a foreign country, the flexibility also decreases with entry strategies associated with high levels of control. For instance, a company can direct their exports to another market if the regulations change in one of their markets, but it would be considerably more difficult for that company to divest from a wholly owned venture without incurring significant costs. Each entry mode, such as licensing or having a subsidiary, indicates different levels of control for the firm. In parallel, each form of entry is related to different levels of resource commitment by the firm (Ghauri and Cateora, 2010).

If the firm is engaged in home-based international trade activities, then it does not necessarily have to commit a significant amount of resources in the host country. The level of this commitment can increase if the firm undertakes considerable levels of global sourcing or exporting, and becomes dependent on these types of activities in its business. At the active or committed stage it is more dependent on exports than are firms at the non-exporting or reactive exporting stages.

Trade-based Entry Strategies

Exporting

When a firm becomes involved in international business for the first time, many anxieties will exist concerning its ability to compete in foreign markets. Indirect channels can be an appropriate form of participation in international business for minimizing risks and overcoming these fears. By using indirect channels, a firm can start exporting with no incremental investment in capital, few risks, and low start-up costs. Such participation can be considered part of a developmental process that takes the firm towards more and more international sophistication and commitment.

Many firms will prefer to use exporting as the initial entry strategy in new markets. In this manner, a firm can test the suitability of its products for the market, and grow its revenues while avoiding the risks of investing in a country directly. Firms will also prefer export strategies due to their flexibility, as a firm can withdraw from the market immediately if the conditions change, or easily redirect their sales to another market depending on the conditions (Bello and Gilliland, 1997). As such, it may also be able to minimize its exposure to the volatility in changes in demand in a single market.

In export strategies, trade barriers will arise as costs for the firm and rapid changes in tariffs or barriers may cause disruptions to its strategy. Export transactions are also very sensitive to fluctuations in currency. An unfavourable movement in exchange rates or an increase in tariffs can easily result in higher costs and the firm's products may not be able to compete in export markets (Daniels et al., 1995).

Firms may also not be able to learn about markets when exporting. As they are not present in a market, they are not able to gain experience in that business environment. In addition they may not be able to gather enough information about customers and especially their changing needs. Thus, solely focusing on exports may limit firms' ability to recognize opportunities in the market or respond to changing customer needs (Albaum and Duerr, 2008).

In exporting their products, firms will need to consider the availability of agents or distributors who can efficiently distribute those products. In doing so, firms will need to decide whether the most efficient choice for them is indirect exporting or direct exporting.

Indirect exporting

The indirect exporting approach, which is exporting through domestic intermediaries, places the burden of responsibility for sales contacts, negotiations and product delivery on the intermediary within a firm's home market. Indirect channels are less expensive in the early stages of exporting because the cost of foreign market penetration is borne directly by the intermediary. However, firms need to consider the 'opportunity cost' – because the intermediary has control over final pricing, a loss of profits may result. Also, the firm's reputation in the host market is dependent on the reputation and actions of the intermediary.

Export management companies (EMCs) or export trading companies (ETCs) are independent firms contracted by manufacturers to undertake export sales, handle shipping and delivery, arrange for payment, and sell products along with other allied but non-competitive product lines. The principal advantage of using an indirect export channel is to have access to foreign markets by 'plugging in' to the EMC's foreign market network. This advantage can be strengthened by carefully selecting the EMC or ETC and then supporting it. Support involves working with the EMC or ETC in formulating a marketing plan for the firm's product line; contributing product information, advertising and technical assistance; and backing up its export operations with the prompt servicing of orders. There are, however, differences between EMCs and ETCs, as explained in Box 7.1.

The primary disadvantage of relying on export intermediaries is the firm's loss of control over foreign sales. This loss can be moderated by specifying in the contract that the manufacturer's approval is required in key decisions and by working intimately with the EMC or ETC. Indirect exporting requires little, if any, foreign market knowledge on the part of the manufacturer, and for the same reason, it isolates the manufacturer from foreign markets.

Box 7.1 What is the Difference Between Export Management Companies and Export Trading Companies?

Export management companies (EMCs) are normally supply-driven; that is, the EMC represents one or more manufacturers or suppliers and manages sales, advertising and promotion in foreign markets. Export trading companies (ETCs) are demand-driven; that is, the ETC identifies demand or needs in foreign markets prior to approaching manufacturers or suppliers. Essentially, both EMCs and ETCs play similar roles as intermediaries in international business.

For multinationals, entering by setting up an export base in an EM is relatively easy. First, MNEs are not faced with local competition, and are incentivized by governments. Setting an export base also does not require high levels of investment. Moreover, they do not create competition within the EM economy, which is especially important for the government if the industry in question is protected.

Direct exporting

Direct exporting – that is, exporting through overseas intermediaries – offers several advantages to the manufacturer:

- partial or full control over the foreign marketing plan
- concentrated efforts toward marketing the manufacturer's product line
- quicker information feedback from the target market
- better protection of trademarks, patents and goodwill.

Direct exporting requires manufacturer familiarity with the procedures of export shipping and international payments. There is a dual problem of developing distribution channel strategies and finding, motivating and supporting overseas distributors in direct exporting. Start-up costs are higher due to greater information requirements and higher risks. In direct exporting, a manager must not ignore the costs associated with international travel, communications, and the need to employ personnel familiar with international business.

Direct exporting offers potentially greater profits and challenges. As is the case for indirect exporting, there are many available options. The basic criterion is control: the amount of authority you choose to delegate to the foreign partner, which is partially dictated by the basic characteristics and technical sophistication of the product and the need for after-sales service. The 10 most common mistakes made by exporters are explained in Box 7.2.

Box 7.2 The 10 Most Common Mistakes of Potential Exporters

1 Failure to obtain qualified export counselling and develop a master international marketing plan before starting an export business.
2 Insufficient commitment by top management to overcome the initial difficulties and financial requirements of exporting.
3 Insufficient care in selecting foreign distributors.
4 Chasing orders from around the world, instead of establishing a basis for profitable operations and orderly growth.
5 Neglecting exports when the domestic market booms.
6 Failure to treat international distributors on an equal basis with domestic counterparts.

(Continued)

(Continued)

7 Unwillingness to modify products to meet the regulations or cultural preferences of other countries.

8 Failure to print service, sales and warranty messages in locally understood languages.

9 Failure to consider the use of an export management company.

10 Failure to consider licensing or joint-venture agreements.

In exporting, the main challenge for companies is in identifying and building relations with the right intermediaries who can be distributors, agents, or sales representatives. Especially in EMs where relations are more pronounced, building business relations with the right agents is key. Companies can identify suitable agents by participating in trade fairs, visiting potential companies, and researching through countries' business directories, or contacting trade associations.

In selecting potential intermediaries, exporters will usually engage in preliminary research and also visit intermediaries in the target market. Such visits enable the exporter to understand the capabilities of the intermediary and start building relations with them. Selecting suitable intermediaries is a key process where exporters need to focus on suitable partners with a good reputation and high quality services. However, intermediaries' expertise in the particular product and their willingness to prioritize the product are also important. Exporters may be confronted by intermediaries with conflicting interests. This may occur if the intermediaries' portfolio is dependent on the other client, or in cases where the intermediary has competing products in their portfolio. As such, exporters may often decide to work with smaller intermediaries to ensure that the intermediary is committed to their operations. An intermediary with specific know-how of the exporter's product is often preferable. Box 7.3 shows some of the criteria that companies must prioritize in selecting a suitable intermediary.

Box 7.3   Exporters' Priorities in Selecting Intermediaries

- The reputation of the intermediary
- Coverage of the market and the intermediaries' access to key areas

- The intermediary's relations with governments and other key actors within the network
- The exporters' share within the intermediaries' portfolio and the intermediary's willingness to prioritize the exporter
- The presence of competing products within the intermediaries' portfolio
- The availability of a skilled sales force
- The availability of inventory maintenance facilities
- Commitment to the protection of exporters' know-how

Source: Cavusgil et al., 2008.

A company's preliminary research is very important in identifying suitable intermediaries. However, long-term success in a market often depends on building relations. Thus, companies often find regular visits to intermediaries beneficial. Other ways in which companies build relations with intermediaries can be by responding to their needs, demonstrating their commitment to a long-term relationship and being responsive to the expectations of the intermediary (Cavusgil et al., 2008). Box 7.4 shows intermediaries' main concerns in dealing with exporters.

Box 7.4 Intermediaries' Expectations of Exporters

- Good, reliable products, and those for which there is a ready market
- Products that provide significant profits
- Support for marketing communications, such as advertising, promotions and product warranties
- Opportunities to handle other product lines
- A payment method that does not unduly burden the intermediary
- Training for intermediary personnel and the opportunity to visit the exporter's facilities (at the exporter's expense), to gain first-hand knowledge of the exporter's operations
- Help in establishing after-sales service facilities, including the training of local technical representatives and allowances for the cost of replacing defective parts, as well as a ready supply of parts to maintain or repair products

Source: Cavusgil et al., 2008.

Entry via exporting presents some challenges for multinationals. Specifically, in exports, multinationals' exposure to foreign currency risk is high. The volatility of EM currencies can lead to losses if not properly hedged. Another challenge in entering an EM through exporting is generated by weak infrastructure which may lead to obstacles in the supply of goods. Moreover, exporting requires dealing with bureaucracy that is eminent in customs' transactions. However, such obstacles have been reduced considerably in many EMs by policies geared towards fuelling foreign trade.

Bidding for global tenders

Many opportunities in emerging markets come in the form of global tenders for infrastructural projects (power, telecommunications, roads, ports, airports, etc.) and bulk purchases of commodities and equipment. Typically, a two-step bid process is followed by emerging economies: the technical bid and the commercial bid. Technical bids may entail preparing a feasibility report, which may then be approved by the buyer, thus enabling the bidder to qualify for commercial or price bidding. Figure 7.1 outlines the process of bidding for local tenders.

It is helpful to conceptualize the marketing process to emerging economies in six phases. The process is typical of the experience encountered by a Western firm selling to private and government sectors. It is much more descriptive of the unusual, rather than routine, major purchases made by emerging economies.

Phase 1: Scanning

Marketing to emerging markets begins with the identification of new opportunities. Most aggressive firms will develop sophisticated market intelligence systems to monitor worldwide sales' opportunities on a continual basis. Information from a variety of sources is sought and evaluated. Internally, managers, subsidiaries and overseas representatives will feed information into a central office. Externally, useful information about new opportunities may be gathered from the Agency for International Development, the World Bank, foreign embassies, international banks, industrial organizations, and other firms. Many publications, such as the bimonthly periodical *Worldwide Projects*, are also helpful.

Although most emerging markets are not socialist countries, buyers must still comply with an annual economic plan or, for example, the implementation of a five-year development plan. These plans will differ in detail and direction from country to country. Nevertheless, most are substantially directive, although they may be called 'advisory' for

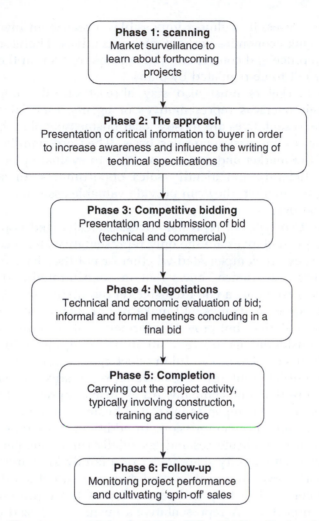

Figure 7.1 The process of marketing in EMs: bidding for local tenders

political reasons. Understanding the process of plan preparation and becoming familiar with the plan itself are the first steps in successful marketing in EMs.

Industrial-sector programmes are usually integral parts of development plans. These are important documents for planning marketing. Note that in many nations, plans can change with governments. Thus, prospective foreign entrants must be familiar with the programmes of political parties.

The situation is not much different for sectors outside the scope of annual plans or for when plans are not direct. Government subsidies, such as tax rebates and low-interest credit, can be more directive than the plan in most cases. It is almost impossible to realize an investment in many emerging economies without such incentives. Therefore, government interference and control are quite dramatic, even in those sectors that appear not to be regulated by plans.

Western marketers must also stay abreast of sales opportunities through their overseas representatives or agents, especially in major markets. Representatives are mostly local businesspeople who ordinarily work on a commission-on-sales basis. They are familiar with the realities of the market and are in a position to evaluate plans and programmes efficiently and identify sales opportunities. In addition to monitoring the market, they can provide valuable assistance in lengthy sales negotiations.

There are two types of representatives: exclusive and non-exclusive. Exclusive representatives are the only representatives for a company in a country. They are compensated whether or not they have anything to do with sales. Experience shows that in concentrated and relatively small markets obtaining a non-exclusive representative may be counterproductive. Some companies will make use of 'scanners', who are not formal representatives but provide information about future contracts.

Several considerations are relevant in selecting an exclusive representative. Firms need to be careful in selecting representatives to ensure there is no conflict of interest. Exclusive representatives may attempt to represent more than one company. An exclusive representative may be an agent for several companies in related businesses in order to secure a certain level of sales commission. In addition, most representatives will have their own businesses and essentially run a 'one-person show'. There is always a majority shareholder or a family known to the locals as the owner(s), even if a professional manager runs the office operations. The personal history and reputation of the representative are extremely important. A representative's business is based on reputation and contacts. Therefore, it is always advisable to check on the representative's history and degree of success with other clients.

Phase 2: The approach

The marketer must approach the buyer with relevant information and attempt to influence the writing of a tender specification, which usually takes the form of a feasibility report, once the opportunity for a specific project is identified. The marketer's aim is to present information on production and technological capabilities, solvency, and the likelihood of successful completion of the project. This is done to establish familiarity and confidence and reduce any perceived risk on the part of the potential buyer.

A key objective of the marketing effort is to achieve a 'first-mover' advantage. A marketer who can pre-empt competitors and be first in supplying relevant information to buyers will have a head start in the selling process. Marketers can tie up prospective buyers through several strategies: (a) a technical solution to buyers' problems; (b) social linkages between buyers and sellers; (c) financial linkages in terms of provision for financing the project; and (d) other informational linkages. In the final analysis, choosing a supplier boils down to human judgement. Hence, the importance of informal social contacts cannot be overemphasized (see Figure 7.2).

Considering of the following issues may prove helpful in determining the desirability of any further commitment to the project:

- Can any information be provided to the buyer that would place you in a stronger position?
- What level of previous influence do you have with the buyer?
- Even if the product offerings are comparable, can you offer a more attractive financing option to the buyer?
- Can you gain a competitive edge by using domestic materials or by directing the end products into export markets?
- Is there an opportunity to tie up the buyer in order to supply managerial/ technical services and other products once the operation is completed?

A major objective of the first-mover is to affect the tender specifications before they are finalized in a feasibility report. The marketer must find out who is responsible for the delineation of tender specifications and

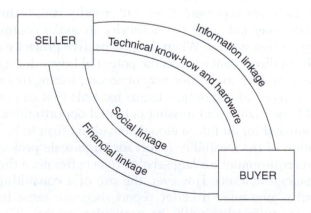

Figure 7.2 Strengthening buyer–seller linkages

then supply technical and other information to the buyer's project team. It is not unusual for marketers to assist buyers with various project-related studies at this stage.

There are several reasons why feasibility reports precede the actual solicitation of bids. Often, buying organizations will have to submit a feasibility report to take advantage of various incentives and obtain credit from local and international sources. Government generally requires a feasibility report to show compliance to plans and overall economic objectives. Favoured projects include building infrastructure; improving the balance of payments, either by import substitution or by creating export opportunities; creating employment opportunities; having high added value; and transferring appropriate technology.

Most feasibility reports are prepared for a specific type of investment with detailed specifications. Although competitive bidding is an accepted practice, many prospective bidders are eliminated because technical specifications are often prepared for a specific group of suppliers. In some cases, the selection of suppliers precedes the preparation of a feasibility report. This means that sales efforts must begin prior to the preparation of feasibility reports.

A feasibility report provides technical documentation of the proposed project. A considerable amount of expertise and technical know-how will be required in order to prepare this report. Usually, the managerial expertise can be found locally. Technical expertise, on the other hand, is usually unavailable, and the customary approach is to consult published reports or international consultants. Because many projects are duplicates of similar investments in industrialized economies, visits to overseas sites by the buyer's project team are also common. Potential clients can be invited to tour the marketer's facilities in the home market and elsewhere.

The local exclusive representatives will usually lack technical know-how, and they may not have the authority to make commitments on behalf of the foreign vendor. When the prospective project warrants it, a team must be in direct contact with the potential buyer during the preparation of the feasibility study. One way of accomplishing this is for sellers in the West to have ad-hoc project teams for EMs that can be organized quickly and hence will avoid missing potential opportunities.

It is not unusual for an international consulting firm to be assigned to the preparation of the feasibility report for large-scale projects. Usually, this is a loan requirement for large-scale projects financed through international financial markets. However, the use of a consulting firm does not necessarily guarantee a better report, because most international consultants are unfamiliar with the particular market. The firm may overlook major factors or rely on incomplete information. Furthermore, political and business considerations can force international consultants to act as mediators in most cases. Consulting firms will rarely be willing to make radical suggestions, because decisions relating to large investment/import projects may result in power struggles and political controversies in emerging economies.

Phase 3: Competitive bidding

A tender is published, and bids are solicited from all interested vendors, once the technical specifications are set. Technical terms and conditions are followed by the so-called administrative terms and conditions (ATC) for large-scale projects, which will spell out the various legal, financial and administrative issues and procurement procedures.

A critical decision by the international marketer at this stage relates to the amount of time and other resources to be invested in preparing the bid. It is expensive to produce bids, particularly for large projects, but the likelihood of a successful bid can be strengthened by tying up the buyer in the previous stage. Purchasing by the government or state-owned economic enterprises (SOEs) is regulated by the law in most emerging economies. This is helpful to the supplier because the organizational buying process and the authority and responsibility for each buying unit are clearly described in such laws. The regulations relating to government procurement state how requisitions are to be placed, who will have decision-making authority, and how the decision will be implemented. Companies need to be familiar with these regulations. However, it should be noted that governments and SOEs are not always obliged to follow the law. This is especially true for certain clauses specifying the conditions under which a contract can be awarded.

There are no such regulations in privately owned corporations. The organizational structure of these corporations is usually centralized. Occasionally, shares of even the largest corporations are controlled by a few individuals or families. This identification is often more difficult with government/SOE purchases. A local representative may provide helpful inside information in this regard.

Some international marketers will concentrate their efforts on the person who appears to be the final decision maker, and neglect or even avoid others in the process. For cultural reasons, this strategy will backfire in many emerging economies. Bureaucrats at lower levels of the hierarchy are generally frustrated and alienated because of low pay, underemployment, elitism, and other factors. Hence, being bypassed by a foreign supplier may be insulting. For instance, a major sales opportunity was lost by a US textile company because of this oversight. An expert in the state planning organization argued that the supplier's technology was inappropriate and convinced the minister

of finance, who was negotiating the financing, not to award the contract, even though the minister of industry and the general manager of
the buying corporation were convinced it was the best offer.

Phase 4: Negotiations

Submitted bids are evaluated by the buyer from both technical and economic perspectives. Typically, bids are shortlisted, and some vendors
are invited for further discussion, which usually marks the beginning of
lengthy negotiations. These meetings provide opportunities for marketers to present additional explanations and details. These can be crucial
in terms of their impact on the outcome.

Due to increasing international competition, emerging economies can
drive a hard bargain. Emerging economy buyers may play Western suppliers off against each other through bilateral or multilateral agreements.
Applying uniform import taxes, pooling commodity imports, and making
cartel-type agreements are common practices. Pooling import purchases,
such as fertilizers and tractors, for commodity production from multinational corporations is one example of such agreements. Many emerging
economies will lack the necessary foreign exchange to finance purchases.
Total financing by the seller is currently a common practice in large-scale
projects. Tight international money markets and the low credit ratings of
many emerging economies force them to look for the best payment terms.
Japanese firms are quite successful in competitive bidding because they
provide emerging economies with complete financial packages.

In certain countries, it will be necessary to deal with intermediaries
close to the government to accomplish any business deal. Their commission (usually around 5–10%) is paid almost automatically. 'Lubrication'
or 'grease payments' are a way of life in most emerging economies, even
though they are considered unethical by some. International marketers
should be prepared to take positions on such issues and make their positions known from the outset. Although such payments are considered
to be bribes by Western standards, intermediaries believe them to be
payments for their services.

Local representatives will be able to advise the international marketer on such matters, and establishing cordial relationships with the
negotiating party may help to reduce this expense. Because many cultures mix interpersonal relations with business, a company with established, friendly relations may reduce risks due to corruption.

Sellers will have a stronger bargaining position in cases in which procurement is related to export-oriented programmes and where assistance
is needed in marketing the final product. Often, emerging economies are

unable to market what they produce because they cannot penetrate international distribution channels. A seller with some control over such channels, or is able to secure the cooperation of a trading company or a broker, has considerable bargaining power in negotiations.

Phase 5: Completion

Once a certain supplier is selected, delivery, installation and the initiation of different components will take place. Typically, a temporary project organization is formed to complete this assignment. Most projects in emerging economies will involve a combination of construction, personnel training, project management and service. The smoothness of the implementation will be critical to the supplier's long-term success. A supplier can experience numerous problems and delays in coping with local subcontractors, local authorities, import regulations, union procedures, and other constraints within the local environment. Successful suppliers will expect such problems and take active steps to deal with them.

Phase 6: Follow-up

The successful completion of a project usually generates a considerable number of spin-off sales. Opportunities will exist for selling a service contract, parts and equipment, software, and other supplementary products. Hence, it is desirable to maintain contact with the customer to ensure satisfaction and learn about developing projects. A company must maintain a reasonable guarantee period, in addition to an adequate level of after-sales service for its customers. Box 7.5 provides some guidelines for marketing to emerging economies.

Box 7.5   Guidelines for Marketing to Emerging Economies

- Follow the development plans and programmes of political parties closely. These are easily accessible in public domain information sources.

(Continued)

(Continued)

- Become familiar with government incentives for investments.
- Select a good exclusive local representative.
- Become familiar with the process of preparing a feasibility report.
- Provide technical know-how during the preparation of technical specifications.
- Maintain close contact with domestic and international consulting organizations who may be preparing technical specifications or feasibility reports.
- Establish friendly relations with potential buyers, even if they are not buying currently. This is an inexpensive but very effective public relations effort.
- Become familiar with regulations related to government and State Economic Enterprise (SEE) procurements.
- Find the 'lion' in each organization. In each organization, one or two people will have the 'final say'.
- Become familiar with the international agreements of the EM.
- Offer a complete deal. Be ready to finance your own sales.
- Leverage strengths to negotiate sales. The ability of the offer to improve the balance of payments, create employment, add value, use local resources, and decrease import dependence can be leveraged.

Global sourcing and outsourcing

Global sourcing refers to the purchase of products or services from external suppliers, while outsourcing is the purchase of value-added activities from external suppliers. In outsourcing, firms will contract their operations and engage in relations with external suppliers who will handle parts of the firm's production process (Luthans et al., 2009).

Managers are consistently faced with the challenge of finding services or products which can help them improve margins or quality. Global sourcing, which is also referred to as global procurement or global purchasing, is an import strategy that entails purchasing products or services abroad for consumption or manufacture at home (Cavusgil et al., 2008). In this way, a firm can enter into contractual relations with multiple suppliers.

Many Western firms will import or source products from emerging markets and be familiar with the process of doing business in such markets. Many firms internationalize, not because they see emerging economies as markets for their products or services, but because they have other motives to source from abroad, as explained in Box 7.6 (Cavusgil et al., 1993, pp. 143–155).

Box 7.6   Motives for Global Sourcing

Competitive firm-specific advantages

Proactive motives

- To exploit technological superiority (unique or differential products)
- To enhance technological capabilities
- To assure organizational flexibility
- To gain a foothold in a promising new market
- To assure delivery and quality improvements

Reactive motives

- To protect proprietary technology leakage
- To cope with intensifying global competition more effectively
- To lock out competitors from a selected competitive base
- To take advantage of more efficient logistics/delivery systems

Comparative location-specific advantages

Proactive motives

- To take advantage of foreign government incentives
- To exploit currency fluctuations

Reactive motives

- To diversify supply sources to spread risks
- To exploit cost advantages, such as cheaper labour, materials and components
- To satisfy local government requirements, such as local content, countertrade and offset
- To overcome protectionist barriers
- To guard against currency fluctuations

In global sourcing, firms will often work with multiple suppliers and continue their search for additional suppliers who can meet their needs better, whether these are in terms of quality or price. However, global sourcing is a low-control entry mode and a firm cannot monitor suppliers' actions or processes. Thereby, supplier selection and building sound relations with suppliers is an important challenge for that firm.

Outsourcing

Outsourcing has been shaping firms' boundaries in the 20th and 21st centuries. It gives companies the chance to focus on their core capabilities while also benefiting from vendor expertise, economies of scale, knowledge base, and standardized procedures (Zhai et al., 2007). The decision to outsource broadly depends on: realizing cost savings, uniting the interests of company and vendor to provide a more satisfactory product for the customer, benefiting from vendors' specialized expertise, and enabling the company to focus on their core competencies (Tiwana and Bush, 2007).

The main types of outsourcing transaction are information technology outsourcing (ITO), business process outsourcing (BPO), and knowledge process outsourcing (KPO). ITO occurs when a company outsources information and communication services-related work to external vendors. Growth in IT outsourcing has led to the establishment of specialized vendors who are able to supply high-quality services.

In IT outsourcing, the vendor does not assume responsibility for the business side, whereas in BPO the vendor assumes responsibility for targeted business results. The vendor implements and manages the business process. Some examples of BPO are accounting, human resources and call centres (Willcocks et al., 2004). BPO enables the company to focus on its core activities and reduces its employees' burden of bureaucratic or administrative processes which can take considerable time and effort. The vendors' inability to meet targets, and the risk of losing important information, are two of the concerns with BPO decisions. Moreover, in many cases, the targets will be very difficult to measure and agreeing on suitable service arrangements can be problematic. In 2009, India, the Philippines and China accounted for 65% of the global revenue from IT-BPO services. These countries attract customers due to their language skills, low-cost labour, and the quality of their information and communication infrastructure (UNCTAD, 2011).

KPO (knowledge process outsourcing) is usually considered to be a form of business process, outsourcing targeting business intelligence activities. This area is growing rapidly and now encapsulates the outsourcing of legal services, engineering R&D, market research and analytics, writing and content development, pharmaceuticals, healthcare, education and training. In these fields, vendors will provide services such as reviewing litigation documents, modelling, secondary and primary research, content writing, R&D, diagnostics, genetic profiling, and tutoring (Sathe and Aradhana, 2007). Despite the optimistic outlook for the KPO market, dilemmas will arise since, by definition, firms which engage in KPO activities are actually outsourcing knowledge which will serve as a competitive advantage (Currie et al., 2008).

Offshoring is a type of outsourcing where the vendor is not located in the same country as the company. The main reasons for offshoring are a reduction in costs, an increase in asset efficiency, and higher profits

(Gottschalk and Solli-Sæther, 2006). Though offshore outsourcing is closely linked to cheap labour, increased specialization and the development of offshore locations reduce the emphasis on cost concerns and give rise to other priorities, such as increasing efficiency and improving services by outsourcing. Generally, companies will focus on lowering costs in the initial stages of outsourcing, and companies who have been outsourcing for longer periods will focus on improving service levels (Marriot, 2008).

In offshore outsourcing, India is still the largest player. India's dominance is due to the English skills of personnel, and a strong legal system. On the other hand, due to increased salary costs and a relatively saturated supply in India, multinationals have started looking at alternative locations. The Philippines, Thailand, Vietnam and Malaysia have emerged as alternative suppliers of outsourcing services (Farrell et al., 2005).

The decision to outsource

In the past few decades, multinationals have been spreading their activities across borders and forming global value chains which consist of a network of affiliates and partners. They coordinate the operations of the network members which are related to the firm through multiple arrangements, ranging from subsidiaries to contracted suppliers. Multinationals will make the decision regarding internalizing and externalizing activities by assessing risks and opportunities while prioritizing the protection of their core competencies. Activities which are externalized or outsourced are then mainly those which are peripheral to their operations. In this way greater efficiencies can be generated, both by increasing the cost-effectiveness and quality of non-core activities and by enabling a management focus on the core activities. As such outsourcing is no longer considered purely on a cost basis, rather as a function of overall business strategy (Van Weele, 2009).

In order to maintain competitiveness within the current business environment, multinationals will need to consider moving each activity to the most efficient locations, whether in terms of a cost advantage or improved quality. On the other hand, spreading activities across a global or even a regional value chain significantly increases coordination and monitoring costs. Internalizing of activities enables the firm to protect its know-how, and eliminates the challenge and cost of finding and managing relationships with partners (Oshri et al., 2009). However, multinationals can be diverted from focusing on their core activities and may face inefficiencies in undertaking non-core activities, as these are often not their specialization. In formulating international value chains, coordination is a key consideration for a firm. Entry mode decisions are affected by the level of control necessary for efficient coordination of the value chain. When firms internalize activities, they are faced with fewer concerns related to control and monitoring. They can also protect their know-how and are not burdened with the challenges stemming from vendor management. In contrast, when firms externalize activities, they may be able to find specialized vendors who can increase efficiency, thus allowing management to focus on other areas and lower costs. However, firms also face the risk of losing know-how and additional burdens related to vendor monitoring and control. Overall, the decision to internalize or externalize an activity is affected by the level of control necessary, and firms prefer to maintain control over activities involving know-how.

Considering that most of the activities which are outsourced are not core to the firm, efficiency and quality can be improved by externalizing the non-core activities to third parties who specialize in those particular activities. In addition, firms can also access third parties' tangible and intangible resources by outsourcing (Oshri et al., 2009).

Managing outsourcing relations

Outsourcing relationships by definition leads to the transfer of management and/or the delivery of a process or a given task to a third party. Most issues will stem from the vendor and the company trying to maximize their own utility instead of acting together in collaboration. A considerable amount of the outsourcing relationship can be managed by establishing long-lasting relationships, thus the success of outsourcing arrangements in part relies on the success of the company's managers and their ability to clarify what is needed, choose accordingly, and handle issues with vendors successfully. In this respect, trust and a minimization of cultural issues gain considerable attention.

Developing trust is a key component in reducing risk in outsourcing relations (Moe and Šmite, 2008). Academics and researchers alike focus on efforts to improve communication in global relations through emphasizing collaboration and continuity (Bhat et al., 2006). Collaboration is working together with the vendor to improve performance; continuity is working with the same vendor over a long time, building a relationship of trust and improving performance through the expectation of a long relationship (Gottschalk and Solli-Sæther, 2006).

Companies also need to be aware of the time and effort needed in creating the outsourcing strategy. In most cases, due to shadowed costs a financially efficient outsourcing process may not be achieved. Factors such as employee turnover, a loss of information through the outsourcing lifecycle, compliance, determining the right targets in line with business metrics, maintaining know-how, and reducing the vendor's tendency to behave opportunistically are major concerns in outsourcing management.

Contract-based Entry Strategies

Multinationals have been increasingly using non-equity modes in cross-border activities. In these partnerships, they can maintain varying degrees of control, depending on the terms of the contract and the relative bargaining power. In configuring the global value chain, non-equity modes which are contract-based entry strategies have become the optimal choice in some industries, such as automotive, electronics and apparel, which require large production facilities. Contract manufacturers have become very efficient in many industries due to their scale and scope. Hence, in some areas multinationals may not be able to attain the same level of efficiency in investing in a manufacturing facility, given the presence of large-scale contract manufacturers specialized in the area.

> The increasing fragmentation of production processes between locations, growing sophistication in codification of knowledge and prevalence of industry standards, improving intellectual property protection regimes worldwide, and growing capabilities and increasing availability of credible and technologically sophisticated partner firms in new markets are all contributing to non-equity mode growth. (UNCTAD, 2011, p. 234)

Following the global financial crisis of 2008, firms' capital constraints, as well as an increased focus on reducing the exposure to business environment risk, have contributed to the increase of non-equity modes of entry. Firms are able to decrease the risks associated with changing demand, as contract manufacturers can adapt production levels relatively easily.

The main risks associated with non-equity modes stem from the lower levels of control which may result in reduced quality in products or operations, or a loss of know-how (Kumar and Annushkina, 2010). These risks are minimized by strong contracts which will include clauses to reduce the risk to various parties. Contracts offer a level of control for multinationals, and enable them to shift some of the risk to the partner; contract entry modes do not strain the company's cash flow due to the relatively low level of investment required. Box 7.7 shows the advantages and disadvantages associated with equity-based and non-equity-based (contract) entry strategies.

Box 7.7 Contract-based (Non-equity) Modes – Key Advantages and Drivers of Growth

Low upfront investment outlays and working capital	• Increasing focus on return on capital employed (ROCE) and the need to de-leverage • Even greater levels of capital expenditure required for the expansion of production and the entering of new markets
Limited risk exposure	• Increasing market and political risk aversion • Limitation of legal liability
Flexibility	• Increasing awareness of the need to anticipate cyclical shocks
Leveraging of core competencies	• Increasing value chain segmentation, combined with improving knowledge codification, the prevalence of industry standards, and improving IP regimes as enabling factors • Growing availability of sophisticated non-equity mode partners in EMs capable of providing core/non-core activities efficiently and effectively

Source: UNCTAD, 2011.

Licensing

Licensing, which is a contractual entry mode, entails a variety of contractual agreements between the domestic firm (licenser) and foreign company (licensee), whereby the licenser provides intangible assets, such as patents, trade secrets, knowledge, trademarks and company name to the licensee in return for royalties and/or other forms of payment. Licensing is commonly undertaken commonly following export or some other kind of international involvement. In licensing, protection and patenting also gain considerable attention. While it is believed to be a low-commitment entry form, for the success of a licensing arrangement, the involvement of the licensor and their continuous support is a prerequisite in maximizing value. In such a continuous relationship, the licensor can also gain more control of the operations of the licensee.

When a firm licenses to an independent foreign firm, the main purpose is to penetrate a foreign market. Licensing offers both advantages and disadvantages to the Western firm. Box 7.8 outlines the advantages and disadvantages of licensing.

Box 7.8 The Advantages and Disadvantages of Licensing

Advantages

- Licensing is a quick and easy way to enter foreign markets and requires little capital.
- The royalties received are guaranteed and regular.
- Western firms can benefit from product development abroad, without the research expense.
- Licensing is especially attractive as a low-commitment entry mode.
- In some countries, licensing may be the only way to tap into the market.
- High transportation costs can be overcome by licensing.

Disadvantages

- Unless the licenser possesses a distinctive technology, a trademark, or a company name that is attractive to potential foreign users, licensing is not the best entry mode to use.
- The licenser lacks control over the marketing plan and production processes in the target market.
- Though royalties are guaranteed, the absolute size of licensing income can be very small compared with exporting to or investing in the target market.
- A licensing agreement usually gives exclusive rights of the technology and trademark to the licensee. The licenser cannot use an alternative entry mode until the agreement expires.
- Licensing is commonly undertaken following export or after some kind of international involvement. In licensing, protection and patenting also gain considerable attention. In such a continuous relationship, the licensor can gain more control in the operations of the licensee.

Franchising

Franchising is a form of licensing in which a company licenses a business system, along with other property rights, to an independent company or person. The franchisee operates under the franchiser's trade name and follows policies and procedures laid down by the franchiser. In return, the franchiser receives fees, running royalties, and other compensation from the franchisee. This type of entry mode has its advantages and disadvantages, as shown in Box 7.9.

Box 7.9   The Advantages and Disadvantages of Franchising

Advantages

- There can be rapid expansion into a foreign market with low capital outlays.
- Marketing is standardized, and there is a distinctive image.
- The franchisee is highly motivated.
- The political risks are low.

Disadvantages

- There can be a lack of full control over the franchisee's operations.
- There are limitations to the franchiser's profit.
- Restrictions can be imposed by governments on the terms of franchise agreements.

Franchising is particularly attractive when a company has a product that cannot be exported to a foreign target country, when it does not wish to invest in that country, and when it has a production process that is easily transferable to an independent party.

Franchising will not work unless the franchiser continuously supports the franchisee. Such support includes supplying equipment, tools, training, finance and general management assistance. The steps to establish franchising systems abroad resemble those of traditional licensing. Franchisers need to assess sales' potential in the target market, find suitable franchising candidates, negotiate the franchise agreement and build a working partnership with the franchisee.

The share of international franchisers in developed markets is generally around 10% of the total franchise, however the share of international franchisers is higher in EMs, approximately constituting between 30% and 40% of the market in Mexico, Russia and Turkey. Yet some EMs such as Brazil have reached a mature level for franchising as the internationals' presence is around 10% which is similar to that of developed countries. The share of franchisees providing value-added services is higher in developed countries. For instance, 37% of the franchising sector in the USA is due to business and personal services. In contrast, the franchising sector in many EMs consists of small franchisees and lower value-added services such as restaurants or retail. For instance in India, 32% of the franchising sector is in retail and 16% is in restaurants (UNCTAD, 2011).

Technology transfer projects

The international transfer of technology is often achieved by means of various situation-oriented, non-exclusive vehicles. Technology and services' expertise can be exchanged by standard export arrangements or project work, licensing agreements, joint ventures, and direct investments. Three fundamental considerations must be combined to determine the financial, legal, and technological character of any transfer transaction. These considerations are: (a) the sellers' business plan, financial considerations and company goals; (b) the nature of the technology/ service and its objective; and (c) the business situation and financial and legal environment of the recipient.

The nature of technology/service is the core consideration of technology transfers. Price, method of transfer, terms of exchange, and buyer–seller relationships all revolve around this centre. The price of a technology/service is usually based on the cost of its development.

A company with a unique product or service can sell that product or service at whatever price the market will bear. A service centred on common knowledge will not be able to command the same price. A technology/ service may be based on a patent, trademark right, company know-how and trade secrets. Even if a firm from a developed market employs a standard manufacturing process, a potential customer may approach the firm to purchase trademark rights that are essential to the success of the end product.

Management contracts

An international management contract gives a Western company the right to manage the day-to-day operations of an enterprise in a foreign market. However, management control is limited to ongoing operations. Management contracts are used mainly to supplement an actual or intended joint-venture agreement or turnkey project.

From an entry strategy perspective, management contracts are unsatisfactory because they do not allow a company to build a permanent market position for its products. Other disadvantages include time-consuming negotiations and the commitment of scarce management talent.

Management contracts are, however, considered a feasible alternative to foreign investments. Transnational firms are not philanthropic organizations, nor do they necessarily have any interest in the political or economic goals of local leaders of emerging economies. They are profit-seeking organizations, and their decisions are based on the firm's goals. All alternative commercially justified routes are feasible.

Contract manufacturing or subcontracting

Contract manufacturing is a cross between licensing and investment participation. In contract manufacturing, a host company secures a product or a manufacturing process from a Western manufacturer and produces under contract for the Western firm. The product can then be exported or marketed locally.

Contract manufacturing requires a small commitment in terms of financial and management resources. It allows for rapid entry into the target country and avoids local ownership problems. It is attractive especially when the target market is too small to justify investment entry and when exporting is not feasible (Lymbersky, 2008). However, it may be difficult to find a suitable local manufacturer. Substantial technical assistance may be required to improve the quality and production levels of potential manufacturers. There is also a risk here that the firm may be creating a future competitor. Approximately a quarter of employment in the automotive industry is in contract manufacturing, which accounted for 30% of global exports in the industry in 2010 (UNCTAD, 2011).

Turnkey projects

Turnkey projects involve contracts for constructing operating facilities, such as power plants, paper-and-pulp plants, and so forth, that will be transferred to the foreign owner when the project is ready to commence operations. The contractor is obliged to provide services such as management and worker training once the construction is complete, in order to prepare the owner to operate the facilities.

The size and comprehensive nature of these projects set this type of business apart from most other forms of participation. The majority of these projects are 'mega' projects involving hundreds of millions of dollars (Hill et al., 2009). Due to the huge financial commitments involved, this kind of business activity is limited to a handful of large firms.

More and more frequently, machinery, equipment, technology and the know-how to handle that technology are sold as a package in the form of complete industrial plants and factories. Sales to EMs with limited local construction and engineering capabilities are often in this form. Apart from the fact that, in some cases, this is the only way to enter a particular market/country, there may be other advantages for firms from developed markets:

- They do not face the constant threat of nationalization or of increasing restrictions by host governments.
- They do not incur any commercial risk while entering a new market.
- They can use turnkey projects as a strategy to charge premium prices for their components.
- They can improve their competitive position relative to their rivals.
- Once they have entered the market through a turnkey project, they can sell the spare parts and components.

Infrastructural projects

Many managers have a misconception that the markets for infrastructural projects in EMs are disorganized and chaotic. However, the significant trend in emerging economies to invest in infrastructural projects involves billions of dollars, and hence buying is often organized and formalized. The fact that EMs are more concentrated and the government is an integral part of most business operations provides opportunities for the international marketer (Qiang, 2010).

Most buying is performed by organizations, either privately owned or government operated. Markets are basically sellers' markets. Buying organizations follow a formal approach in their purchases, which are based on a feasibility plan that contains a strong macroeconomic orientation for development.

Countertrade

Countertrade is an ancient form of trading that has emerged at different times in world commerce. It refers to a transaction characterized by a linkage between exporters and importers of goods or services, in addition to or in place of financial settlements. In ancient times, countertrade took place in the form of barter, so that goods of approximately the same value were exchanged without any money being involved. Naturally, these transactions took place at a time when money as a common medium of exchange was not available. This kind of trade is experiencing a resurgence. Countertrade has been used in circumstances in which it was more efficient to exchange goods directly than to use money as an intermediary. In EMs, this form of trade can often be observed. For instance, Caterpillar received iron ore from the Venezuelan government in exchange for machinery. Other examples are Coca-Cola's agreement to receive tomato paste from Turkey and oranges from Egypt in order to contribute to the export levels of the countries where the company is active, or the agreement of Control Data Corporation with Russia to accept Christmas cards as payment (Cavusgil et al., 2008). Several studies reveal that a shift is occurring from using countertrade reactively to using it proactively, as a new tool for financing and marketing internationally. Another conclusion is that countertrade is here to stay for the foreseeable future, and that Western companies should be prepared to participate in this non-traditional form of trade (Fletcher, 2009).

EM firms and governments will often favour countertrade transactions when they are faced with a shortage of cash. EM firms may be unfamiliar with the business environment in developed countries and have issues in terms of marketing their own products, so will choose to enter such markets through countertrade. However, difficulties in measuring the value of the goods exchanged, as well as determining the quality of the goods received as payment, make countertrade transactions very complex indeed (Stolt, 2010).

In some cases, countertrade may arise as the only option for companies entering a market. Thus, firms may have to consider countertrade transactions despite their complexity. At the same time though, such transactions are also associated with significant advantages, as firms may be able to secure a sustainable supply of goods that they need in their manufacturing processes or build relations with new customers (Hill, 2011). Multiple types of countertrade transactions such as barter, counter purchase or offsets can be observed (Mühlbacher et al., 2006).

Barter

Barter transactions involve a direct exchange of goods without involving cash transfers. They are often one-time transactions which do not require a significant commitment of resources (Aggarwal, 1989).

Clearing

Clearing involves the establishment of clearing accounts to hold deposits and to make withdrawals for trade. Countries will buy and sell different goods and services with the goal of restoring a balanced account in the long term. This practice was common in the former Eastern Bloc countries.

Counter purchase

Under traditional barter trade, goods are exchanged with goods (e.g. cars for toys, sugar for bananas, or machinery for agricultural products). However, a sophisticated version of countertrade, known as counter purchase, is now emerging. In such an agreement, the parties will sign two separate contracts specifying the goods and services exchanged (e.g. Pepsi Cola for vodka). If the exchange is not of equal value, a partial payment will be made in cash.

Buyback

In another form of countertrade, a Western company agrees to supply technology and equipment and receives payment in the form of goods produced by the same plant until a final payment is made for the technology (Aggarwal, 1989). This is known as a buyback agreement.

Offset

Offset is often found in defence-related sectors and in sales of high-priced items, such as aircraft. For example, a developing country purchasing aircraft from France requires that certain parts of the aircraft to be produced and assembled in the purchasing country (Mühlbacher et al., 2006). Such conditions are very commonly placed on defence and other large-scale contracts and can take many forms, such as co-production, licensing, subcontracting, and joint ventures.

Non-equity collaborative ventures

Collaborating with a partner enables the firm to access complementary resources, as well as enter into large-scale projects which may not be possible alone. The firm can also engage in collaborative ventures in research and development activities, which can reduce the time needed for product development, increase efficiency, and spread costs (Talay et al., 2009).

In non-equity collaborative ventures partners do not form a new entity, rather they engage in a project-based contractual relationship. Each partner is expected to contribute to the project as defined by the contract. Thus, contract management and partner selection are especially highlighted in considering non-equity collaborative ventures (Hacklin et al., 2006). Managers need to ensure that partners have complementary skills and common objectives, and are willing to commit the resources required by the project to the venture. Entering into a collaborative venture can often imply working with partners who can be competitors outside of the venture. Thus, managers need to assess the risks extensively before entering into such relations. Non-equity collaborative ventures can take the form of strategic alliances, consortia, and cross-licensing agreements.

Strategic alliances

As it is difficult for a single company to meet the demands of fast-changing technology efficiently in a sustained manner, many companies will choose to form alliances in order to increase their efficiency. Strategic alliances are formed by two or more companies in the quest to utilize each other's competitive strengths and achieve their targets more efficiently or at a lower cost (Hess and Rothaermel, 2011). Box 7.10 shows companies' main motives when engaging in strategic alliances.

Box 7.10 Motives for Entering into Strategic Alliances

A strategic international alliance implies that:

1 there is a common objective
2 one partner's weakness is offset by the other's strength,
3 reaching the objective alone would be too costly, take too much time, or be too risky, and
4 together their respective strengths will make possible what otherwise would be unattainable. In short, a strategic international alliance is a synergistic relationship established to achieve a common goal where both parties benefit.

Opportunities around the world are numerous, but in order to benefit, firms must be current in new technology, have the ability to keep abreast of technological change, have distribution systems to capitalize on global demand, and

---

also have cost-effective manufacturing and the capital to build new systems as necessary. Other reasons to enter into strategic alliances are to:

- acquire the necessary market bases
- acquire the necessary technological bases
- utilize excess manufacturing capacity
- reduce new market risk and entry costs
- accelerate the product introductions demanded by rapid technological change and shorter product life cycles
- achieve economies of scale in production, research and development, or marketing
- overcome cultural and trade barriers
- extend the existing scope of operations.

Source: Ghauri and Cateora, 2010.

Multinationals will often seek alliance partners in EMs in order to access institutional networks as well as customer and supplier bases. Governments play a major role in the economy, and forming ties with the authorities can be a competitive advantage. Alliances can enable foreign investors to access a network of EM partners (Wu and Pangarkar, 2006). The failure of cross-border alliances is mainly due to the incompatibility of the partners' objectives. Cross-cultural factors and an inability to establish clear objectives and communicate them efficiently contribute to the issue (Bonaglia et al., 2007).

Consortia

Consortia are large-scale projects where different firms will fulfil different tasks and share the profit as defined by a contract. In industries where innovation is especially pertinent and the cost of developing and marketing the product is high, this form is often preferred. Alternatively, firms will form consortia to bid on large-scale projects which are too large for an individual firm to undertake (Ghauri and Cateora, 2010).

Cross-licensing agreements

In cases where two partners have technology which they can license, they may form cross-licensing agreements to gain access to each other's technology. Similarly, firms may also form a cross-distribution agreement, enabling each firm to distribute the products or services of an other firm (Arora et al., 2001).

Investment Entry Modes

Marketing subsidiaries

Some firms prefer to have only a marketing and distribution network in foreign countries to exploit the potential of spin-off sales (generated by spare parts, etc.) and to create a mechanism to offer good after-sales service facilities. This can usually be done in the case of technology-intensive products, in which an after-sales service may be a key criterion in purchasing decisions. The same facilities used for marketing and so forth can be used as powerful information-providing assets so that the firm can keep 'learning' about the foreign market (Hägele, 2010).

Joint ventures

Joint ventures are a special type of ownership-sharing in which equity is owned by two or more companies. Joint ventures are a common form of participation for firms moving beyond the exporting stage to regular overseas involvement, in which local participation is advantageous. Depending on the equity share of the companies, they may be classified as majority, minority, or 50–50 ventures. Joint ventures, in many cases, may be the only feasible form of investment participation in countries in which sole ownership is prohibited or discouraged.

Joint ventures provide a mutually beneficial alternative for foreign and Western businesses to join forces. For both parties, ventures are a means by which to share both capital and risk and make use of each other's strengths. Problems may arise in these ventures when more than one party is involved in the decision-making process. Joint ventures can be managed successfully with the patience and flexibility of both partners. Usually, however, one of the partners must play the dominant role in order to steer the business to success.

The most critical decision in a joint venture involves the choice of a local partner. For that reason, joint ventures are often compared to marriages. Likewise, joint ventures can frequently end in divorce when one or both partners conclude that they could benefit more by severing the relationship. In EMs which are relatively unfamiliar to multinationals, the importance of partner selection is further highlighted (Li et al., 2009). As networks and relations are very important within these markets, forming informal relations within the selection process becomes essential.

Forming a joint venture with a local company in EMs provides multiple advantages for multinationals, such as the ability to access local know-how related to the market and the consumer. Moreover, joint ventures may also provide access to networks such as suppliers or distributors and thereby contribute to the efficiency of the operation. Networks can also take the form of regulatory authorities or interest groups, and the ability to leverage local partners' relationships within such networks can significantly accelerate the multinational's operations in the market (Hitt et al., 2000). In some cases, in an effort to protect local firms and boost their operations, governments may demand compulsory joint ventures as a condition of entry (Onkvisit and Shaw, 2008).

Each partner enters a joint venture to gain the skills and resources possessed by the other. The contribution of the foreign entrant to a joint venture depends on both its own capabilities and those of the local partner, as well as the joint venture's purpose and scope. Usually, the key contribution of the partner from a developed market consists of technology and products, while the local partner provides the knowledge and skills necessary to manage the operation. In this scenario, both partners face risks (Rui and Yip, 2007). Alternatively, the local partner, having accessed the know-how, may default from the venture and continue operations using the knowledge gained. In order to prevent the local partner from accessing knowledge and disrupting the venture, many multinationals will try to limit the transfer of technological know-how to the local partner. In such cases however, the level of contribution of the foreign investment in the local economy is restricted (Saebi and Dong, 2009). In order to prevent such occurrences, a pre-selection period becomes integral to forming a joint venture in an EM economy. In this process, a multinational needs to ensure that its goals are aligned with those of the local partner, and that they both envision the venture as a long-term partnership (Hite and Hesterly, 2001).

In operating joint ventures, each firm takes an active role in decision making. This may include distribution, manufacturing or R&D arrangements. Joint ventures have costs for each partner but if both partners recognize that cooperation will result in a better performance, they will engage. In joint ventures, the resources of a firm can improve its bargaining power, however the firm's need to cooperate can decrease its bargaining power. Bargaining arrangements will determine the conditions of the joint venture, the inputs necessary, the outputs expected, and the control mechanism the partners need to use to ensure that the benefits expected are received (Kamminga and Van der Meer-Kooistra, 2007). Particularly in developing countries, joint ventures have been used to cope with uncertainties and the need to meet the demands of local markets.

Wholly-owned entry strategies

Wholly-owned entry strategies are associated with high levels of commitment and control. Such investments involve the transfer of an entire enterprise to the target market, and enable the company to exploit its competitive advantages in that market. Once a company has decided to enter a market with a wholly-owned subsidiary, it has two choices in entering that particular market: (a) an acquisition, or (b) a greenfield investment. By entering a market with a wholly-owned subsidiary, firms can prevent the loss of know-how, realize location economies, maintain control, and establish a strong presence in the selected country. Wholly-owned subsidiaries are also often associated with higher costs and risks (Hill, 2011).

Advantages

The main advantage of wholly-owned entry modes is the protection of the firm's know-how. Especially if the firm's core capability rests on technological know-how, protection of the knowledge becomes a priority for the firm and, thus, wholly-owned entry strategies are the most suitable (Morschett et al., 2009b).

Apart from maintaining control over know-how, the firm can also maintain control over operations in wholly-owned structures. Such control is often necessary if the firm is pursuing a global expansion strategy and is trying to coordinate the activities of each subsidiary (Demirbag et al., 2008). Many firms locate activities within the value chain in different locations to maximize cost efficiencies and benefit from the country-specific advantages in each location. In such cases, production needs to be carefully planned and the firm needs to be able to control, coordinate and monitor the activities at each location (Hill, 2011).

Local production may lower costs, compared with export entry, because of savings in transportation and customs duties, and lower manufacturing costs due to less expensive local inputs of labour, raw material, and energy. Direct investment can also create marketing advantages, due to the easier adaptation of products to local preferences and purchasing power (Mühlbacher et al., 2006). Another advantage is the opportunity to build strong relations with the authorities in the selected market, as the government welcomes foreign investment due to the investment's contribution to the country's economy.

Disadvantages

Wholly-owned entry requires substantially more capital, management and other resources, when compared to alternative entry strategies. The company incurs direct costs in establishing its operations and indirect costs in operating in an unfamiliar environment. The risks of international business are higher where wholly-owned entry strategies are concerned as the company's investment is considerable. Moreover, exiting from the market is often harder in such cases due to substantial investment, as well as the commitments made as an investor and employer. Another disadvantage of choosing a wholly-owned entry strategy is the amount of time the firm needs to commit before it can start reaping profits. Creating a new subsidiary can be a lengthy process because of the time required to build or adapt facilities and the time needed to organize the new operation (Hill, 2011).

Whenever possible, a company should gain experience in a target country first (through exports) before opting for direct investment. Such an investment project must be analysed in the context of its political, legal, economic, social and cultural environments. In wholly-owned entry strategies, many features of a target country's investment climate need to be assessed by managers; these are summarized in Box 7.11.

Box 7.11 Factors Affecting FDI Location Decisions

The political environment

- Openness to foreign investment
- Incentives that the government is willing to provide to attract investment
- Political stability in the country
- Monetary regulations
- Government bureaucracy

The legal environment

- Regulations related to foreign investment
- Regulations regarding the transfer of profits or funds outside the country

(Continued)

(Continued)

- Trade barriers and content requirements
- The protection of foreign investors' rights
- The protection of IP
- Tax regulations
- Laws and regulations on the employment of locals and expatriates

The social environment

- The size of the market and its growth
- The demographic characteristics of the market and trends among the population
- The prevalence of dominant interest groups and their effect on the authorities
- The attitude of the market towards the foreign investor

The economic environment

- The cost of land and labour
- The availability of skilled labour
- The infrastructure level within the country, and the availability of distribution channels and utilities

The business environment

- The presence of dominant players and their ability to influence authorities
- The ease of doing business, getting permits and opening/closing businesses
- The availability of suppliers and supporting institutions
- The ease of access to raw materials and goods

Location

- The proximity to target consumers and target regions
- The ease of export and the proximity to main export hubs

Acquisitions

Wholly-owned entry can be made through acquiring an existing operation. In the case of an acquisition, a company can increase the speed of entry because the business already exists and has a certain position in the local market. Companies can avoid start-up problems, such as the hurdle of getting bureaucratic permits and fulfilling local rules and regulations in an unfamiliar environment and save time. An acquisition promises a shorter payback period by creating an immediate income for the investor (Slangen and Hennart, 2008).

Acquisitions enable firms to access location-bound assets such as relational assets and knowledge of the market, and overcome some of the challenges associated with market know-how. In some cases, companies have chosen to acquire local businesses in order to establish a presence in the market and capture the market rapidly. An example would be Amazon, which entered China by acquiring the local competitor Joyo because the company felt that building a brand would take too long. Amazon first improved the quality standards of Joyo and then integrated it into the Amazon website, starting to use both names (BCG, 2011). In some cases, firms will also use acquisition as a strategy in order to deter their competitors from a market, especially if that market is globalizing rapidly. In such cases, firms may be able to achieve success on a global scale and capture the market rapidly through acquisitions.

Another possible advantage is that new product lines can be acquired. However, this can turn into a disadvantage if the investor has no experience of the new product lines. Thus, although acquisition may have the aforementioned advantages, a potential investor may not necessarily be able to gain them.

Managers will often view acquisitions as less risky than greenfield investments, as the entry takes less time and a revenue stream is expected in a short period. Moreover, the firm gains access to intangible assets such as know-how of the market or consumer awareness of the brand. However, acquisitions are associated with other risks. First of all, the acquirer may often overpay if the acquisition is through a bidding process and the management's view of the firm is too optimistic. The process of fitting the acquired company into current operations and policies can constrain performance and earnings (Child and Rodrigues, 2005). For example, personnel and labour relations may be difficult to change, 'bad will' rather than goodwill may be accrued to existing brands, and facilities may be inefficient and poorly located in relation to future potential markets.

In acquisitions, a major problem is integrating the acquiring firm into the acquirer firm's operations. These difficulties stem from differences in management culture, as well as in the national culture of the firms. In fact, following an acquisition, employee turnover in the acquired company tends to increase due to employee dissatisfaction with the new management (Hill, 2011).

Greenfield investments

Companies are not faced with issues related to changing the routines, culture, and operations of the acquired company in establishing subsidiaries.

By engaging in greenfield investments, firms are able to control the establishment of the subsidiary, building up its operations as well as its culture according to the firm's needs and standards (Onkvisit and Shaw, 2008). A company may even end up with a relatively cheaper entry because it invests only as much as needed. It can later expand successively as the demand increases. It will not inherit any problems, which might be the case if it were to take over an existing company.

A greenfield investment is also welcomed by local governments because it creates new job opportunities and is considered to be of help in infrastructure development. In this case, the company can efficiently choose a location that provides the most benefits. Moreover, companies can benefit from incentives offered by governments which aim to increase the investment in their countries (Cavusgil et al., 2008). However, high levels of investment are required and difficulties in estimating the timing and amount of revenue by the subsidiaries are major considerations in selecting this type of entry strategy.

All entry strategies have advantages and disadvantages, and the entry choice of the firm is dependent on many factors which concentrate around the capabilities of the firm, the motives of the firm, the opportunities available in a given country, and the risks inherent in the host country or the host market. Table 7.1 summarizes the advantages and disadvantages a firm may encounter with various entry strategies.

Factors Influencing Entry Strategy

Doing business with emerging economies brings with it several challenges for companies. New tasks, unfamiliar environments, and greater uncertainty mean that a company needs to assume additional and greater risks (Meyer et al., 2009). Choosing a suitable mode of entry is dependent on many factors, both on the side of the company and that of the host economy. As conditions change, suitable modes of entry will change as well. The local environment of the country, changing aspirations, and the experience of the company are some of the main drivers leading to the change of entry mode.

Common reasons for this mode change are modifications in firm strategy in order to realize growth objectives, and differences in the resource portfolios of firms. Management attitudes regarding the perception of costs and benefits, as well as changes in the perception of market benefits and constraints, will stimulate mode changes (Calof and Beamish, 1995).

The job of companies in international business is much more challenging than that of domestic companies because of cultural disparities

Table 7.1   Summary of advantages and disadvantages of different entry strategies

	Advantages	Disadvantages
Export	Low-cost entry as the firm does not invest in the market	Sensitive to trade barriers
	Low risk as the firm can withdraw from the market	Limits possibilities for local responsiveness
	Enables the company to enter the market rapidly	Hinders the firm from learning about the market
	Less risk of loss of know-how	Higher distribution costs
	Hedges against dependence on a single market	Prone to issues related to distribution networks
Contractual agreements	Low capital requirement	Risks due to knowledge transfer
	Can be used to overcome ownership restrictions	Lower levels of control
Strategic alliances	Enable the firm to benefit from the complementary assets of the partners	May result in the loss of know-how
	Increase the efficiency of the firm	Managerial issues among partners
	Reduce the cost of the project by spreading costs among partners	Mismatch between the objectives of partners
Joint ventures	Lower political and economic risk	Risk of creating a potential competitor
	Enable companies to utilize local know-how	Risk of losing know-how
	Enables companies to access markets which restrict foreign entry	Managerial challenges among partners
Wholly owned	The company can maintain control over operations	Length of time necessary for establishing operations
	Can capitalize on low-cost labour	High levels of investment are necessary
	Avoids import costs and transportation costs	Entry barriers in the target market
	Ease of access to raw materials and supplies in the new location	Lack of local market knowledge
	Reduced risks of losing know-how	Vulnerability to political stability and economic sanctions
Acquisitions	Take less time than establishing a greenfield subsidiary	Risk of overpaying if the management is too optimistic
	Can gain access to intangible assets of the acquired company	High levels of investment required
	Reduce market risk by accessing the local customer base of the acquired company	Issues related to integrating the acquired company into the parent firm

and also variance in the demand patterns and behaviour of firms and authorities in different markets. Table 7.2 summarizes some of the challenges encountered by firms engaged in international business.

Cost in entry decisions

In choosing an entry mode, cost plays an important role. First, the geographic distance makes physical distribution more difficult. Second, firms have to deal with multiple environments, such as public policy, traditions of trade, barriers to trade, and competitive forces. Third, firms engaged in global marketing have to deal with multiple currencies and exchange-rate variations; and transactions in various currencies entail administrative costs and difficulties. Fourth, firms engaged in international marketing are often in conflict with their home governments, because they take employment opportunities and other resources out of the country. These firms are also often in conflict with host governments in regard to remittance of their profits back to their home countries or head offices, ownership of local facilities, and competition with local firms.

The cost of the investment itself affects the choice of entry mode. Equity-based ventures require significant levels of human and financial capital. Apart from the direct costs of acquisition or investment in a joint venture, the company is faced with decisions such as the cost of acquiring market knowledge via acquisition versus the cost of building market knowledge. These decisions may have financial implications, as well as implications due to the time and costs stemming from the lengthier process of building market knowledge (Hill, 2011). In joint ventures, the time needed to build trust may arise as a cost, or the lack of trust between the partners may create additional risks. Entry can be shaped by the changing structure of costs. For instance, a change in tariffs or transportation costs can lead to a reduction in exports and a company decision to enter a contractual agreement or joint venture. In contrast, changes in IP protection regulations within a country can lead the potential entrant to choose an acquisition or a licensing strategy in favour of a greenfield option. The increased cost of building trust prevents acquisition and gears the firm towards a greenfield or contractual arrangement. The high cost of marketing leads towards the acquisition of a firm, licensing or franchising, or the high cost of a technology transfer may mean foreign direct investment. In general, subcontracting is not a very effective choice for the entrant because of the advantage offered to rivals and the lack of benefit from the rivals' marketing experience (Buckley and Casson, 1998).

Table 7.2 Examples of challenges in doing business internationally

Challenge	Impact minimized by
Distance: Separation of buyers and sellers by great geographical distances may create difficulties in communication and physical distribution. The exporter, for example, has to rely upon a large number of intermediaries. These may include a domestic carrier, an international freight forwarder, a foreign distributor or agent, and local transportation companies. The delivery may take longer and the export transaction may be financed over a longer period.	• Advances in transportation technology. • Development of multimedia, and economical communication technologies. • Increase in information available on EMs and business conditions there.
Multiple environments: a company seeking a supplier in a foreign country is faced with a new set of public policies, and competitive, resource, and market environment constraints. Different political regions, barriers to trade, higher inflation rates, and greater government involvement in economic affairs are just some of the environmental difficulties involved in doing business with another country.	• In-depth research of the political, economic, social, and competitive environment of the countries of interest. • Knowledge of expert opinion on the risks of doing business in or with such countries. • Awareness of cultural norms, traditions, beliefs, etc., of foreign countries.
Multiple currencies: apart from the administrative cost of handling transactions in various currencies, exchange rate fluctuations pose special difficulties. Exchange rates, the value of one currency expressed in terms of another, are subject to fluctuation as demand for various currencies changes. Therefore, quoting prices in the foreign currency or estimating the profitability of an export transaction is difficult, especially when selling to countries that are experiencing high levels of inflation.	• Availability of financial instruments like forex hedges, options, futures, etc. • Signing contractual agreements at a predetermined exchange rate.
Conflicts with home and host countries: on one hand, home countries will accuse their own companies of taking employment, R&D and taxes out of the country (e.g. some union officials have labelled US multinationals as 'runaway' corporations). On the other hand, the direct investment presence of a company in a host country makes it more vulnerable politically.	• Avoiding countries with adverse relations with home country as target markets. • Creating a positive image in the host country through managing relationships with the host government, communities, and customers.
Social and corporate culture differences, business customs and language: stepping into a different social and cultural environment, the international manager encounters one or more foreign languages, different values and beliefs, changing lifestyles and norms, varying aspirations and motivations, and a new set of consumption, use, and shopping behaviours.	• Understanding the social and cultural aspects of the foreign country before making business decisions, especially in marketing. • Involving an employee with a foreign country origin in negotiations. • Training managers in intercultural and international business negotiations.

Cultural and institutional distance

Cross-cultural interaction also creates challenges for international business. Differences in language, business customs and ethics, lifestyle and values, and other cultural dimensions will often cause uncertainty and psychic distance (Conway and Swift, 2000). This type of distance is related to how we perceive a certain market and is different from physical distance. For example, for a US firm, in psychic distance terms the UK is a closer market than Brazil or even Mexico.

Many authorities contend that Western businesspeople are ill-prepared to conduct business in any culture other than their own. They are unfamiliar with the 'hidden dimensions' that frequently play a fundamental role in international business transactions. Different cultures require different behaviour patterns from a firm, because the strategies, structures and technologies appropriate in one cultural setting may fail in another. Therefore, one of the primary challenges of international business transactions is to operate effectively in a multicultural setting (Ghauri and Cateora, 2010).

The liability of foreignness

Firm-specific difficulties that internationalizing companies face in new environments stem from the liability of expansion which increases operational and scale costs, the liability of newness in the presence of competition, and the liability of foreignness in a new institutional setting with new customers (Cuerva-Cazurra, 2007).

Liability of foreignness (LoF) is generally defined as the extra cost incurred by the international firm in the host economy. Such costs may arise due to distance, and an unfamiliarity with the environment, market, know-how, and institutions of the host country (Zaheer, 1995). LoF encapsulates the costs of learning about new cultures, as well as the costs related to operating an international firm and functioning within a different institutional framework (Contractor, 2007). In a different country, firms are faced with different customers who are not necessarily knowledgeable about the firm's products and whose consumption needs are already met by existing firms in the domestic market. Moreover, these firms do not have relations with members of the value chain such as suppliers, agents, or distributors. Foreign entrants face costs in acquiring knowledge about network members, and do not enjoy the advantages of long-term relations that locals enjoy, and may incur costs in organizing their activities efficiently (Cuervo-Cazurra and Genc, 2008).

In deciding on an entry strategy and assessing their options, firms then need to consider the liability of foreignness and the additional costs that will be incurred due to their unfamiliarity with the country. In minimizing the costs of LoF, multinationals must assess their strengths and weaknesses (Enderwick, 2007). For instance, if a multinational needs to transfer their business structures to gain a competitive edge, they may opt for a wholly-owned structure. Through this structure, the company can install their practices and transfer and protect know-how, as they have control over the new establishment. On the other hand, if cultural distances are high and difficulties arise from an unfamiliarity with members of the value chain, multinationals may prefer a joint venture entry mode through which local know-how regarding the customer and the business landscape can be obtained from the partner. Effective strategic alliances formed with the right partners can compensate for this gap, providing access to diverse information and opportunities for learning that will help the firm overcome its liability of newness (Li, 2007). As a result, alliances can be used to overcome the liability of foreignness (Wu and Pangarkar, 2006), and provide access to the new market's resources (Bausch et al., 2007). High cultural distances can also be minimized through local partners, as the partner can help reduce the cultural distance and enable the company's acceptance by the host economy consumer.

Control and commitment

For markets where a firm can recover fixed costs by entering in a high control mode, the firm makes a decision, considering transaction-specific assets, external/internal uncertainty and free-riding potential. In this manner, transaction cost analysis prefers a low-level involvement (and commitment of resources) unless there are more profits to be made otherwise. However, firms will choose greater control options for products with high-asset specificity, such as technologically sophisticated products with a high proprietary content (Zhang et al., 2007). High modes of control are also preferred if the firm is engaging in first-time transfers and the learning curve for transfers is not developed. Moreover, high control is necessary for customized products, since the entrant needs to work with the customer to develop solutions. Similarly, the firm also needs to protect its knowledge when working with immature products and choose high-control entry forms. Under normal circumstances, in volatile environments, firms will choose low-control entry modes; however, if there is asset specificity, a firm may use a high-control entry mode in order not to be locked in by partners or agents (David and Han, 2004). Likewise, if there is internal uncertainty and the firm is unable to assess the agent's performance, high control modes will be selected. Since control is associated with ability and appetite to take risks, it is also linked to a firm's experience in international markets. In choosing an entry mode, a firm should also take into consideration the similarity of the market and consider whether the entrant's strategy or organizational patterns may not be suitable for the market. However, in instances where the brand image of the company is in question, companies will prefer high control modes in order to avoid free riding by agents (Anderson and Gatignon, 1986).

Some companies prefer to operate under strict contracts, work with worldwide suppliers and maintain full control over the operation through high-control entry modes, as well as offer standardized products in order to minimize the effects of institutional distance. In this manner, the company is able to achieve a level of autonomy and independence from the local framework. Although this strategy may prove to be safer in some circumstances, the company may also lose opportunities from growing operations, like appealing to a larger customer base or establishing a leaner structure, by taking advantage of a country's resources. Thus, many companies will try to reduce LoF by establishing a local presence via local partners or in some cases local personnel. Another way of building a local presence may be by committing resources or sourcing a locally to gain institutional support and market power (Enderwick, 2007).

Timing of entry

Deciding when to enter an EM poses a challenge to multinationals. First, evaluating EMs is not an easy task given the lack of data which multinationals take for granted in their domestic economies. Within the available data, a multinational may also be misled due to the presence of non-registered parts of the data. Moreover, EMs are by definition undergoing rapid changes. These indicate shifts in income levels, which in turn affect consumption levels and patterns. Such shifts are very difficult to predict in advance.

First-mover advantage

First entrants to a market can gain access to resources, and may be able to purchase assets at lower prices in the absence of any competition. First movers also have the ability to set standards for the product and shape consumers' image of that product in terms of its advantages.

The multinational can create the market and establish its brand rapidly as a first mover. In the absence of similar competitors, the multinational can gain a large market share within a relatively short period. For example, an Italian company named Bisleri was a first mover in India for selling bottled water in 1967; the brand became a generic name for the product and the company now enjoys a 60% market share (Rahman and Bhattacharyya, 2003).

The accumulation of R&D, information, and market know-how establishing scale and scope before the entry of competitors can also be a barrier for competitors (Luthra et al., 2005). As a first mover, a company can attract talent and build relations with network members in the market, such as suppliers, distributors, and agents. Especially in EMs, where governments are relatively more involved in the economy, first-mover advantages, such as establishing relations with the government and building government support, may prove to be a significant advantage.

On the other hand, first movers are faced with the risks associated with creating a new market, and creating consumer awareness for a new product may be too costly. Moreover, the product may not appeal to consumer tastes. First movers are also disadvantaged in terms of their knowledge of the business network in a market and may face increased costs in establishing a presence and an efficient value chain.

Building a logistics base and supplier network, and adapting value-chain activities to the country's environment in the absence of benchmark practices, can all lead to increased costs (Hexter and Woetzel, 2007).

As such, first entrants may face increased costs in establishing their operations, appealing to the consumer and gaining acceptance, however they will also be able to gain precedence in building their brands and establishing a customer base. For instance, the first entrants to South Africa and China as mobile operators were very successful as they were able to build their brands at relatively low costs. Such companies set pricing levels and built a customer base. Companies entering the product segment later were not able to build a customer base as efficiently, as they were faced with higher costs in attracting custom (Beardsley and Evans, 1998).

Latecomer advantages

Firms which enter the market later are able to analyse the strategies of the first entrants. If the first mover has invested in infrastructure and created awareness among consumers related to the product, then those firms which enter later can benefit from such efforts and investments.

Table 7.3 Locational determinants and relevance for FDI and non-equity modes

Relevant for FDI and non-equity	More relevant for FDI	More relevant for non-equity
Policy framework		
Economic, political and social stability Competition policy Trade policy Tax policy	Rules regarding entry and operations Standards of treatment of foreign affiliates International investment agreements Privatization policy	Stable general, commercial and contract law Specific laws governing non-equity mode contractual forms (e.g. recognizing licensing, franchising contracts) Intellectual property protection
Business facilitation		
Reduction in 'hassle costs' (e.g. cost of doing business)	Investment promotion Investment incentives Provision of after-care Provision of social amenities (e.g. quality of life)	Facilitation efforts aimed at: • upgrading technological quality and productivity standards of local firms • enterprise development, increasing local entrepreneurial drive, business facilitation • subsidies, fiscal incentives for start-ups • information provision, awareness-building on non-equity mode opportunities with local groups • supporting minimum standards of working conditions and CSR in local firms
Economic determinants		
• Infrastructure • Market size and per capita income • Market growth • Access to regional and global market • Country-specific consumer preferences • Access to raw materials • Access to low-cost labour • Relative cost and productivity of resources	Access to strategic assets: • created assets (e.g. technology, intellectual property) • strategic infrastructure	• Presence of credible local entrepreneurs and business partners • Access to local capital

Source: UNCTAD, 2011.

Latecomers are able to utilize advanced technologies more easily. They can move through the learning curve more efficiently, benefiting from the incumbent's prior experience with the technology, as well as support from other actors. As such, latecomer advantages may help these firms to catch up with the incumbents (Mathews, 2002). Latecomers can also benefit from a more efficient value chain, as members of the chain will have accumulated knowledge and experience.

A latecomer may be able to insert itself into the global value chain by accessing resources through partnerships, joint ventures, or other forms of network (Mathews, 2002a, 2006). Other strategies which can be successfully employed by latecomers may be responding to changing consumer preferences by shortening investment periods, benchmarking against established industry parameters, investing in new technology and using enhanced information to buffer demand (Cho et al., 1998).

Latecomer advantages have mostly been discussed in relation to explaining the success of firms from EMs which became global leaders and major competitors for incumbents in a relatively short period of time. These firms can utilize latecomer advantages by benchmarking against best practice as well as cornering niche markets (Bartlett and Goshal, 2000). The development of existing technology and products can also lead EM firms to move along the learning curve more quickly (Accenture, 2008).

There are many factors that firms need to consider in choosing an entry strategy in a new market. The suitable strategy depends on the type of firm, its characteristics and objectives. In addition to analysing internal capabilities and objectives, firms must also perform a thorough analysis of the locations and markets they are planning to enter. Table 7.3 summarizes the main considerations which firms need to make in analysing their prospects for internationalization.

Chapter Questions

1 Discuss trade-based, contractual, and equity-based entry modes in terms of control and commitment.
2 What are the motivations of multinationals from developed markets in entering joint ventures with locals in EMs? What are the motivations of EM partners? How do these motives affect the venture?
3 Discuss the costs involved in entering different markets. How can these costs be managed and reduced?
4 Discuss the advantages and disadvantages of outsourcing. How do firms make decisions related to outsourcing?

EIGHT   The Negotiation Process and Strategies in International Business

Two elements must normally be present for negotiations to take place: (a) common interests and (b) conflicting issues: 'Without common interests, there is nothing to negotiate for, without conflicting issues nothing to negotiate about' (Ikle, 1964, p. 20). In other words, although the parties might have a number of conflicting issues, both of them would hope to achieve a common objective (i.e. a transaction). Therefore, *negotiation* is defined as an interactive process of resolving conflicts and reaching agreements to provide terms and conditions for the future behaviour of the parties involved. Little research has been carried out on international business negotiations, despite the increasing importance of international business. In the past, the ability to negotiate was considered innate or instinctive, but studies have shown that negotiation is a technique that can be learned.

Basic to understanding negotiation is the concept of *process*. Most professionals and academics agree that negotiation is an activity fraught with difficulties. Very few negotiations will exactly replicate previous experience, especially when they are undertaken with different parties coming from different countries and cultures. However, we can identify some elements of the process that constitute business negotiations and the factors that influence these negotiations.

Business negotiations – especially cross-cultural business negotiations – are often a frustrating and stressful process. Negotiating involves perceiving and interpreting a wide range of factors on the basis of a limited amount of information. And by their nature, *international* business negotiations are even more complex in that they involve more unknowns and often much higher stakes (Moran and Stripp, 1991). If you become perplexed by these difficulties, the sheer fear of negotiating a bad deal for yourself or for your company may cloud your perceptions, negatively affecting the negotiating process itself.

Yet negotiating is a basic human activity. Every day, we will enter into a series of negotiations, both big and small. We will negotiate where we should eat lunch, what time our proposals are due, and when we will arrive home. Negotiations are a process of managing our relationships and resolving our differences. Often, they are activities undertaken and completed without much thought or difficulty. So what makes these everyday negotiations different from resolving international business agreements?

Obviously, international business negotiations will occur between two different business organizations in two or more different countries. Less obvious, however, are the deeper implications of the word *different*. Negotiations are inherently a perceptual and interpretive process, and, thus, they are dictated by what we perceive and interpret as being different or the same (Usunier, 2003b).

First, when we must negotiate with our co-workers regarding what time our proposal will be ready to be discussed, we will generally perceive that negotiations will occur within a single organization and among people with similar goals. Here, we enter into this process with an expectation of success: that a mutually agreeable solution can and will be found. Because we are all working for the same organization, we assume that everyone is working toward the same goals and will be willing to make reasonable concessions toward this end.

However, when dealing with negotiations in which we perceive ourselves to be different from the other negotiating party, the whole process of negotiating becomes suspect. Negotiating with strangers is not the same as negotiating with friends. Within the realm of business, businesspeople tend to view things in terms of competition ('What are our competitors doing?'), competitive standing, competitive intelligence, and so on. We believe that the other party might be looking out only for themselves, and thus we adjust our bargaining position accordingly. We pad out our proposals with stipulations that we plan to concede later, mask our true intentions, and generally take a more hard-line stance toward making concessions.

Second, because these agreements are international, we are also working with differences across a much larger realm of assumptions. Our everyday negotiations have the advantage of sharing many things in common. Despite differences in our positions, we are still working within the same culture. We have similar expectations for protocol, use the same language, and understand each other's idioms. Furthermore, we both draw on a common history and more likely than not will use similar tactics and logic to resolve our differences (Ghauri, 2003).

In international negotiations, we will lack these shared experiences and expectations. An Eastern person may approach problems with a mindset that is entirely different from that of the Westerner, and arrive at a completely different set of conclusions. Business protocol in Arab countries often differs greatly from what we may expect, and business organizations in Eastern Europe may be completely at adds with the way we might want things run. Failing to meet each other's expectations often leads to unintended insults or simply a lack of communication. For example, many countries differ in their perception of time. In some countries, promptness is always to be expected. For instance, 8 o'clock in the morning means being at the designated place exactly on time and ready to conduct business. Being 15 minutes late might be considered an insult or, at the very least, sloppy business practice. In other countries, however, 8.00 a.m. might be more negotiable – it could perhaps mean closer to 9.00 a.m., or even involve a last-minute change of location or cancellation. In these countries, such changes happen all the time and would not normally be interpreted negatively.

Countries and cultures also differ in their levels of formality and familiarity (Plester, 2008). On arriving in a host country for a round of negotiations, some businesspeople may be required to dine before discussing business. Discussing business during such a meal may be considered rude or in poor taste. In other countries, negotiations might start right away and delays might be seen as a tactic by which to avoid or stall negotiations (Schein, 2009).

The primary obstacle to successful international negotiations is the perception of difference among the parties and difficulties in making the negotiations process a cooperative effort. 'Win–lose' bargaining styles, in which gains must be offset by an opposing party's loss, are generally considered outdated. Opportunist and competitive perspectives in negotiation limit the benefits both parties can achieve by working together, especially considering the advantages and opportunities of international cooperation. Although you should always be wary of being taken advantage of, we suggest that you adopt a 'win–win' technique, often referred to as *integrative negotiating*. This technique approaches coming to an agreement as a problem to be solved. Both parties work together to find a solution that leaves each one better off. The benefits of this type of negotiation have been studied by many authors (Ghauri and Usunier, 2003; Zhang et al., 2006; Acuff, 2008).

Win–win negotiating can be characterized as follows (Ghauri and Usunier, 2003):

- having a more open information flow between parties – both must sincerely disclose their objectives and try to find overlapping goals
- recognizing that the parties have common as well as conflicting interests that will affect an agreement – both must agree to achieve common and complementary objectives as much as possible
- sincerely and truly trying to understand the other party's point of view.

The purpose of negotiation is to reach an agreement on different needs and wants. Thus, within the negotiation process between the parties – whether there are two or more – is a process of understanding each party's position and offer in an effort to reach an agreement (Kamran, 2011). The conclusion of a negotiation process is often the initiation of a business relationship, and for this relationship to be successful both parties need to be satisfied with the negotiation agreement. Hence, both parties need to 'win' in a way, meaning their interests need to be satisfactorily met throughout the process by collaboration and mutual trust. As such, a successful negotiation process entails understanding the needs and interests of all parties, building trust and collaborating, which is more difficult in cross-cultural settings due to different cultural backgrounds and business processes (Acuff, 2008).

Studies show that firms may take different approaches to foreign markets and cultures, which can by summarized in three major profiles referred to as ethnocentrism, polycentrism, and geo-centrism (Morschett et al., 2009a). Firms with ethnocentric strategies view foreign operations from the home-country perspective. Their focus is on home-country business practices and standards in interacting with foreign countries, and they will export practices to their international businesses while refraining from adaptation. In parallel, negotiators from such firms will focus on the needs of their own HQ and will not make an effort to understand the needs of the foreign team. In contrast, firms adopting the polycentric approach will analyse each country and culture separately, trying to find optimal strategies and behaviours suitable for each country. In a geocentric approach, instead of considering locations and cultures separately, companies will view the world as a whole and try to formulate practices which are beneficial globally. Thus, negotiators and managers of firms with geocentric approaches need to know the culture and business environment of all the countries involved, and try to formulate solutions and strategies which can be beneficial throughout. Within these approaches, an ethnocentric stance may lead to frequent failures due to a tendency to judge other cultures by the values and rules of the home country. In parallel, a polycentric approach may be ineffective considering that firms today are much more culturally diverse, and it is difficult to identify a unique negotiation style in teams which are multicultural themselves. Thus, a geocentric approach which recognizes cultural differences and similarities while taking a more global approach can be most effective. Negotiators with a geocentric approach are defined by the depth of their international experience which enables them to communicate effectively across cultures (Rudd and Lawson, 2007).

Preparing for Success

With an amazing number of differences between cultures, it is easy to think that international business executives would be well served by a comprehensive resource describing the necessary etiquette and protocol for each country. Indeed, there are many good resources that provide this information. Although this kind of knowledge is often very helpful, there is a distinct danger in relying on a 'dictionary' of culture. People will appreciate a visitor's efforts and will try to learn more about their culture, but most people will distinctly dislike being defined or stereotyped by a 'typical' behaviour pattern. Cultural research should aim to help firms understand the negotiation partner but this should not result in mimicking or role playing his or her expectations.

An open mind, a friendly attitude, and a general sensitivity for cultural difference will go a long way toward facilitating negotiations. Being aware of a culture's customs is less a quantitative or qualitative strategy for negotiating than it is a gesture of goodwill. Your partner will probably recognize your cultural differences and allow you a few well-meant mistakes. The effect of shaking hands versus bowing, for example, is probably negligible.

With this in mind, the best strategy for a successful negotiation is good preparation (Zhang and Zhou, 2009). Knowing as much as you can about your partner's position as well as your own will help reduce anxiety, as well as provide you with more insight towards achieving your goals. As with all negotiations, stress and pressure are the real enemies when making a good deal. Stress makes us tired, and when we are tired, we make mistakes. It is important to analyse every offer for what it is worth, rather than accept or reject it because we feel the need to reach some kind of conclusion. Negotiation teams need to try to learn about the other party, focusing on issues such as the other party's culture, the organization's culture, and their options. In this manner, the negotiating team can 'gain an understanding of the other party's major interests, goals and needs' (Rudd and Lawson, 2007, p. 51).

Self-knowledge

While negotiators do not need to consider factors such as culture and language in the domestic environment, they do need to think about such differences in the international environment. Differences in culture and business customs can affect the negotiation process. Each negotiator is partially affected by his own culture and customs, even before starting the negotiation process. Thus, each negotiator faces the risk of misinterpreting the other side's attitude or motives if he evaluates the other side solely on the basis of the norms of his own culture (Ghauri and Cateora, 2010). Negotiators must therefore be able to understand their own style and the effects of culture on their own approach in order to prevent the process from being affected by cultural biases or tendencies. By adopting a multicultural view and foregoing notions that one's own culture is superior, negotiators can better view the issues of negotiation and work towards a mutually beneficial solution (Rudd and Lawson, 2007).

The axiom 'know thyself' cannot be overemphasized. This means knowing not only your bargaining position but also the cultural biases you are bringing to the table. Recognizing your own expectations regarding protocol and business behaviour will also help you recognize cultural differences and avoid miscommunication. For example, American business style tends to be direct and to the point. Recognizing this, you will know that you can expect a less direct negotiating style in some parts of Asia and make a conscious effort to adapt your style and expectations. You might re-word your criticisms of your partner's offer to avoid offending them inadvertently, or simply pick up on subtleties that they might have implied but did not state directly.

Understanding Your Partner

An acute knowledge of your negotiating partner is also very important (Galinsky et al., 2008). This includes information about the company, as well as *political, social, cultural* and *strategic* factors. These things make up the background against which negotiations are played out. A more complete understanding of the environment in which your partner operates will help you understand their position and lend insight into how they will approach negotiations (Das and Kumar, 2011). For example, many Western executives are frustrated by their inability to extract firm commitments from their foreign partners. Westerners are accustomed to making binding, long-term deals. However, in some Latin American countries in which political and economic conditions fluctuate rapidly, local companies may find themselves unwilling or unable to commit beyond a few months.

Political and social factors

Knowing the political climate of a country is extremely important, not only because affects the stability of your investment but also because it shows how a foreign partner might approach a binding agreement. In countries without a strong legal system, a company may see a written agreement as an indication of intention. Trying to hold a company to an agreement in a country with a weak legal system may be difficult or impossible. Moreover, in many countries in which businesses cannot rely on legal recourse, the business culture may insist on more rapport-building efforts in order to establish a relationship (Danis et al., 2010). Finally, it is always wise to understand the possible political impediments to doing business with a foreign company. Businesses must often operate under a variety of restrictions and regulatory procedures that may affect what a business will seek in negotiations (Elg, 2008).

Multiple business processes, standards, regulations and, most importantly, cultures are involved in international business negotiations, thereby increasing the complexity of the process. In order to be successful in such negotiations, negotiators need to know about the structural differences between the various nations in terms of process and regulation, as well as being able to communicate with and influence members of the counterparties (Saee, 2008). It is vital for companies to familiarize themselves with negotiation patterns in the host country and identify all the players that may affect the process. Different players such as the government, labour unions, shareholders, management, special interest groups or trade commissions may have the authority to influence the negotiation process. Knowing the players and their interests can prepare foreigners for potential challenges and enable them to cope with these challenges more effectively (Sebenius, 2002).

Finally, businesspeople must realize that foreign executives may emphasize different goals in negotiation. Many emerging markets have placed a particular emphasis on supporting their long-term growth and development. Many also have a long history of colonialism or other actions of Western powers that may affect their attitudes toward the West. They may be especially suspicious of Western companies that could take advantage of them and leave. Although this may not be true, you might have to spend a considerable amount of time in establishing a relationship based on goodwill. For example, China has been particularly shrewd when dealing with the West, often to the frustration of its would-be partners. As one of the world's oldest civilizations, it has a long history of repelling invaders and resisting foreign influence. In the past, its relations with the West had been particularly strained by imperialism, as well as by more recent rifts in ideology. Today, recognizing its importance as the world's largest untapped market, China can be expected to drive a hard bargain in exchange for opening its doors. The Chinese have worked very hard to increase competition between those searching for access and have played firms off against each other in order to negotiate some very favourable deals for themselves. Combined with considerable cultural barriers, Western business executives will face tough negotiations when dealing with this country (Leung et al., 2011).

Cultural factors

Negotiating in international business starts by building relations, a process which is highly influenced by cultural difference. Such differences may occur at the individual level of the organization, since people are inadvertently affected by different norms within their national culture, social culture, and organizational culture. The international negotiator is then faced with the challenge of understanding the counterparty without cultural bias (Rudd and Lawson, 2007).

To communicate efficiently, negotiators need to understand the culture of the other parties. Such understanding also entails nuances stemming from the silent language displayed through manners, gestures, and customs. As such, negotiators will need to prepare for and learn about the host's culture, from their values, ethics and religion to their political structure (Ghauri and Cateora, 2010).

A familiarity with the social and cultural conventions of a given country will prevent you from inadvertently offending your partner during negotiations and will also facilitate the methods and strategies you might employ (Adair et al., 2004). An international business executive quickly learns that business in one country is simply not like business in another. Despite the universality of basic business motives and methods, culture plays a large role in how people perceive and evaluate things.

Culture and belief systems affect how we perceive, judge, and think about and decide on the world. Normally, culture plays only a very subtle role in our daily communications because we are surrounded by people from the same culture. However, when we are placed within the vicinity of another culture, negotiating these differences becomes a very dynamic process. Human beings tend to project a cognitive similarity onto other people. This means that we assume that other people will think the way we do, which is not always the case (Ferraro, 2002).

For example, given the emphasis on teamwork and social harmony in Japan, the role of the individual is often downplayed. In cultures like this, direct confrontation will probably be avoided and regarded as distasteful or uncomfortable. Rather than rejecting a proposal directly, a Japanese negotiator might sidestep giving an answer, stall, or simply fall silent. In contrast, Americans are very often outgoing and direct. Not hearing a definite 'no' might be interpreted as a 'yes', or perhaps not be acknowledged as an impasse. In order to mitigate the issues stemming from such misunderstandings, it is pertinent for negotiators to familiarize themselves with the business customs and culture of the counterparties. Some of the main concepts that need to be understood in thinking about cross-cultural negotiations are time, decision making, communication patterns and personal relations (Ghauri and Cateora, 2010). Table 8.1 shows how the negotiation process can be influenced by cultural differences.

Time

A main cultural factor which needs to be highlighted within the context of international business negotiations is the perception of time. Time has

Table 8.1 Cultural dimensions in the negotiation process

Considering cultural factors, Jeswald W. Salacuse has identified 10 areas where culture can influence negotiation. According to his work, some cultures view the purpose of the negotiation as a means to sign a contract, whereas other cultures view it as the process of forming a relation. Cultures can also have different attitudes towards negotiation. For instance, while some cultures view negotiation as a process whereby a mutually beneficial arrangement can be reached, other cultures focus on confrontation and winning.

Goal	Contract	←——→	
Attitude	Relationship Win/Lose	←——→	Win/Win
Personal style	Informal	←——→	Formal
Communication	Direct	←——→	Indirect
Time sensitivity	High	←——→	Low
Emotionality	High	←——→	Low
Agreement form	Specific	←——→	General
Agreement building	Bottom up	←——→	Top down
Team organization	One leader	←——→	Consensus
Risk taking	High	←——→	Low

Source: Salacuse, 2004.

different meanings in different cultures, as identified by Hall and previously discussed. Cultures may view time differently. They can have a 'monochromic' or linear approach to time and prioritize the task at hand. Members of such cultures will then focus on timeliness, and adhere to schedules. Other cultures may have a 'polychromic' approach and will focus on the overall process and relations, instead of completing the task at hand in a timely manner. The Western perception of time, which is mostly monochromic – concentrating as it does on scheduling and completing tasks – is different from the view in most EMs which have a polychromic perception of time. Those need to understand the perspective of time in emerging markets and plan accordingly (Adair and Brett, 2005). Those from cultures with a linear perception of time can be perceived as untrustworthy and unfriendly within EMs due to their emphasis on resolving issues quickly (Ghauri and Cateora, 2010).

In most emerging markets, time must be set aside to establish personal relations and get acquainted prior to opening negotiations. On the other hand, many Western businesspeople will view time as a resource that should not be wasted and will try to minimize the amount of time spent on building relations, which is viewed as a necessity in many cultures. Another major issue stemming from the perception of time is scheduling, as Westerners will prefer a sequential process. In most EMs, negotiators would prefer to discuss issues all together, without sticking to an agenda (Usunier, 2003a).

Communication patterns

The communication patterns of different countries will differ due to cultural characteristics as well. (Communication types will be discussed further within this chapter.) In terms of pattern, cultures may lean towards explicit/implicit and direct/indirect methods which can create difficulties when communicating with other cultures. Some cultures may make use of implicit communication which is rather vague, and failing to interpret this vagueness appropriately can lead negotiators to the wrong conclusions. For instance, in some cultures 'maybe' can mean 'yes', whereas in others it can mean 'no' (Ghauri, 2003).

Different countries' speech patterns also differ in their treatment of silence. American executives are often uncomfortable with silence and will seek to fill the void with more dialogue. Often, this leads to a quick concession that might not have been needed or another attempt at a persuasive appeal. Long pauses in American culture are signs of an impasse but may simply indicate careful consideration in other cultures. Brazilian negotiators may deal with silence even less successfully than US negotiators. While US conversational style is relatively orderly and efficient, Brazilians will often speak simultaneously, fighting for the floor. US executives might perceive Brazilians as poor listeners, when the real problem is a clash of styles.

Negotiators also need to understand that in many countries learning about the national culture is not enough. In emerging markets such as India and China, sub-regions differ from each other significantly in terms of many layers of culture such as beliefs, rituals, and even languages. Thus, companies need to be careful about the difference between the regions and not assume that they are familiar with a nation's culture solely on the basis of having done business in one area (Rudd and Lawson, 2007).

Strategic factors

In preparing for negotiations, negotiators will have to learn about the other parties, especially in terms of essentials such as the preferred decision-making process, accepted norms in presentation, and the negotiation strategy commonly employed (Ghauri, 2003). Presentation styles are very different in a large number of countries. For instance, in many African and Latin American countries informal presentations are preferred, while most Asian and Eastern European countries prefer a formal style. Particularly in countries such as India, Russia and China, providing information on technical aspects is necessary, whereas in countries such as Peru and Brazil, focusing on emotions and goals throughout the presentation as opposed to solely providing facts may be a better approach (Acuff, 2008).

Negotiation strategies also differ between countries and negotiators. Some will focus on tough strategies whereby a very high offer is made initially and concessions are expected from the other party. Other nego- tiators may use soft strategies, where a party may give the first conces- sion, hoping for a reciprocal response from the counterparty (Yang et al., 2009). Negotiators need to understand the other party's strategy in order to prepare and create options and offers that can be presented as a response during the process (Olekalns and Brett, 2008).

The decision-making patterns of the counterparty are also important in preparing for negotiations, as negotiators will need to understand issues such the other party's influence or power in making final deci- sions, or their focus on rationality or impulsiveness in making deci- sions. In analysing the other party thoroughly, negotiators can also decide whether they need an agent or an intermediary throughout the negotiation, as in some cases utilizing agents or consultants who spe- cialize in different locations may be necessary or advantageous (Saorín- Iborra, 2008).

Creating alternatives

Creating alternatives ahead of time is one way of remaining flexible. Your ability to appear willing to do business and work toward a mutually acceptable agreement will be easier if you know your position ahead of time, have a good idea of the other party's position, and can readily present alternative solutions to expected impasses. Anticipate things beforehand because it will be harder to come up with solutions when under pressure. Keep asking yourself, 'What should we do if they won't accept this?'

Western negotiators often believe they only have three options: persuasion, threats, or concessions. In fact, there are many alternative solutions to a problem. A problem-solving attitude is key; it is not only a question of win or lose. Different issues can be combined to produce numerous alternatives. If the customer demands a 5% concession on the price, the other party can ask them to pay cash instead of the one-year credit proposed. Negotiators can also ask customers to pay interest on the demanded loan. In one case, a buyer demanded a 5% concession on the contract price after everything else had been agreed on. The seller instead proposed that he was willing to give a 10% rebate on all the spare parts bought by the buyer during the next three years. This offer was gladly accepted by the buyer (Ghauri, 2003, p. 519).

Knowing one's best alternative if the negotiation fails may establish a guideline during the process and enable the negotiator to prevent inefficiencies, such as accepting less favourable conditions than the alternative or refusing a more advantageous agreement. 'BATNA' – best alternative to a negotiated agreement – strengthens the negotiator's position and acts as a benchmark from which the negotiator can focus on more favourable terms. In parallel, negotiators can also gain an advantage by identifying the other side's BATNA and argue their position accordingly (HBR, 2003). Analysing the alternatives can also help negotiators assess the conditions in which they are not willing to accept a deal, and the conditions in which they are willing to negotiate (HBR, 2005).

A Framework for International Business Negotiations

An overall framework for business negotiations has three groups of variables: background factors, process and atmosphere, as shown in Figure 8.1. Because the negotiation process is inherently dynamic, a certain perception of the parties or a particular development in the process may influence a change in the background factors.

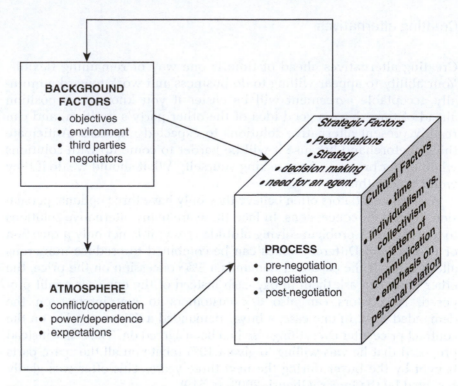

Figure 8.1   A framework for international business negotiations
Source: Ghauri and Usunier, 2003.

Background factors

This group of variables serves as a background to the process. They influence the process of negotiation and atmosphere. The effect of different variables on the process and its different stages varies in intensity. One of these variables may influence one stage positively and another negatively. A positive influence means that the process saves time and continues smoothly, while a negative influence causes delays and hindrances. Background factors include objectives, the environment, market position, third parties and negotiators.

Objectives are defined as the end state each party desires to achieve. They are often classified as common, conflicting, or complementary. For example, the parties will have a *common* interest: both will want a successful transaction to take place. At the same time, their interests may *conflict* because profit to one may be cost to the other. In terms of *complementary* interests, buyers in international deals are concerned with acquiring the appropriate technology to build an infrastructure. Sellers will want to enter a particular market and will also expect to do future business with it and the surrounding countries' markets. Common and complementary objectives will affect the negotiation process directly and positively, while conflicting objectives will have negative effects. These effects in turn will influence the atmosphere and outcome. The opportunity for an agreement decreases as conflicting objectives dominate in a relationship; it increases as common and complementary objectives dominate.

The *environment* refers to the political, social, and cultural milieu of the parties. There is a greater chance of interaction interference when unfamiliar parties, having different behaviours, interact with one another. Some of the characteristics will directly affect the process, while others will directly influence the atmosphere. Political and social aspects will affect the process, and cultural aspects plus the behaviour of the parties will influence the atmosphere.

The party's *market position* is another background variable influencing the negotiation process. The number of buyers and sellers in the market determines the number of alternatives available to each party, which in turn affects the amount of pressure imposed by counterparts within the market. The process and bargaining position of the buyer or seller can be affected if either one has monopolistic power in the marketplace; for example, if there is a large number of sellers and only one buyer, the latter can dominate.

Most international business deals involve *third parties*, that is, parties other than the seller and buyer, such as governments, agents, consultants and subcontractors. These parties may influence the negotiation process because they have different objectives. Often, governments from emerging economies are involved and they will influence buyers toward complementary objectives, such as infrastructure, employment opportunities, foreign exchange considerations, and any other prospective relationship between the two countries. The seller's agents will play an important role, because they can help bridge differences and prepare the groundwork for negotiations. Financiers may also be involved as third parties, for example the World Bank. These financiers will influence the negotiation process by demanding different types of guarantee and documentation that may delay the process of negotiation.

Negotiators influence the negotiation process with their own experience and negotiation skills and they operate within two limits. First, they act to increase common interests and expand cooperation between the parties; and second, they act to maximize their own interests and ensure an agreement that will be valuable for them. The personality of the negotiators may also play a role, particularly when information about the other party is lacking and there is a lot of stress. Negotiators from the seller's side can handle the situation effectively, due to experience and personality. A 'good' personality is defined as an individual with the ability to make others understand a position, approach strangers with ease and confidence, and appreciate the other person's position. However, their skills are related to different objectives and motivations pertaining to different people and professions. Negotiators with a technical background may place more emphasis on technical issues, while those with a business background might consider other issues to be more important.

Atmosphere

The relationship developed during the negotiation process between the parties is characterized by an atmosphere that is of basic importance to the process as a whole. The atmosphere and the process affect each other through interaction at each stage. *Atmosphere* is defined as the perceived milieu around the interaction, how the parties perceive each other's behaviour and the properties of the process. It enhances the dynamics of the process. Some atmosphere characteristics will be dominant at one stage, others at another stage. The offer stage will be dominated by cooperation rather than conflict as parties look for technical solutions for buyers. The dominance of various atmosphere characteristics will change from process to process. These characteristics are conflict/cooperation, power/dependence, distance and expectations.

The existence of both *conflict* and *cooperation* is a fundamental characteristic of the negotiation process. On one hand, parties will have some common interests in finding a solution to the problem that fits both the supplier's ability and the user's need. On the other hand, a conflict of interest may arise because cost to one may be income to the other. The magnitude of conflict or cooperation in the atmosphere will depend on the objectives of the parties during the negotiation. Some relationships will be more complementary than others and, consequently, less conflicting. The degree of conflict or cooperation during different stages of the negotiation process is often a function of which issues are dealt with, while the degree of conflict or cooperation in the atmosphere is a function of how the parties handle various problems. Conflict is sometimes perceived without the existence of real conflict, due to misunderstanding each other's behaviour. The more unfamiliar the parties are with one another, the higher the risk for such perceived conflicts.

The *power/dependence* relation is another basic characteristic of all negotiation processes. It is closely linked to the objective power relation, which is influenced by the value of the relationship to the parties and their available alternatives. Background factors (e.g. the market position) can influence the power/dependence relation. The ability to control a relationship is linked to the perceived power of the two parties, their relative expertise, and access to information. This power is a property of the relationship and not an actor attribute. In fact, it is closely related to dependence. Therefore, the power relationship is in balance if both parties have equal power, and the power relationship is unbalanced if one of the parties has more power or if one party is dependent on the other.

The last aspect of atmosphere concerns two types of *expectation*. First, there are long-term expectations, regarding the possibility and value of future deals. The stronger these expectations are, the more inclined the negotiators will be to agree on the present deal. Second, there are short-term expectations, concerning the prospects for the present deal. Long-term expectations will be related to primary objectives. The parties' decision to enter negotiations and continue after each stage implies expectations of a better outcome from participating than from not participating. This compels the parties to proceed from one stage to the next. Expectations develop and change in different stages of the process and can also be related to expectations in organizational problem solving.

The negotiation process

The process of international business negotiation presented here is divided into five different stages. A *stage of the process* refers to a specific time and includes all actions and communications by any party pertaining to negotiations made during that period. Parties communicate with each other to exchange information within each stage. A particular stage ends when the parties decide to proceed further into the next stage or to abandon the communication if they see no point in further negotiations. In the offer stage, the parties will attempt to understand each other's needs and demands, and will decide either to proceed with the following stage (informal meetings) or not to proceed further due to the incompatibility of each other's demands, whereupon the negotiations will end without agreement.

Process development depends on three dimensions: time, issues, and contacts. The more time a process/stage takes, the more conflict and distance is perceived by the parties. As discussed earlier, some issues, such as technical details, will create a positive atmosphere, while others, such as price and terms of payment, will create a negative atmosphere. Contacts, as well as time and issues, are crucial aspects in understanding the negotiation process. This factor refers to the people who meet during each stage of the process, whether on a technical or commercial basis. Technical people tend to stress technical details and specifications; commercial people tend to focus on price, terms of payment, and guarantees.

Stage 1: Offer

The offer stage begins with the first contact between parties concerning a particular venture and ends when the vendor submits a final offer. During this stage, some negotiations will take place, and counter-offers will be made, often resulting in a revision of the vendor's offer. The dynamism of the process can be observed at this early stage, when the parties begin to understand one another's needs. It is important that the vendors realize that in submitting an offer, they are committing themselves to their part of the deal. It may be necessary to make concessions on many issues.

To gain greater power, parties should gather as much relevant information as possible about each other, the operating environment and the involvement of other third parties, influencers, competitors, and the infrastructure. They need to be aware that their relative power relationship can be altered at any time by events such as the repositioning of competitors or changes in exchange rates. We have defined this negotiation process as being problem-solving in nature, so the main issue here will be to define the problem to be solved. It is important to do this jointly because it will not only reflect each party's expectations but will also acquire the necessary commitment from both parties. The parties should thus truly and openly discuss each other's objectives and expectations to achieve such positive problem solving.

Stage 2: Informal meetings

The parties will meet to discuss the offer and get acquainted. After the buyer receives the offer, informal meetings will take place as the parties examine each other's positions. Whether the parties continue to the next stage of the negotiation process will depend on the perceived level of cooperation or conflict, power or dependence, and the degree of distance. The process will often end in failure if excessive conflict or distance is sensed or if a successful future relationship seems doubtful. At this stage, the parties should truly see how they are going to solve the problem, whether it is realistic to achieve the objectives of both sides, and identify the obstacles that have to be overcome to achieve their objectives.

The selling firm must realize that a government buyer in emerging countries has objectives that are different from those of a private business firm. Objectives such as job opportunities, an increase in the capacity of the industry, a balance of payments, or other matters of policy will be dominant if the buyer is a government organization. This was the situation that existed in the negotiation process for a paper-and-pulp plant in which the buyer was a large, state-owned company. The right to reject the seller's subcontractors was reserved in this deal. The aim was to accept the offer that used local subcontractors, thereby solving regional unemployment problems.

Informal meetings are often more important than formal negotiations in many emerging markets. Social, informal relationships that develop between negotiators at this stage can be of great help. Trust and confidence gained from these relationships will not only increase the chances for agreement but also decrease the psychic distance between parties. One method of establishing such contacts is to invite individuals from the buyer's side to visit the seller's office/factory in an attempt to develop trust. The prime objective here is to discover each other's priorities. It is important to understand what the other party wants and why they want it, along with their underlying interests and objectives, because this information will help the parties find solutions that are acceptable to both sides.

Stage 3: Strategy formulation

Parties can begin to formulate their strategy for face-to-face negotiation if Stage 2 has ended in success and they decide to continue the process. By *strategy*, we mean a complete plan regarding problems, the solutions available, and the preferred choices relative to the other party's choices and preferences. At this stage, the parties will try to build up their relative power. The buyer compares the offers submitted by different vendors, makes checklists, and assigns pro and con arguments or competitive advantages to all competing vendors. The seller decides on possible points of concession and their extent. A volatile environment can severely upset established relative power positions. It is essential that negotiators continue to monitor changes in the environment to protect their power position at this stage.

It is often assumed that information exchanged in the offer and during informal negotiations can replace face-to-face interaction, but this is not the case. The remittance of funds, taxes and import duties, and issuance of work permits are just some examples of the rules and regulations of the particular country that must be researched at this stage. An understanding of the infrastructure of the country and the company is also critical at this point. In some countries, especially when the public sector is the buyer, purchasing organizations will issue a *letter of award* (also called a *letter of intent* or *acceptance*) after offers have been received. This document states that the order for the project has been awarded to 'Company ABC', and that company is called for formal negotiations. Vendors from Western countries often perceive this letter of award as the granting of a contract. This is an incorrect assumption, because other competitors might also have received a similar letter. The letter merely indicates the buyer's intention to negotiate further following their receipt of the final offer.

There are several dimensions to strategy in business negotiations, such as tough, intermediate, or soft. In using a *tough* strategy, a party will start rather high and remain firm on its stand and would expect the other party to make the first concessions. In using a *soft* strategy, a party will offer the first concession in the hope that the other party reciprocates. In using an *intermediate* strategy, a party should not start high, and as soon as an offer is made that is within its expectations, that party should accept. Other dimensions of strategy are voluntariness, structure, informational locus, and opportunism (Lewicki et al., 1994, pp. 110–111).

In a *voluntary* strategy, we have to make a choice of what to pursue, how to pursue it, and whether to have a strategy at all. In government projects, for example, strategies can be more or less structured. A *highly structured* strategy would provide control, a sense of direction, and guidelines. The *informational locus* dimension refers to the fact that a strategy is based on incomplete or unreliable information and can be changed or adjusted as the information, for example on the other party, emerges as the negotiation proceeds. Here, the negotiators should try to adapt their strategies as early as possible to achieve better results. *Opportunism* refers to the fact that not having a strategy is itself a strategy. When done intentionally, it is referred to as *adaptive, emergent* and *opportunistic*, and it enables negotiators to exploit opportunities as they recognize them.

Whatever the dimensions, at the outset, parties to international business negotiations should have an initial strategy, which is dependent on the information attained up until then and on the expectations. Negotiators should list the problems and issues, especially the conflicting issues, and form strategies and choices for all the possible solutions they or the other party could suggest. These solutions should be ranked, for example, as *preferred, desired, expected*, and *not acceptable.* If not acceptable, then a solution should be developed that is acceptable to the other party. It is thus important to have several solutions to hand for each problem or issue.

Stage 4: Face-to-face negotiation

The parties should be aware that each side will view the situation, or the matter under discussion, in its own way. Not only will they have a different perception of the process, they will also have different expectations for the outcome. It is therefore necessary to start face-to-face negotiations with an open mind. At this stage, the parties should evaluate the alternatives presented and select those that are compatible with their own expectations. The best way to do this is to determine the criteria for judging the alternatives and then rank each alternative against these criteria. Here, the parties can even help each other in evaluating these alternatives and discussing the criteria for judgement. The main issue is to explore the difference in preferences and expectations and then try to reach an agreement.

The negotiation process is controlled by the partner who arranges the agenda, because each can emphasize its own strengths and the other party's weaknesses, thus putting the other party on the defensive. However, the agenda may reveal the preparing-party's position in advance and hence permit the other side to prepare its own counter-arguments on conflicting issues.

Experience suggests that it is often the partner with the greater relative power who arranges the agenda. Some negotiators will prefer to start negotiations by discussing and agreeing on broad principles for the relationship. Another way to ensure success at this stage is to negotiate the contract step by step, discussing both conflicting issues and those of common interest. In particular, discussions on items of common interest can create an atmosphere of cooperation between parties. The choice of strategy will depend on the customer or supplier with whom one is negotiating. It is helpful to anticipate the other party's strategy as early as possible and then choose a strategy to match or complement it.

In Stage 4, both parties will take the initiative by asking questions about the other party: aspects of the offer, price, quality, delivery, and credit possibilities. These questions will clear the negotiation range, that is, the gap between the minimum point of one party and the acceptable point of the other. The negotiator should not agree to a settlement at once if there is considerable overlap between his or her position vis-à-vis the other party. The negotiator may obtain further concessions by prolonging the negotiation process. A number of studies have revealed that negotiators who submit a 'final offer' up front can be at a disadvantage. In view of the diverse cultural and business traditions prevailing in different countries, international negotiations will inherently involve a discussion of environmental differences. It is very difficult for parties to comprehend or adjust to each other's cultures or traditions, but it is crucial for them to be aware of these differences. In many emerging markets, the social contact developed between parties is far more significant than technical and economic specifications. Negotiators from these countries will take their time and be very careful not to offend or use strong words, and the other party will be expected to follow suit.

Negotiations with the public sector in emerging economies often involve negotiating with civil servants and politicians. These negotiators are bound by rules, regulations, and government policy. Vendors must take these rules and regulations into account. A balance between firmness and credibility is essential in all types of negotiation. It is important to give and take signals of preparedness in order to move on from the initial stage without making concessions. Negotiators who have had prior dealings with each other can easily send and receive signals, but this is very difficult for those who are meeting for the first time. The timing of a move is crucial, but the attitude and behaviour of both parties can also be decisive factors. A positive atmosphere may be developed by a negotiator who is firm and at the same time exhibits a courteous, problem-solving attitude.

Negotiators from Western countries will frequently adopt a tough attitude in negotiations that is perceived as a 'big brother' stance and proves very offensive to the other party. Negotiators will often send conditional signals such as 'We cannot accept your offer as it stands', or 'We appreciate that your equipment is quite suitable for us, but not at the price you mentioned'. The seller might say, 'I understand, but you know that this is the lowest price I can offer. Otherwise, I will have to call my head office and discuss the price with them'. This is a tactic used to test each other's commitment as well as the resolution of the offer. It is also common that the party perceiving that it has greater relative power makes fewer concessions and that the weaker party yields more often to create a better atmosphere.

Maintaining flexibility between parties and issues is of great importance in regard to terms of payment, price, and delivery time. For example, the price can be reduced if the party offers better terms of payment. Other elements can be traded off, but there may not be a way to evaluate them in accounting terms. For example, obtaining a reference or an entry into a huge, protected market may be strategically more important than gaining handsome profits on the present deal. A point will be reached at which the negotiators must make a final move. It is usually a poor strategy to announce that they do not have the final authority to conclude the contract, but this is quite effective when used as a tactic to check the other side's final move.

Stage 5: Implementation

At this stage, all terms will have been agreed on. The contract will have been drawn up and ready to be signed. Experience has shown that writing the contract, and the language used, can be a negotiation process in itself, because the meaning and values may differ between the two parties. In cases involving Western firms and emerging-economy parties, the language used and the writing up of issues previously agreed on can take a considerable time. This stage can lead to renewed face-to-face negotiation if there is negative feedback from background factors and atmosphere.

Discussion should be summarized after negotiations to avoid unnecessary delays in the process. The terms agreed on should be read by both parties after the concessions are exchanged and discussions held. This is facilitated by keeping minutes of meetings. This is helpful not only in writing and signing the contract but also in its implementation. Trouble may arise later during implementation of the contract if the parties are too eager to reach an agreement and don't pay enough attention to details. The best way to solve this problem is to confirm that both sides thoroughly understand what they have agreed on before leaving the negotiating table.

What is a good outcome?

A good agreement is one that leads to a successful implementation. There are many examples of firms getting into trouble because they could not implement the contract conditions of a particular project. Therefore, in some cases, not reaching an agreement may be a better outcome for a firm. A good outcome benefits both parties and does not make either party feel that it has a less advantageous contract. This type of arbitration was one of the reasons for deadlock in a case between a Swedish seller and a Nigerian buyer. The buyer wanted local arbitration, but the seller wanted a Swedish or international arbitrator. The buyer commented, 'Well, if they are sure that they are going to fulfil the commitments of the contract, then why are they afraid to accept arbitration in Nigeria, because in that case there will be no conflicts and no arbitration?' Sometimes negotiators will want to avoid specifying some issues and keep them ambiguous. It is important to understand that on one hand, ambiguity can lead to a reopening of the conflict later on, and on the other hand, if we want to specify such issues, it might prolong the negotiation process or prevent an agreement. Sometimes this ambiguity is unintended, and sometimes it is intentionally done to speed up the process or to give the impression that the particular issue needs to be renegotiated (Ikle, 1964, pp. 8–15).

A good deal is one that provides financial gains. But what were the objectives of the firm when it decided to enter into negotiations? Was the present deal the most important outcome, or was it future business? The outcome must be related to the firm's objectives. If these have been met, then it is a good outcome. A successful negotiation is not a question of 'win–lose' but a problem-solving approach to a 'win–win' outcome.

Building Bridges:
The Negotiating Process

As mentioned earlier, negotiating is a process of managing relationships. Many businesspeople, especially in Western civilizations, expect contracts and other agreements to be negotiated within the space of a few days. Although this may be common in the West, in many other cultures, businesspeople may expect to take their associates out for dinner and participate in other rapport-building activities before entering into an agreement. Personal relationships with partners and clients are relied on more heavily in other parts of the world, and the more experience you gain doing business abroad, the more skills you will acquire for negotiations.

Communication types

Communicating with other people can be a very complex task. It can be both verbal and nonverbal, subtle and straightforward. In addition, within the process of communication, there are many subtasks or stages that will occur as the participants attempt to understand each other. Communication can be broken down into four categories based on purpose: phatic, informational, persuasive, and cathartic (Ghauri and Usunier, 2003).

Phatic communication consists of preliminary discussions intended to build binding relationships (Vetere et al., 2009). Though this is often overlooked, it is particularly important because we communicate better with people with whom we have created a personal bond. Greetings and small talk, for example, are key examples of phatic communication. These help put us at ease with each other and allow us to connect on a more personal level. Phatic communication in different cultures varies in its formality, length, and subject matter. What is appropriate in one culture may not always be appropriate in another (Bytyci, 2009). For example, in the USA, businesspeople tend to think that being informal is a friendly form of confidence. In other countries, however, a lack of formality and use of titles might be considered rude or make others feel uncomfortable. Americans also have a reputation for expedience. They want to appear on the scene, begin negotiations right away, and then leave. Often, they will not realize that the round of golf their host wants them to play is actually part of the phatic round of negotiations. Until a relationship has developed, many cultures will not discuss matters of substance. A good negotiator must learn to take cues from his or her host and adapt accordingly.

Informational communication is speech which is intended both to request and receive information. Although this seems fairly straightforward, informational messages must still be applied within the appropriate context to be understood (De Mooij, 2009). Idioms, catchphrases and adages, often used in the business world to elucidate meaning, can sometimes confuse issues even more. Even simple phrases or references can be misunderstood. For example, in the USA, an octopus is said to have several 'arms'. In Japan, however, it is said to have several 'legs'. 'Next Sunday', if you are talking to a Swede, does not mean the coming Sunday, but the Sunday after that. In India, however, 'next Sunday' means the coming Sunday. Likewise, 'nice weather' in Europe usually means sunshine, but in African and many Asian countries 'nice weather' means cloudy or rainy weather.

The third category, *persuasive* communication, includes all activities meant to persuade another person. It is most effective when the other person is a willing and able listener (Pietroni et al., 2008). This, of course, is the trick. The right kind of phatic and informational communication will play a large part in making someone receptive to your ideas. It also helps you to understand how the other person perceives and evaluates new information. Obviously, different individuals and cultures will approach things differently.

Finally, *cathartic* communication provides a release of emotions. Both positive and negative emotions will supply important feedback for communication, allowing you to adjust your negotiating strategy for success and failure. For this type of communication to be effective, the other person must be willing and able to accept the conduct of the person seeking cathartic release.

By understanding your partner's communication in terms of these four communication types, you will be able to better understand what your partner is saying and how it fits in with what he or she means. Effective negotiations will rely on the negotiator's ability to accurately interpret the other side and respond with an appropriate message (Ghauri and Usunier, 2003).

Verbal versus nonverbal communication

Approximately 70–80% of all communication occurs on a nonverbal level. Although some studies conclude that only 7% of the message we speak goes through language, much of our meaning is conveyed in the tone of our voice, how quickly or slowly we speak, and our posture and body language (Ghauri, 2003, p. 519). Paying attention to nonverbal cues can be a particularly helpful tool for international negotiators because many of these habits are in our unconscious behaviour (Semnani-Azad and Adair, 2011). Whereas our verbal language is carefully formulated ahead of time, our nonverbal language is generally more spontaneous and possibly more sincere or insightful. For example, sometimes people will lean forward when they like what you are saying, or will lean back and cross their arms when they don't. Excessive blinking may be related to feelings of guilt or fear. Other signals include blushing, strained laughter, or silence. Although body language is often ambiguous, it can prove valuable just to note at which point of your communication your message receives a reaction. Conversely, being aware of your own nonverbal patterns may help you suppress any information you might not want to give away. Sometimes rephrasing a proposal or a different approach to a problem can help fine-tune the presentation of your message. Acting physically confident may also help you feel emotionally confident as well.

Body language can vary by culture (Goman, 2008). For example, US business executives will often require more personal space than their Latin American or Arab counterparts. Asian associates may stand even further apart. In the West, a lot of eye contact is taken to be a sign of honesty and sincerity. In Southeast Asia, however, direct eye contact should be avoided until a firm relationship has been established. Personal space and eye contact may vary due to the level of intimacy in many cultures.

Each culture also has a number of signals that are distasteful to them, although they may seem innocuous to outsiders. In Malaysia, for example, you should never touch the top of anyone's head. Malays believe this is where their souls reside. In Arab countries, it is almost impossible to sit with your legs crossed without offending someone. Showing the sole of your shoe (or pointing it at someone) is considered an insult. And in Muslim countries, one should refrain from using one's left hand – it is reserved for personal hygiene and thus is considered dirty (globalEDGE, 2011).

Conservative behaviour is almost always a wise choice, at least until one has a good idea of what is going on. American culture is relatively informal compared with much of the world, so being more formal than you think necessary is better than taking undue liberties. Until you get a feel for what is expected of you, remain perceptive and refrain from making a judgement on things you do not yet understand.

It's all in the tongue

If you plan on doing a lot of business in a particular country, consider learning the language. Although English is rapidly becoming the business language of choice, you may be putting yourself at a disadvantage if you don't speak your partner's language. Interpreters are also often cumbersome to work with and may not be completely reliable. Speaking for yourself is always a good choice.

The dominant position of the British and US economies has made English a popular language with foreign executives. Many countries require their students to have at least some competency in this important language. Conversely, although foreign language training is very popular in these two countries, few people reach an adequate level of fluency. If your partners understand English but you don't understand their language, you're giving them an edge.

In trying to negotiate in foreign languages, parties run the risk of being misunderstood. Though English is widely accepted globally, there may be differences in meaning and the fluency level of the partners may cause delays and misunderstandings as well. Many companies try to prevent such problems by involving translators. Still, in doing so, they will need to be careful and check the credentials of the translator from independent sources, and explain the context of the meeting to the translator beforehand, so as to facilitate meaningful interpretations throughout the meeting. In some cases, companies may use intermediaries as translators, however in doing so they will need to take into consideration the interests of the intermediary and whether those interests would lead the intermediary to direct negotiations in other directions (Salacuse, 2004a). The use of translators allows foreign executives to help verify the accuracy of what they hear. It also gives them twice the amount of time to analyse information while they are waiting to hear the translation. More importantly, while the translator is giving the English version of their message, they can focus on watching your reactions.

Bargaining in English also creates a substantial loophole for foreign executives. Although negotiating in English may seem like an advantage to us because we are more comfortable quickly formulating arguments, it can also backfire on us. The other side can always say that they did not understand our complex arguments, or may use selective understanding to misinterpret what we have said. They may also dissolve previous commitments by claiming a misunderstanding between what they said and what they meant. When facing a group of foreign executives, we can also have a tendency to think that the one who speaks English the best is the most intelligent and influential person in the party. We will then aim most of our persuasive efforts at this person. If that person is not the brightest or most influential in the party, our efforts will become somewhat misguided.

Finally, learning the language represents an excellent show of goodwill. People appreciate the effort and feel more comfortable when speaking in their own language. Also, native idioms and constructions can provide a lot of insight into how people in a different culture may think.

Safety in numbers

Western executives are almost always outnumbered in international negotiations. As a result, they may be at a disadvantage. Negotiating involves handling several activities at one time, including formulating arguments, thinking up questions, issuing explanations, and, of course, listening. No matter how well you think you can do all of this, the chances are you can't do so as well as several people working together. In selecting negotiators, traits such as cultural understanding, knowledge, flexibility, and empathy are considered important (Ghauri, 2003, p. 519). As negotiations are essentially relationship-building processes, the presence of teams as opposed to an individual becomes more crucial. Moreover, the team can more easily gather information and influence progress within the process (Saee, 2008). A negotiator needs to collect information and understand the view of the other side in order to create a solution; thus, assigning one person just to take notes can be a good idea. In many cases, the negotiation items and views will need to be discussed with HQ who may often need to be persuaded. Thus, involving senior executives may speed up this process and also increase the team's credibility in relation to the other side (Cateora et al., 2009).

Including more members on your team might raise the cost of your mission a bit more, but it could pay off in the long run. It is difficult for a single individual to have all the necessary technical know-how, in addition to good negotiating skills, to be able to evaluate proposals. Having extra personnel there will allow you to operate more effectively. Not only will you be better prepared and have greater expertise available to you, you will also be able to pay more attention to nonverbal cues. Assembling your negotiations team will be a vital part of your preparations. You will need to have input from of all the departments that might be seriously affected by an agreement. International business negotiators can do more harm than good if they lack integrated knowledge of the firm and how different parts of the firm will be affected by a deal (Ghauri, 2001, p. 548).

Team members should have a clear idea of the role they are expected to play. For example, you may want to assign roles for spokespersons, technical experts, note takers, observers, and so on. All team members should understand the tactics and strategies you plan to employ. There should also be some organization of how the team will handle first offers, concessions, caucuses, and other issues that may arise. It is important that the team can work together well. You don't want to have part of your team fighting other parts at a crucial point in negotiations.

It may also be worthwhile to seriously consider hiring outside help. An outside agent can be particularly helpful when a firm is entering a new market in which it has no previous experience. Consultants need not act as a firm's negotiators, but they may be able to offer assistance and advice in formulating strategies or providing information regarding environmental factors. A lawyer with expertise in that particular market can often provide a lot of help.

Finally, when considering who should be on your negotiating team, you should always factor in who the other team will bring. The size of the team is often affected by culture. For instance, in China, where consensus is prioritized, negotiation teams are often larger and will include representation from all interested parties. In contrast, in countries where an individual has the decision-making power, such as the USA, negotiation parties are relatively smaller (Rudd and Lawson, 2007). Status plays a key role in doing business abroad. If the other side brings an important key player, such as a vice president or president of the firm, you should always have a suitable counterpart for that person. In cultures where seniority and rank take precedence, involving young and inexperienced negotiators may be a mistake. In China and other countries in which the Chinese community is very strong, CEOs are almost always present in the final round of negotiations. The CEO of a family-run business is almost always that family's father (Ghauri, 2001, p. 549).

Strategies for the Global Negotiator

Skilled negotiators can offer many different strategies towards dealing with international negotiations, all of which may be practised with varying degrees of success. A win–win approach stresses meeting the needs of both parties but does not exclude a firm negotiation stance. A wise negotiator can manage being shrewd, reasonable, and willing to adapt to each situation.

Firms in some countries may take a particularly hard-line stance toward negotiations. Others may be more willing to work cooperatively.

Regardless of what their attitude is, it is vital to remember that you are never obliged to reach an agreement. If the other party senses your need to conclude the session with a deal, a common tactic is simply to wear you down. The greatest power you have in any negotiation is your ability to walk away.

Understand the needs of the other party

Negotiators need to consider the position of the other party and understand this. In doing so, a negotiator may better prepare for the other parties' reactions and deal with them. In doing so, the negotiator can prepare to argue their position more effectively and offer alternative solutions throughout the negotiation process, which can more effectively lead to a resolution. In trying to understand the point of view of the other side, negotiators first need to prepare beforehand and, second, be attentive throughout the negotiation process – not just to what is being said but also to what is being implied. Negotiators' ability to understand the other side and offer alternative solutions can also add to the positivity of the atmosphere and increase the other side's openness to alternative solutions (Ghauri, 2003).

Throughout the process, negotiators also need to consider the informational needs of the other party and be careful about how to present such information. Often, presenting technical specifications as well as the proposals in the local language can be an effective way of overcoming communication barriers.

Stick to the issues

It is important for the negotiator to stick to the salient issues at hand and not let the differences between cultures unduly interfere with making an agreement. This means that culture is non-negotiable. Culture makes up a large part of a person's personal identity, and it is not easily changeable. A negotiator needs to accept the other party as they are or not do business with them at all. It would be unreasonable and unrealistic to enter into business with another party that the company or the negotiator does not respect and expect them to change.

A large part of negotiating is persuasion and, to all intents and purposes, when the goal is to persuade someone, the person to be persuaded is always 'right'. No matter how much sense a company's proposal makes to them, if the party negotiating rejects it, the company has failed to achieve their objective. Convincing the other party is always the only solution and, in this process, enforcing the negotiators' own opinion is not helpful.

Build up relative power

Negotiators can determine who has the relative power advantage by gathering information about the other party, considering each party's position, and developing different alternatives. They can try to build their own relative power by developing arguments against the elements of power and improving their own position. In the negotiation process, this kind of power may be exercised by mentioning the other party's weak points: 'What happened to the project you sold in Poland? We heard that they had lots of problems with your machines, and there was some dispute about guarantees ... '.

Another good example would be addressing uncertainty regarding infrastructure and exchange rates in an emerging market. You may want to include stipulations for adjustments in the event of exchange-rate variations. In this kind of negotiation, the party with more information automatically acquires more power.

Box 8.1   Potential Irritants – Words and Phrases to Avoid

Be careful of any subtle overtones you might be conveying in your language. Some words and phrases might set the other negotiating party against you, rather than persuade them to your way of thinking. The following is a list of possible irritants:

  'You always/never ... '

These are pretty strong words that are rarely true. While you may just be venting your frustration, people don't react well to being told that their behaviour is predictable.

  'What you need to understand ... ' or 'Be reasonable ... '

Statements like these have a tone of superiority. You are implying that they don't understand or they aren't being reasonable. Most people think that they do understand and that they are reasonable. Telling them otherwise won't make you any friends.

  'Calm down!'

(Continued)

(Continued)

This statement is more likely to infuriate the other party than to have any calming effect. No one likes being told what to do and certainly not how to feel.

'Obviously ... '

Be careful that you are not implying that your partner is incapable of seeing the obvious. Things that are obvious probably do not need to be pointed out to them.

'You can't tell me ... '

You are undercutting their position. They can and will tell you anything they want. Why would you say this unless you are looking for a direct confrontation?

'Most people would ... '

You are devaluing the person's identity with this statement. Some people consider *not* being like 'most people' a virtue. Others might resent the implication that there is something wrong with them because they don't agree with you.

Source: Acuff, 1993.

The negotiator may have to work like a detective to ascertain the buyer's needs, their strong and weak points, and the strong and weak points of their competitors. An experienced negotiator can build up information in order to gain relative power by being active in the negotiation process. This can be done by asking the other party questions. It can also be done by giving conditional answers, such as *'If* you agree to pay cash, *then* we can consider looking at our price' or *'What if* we agree to pay cash? Perhaps then* you can lower the price by 5%' (Ghauri, 2003, p. 101).

Don't reduce your own bargaining position

Negotiators need to be reasonable, but should not be afraid of setting a high initial demand. It's not sensible to reduce the negotiator's own option, and sometimes a negotiator can be surprised by what can be achieved. High initial demands teach others how to treat the negotiator and also give the negotiator some room to make concessions. Negotiators can always lower their offerings later, at a suitable time.

In negotiations, some amount of haggling is expected and negotiators will need to leave some room for manoeuvre. Furthermore, there is an emotional imperative to 'extract' concessions out of the negotiator. By starting out high and then gradually lowering demands, a negotiator can fulfil the other party's need to engineer a bargain. Giving in immediately, on the other hand, may arouse suspicion or perhaps be interpreted as a weakness in the negotiator's position.

Timing is a key factor in negotiations. Where and when the negotiator makes concessions will give the other party valuable information about their negotiating style, resolve, and so on. Negotiators should make their concessions very strategic events. Some key points to remember are as follows:

- Expect to make some concessions.
- Save concessions until the end.
- High initial demands leave room to bargain; also, an emotional imperative for the hard sell does not always work.
- Emphasize relationships.
- Emphasize mutual problem solving and gains.

What Makes a Good Negotiator?

A number of studies identify the characteristics of a good negotiator. Ikle (1964) defined someone who can have a 'quick mind but unlimited patience, know how to dissemble without being a liar, inspire trust without trusting others, be modest but assertive, charm others without succumbing to their charm, and possess plenty of money' (p. 253). Successful negotiators often plan diligently and come up with a wide range of options beforehand. In parallel, they are also more focused on establishing a common ground. Prioritizing and defining objectives in advance can also increase flexibility (Saee, 2008).

Empathy and respect for different perspectives are of utmost importance. It is not necessary to adapt or change yourself because of local environments. It is more worthwhile to be aware of these differences and to show them due respect and acceptance. Asians and Arabs attribute huge significance to social contacts and informal relations. A marketer's personality and social behaviour are as important as these personal relationships in many emerging countries. His or her decision in favour of a deal is often based on the salesperson's personality and not on the quality of the deal.

Negotiators can often be grouped into different categories depending on their behaviour, such as 'bullies', 'avoiders', or 'acceptors'. Bullies want to threaten, push, demand, or attack. Avoiders like to avoid conflicting situations and would rather hide than make a wrong decision or be held responsible. They will normally refer to their superiors for a final decision: 'I have to call my head office ... '. Acceptors will always give a very positive answer and say 'yes' to almost anything, which makes it difficult to work out which 'yes' is 'yes' and which 'yes' is 'maybe', and whether what is being promised can be delivered. The best way to handle these behaviour types is to identify them first and then confront them by establishing a limit, helping them feel safe and asking them how and when they would be able to do what they are promising.

It is essential to know the negotiator's precise authority. In Eastern Europe and China, one team may negotiate one day followed by a fresh team the next day. When this process is repeated a number of times, it becomes very difficult for the Western firm to establish who is the negotiating party and who has the final authority.

One of the characteristics of a good negotiator is the ability to discover the timetable of the other party and allow plenty of time for the negotiation process. It is usually not feasible to expect to fly to a distant country, wrap things up, and then be home again in a week. Nor is it reasonable to coerce a party that is not ready to reach a decision. Negotiations with EM customers will take a long time! Patience and time are the greatest assets a negotiator can have while working with customers from these markets (globalEDGE, 2011). Some negotiators will take their time, discussing all the issues and justifying their roles through tough negotiations. Negotiators must be in a position to change their strategies and arguments, because the process of negotiation is highly dynamic. They must be flexible. The other party will often ask questions, probing the seller's weaknesses, just to provoke and obtain more concessions. It is important to keep calm and find out first if the questions asked are relevant and justified. Negotiators can use this in their favour when the questions are not justified and the buyer had incorrect information. A good negotiator is not just a person who can conclude an apparently good contract for the company or one who can arrive at a contract in a short time.

Building relationships

In many cultures, building relationships is considered an essential part of doing business. Thus, Western negotiators, especially when dealing with emerging markets, need to invest time and effort in building relations (Jansson, 2008). As such, respecting the culture and business customs of the counterparty can both help build relations and minimize misinterpretation between the parties (Ghauri and Cateora, 2010).

Business between companies increasingly focuses on establishing long-term arrangements. Parties engaged in the transaction can often increase their benefits by building a long-term relationship. First, trust enables companies to lower monitoring costs. Second, by viewing the party as a long-term partner, each side increases their commitment. Moreover, companies are less willing to engage in risky or greedy behaviour in anticipation of future benefits. A partnership also increases reciprocity through which both sides can benefit. Thus, in building relations as well as through negotiations, emphasizing a long-term vision can be advantageous.

Chapter Questions

1 Discuss the strategies that negotiators need to consider in international business.
2 How does culture affect the negotiation process?
3 What are the steps in the negotiation process? What should international negotiators consider at each step?
4 Discuss background factors in the framework for international business negotiations. How would these factors be in an EM setting?

NINE Negotiations and Building Relationships in Emerging Markets

Negotiations in Emerging Markets

Culture and the business environment affect each aspect of the negotiation process. Even within a given market there are differences which can influence negotiations. Despite major differences between EMs, there are some common traits which firms need to consider within the process. Table 9.1 shows how various aspects of culture can affect the negotiation steps in a number of regions.

Negotiation outcomes are assessed differently depending on the collectivist or individualist values within the culture. For instance, in China or Indonesia, group decision making is the norm and decisions are made through a process of building consensus. Pakistan, Peru, Mexico, the Philippines and Turkey also emphasize reaching a group consensus in their decision-making processes (Moore and Woodrow, 2010). In collective cultures, indirect confrontation can be a better route to resolving conflicts, as such cultures often emphasize social harmony. Harmony can be damaged by conflict, and direct confrontation can disturb harmony by leading to aggressive communications and implications of blame. With indirect confrontation, negotiators can avoid blaming and disrespecting the other side while resolving issues (Brett and Gelfand, 2005). Instead of a direct confrontation, negotiators can seek help from third parties who have relationships with both sides in order to overcome

Table 9.1 Regional differences in the negotiation process

	Asia	Sub-Saharan Africa	Latin America	East Europe	ME and North Africa
Pace of negotiations	Slow	Moderate	Slow	Slow	Moderate
Negotiation strategy					
Opening offer	Moderate to high initial demands	High initial demands	Moderate initial demands	High initial demands	High initial demands
Presentation of issues	Group of issues may be presented	One at a time	One at a time	Group of issues may be presented	One at a time
Presentations	Fairly formal	Informal	Informal	Fairly formal	Informal
Dealing with differences	Polite: quiet when right	Direct	Argumentative, passionate	Argumentative	Usually passionate
Concessions	Slow	Slow	Slow	Slow	Slow
Emphasis on personal relationships	High	High	High	Very low	High
Emotional aspects					
Sensitivity	Valued	Moderate	Valued	Not highly valued	Valued
Degree of emotions	Usually not visible	Moderate	Passionate	Moderate	Passionate
Decision making					
Overall method	Group consensus	Group consensus	Impulsive, spontaneous	Somewhat impulsive	Group consensus
Emphasize	Logic	Concepts	Concepts	Logic	Consensus
Emphasis on group/team	High: decisions from middle- and lower-level groups	Low: decisions from top level	Low: decisions from top level	Moderate: decisions from top level	Low: decisions from top level

(Continued)

Table 9.1 (Continued)

	Asia	Sub-Saharan Africa	Latin America	East Europe	ME and North Africa
Emphasis on face saving	Extreme	Extreme	Extreme	Fairly high	Extreme
Influence of special interests on decision makers	Openly influenced	Expected, condoned	Expected, condoned	Usually not condoned	Expected, condoned
Contractual and administrative factors					
Need for an agent	Average	High	Average	Average	High
Degree of contract specificity	Moderate	Moderate	Moderate	Moderate	Low
Degree of paperwork/ bureaucracy	Moderate	Moderate	Moderate	High	Moderate
Need for an agenda	Moderate	Low	Low	Moderate	Low

Source: Acuff, 2008.

cultural gaps or express their concerns privately. They need to be patient and focus on expressing the benefits of the relationship throughout the negotiation process and handle any disputes progressively. Cultures emphasizing harmony will often prioritize 'saving face' and preserving everyone's honour. To this effect, negotiators should refrain from openly criticizing and disagreeing with the other side throughout the business relationship (Katz, 2006).

A major difference between many EMs and Western cultures is the emphasis on hierarchy. In most cases, EMs tend to be more hierarchical and bureaucratic. In terms of Hofstede's cultural dimensions, this can be interpreted as having higher power–distance scores. Decision making in hierarchical structures is often by top management and subordinates will need to consult with multiple authorities throughout the negotiation process. In bureaucratic societies, such as Russia or India, continuous exchanges and approvals are often needed to reach decisions. In contrast, in individualistic societies, decisions are made by autonomous individuals or an autonomous group, so gaining consensus through the hierarchy or gaining the approval of the sole decision makers at the top is not necessary (Moore and Woodrow, 2010). When faced with hierarchical structures, negotiators need to consider the process of reaching consensus through the levels of the hierarchy or obtaining approval from external influences. Foreign negotiators need to account for the time necessary for the approval process and also consider meeting the needs of each stakeholder by providing comprehensive information. Another challenge is identifying decision makers and contacting them through the negotiation process, or trying to reach a mutual agreement even before negotiations start. In hierarchical societies, negotiators also need to consider the necessity of involving senior executives in their organization, at least in the initial stages of the negotiation process in order to show respect and commitment (Katz, 2006).

A culture's approach to time influences the negotiation process. Many EMs have a polychromic perception of time, thereby schedules may not be as rigid as in Western nations. However, foreign negotiators need to take into account that they are expected to be on time for meetings and schedule their meeting ahead of time in these markets. Still, due to different perceptions of time, the meeting may not start or end on time, or follow an itinerary. Another aspect of a polychromic perception of time which influences the process is the negotiation style. Cultures with a polychromic perception do not single out and discuss selected topics in order, rather issues are discussed simultaneously during the meeting (Morrison and Conaway, 2006).

The business environment in EMs is strongly affected by relationships (Constanza, 2009; Black and Morrison, 2010). In parallel, foreign firms trying to do business in these markets need to concentrate on building relationships which may translate into a longer-term commit-ment, as building relations takes time and requires frequent communication with prospective business partners (UKTI, 2011b; US Commerce, 2011a). Negotiators will then need to account for the time and effort required to build a relationship and gain trust. To this effect, seeking the help of outside contacts who can make the necessary introductions to initiate relationships may be helpful. In most EMs, changing members of the team during the negotiation process may be damaging where relationships are concerned (Katz, 2006).

Negotiating in BRICs

Brazil

In negotiations, Brazil is typically a price-driven market. Negotiators consider price and price discounts to be crucial, although awareness of quality and after-sales service is increasing. For consumer products, branding and advertising are extremely important. Foreign firms are thus advised to establish their corporate identities in the market before coming to the negotiation table. Trade fairs are one way of building a corporate image.

Similar to many EMs, Brazil has a business culture based on relationships. Thus, companies which do business in the country need to build relations and invest time in this area (Hadjikhani et al., 2008). Due to the emphasis on relations, firms need to try to maintain the same team throughout the negotiations. Trust is very important in the business environment. Obtaining references from people or firms known to the Brazilian counterparts, using local agents and lawyers to access local companies, as well as focusing on relations throughout the negotiation process in meetings and in social interactions, can be helpful in gaining trust (globalEDGE, 2011). Though most Brazilian businesspeople are indirect at first, they prefer direct communication once a certain relationship and trust have been established (Katz, 2006).

In negotiating with Brazilian counterparts, being passionate and enthusiastic is advisable. As Brazilians like to bargain, foreigners should also prepare for a long negotiation process where counterparts do not give concessions easily (Acuff, 2008). Brazilian negotiators can be tough and sometimes aggressive. Negotiators need to be careful in leaving room for concessions and focus on the relationship throughout the process. Subjective feelings can also influence the decisions made by Brazilian negotiators (Morrison and Conaway, 2006).

In Brazil, people in large cities will generally have some international experience and be quite open-minded, however populations in more rural areas and older generations are often conservative and will expect foreign counterparts to follow their process (Katz, 2006). In negotiating with the government, it is often advisable to work with locals who may help with the bureaucracy (Acuff, 2008). Engaging foreign lawyers may cause resentment, so hiring local lawyers to help with contract issues may be necessary (Morrison and Conaway, 2006).

Russia

In Russia, ensuring that the firm deals with decision makers in the negotiation process is important due to the hierarchy entrenched in the business culture (globalEDGE, 2011). In most cases, Russian parties will expect the presence of senior management in negotiations. Foreign firms also need to consider that the business environment is affected by external parties such as the authorities and bureaucrats who can influence negotiations (Katz, 2006). They should account for the delays due to bureaucratic hurdles and tactics due to the presence of external influences. In most cases, Russian negotiators will need to obtain confirmation from HQ frequently during the negotiation process. Foreign firms will also need to be prepared to defend their position to multiple stakeholders (Acuff, 2008).

Russian negotiators will focus on obtaining information in order to gain power over their counterparts, and in parallel they are usually not willing to give out information in order to preserve an upper hand. Reluctance in giving information is also due to the bureaucratic nature of organizations and the difficulties associated with accessing information. As Russia is regarded as a high context culture, Russian negotiators will often communicate indirectly and focus on general information as opposed to being specific. Specific aspects are often left to the final stages of the process. Often, negotiators from other cultures try to gauge the views of the Russian negotiator through their reactions to different proposals (Moore and Woodrow, 2010).

Russian firms will look for detailed plans in which the technical aspects related to a deal are clearly presented and explained. During the process, they will try to understand the exact nature of the deal, therefore involving technical personnel may be helpful (Acuff, 2008). Similarly, providing and supporting arguments with facts and technical details can be a sound strategy, especially considering the Russian negotiator's need to gain approval from multiple stakeholders (Morrison and Conaway, 2006).

Russian negotiators will often try to obtain a superior position by defining the situation in favourable terms and trying to establish parameters to guide the process. Negotiators from other cultures will need to be careful in preserving their own stance and avoiding any actions which may be interpreted as a weakness. Russian negotiators may present aggressive arguments and push their position throughout long discussions to maintain control over the relationship. Along the way, they will try to assess their counterparts' commitment, as well as their weaknesses and strengths. They may try to stall the process to weaken opponents' positions and obtain concessions (Moore and Woodrow, 2010). Russian negotiators will often avoid making concessions as these can be regarded as a sign of weakness. The process for them can be aggressive and confrontational. If disputes or conflicts arise, it is advisable to allow some time before attempting to reach a resolution. Making a different proposal, presenting supporting information, and focusing on technical details can be helpful in convincing Russian negotiators (Katz, 2006).

Russian law changes frequently and may sometimes be open to interpretation. Hence, even local Russian firms may not have a full grasp of the legal perspectives (Morrison and Conaway, 2006). Consulting with specialists on Russian law may be helpful throughout negotiations as a result (globalEDGE, 2011).

India

The autocratic nature of Indian institutions influences the negotiation process in several ways. Decisions are made at the top level, thus foreigners need to focus on meeting those in top management. Local agents with connections may be helpful in facilitating such contacts. This autocracy also means the negotiation team has a consistent need to obtain confirmation from superiors, or involves multiple negotiations through which foreign must firms must move through the ranks of the Indian organization (Acuff, 2008). High levels of bureaucracy in India can drag out the negotiation process over a long period, especially in transactions with the government (US Commerce, 2011b). Foreign firms must respect the hierarchical nature of the business environment (Forsans and Nelson, 2008). In parallel, foreign negotiating teams must also be aware that Indians do not appreciate disagreements with or criticism of superior executives (Katz, 2006).

Building trust and gaining respect are very important at the onset of negotiations in India. The time necessary to build relations is generally shorter when compared to other Asian countries, as Indian negotiators prefer to begin talks fairly quickly. Relations are often cultivated throughout the business proceedings. Indian negotiators will often focus on an ordered progression within the process and expect information which includes data and facts. Foreign negotiators in India need to focus on being clear and direct and refrain from displays of extreme emotion and direct confrontation. They also need to be prepared for a competitive negotiation process, in which displaying a predictable and solid approach while offering low-risk solutions may be helpful (Moore and Woodrow, 2010). Friendliness and a willingness to compromise can prove effective in resolving disputes (Katz, 2006).

A foreign firm's ability to provide technical support and training can be critical in the Indian partner's decision-making process (Morrison and Conaway, 2006). It is often advisable to give detailed presentations beforehand (globalEDGE, 2011).

Negotiators are expected to be flexible in India and a rigid position may not be perceived favourably (globalEDGE, 2011). Prices may move by over 40% in negotiations as Indians are often hard bargainers. Hence, firms will need to leave room for concessions and ask for reciprocation (Katz, 2006).

China

Negotiating in China begins with contact with the Chinese authorities. A Western firm must make presentations for a number of groups. In these sessions, the firm must convince the Chinese that it has the technology they need. The process of negotiation can be divided into the following stages (Ghauri and Fang, 2001):

1 *Lobbying:* the firm must understand the objectives of the Chinese. Calculations must be made as to what the firm might gain or lose in tangible and intangible terms. Negotiators should try to identify the decision makers on the other side and develop relationships with them. The Western firm should also find out who the competitors are and convince the Chinese side of the firm's advantages over its competitors. Presentation materials should be available in ample copies and distributed in English and in Chinese. The Western negotiators should build up trust both in the products that are the subject of trade and in the individuals who are negotiating.
2 *Offer:* after establishing the objectives and consequences of the deal, the firm should make an offer outlining its general principles, technology, equipment and price, and the terms and conditions of the deal. At this stage, it is very useful for a Western firm to invite the Chinese team to their home country to show them their manufacturing plant

and technical capabilities. This invitation will help the firm gain an edge over its competitors and build trust.

3 *Formal negotiations:* due to increasing decentralization, it is possible for Western firms to negotiate directly with Chinese firms and organizations. The Chinese will use different tactics to get the most out of their counterparts, such as flattery, embarrassment, and the use of historical facts. They will also create a more competitive environment by revealing selective information on competing offers. The Chinese want the best and latest technology. The firm should be specific about patents and copyrights. In joint ventures, the contributions of each partner should be very clearly specified.

4 *Implementation:* experience shows that the real problems start following formal negotiations. The Chinese normally like to agree on principles and broad terms in formal negotiations and leave the details for the implementation stage.

While Westerners view communication as an exchange of information which stops when the deal is completed, Eastern cultures, especially in China, view communication as a process leading to a long-term relationship (Thomas and Chen, 2003). As a result, Chinese culture focuses on the context as opposed to the direct information provided verbally, which is in contrast to the Western approach. Box 9.1 shows an example of how communication patterns may differ between Western and Chinese culture.

Box 9.1 The Chinese 'Yes No'

The emphasis on building Guanxi, promoting group harmony, and maintaining face explains the reluctance of the Chinese to say no. The meaning and use of the word 'no' represents a fundamental difference between Chinese and Western communication practices. Westerners interpret and use no literally, as an indication that something will not happen, that a request will be denied, or that the issue should not be pursued further. From the Western point of view, no usually means no – end of story. This meaning presents certain challenges in the Chinese context. While the Western use of no in either business or cultural situations usually pertains to a separate transaction or demand, the Chinese have difficulty in translating the Western nuance of the word's meaning into their own way of communicating because they do not readily split business or cultural exchanges into finite parts or disconnected concerns. The Chinese are much more interested in communication as a fluid element that supports the ongoing formation and refinement of a relationship. This means that the Chinese are reluctant to use the word at all, because it signals that the overall relationship, rather than simply one request or dealing, may be in jeopardy.

The Chinese communicate no through a range of phrases and supporting facial expressions, gestures, silence, and deferral of the issue at hand. Essentially, the goal of a Chinese speaker is to remain polite and save face for everyone involved in the discussion. This means that rather than saying no outright, a person may hesitate when responding to a specific request, couch a reply in vague terms such as 'perhaps', or change the subject completely. The Chinese speaker expects his or her counterpart to pick up on these subtleties and reach an understanding accordingly by neither engaging in confrontation nor pursuing the issue further. From the Western point of view, this indirectness can be interpreted, at worst, as indicative of secrecy or dishonesty, and at best, as showing disinterest or incompetence. The simple word 'no' carries the potential, therefore, for long, complicated misunderstandings between Chinese and Western business associates.

Source: Thomas and Chen, 2003.

Guanxi is an effective force in influencing negotiations in China and social capital becomes important within the process. Guanxi is also strengthened by the system of reciprocity and a favour is never forgotten but returned in the long run (Graham and Lam, 2003). Building trust is essential in business relations and one route to accomplish this is by using an intermediary and thereby using Guanxi in a way. In order to build trust and loyalty, informing the counterpart of the firm's intentions beforehand can be a helpful strategy, signalling openness and goodwill. Firms may also focus on providing detailed material and presentations in order to reduce trust issues (Ghauri and Usunier, 2003). Negotiators need to focus on building personal relations which may in many instances lead to reciprocal expectations. However, they must be careful about the receipt of offers which may mean they have to provide concessions in the future in order to reciprocate (Moore and Woodrow, 2010).

Intermediaries can help in interpreting the Chinese representatives' approach, as Chinese culture is not very confrontational and natives can understand the mood and approach of the other side better than foreigners. Moreover, an intermediary can also obtain a more direct response from the other side and settle differences, as it is easier to express one's position to the intermediary than the other side (Graham and Lam, 2003).

The Chinese often view business relations as a long-term commitment, and thereby negotiations can cover a lengthy period during which foreigners may find focusing on long-term benefits, their commitment, and the intention of cooperation beneficial. Bureaucracy, the requirement to gain approval of all the members of the group, and the need to further understand the foreign firm may be other factors which prolong the negotiation process (Acuff, 2008).

Negotiating in Asia

Asia's cultures are as diverse as they are interrelated, and this can make negotiating there a difficult process. While Westerners prefer dividing the negotiation process into separate parts and moving along the process step by step, Asians are used to negotiating in an holistic manner. Generally, they do not discuss issues in a particular order in negotiation meetings and prefer to go over multiple issues at once and agree on concessions at the end of the discussion. This is due to the Asian focus on building long-term relationships and the relative unimportance of a single issue within this context.

Most Asian countries can be described as consensus cultures. Negotiations will often involve a long process where different stakeholders within the firm, as well as external stakeholders, need to reach an agreement. As consensus cultures often focus on relationships in business, the negotiation process in Asia is affected by the Asian team's focus on forming a relationship with the other side as a prerequisite of doing business with them. The negotiation process with many Asian companies can be accelerated by a friendly approach and the timely provision of information and explanation to each unit when necessary. In many cases, interacting with stakeholders before the negotiation process and addressing their concerns before they reach an internal consensus can prove effective approach (Sebenius, 2002).

In many Asian cultures, it may be helpful to engage local intermediaries in contacting local firms. Intermediaries can leverage relationships, help overcome cultural and communication gaps, and even provide access to senior management (Katz, 2006). In Asia, it is essential to respect social traditions, focus on excessive politeness, show commitment, and avoid direct confrontation. Foreigners need to be considerate of values such as modesty and humility. Otherwise, they may be perceived as rude, disrespectful, untrustworthy, or aggressive (Morrison and Conaway, 2006).

Thailand

During the negotiation process in Thailand, firms need to focus on cooperation and friendship, and display a level of humility to avoid being perceived as disrespectful (Acuff, 2008). Similar to many EMs, local businesses in Thailand are accustomed to local practices which rely on relationships in doing business (US Commerce, 2011d). In Thailand, negotiators must be careful to be polite and respectful. Bringing up regional politics, talking about the rulers or issues of the country, and comparing Thailand with Western nations may be perceived as being rude (Acuff, 2008). Building trust is vital in negotiations and the due diligence process also gains significance here (US Commerce, 2011d).

Thai negotiators will often avoid direct confrontation. They can sometimes focus on small details as problems in order not to offend their counterparts. Decision making is affected by outside influences such as government authorities, the military, and bureaucrats (Katz, 2006). Hence, the negotiation process may take time as Thai negotiators will often consult different stakeholders before making decisions (globalEDGE, 2011).

Malaysia

In Malaysia, building trust and focusing on building relations is key. The communication style of the Malays is generally indirect, thus foreigners need to be mindful of direct comments which may be insulting and should not expect a clear statement of a Malay firm's position on a given issue. Foreigners should also focus on providing clear and extensive information as Malays are generally detail-oriented and may wish to engage in lengthy discussions regarding each aspect of the proposal (Acuff, 2008). Meetings in Malaysia are also rather formal (globalEDGE, 2011).

It is not advisable to be passionate and too animated during negotiations. Rather, a gentle approach is expected (globalEDGE, 2011). Politeness and courtesy are very important in Malaysia. Politeness may hinder Malaysian negotiators from openly disagreeing with the proposals and lead to a more indirect communication process. In parallel, foreign firms trying to do business in Malaysia should avoid direct confrontation (Morrison and Conaway, 2006).

Unlike in the West, silence is not uncomfortable in Malaysian culture. Thus, during negotiations, there may be pauses during which Malaysian counterparts will contemplate the situation (Morrison and Conaway, 2006).

Indonesia

Bargaining is a part of the daily lives of Indonesians, thus foreign firms will need to act professionally and avoid giving concessions too soon, in order to gain respect and prevent being perceived as naive. Within the negotiation process, managers of relevant departments can be included to negotiate their own terms. In dealing with the government, working with a local agent may be helpful in sorting through the bureaucracy (Acuff, 2008).

Indonesian negotiators usually start by providing general information and move on to more specific discussions throughout the negotiation process. Indirect communication patterns and their general approach may often leave the other party with a need to deduce the answers to their questions. As the culture emphasizes harmony, respectful interaction and non-confrontational approaches are preferred. Foreign negotiators faced with Indonesian counterparts need to focus on building a positive environment and avoid negative and coercive approaches. Saving face is very important, thus private discussions in dealing with issues may be helpful. Intermediaries may also be helpful in avoiding direct confrontation and delivering messages without leading to visible conflict (Morrison and Conaway, 2006).

Informal discussions are vital throughout the negotiation process, as the parties can indirectly discuss solutions to issues and try to find a favourable one (Moore and Woodrow, 2010). Negotiators need to be careful to control emotions and maintain composure during the process as losing face is a very important concept within the culture. Expressing extreme emotions or anger may lead to losing face and the negotiator may be perceived as untrustworthy (globalEDGE, 2011).

Building relations based on trust and respect is essential. As such, a friendly approach and a commitment to visit the country and spend time on the process is necessary (globalEDGE, 2011). Though Indonesian negotiators are often indirect, they are hard bargainers. And while they are competitive, they also focus on building long-term relations and benefits for both parties. It is often advisable to be patient, maintain a calm approach, and emphasize points which both parties agree on throughout the bargaining process (Katz, 2006).

Indonesian culture focuses on hierarchies. Therefore using information obtained from experts and high-level executives can be advantageous during the negotiation process. Indonesians value status and presence, and the support of senior executives can also be helpful (Moore and Woodrow, 2010). Meetings are formal and showing respect for the hierarchy within the negotiating team is essential (globalEDGE, 2011).

Pakistan

Pakistan has a group-oriented culture and building relations is a crucial aspect in doing business. As such, a long-term commitment is necessary. Relations are often viewed as between people and not firms. Hence, a foreign firm will often not be trusted by the Pakistani partner based on an individual relation. Local intermediaries or mutual contacts can be helpful in the initial stages in overcoming cultural gaps and establishing relationships. In Pakistan, negotiations by individuals as opposed to teams may be preferable (Katz, 2006).

Punctuality is also important as locals are aware of Western habits of timeliness. Negotiations may be prolonged as Pakistanis will continually go over their decisions, be slow to make concessions, and may take extreme views on some of the issues (Acuff, 2008). The process can take time, especially if a firm is dealing with the government. The government is a big player and firms will need to consider the various bureaucratic procedures of each public or semi-public entity they are dealing with (Morrison and Conaway, 2006). During the negotiation process, pressuring counterparts is often not effective as Pakistani negotiators may perceive this behaviour as an unwillingness to commit to long-term relations (Katz, 2006).

The Philippines

Building relations is very important in doing business in the Philippines. Sincerity and sensitivity are crucial in building relations and successfully negotiating with Filipinos. Radical proposals or innovations may not be well received and be perceived as suspicious, thus foreign firms can be more successful by focusing on practical and conservative proposals (Acuff, 2008). In the case of conflict, it is advisable to be patient and friendly (Katz, 2006).

In negotiating in the Philippines, it is necessary to create teams in which the role of each member is specified, and to ensure the continuity of the team as changing members in the process may hurt relations (Katz, 2006). It is often considered rude to leave after meetings and the foreign team is expected to stay a while longer and chat (globalEDGE, 2011).

It may be difficult to meet decision makers without an introduction from mutual contacts. To this effect, many firms will use representatives who can reach senior executives. Engaging a mutual friend or business partner for an introduction before negotiations start can be helpful (globalEDGE, 2011). Otherwise, foreign executives are expected to build relationships with different levels of management formally and socially before meeting senior executives (Morrison and Conaway, 2006). Decisions will be made by the upper management team, however subordinates can affect decisions considerably. Seating arrangements will usually reflect the hierarchy of members (globalEDGE, 2011). When compared to other

EMs, Filipinos are more punctual. However, the pace of negotiations is often slower than with Western nations (Morrison and Conaway, 2006).

Negotiating in Latin America

Cultural expectations in Latin America can be quite diverse. However, some similarities and generalities can be drawn between many Latin American countries. General attitudes toward time, the pace of negotiation, decision making, and the emotional aspects of business relationships are often held in common. In Latin American countries, foreign negotiators especially need to focus on the importance of dignity and be careful in choosing their words and actions as these may easily be interpreted as insults. Most countries within the region have populations of different social standing which leads to a complicated form of diplomacy and etiquette. Successful business outcomes and negotiations are highly dependent on building relations. During the negotiation process, Latin American parties may start with moderate initial demands, however they can be rather slow in giving concessions and display argumentative and emotional behaviour (Acuff, 2008).

Mexico

Mexican culture places a high value on status. Negotiators need to be aware of how they approach their Mexican counterparts and take their rank into consideration. Within the decision-making process, members with similar ranks are expected to work together. Top managers are often decision makers and the process can be autocratic. It is important to have a senior member attend the initial meetings (Katz, 2006).

Building relations, winning favours, and cultivating relationships are vital for doing business successfully in Mexico (globalEDGE, 2011). Initially, Mexican businesspeople may seem indirect and suspicious. However, firms can initiate long-term relations based on trust and reliability as they commit time and effort in building relationships. In the end, personal relationships can be more effective than the attributes of the firms that the foreign entrants represent (Morrison and Conaway, 2006). It is often a good idea to focus on the achievements of the country and the country's culture, as most Mexicans are very nationalistic. Foreigners also need to provide detailed presentations and information to build trust (Acuff, 2008). The risk-averse nature of the culture may prevent Mexican negotiators from giving sensitive information initially, which they may disclose later on depending on the level of trust gained (Moore and Woodrow, 2010).

Though Mexicans prefer to avoid conflict they are also hard bargainers, which may lead to long and inconclusive discussions. Mexican negotiators are often reluctant to give concessions, and pushing for these directly can be misinterpreted and insulting (Katz, 2006). In order to preserve a productive business environment, foreign negotiators need to refrain from criticism and direct confrontation which may lead to a loss of face. Focusing on mutually beneficial solutions may be helpful in the process (Moore and Woodrow, 2010).

Peru

Though negotiations in Peru are often competitive, the culture is collectivist and focuses on building relationships. Firms and negotiators in rural areas are more cautions and indirect when compared to urban regions (globalEDGE, 2011). Negotiators prefer a straightforward style, however they may sometimes use pressure techniques in order to reach agreements (Katz, 2006). During the process, negotiators may also focus on relatively unimportant issues and spend a great deal of time discussing data. In parallel, it is often advisable to provide a variety of materials in presentations and be prepared to discuss the topics extensively (Morrison and Conaway, 2006). The bargaining process may be long and negotiators may often find it difficult to change their position and make compromises.

Chile

In Chile, society is formal and negotiators should be careful in maintaining a professional attitude and engage the help of upper-level executives at the preliminary stages. The business culture is hierarchical and negotiators need to make sure that they show respect to the senior executives of Chilean firms and take their concerns seriously (globalEDGE, 2011). Following the initial meeting, senior executives will not be expected to attend, however Chilean negotiators will expect the foreign firm's team to be composed of relatively senior executives with a thorough knowledge of the firm (Katz, 2006).

Commitment is important in business relations. A willingness to provide training or continued services can be an effective strategy in showing a firm's interest and commitment to Chilean partners (Morrison and Conaway, 2006).

Chilean negotiators tend to be straightforward and expect similar approaches. They also do not like extensive bargaining processes. Within negotiations, aggressiveness and open confrontation can be harmful. Though Chilean negotiators do not like to be rushed, the process is often faster when compared to other Latin American countries (Katz, 2006).

Negotiating in Africa

Africa is a large continent with a diverse population, thereby it is difficult to generalize the attitude toward negotiations. However, most Africans will emphasize building relations based on trust and sincerity between the parties at the onset of negotiations, as such initial meetings will centre on informal discussions. Parallel to the value placed on respect, saving face is generally a concern. Foreign negotiators will need to try to get to know their counterparts personally and also try to avoid direct conflict, focusing on preserving respect and decorum (Moore and Woodrow, 2010). In Africa, punctuality is more important than in other EMs. Due to their ethnic origins, tribal associations may be emphasized in many cases. The approval of all group members may also be necessary in reaching agreements. Building relations through formality and respect is a key aspect of negotiations in Africa (Acuff, 2008).

South Africa

When negotiating with South African counterparts, Western firms should feel quite comfortable. The infrastructure and business environment are quite compatible with the Western world. Printed material aimed at the non-white population is mostly in the English language. South Africa is not a typical African country. A well-developed industrial and trade infrastructure has influenced the mentality of its people. The managers and executives with whom Western firms transact are often well-educated and experienced negotiators. In South Africa, negotiation patterns may be similar to the UK if business dealings are with people of British descent. However, before entering into negotiation, firms will still need to establish connections and make sure that they can reach the top level of the organization where the decisions are made (Acuff, 2008).

In order to protect know-how and intellectual property, firms entering into partnerships in South Africa will need to focus on due diligence prior to negotiations, and emphasize the incentives in honouring contracts during the process. In fact, in South Africa, the basis of sound negotiations is often a due diligence process (US Commerce, 2011c).

Meetings are generally social and friendly (globalEDGE, 2011) and negotiators are often straightforward (Katz, 2006). Foreign negotiators will have to consider concessions and prepare alternative options. Concessions are often reciprocated. Focusing on the mutual benefits for both parties and win–win strategies is important in South Africa.

The pace of negotiations will vary between different types of firms. Traditional firms may be slow while modern firms will be decisive. Often, the process of gathering information and the discussion of details will take time before the bargaining stage can begin (Katz, 2006).

Egypt

Relations are crucial in Egypt, thereby negotiations will often involve social conversations on general issues and information will be shared gradually (Moore and Woodrow, 2010). The pace of business and hence the pace of negotiations will be slow (globalEDGE, 2011). Trying to rush things may prove counterproductive for foreign parties (Morrison and Conaway, 2006).

Firms engaging in negotiations in Egypt need to account for the time necessary to establish relations and trust, and be ready for long arguments related to the Egyptian party's position (Moore and Woodrow, 2010). Egyptians are often hard bargainers, and negotiators will need to leave room for concessions. Due to the focus on building long-term relations, foreign firms can be more successful by emphasizing the long-term benefits of the partnership during the negotiation process (Katz, 2006). Egyptian negotiators will often start the process from an extreme position which is the initial step in working towards an acceptable solution. The reason for this approach is generally to display the negotiator's authority and strength. Despite starting with an extreme initial position, Egyptian negotiators are often committed to reaching agreements and will keep on advocating their position further, even when the other side is negative, which may result in extended discussions. In such cases, intermediaries or mediators could help parties to show gestures of generosity, agree on general principles, and reach satisfactory conclusions (Moore and Woodrow, 2010).

Negotiating in Turkey

Many businesses in Turkey are controlled by business groups or families. Hence, firms will need to identify the relevant stakeholders and their influence before initiating negotiations (Katz, 2006). Decision making can be slow due to the need to meet the less senior members of a family or firm first and then move on to more senior managers after gaining their approval (globalEDGE, 2011).

In dealing with Turkish businesspeople, firms need to ensure that they present clear proposals demonstrating mutual benefits (globalEDGE, 2011). Building relationships is very important for doing business. In fact, negotiation outcomes are often affected by the level of trust that the foreign negotiators have managed to generate (Morrison and Conaway, 2006). In Turkey, written exchanges regarding the outline of meetings can be useful. The final contracts will often be detailed, however maintaining relationships is necessary to ensure commitment to the contract (Katz, 2006).

Developing and Managing Relationships in EMs

In entering an EM and in negotiating with counterparts within the market, foreigners need to build relations with the right actors and cultivate such relations. In this respect, many of the developed nations differ from EMs in their emphasis on relations in doing business. Managers are often aware of the importance of establishing, developing, and nurturing productive business relationships. But when applying these aspects to doing business in EMs, they may not realize the extent to which cultural differences can affect their ability to manage relationships (Ghauri, 1999). Not all business relationships are of equal importance, or will create the same impact on the focal relationship between a customer and a supplier. Figure 9.1 describes a few key business relationships that may have more than a marginal impact on buyers and sellers.

In international settings, it is extremely important to manage business relationships with cross-cultural differences in mind. Foreign entrants in EMs should try to master the ability to communicate well, both verbally and nonverbally; should be capable and willing to take action with insufficient, unreliable, and often conflicting information; should inspire trust and confidence; and should be able to view problem solving as a social process involving consensus and interpersonal influence rather than correct answers (Ghauri and Usunier, 2003). Adjusting to a foreign country depends on understanding the behaviour of foreigners, which in turn is predicated on being nonjudgemental (Ones and Viswesvaran, 1999). A few predictors for the success of a Western manager operating in an EM can be relational characteristics such as tolerance for ambiguity, behavioural flexibility, a nonjudgemental attitude, interpersonal skills, cultural empathy and enthusiasm or motivational characteristics, such as an interest in overseas experience, an interest in the specific host country's culture, and a willingness to acquire new patterns of behaviour and attitudes (Franke and Nicholson, 2002).

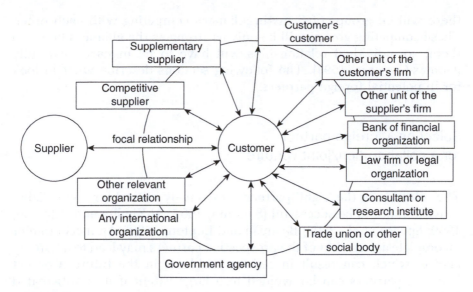

Figure 9.1   Facilitative relationships in emerging markets

Selecting Partners and Distributors in EMs

The formation of global business alliances and partnerships has been increasing over the last two decades. Sheth and Parvatiyar (1992) identified purpose and parties as two dimensions in describing the formation of alliances. Each isomorphically represents uncertainty and trust, respectively. Based on this dichotomy of purpose and parties, a typology of business alliances has been created:

- *Cartel:* if a business alliance is formed for operations efficiency among competitors, it is called a cartel.
- *Cooperative:* if a business alliance is formed among noncompetitors (suppliers, customers and noncompetitive businesses), it is called a cooperative.
- *Competitive:* if a business alliance is formed for a strategic purpose among competitors, it is called a competitive alliance.
- *Collaborative:* if a business alliance is formed among noncompetitors for a strategic purpose, it is called a collaborative alliance.

A major trend in management is to form virtual organizations, made up of various firms performing activities related to their core competencies, interacting together to gain the maximum benefits of business opportunities that will arise in a very short timeframe. In fact, in the future, there will be groups of firms in alliances competing with each other. These competing groups will be only as strong as the alliances between them, so individual relationships will have to be managed carefully (Gomes-Casseres, 1994). The following sections describe what to look for in potential foreign partners.

Selecting a foreign partner for a collaboration/joint venture

The selection of the 'right' partner is extremely critical for any collaborative venture to be successful (Simonin, 1997; Al-Khalifa and Peterson, 1999; Spence et al., 2008; Beamish and Lupton, 2009). An inaccurate or incomplete assessment of the prospective partners may lead to a 'wrong' choice, which can result in serious problems in the future. Conflict between partners can be avoided to a large extent if it is anticipated before the venture is established. As a minimum, the partners should be able to provide complementary capabilities that in both the short and long term will be necessary to enable the venture to be competitive (Langfield-Smith, 2008; Culpan, 2009). The partner chosen for the venture can influence the overall mix of available skills and resources, the operating policies and procedures, and the viability of the venture. Hence, even if one or a few viable partner prospects exist, screening these firms for suitability as collaborative venture partners is still a critical task (Duisters et al., 2011).

Partner-related criteria

These criteria refer to the qualifications of the partner, both tangible and intangible, that are not specific to the type of operation but will affect the risk(s) faced. More specifically, they include what we might call the 'personality traits' of the partner, such as their business philosophy, reliability, motivation, commitment, intellectual property protection approach, and some general characteristics, such as experience, reputation, and political connections.

- *Partner characteristics:* several background characteristics of a prospective partner are perceived by managers as key factors for evaluating the potential contribution of that partner to the venture (Roy and Oliver, 2009). Examples of these characteristics include reputation, experience, complementariness of resources to the venture, and political connections. In EMs, the business environment is reliant on relationships. Thus, in selecting a partner, foreign firms will need to assess that prospective partner's networks. To this effect, the local partner's relationships with governments, bureaucrats, authorities and other interest groups are very important (Meyer et al., 2009).

- *Property rights protection:* technological know-how or other intellectual properties may constitute a key competitive advantage. Hence, firms with valuable intellectual property that enter cooperative ventures face a dissemination risk. This refers to the risk that a firm's specific advantages in intellectual property will be expropriated or exploited by the venture partner(s). Thus, the partner's approach to and mechanisms of enforcement for property rights protection are particularly important if one brings valuable intellectual property into the venture.

- *Compatibility of business philosophies:* one of the main reasons for failures in collaborative ventures is disagreements over operating strategies, policies, and methods (Chen et al., 2008). Such conflicts can be resolved to the extent that the business philosophies of the partners are compatible. The venture will be doomed to fail unless the partners have compatible business philosophies (Ozorhon et al., 2008).

- *Commitment:* a partner's commitment to the venture is crucial for its viability and success (Ramachandran et al., 2011). The more committed partners are, the more quality time and resources they are likely to put into the venture. Committed partners will make more of an effort and try harder to make the venture a success.

- *Motivation:* the major benefits of entering international collaborative ventures are risk sharing, complementary resources, market access, economies of scale, and competitive leverage. One or more of these benefits may be a source of the partner's motivation to enter the venture. In international cooperative ventures, a major motivational factor for a firm is to have access to the key resources and skills needed for undertaking business. Ideally, these resources and skills will be complementary to the firm's own resources and skills. Hence, a partner will be more highly motivated if the resources and skills one brings to the venture will be complementary to those of the partner (Deitz et al., 2010).

- *Sharing:* cooperative ventures may result in substantial cost savings and greater efficiency through the sharing of resources, and the concentration of partners' efforts in areas of expertise and scale efficiencies. Potential synergies may be created through sharing manufacturing facilities, technology and other physical assets; marketing synergies may be created through sharing brand names, products, support services, distribution channels, sales forces, and other marketing facilities. Some other key strategic benefits may include market access, risk reduction, blocking competition, and economies of learning.

- *Reliability:* a prospective partner's reliability refers to their focus and capability in undertaking the agreed task. This is a significant variable because it shows how much you can trust and count on the partner (Tatoglu, 2000). One of the questions managers may ask themselves in evaluating a potential partner is: 'Is this partner concerned with obtaining gains only for itself?' If the answer is 'yes', that partner may be inclined not to deal fairly. Partner characteristics such as reasonableness, honesty, and trustworthiness will not generally become evident until you have had some business experience with the partner. Other things being equal, you should choose a firm that you know well from previous positive business dealings to be your partner.

Task-related criteria

Task-related selection criteria refer to those variables, both tangible and intangible, human and nonhuman, that are relevant for the venture's viability in terms of its operational requirements. Hence, these variables are specific to operational resources and skills related to the venture (i.e. financial, marketing, organizational, production and R&D resources, and customer service). In looking at such variables, assessing the complementarity of the resources among the partnering firms becomes critical (Rothaermel and Boeker, 2008). Resource complementarity in acquisitions or alliances enhances performance (Hitt et al., 2002; McCutchen et al., 2007; Lunnan and Haugland, 2008; Schreiner et al., 2009).

Financial resources are important: the current availability and future outlook of the financial resources that the partner can provide to the venture are key considerations (Nielsen, 2003). A partner should have a sound and healthy financial status in order to provide their share of venture's funding. Partners who are not able to provide their share of funding will slow the venture's growth and development, and put additional financial burdens on the other partner(s).

Financial ratios (e.g. profit margin on sales, return on total assets, and return on firm equity) show the relationship for figures found in financial statements. By comparing the potential partner's ratios with those of its principal competitors in the same industry, it is possible to identify the relative strengths of that partner. The analysis of ratios includes an assessment of absolute values and trends. Ratio analysis has its limitations, but if used with care and judgement, it can be helpful.

A credit rating is an overall measure of how well a firm manages its financial resources. You may refer to Dunn & Bradstreet International and the US Department of Commerce World Traders Data Reports (WTDR), which provide ratings for the overall soundness of firms. For example, WTDR gives information such as financial and trade references for specific foreign firms on request, at a nominal cost.

It is vital that any partner for a cooperative venture has a prospective future in terms of growth and profitability (Chen et al., 2008). Any sign that the partner might have financial problems in the future is a warning for any firm that considers working with that partner. If the partner has a healthy outlook for continuous growth and profitability, then most likely it will not have a hard time generating the financial resources necessary for the continuity and success of the cooperative venture.

An organization's leverage vis-à-vis other firms is often enhanced if it possesses superior technology, as well as good R&D and technical resources. These are particularly important if the venture is primarily based on R&D (e.g. joint R&D). Moreover, firms will often expect a potential partner to have a minimum level of R&D and technological resources and capabilities. In cooperative ventures involving technology transfer or sharing, the transfer of technology is a major component of the venture. To identify how easy (or difficult) the transfer of technology will be, an assessment of the level of a partner's technical resources is required. The higher the level of R&D and technical resources, the easier the transfer of technology will be (Chen et al., 2008).

In evaluating the partner's performance in new-product development and process enhancement, it is advisable to check on their record of new-product developments, available facilities, and new-product organization and coordination. The quality of the R&D and technical personnel is far more important than how many of them there are. Verifying the educational qualifications of the scientists (as well as the total number of them) working for the partner, or checking outside evaluations, such as those provided by Dunn & Bradstreet, may be helpful in this regard. Investigating the patents owned by the potential partner may also be helpful.

Market access, along with capabilities in marketing, promotion and sales, and distribution, are viewed as important critical success factors, particularly within the context of a local or regional target market. If your partner's role is to bring key marketing resources to the venture, then a careful assessment is essential. In particular, it is essential to determine their strengths vis-à-vis their competitors.

It is crucial to ascertain whether a potential partner has coverage of and access to key customers and distribution channels in the target market(s). Their relations with master distributors and affiliates in the market are very important to facilitate access to the channels.

Marketing of the products will be done much more efficiently and effectively if a partner has a sound, established, and well-structured marketing organization (US Commerce, 2011a). In evaluating the sales force, the partner's experience in the market and of the products, past performance in the market, reputation among customers, and knowledge of the market and customers are key factors. If the image of the potential partner is well established, and its trademarks and brand names are successful in the target market, this will imply that the partner has been a good marketer of its offerings.

In some collaborative ventures, particularly those involving manufacturing, the production resources (both tangible and intangible) of a prospective partner may be significant when selecting a firm as a partner. For instance, they may provide a good location for plants and fixed assets for the venture or have a highly productive and efficient workforce. The current condition of their production plants and fixed assets must be assessed by you as adequate to produce quality output efficiently. The relevant question you must ask yourself is this: 'How do the production facilities and assets of this potential partner look to a casual observer?' In many instances, the formation of a cooperative venture may be stimulated due to the availability of 'good' production facilities and assets. The more competitive, well maintained and available these facilities and assets are, the more they will represent an opportunity to invest to some at an advantage.

Particularly in the case of manufacturing-related ventures, the characteristics of a partner's production workforce will be an important criterion in assessing their production resources. These characteristics may include factors such as education level, turnover, absenteeism, trainability, and flexibility. Any incentives that the partner is able to secure from the government for local production will be part of its production resources. The more a partner is able to obtain incentives from the government of the country in which the production is going to take place, the more attractive that partner will be to work with.

Organizational resources are another key aspect: the existing managerial skills and resources of a prospective partner may have an impact on the selection of that partner (Fang and Zou, 2009). Some of these managers may become operating managers, directors, or important officers within the collaborative venture. Hence, it is important that the partner has competent, experienced people to assign to the venture, as well as an effectively run organization.

The analysis of a partner's organization provides an overall measure of: (a) its approach to business transactions; (b) its measures of performance; (c) its levels of planning and control; and (d) its management and selection of personnel. In some of these areas, disagreement between the partners can lead to serious difficulties in daily decisions and management of the venture.

The way a partner establishes a course of action can provide information on whether a firm has a compatible approach to managing and conducting business. For example, it may check the reporting system in a partner's organization. It is important that a foreign firm understands the planning and control system in a partner's organization. The more similar the planning and control system is to a firm's own, the easier it will be for that firm to understand it.

Senior personnel turnover refers to the number of times senior employees are replaced in a year. This number suggests the level of employment stability and thus the likelihood of continuing with the goals, objectives, and policies set by senior staff. It also represents an indicator of the firm's overall efficiency. The higher the turnover, the lower the efficiency.

Customer service, including after-sales service, warranties and reverse distribution, is another critical factor, especially for prolonged success in the market. Good customer service will increase the likelihood of repurchases by customers, which are necessary for a continued presence and success in the market. Customer services can become a competitive weapon in certain circumstances and for some industries. If the characteristics of a product or technology require considerable support from a partner, then a good assessment of the level of customer service provided by your partner is vital. The partner must have capable personnel to perform the customer service function, including after-sales service, on request by customers. The amount of geographical market coverage the partner has is a key factor in assessing its customer service. In emerging economies, an assessment of geographical coverage must include the extent of paved roads and the condition of the service fleet.

Selecting a foreign distributor

There are five major dimensions that influence the selection of a foreign distributor (see Figure 9.2): (a) level of commitment; (b) financial and general firm strengths; (c) marketing skills; (d) product-related factors; and (e) facilitating factors. Although the final three factors should be weighted less than the distributor's level of commitment and financial and firm strengths, they are still important because they relate to the distributor's specific marketing capabilities, product, and target market knowledge.

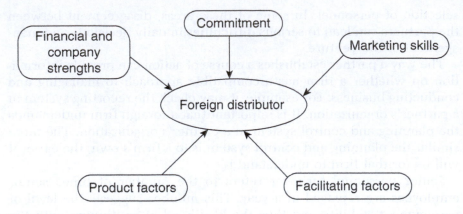

Figure 9.2 Selecting a foreign distributor

Commitment

Commitment is the most crucial factor in the evaluation of a foreign distributor. A highly committed distributor will take your product to heart and will also make it a personal objective to make the sale of your product a success in that particular country (Doney et al., 2007). Firms need to be careful in choosing distributors whose product mix exhibits extreme volatility over time. Considering distributors who have stable product portfolios can be a less risky approach. This stability suggests that the distributor has a long-term commitment to its product lines; that is, it has grown by focusing its efforts on a few product lines at a time. In addition, firms need to look at the sales performance of the distributors and be very careful in cases where a large percentage of sales comes from a single supplier. This often means that the distributor is already committed to the product lines of this supplier and may not give the firm necessary attention.

Although the distributor may be willing to maintain a satisfactory level of inventory, firms should also determine their ability to do so. Firms need to check to see whether the distributor has the warehouse space available to carry the required level of inventory. It is also advisable to check to see whether the distributor has access to contingency space that would enable quick access to additional space when needed.

Firms also need to assess the capability of the distributor to provide them with financial support for advertising and promotional activities (Nevins and Money, 2008). The distributor may provide support for translation, trade fairs, and so on. Some products, because of their characteristics, will be difficult to sell unless the potential buyer has an opportunity to examine them in person. In this instance, trade fairs and shows are most useful for bringing buyers and sellers together. In such cases, firms should ask the distributor for a list of trade fairs in which they have participated, as well as inquire about their plans for the coming year.

If some form of sales and technical training is required for the firm's product, firms will need to choose a distributor who is willing to commit to a joint effort in the training of its sales personnel. If the product is of a technical nature training can be expensive, and it is better to seek a distributor who is willing to share these costs with the firm.

It is important for potential distributors to have a clear understanding of the firm's objectives and expectations from the outset. One of these objectives should be the target sales volume of the distributor for the firm's product. One way to evaluate the level of commitment is to ask the distributor whether minimum sales-level provisions are acceptable in the contract.

Financial strengths and performance

The financial standing of the distributor is the second-most-important criteria. To begin with it shows the distributor's ability to make money as well as be in business. Second, it indicates their ability to perform some marketing functions, such as the extension of credit to customers and risk absorption. Therefore, firms will need to seek distributors who are well capitalized. Their financial statements should clearly indicate their earning potential and ability to invest in the venture. Immediate investment may be necessary for certain up-front expenditure, such as the hiring of additional salespeople. In addition, firms should choose distributors who have the working capital to handle rapid sales increases when the need arises.

The capability of a distributor to borrow money and obtain credit indicates a strong financial position. A distributor who has the support of the local financial community is usually one whose business performance suggests strong sales and profits. The basic issue that this question addresses is whether they are capable of securing any additional funding that is needed immediately or that may be needed in the future as the business takes off.

One way to evaluate the size of the distributor is by assessing whether they have a critical mass of organizational capabilities to support the firm's product in the local market. If the distributor is too small, it may not be able to provide sufficient organizational support for the product or be able to push the product through the relevant market channels.

The way the distributorship is managed is a critical factor here. The quality of the senior management can be assessed through objective measures, as evidenced by their experience level and strong performance measures, or through objective evaluation methods, such as the motivation level of their employees and the care and attention given to the distributor's workplace.

Although the quality and level of technical support is less important for consumer and other nondurable products, this factor is critical for industrial and consumer durables. If a firm exports either type of product, it is important for them to consider distributors who can provide an acceptable level of technical support in their product line.

To help facilitate the distributor's assessment, firms can obtain verification about the distributor's reputation and effective performance. It is wise at this point to talk with customers such as retailers and other end users who have dealt directly with the distributor. They can be a good source of information concerning the distributor's work ethics, their financial standing in the marketplace, and their general reputation in the business community.

Trade associations and other business groups have a key role in promoting, fostering and protecting the interests of corporations and individuals engaged in business in many countries. In addition, they also facilitate coordination and cooperation among their members. Hence, distributors who are actively involved in these trade associations are likely to be highly committed and involved businesspeople. Firms can determine which trade associations a distributor belongs to and then check with those associations to see whether the distributor is a member of good standing.

Marketing skills

Firms should consider the level of motivation and commitment in evaluating distributors, however these factors by themselves are not sufficient. The extent of geographical coverage and knowledge of the target segments is also equally important in selecting distributors. Distributors who are knowledgeable about their markets are very often also familiar with customer requirements. The quality of management, size of the distributor and experience of the sales force will also bear directly on the marketing ability of a distributor (Zou et al., 2011).

Firms should consider the distributor's level of experience with the marketing channels relevant to their product. They should also check to see whether a potential distributor has the necessary connections with industry leaders, retailers, final customers, and consumers.

A well-articulated marketing plan is a strong indicator that the distributor has long-term goals and visions for the business. Firms should avoid distributors who do not have the ability to chart out future strategies and implement them. Firms can ask a distributor how marketing is planned with suppliers. In doing so, they will be able see whether some process is in place that has objective task-budget control.

Most distributors will claim that they cover their entire national territory in EMs. Benchmarks to look for are the distributor's physical facilities, the size and training of the sales force, and the number of sales outlets. Firms will need to try to determine the particular market segments a distributor services and their extent of market share in each. A distributor's geographic coverage can be evaluated in terms of principal market areas. The extent of market coverage by a distributor and how well these markets are served are often good indicators of an experienced sales force.

Market share is often an indicator of marketing performance. A high market share has also been shown to be correlated with high profitability. Distributors with a high market share will frequently have strong marketing skills and may also have stronger financial resources vis-à-vis other distributors with a smaller market share. Distributors with more experience will often tend to have a higher market share than newer distributors.

Distributor access to local media placement and scheduling is of great importance for a firm's advertising campaign. The distributor may also support that firm's efforts by preparing promotional materials (e.g. brochures, handouts, etc.). In such cases, firms can ask for samples of promotional materials that have been previously produced.

Firms will need to consider distributors who have the capability to provide on-time and complete deliveries. These capabilities will often reflect the quality of the distributor's logistics management. A customer-oriented distributor would attend to customer requests, complaints, and concerns as quickly as possible (i.e. within 24 hours).

Product factors

Product-related factors include knowledge about the product, the characteristics of a distributor's existing product lines, and the extent of their service and stocking facilities. Establishing a relationship with a distributor who is unfamiliar with the firm's product may result in marketing problems. Training their sales force in the type of servicing and marketing necessary may compensate for the distributor's shortcomings in being unfamiliar with the product. Firms can check the number of product lines carried by the distributor to see whether the product range is spread too thinly. This can show whether the distributor only concentrates on products that provide the best compensation. Firms should also avoid distributors who handle direct competitors' products and concentrate on those who handle complementary product lines and have already achieved some degree of specialization in sales and service.

Facilitating factors

Firms should also look at the quality level of the product lines currently carried by a distributor. The quality match for products is significant for product-positioning reasons (e.g. a high-quality product may suffer from a bad distributor reputation). It is important to realize that quality is very hard to assess; however, a few guidelines can help firms make a better assessment. For instance, if the distributor is a manufacturer, firms may use ISO 9000 quality standards or inquire about the distributor's brand name in the sector.

Violations of intellectual property rights are a problem in many countries that do not provide stringent intellectual property protection laws or impose strict sanctions against violators. Firms will need to select distributors who are willing to invest money in ensuring this protection. Note, however, that in certain countries, the distributor's hands may be tied and he or she may be unable to bring about effective enforcement. Firms must consider the existence of an intellectual property protection law, the efficacy of that law, its enforcement, and the distributor's ability to protect a firm's intellectual property, regardless of regulations and enforcement.

Managing Relationships in EMs

Managing relationships with foreign partners

A firm may decide to enter an EM in a joint venture with a foreign partner, appoint a foreign distributor, or use a foreign firm for sourcing. In this section, we refer to all the above-mentioned foreign counterparts as partners. Firms will need to build relationships at both a formal and informal level with a foreign partner's firm. In many cases, it is important for the foreign firm to identify the decision makers in an organization. The best strategy for managing relationships is to have cross-functional teams from various organizational levels building relationships with each other. This makes it more certain that if the principal contact of the foreign firm leaves for some reason, the business relationship between the two firms will continue to survive. There are various benefits to maintaining and developing good relationships with a foreign partner:

- If the foreign partner is better than the firm in managing a specific business process, they may agree to undertake a mutual benchmarking initiative.
- The foreign partner can provide the firm with invaluable leads and contacts voluntarily if that firm can establish trust and confidence.
- Training a foreign partner in quality management or statistical process control becomes easier within a strong relationship. This is especially true for supply chain management in emerging economies.
- Working toward common goals in the long term becomes easier if a sound working relationship is built with a foreign partner.
- Conflict resolution becomes faster within a good relationship with the foreign partner.

Managing relationships
with foreign customers

A firm striving for excellence never loses sight of its customers and their needs, and considers all its customers as equals. To be successful internationally in the long run, firms need to be aware of the complaints and feedback customers provide. A strategy to manage relationships with foreign customers should include the following:

- Providing the customer with the promised levels of price, quality, delivery and reliability and letting the customer know that the firm is in the country to do business in the long term and will not leave after extracting short-term profits.
- Communicating that customer views and feedback about the firm's products are extremely important and are taken seriously by the firm – having a toll-free customer telephone line and listening to complaints can be a good idea.
- Maintaining respect for cultural differences in taste or choice that the customer may have about specific features of the product and removing the features that may be culturally undesirable. For example, when McDonald's entered India in 1993, it had to abide by Indian religious preferences and not make burgers using beef or use animal fat when cooking its fries.

Managing relationships with foreign governments

Managing relations with foreign governments is vital for foreign businesses, especially in EMs, because small changes in a foreign government's trade policy can create a tremendous impact on the firm's business (Luo, 2001). A good example here is Coca-Cola in India. In 1977, the Janata Party came to power in India, and the new government demanded that Coca-Cola reveal its secret formula for the soft drink if it wanted to do business in India. Rather than comply with this unreasonable demand, Coca-Cola chose to leave India in 1977, and not to return until 1992, when government policy became more reliable and attractive to foreign investment.

Foreign entrants need to find a fit between what they can offer (capital, infrastructure development, technology, new jobs, etc.) and what the foreign government needs for its economic, political and development programmes (Zou et al., 2011). The priorities of a foreign firm and EM government may not match, and in such cases foreign firms can use the following strategies to manage their relations with government (Ghauri and Holstius, 1996; Austin, 2002):

- *Alter:* the firm can bargain to get the government to alter the policy, the instrument, or the action of concern.
- *Avoid:* the firm can make strategic moves to bypass the risk or impact of the government's action.
- *Accede:* the firm can adjust its operations to comply with a government requirement.
- *Ally:* the firm can insulate itself from risks by creating strategic alliances.

Depending on the relative importance of the issue to the firm and the relative power of the firm, one of the four approaches in Figure 9.3 can be used. If the issue is vital to the firm and it has the type of power needed to alter the foreign government's action, it should choose the *alter* strategy. The firm should choose the *accede* strategy when the issue is of little importance and it has low power. The firm should choose the *avoid* strategy to step back from a confrontation with the foreign government when dealing with issues that are of low importance to the firm, high importance to the foreign government, and the firm is in the position of high power. The firm may choose the *ally* strategy when the issue is highly important to the firm but it is in a low position of power.

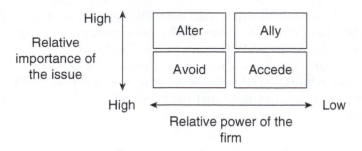

Figure 9.3   Strategic approaches to government relations

While preparing for negotiations with government officers, foreign managers must remember that all four strategies require some give and take. Minimizing conflict and building a common ground for negotiations remain the two most important first steps toward successful business in EMs.

Managing relationships with expatriates

Many firms will ignore the need to manage relationships with expatriates working in emerging economies. Merely providing a good monetary incentive system to motivate expatriates may not be enough; poor relations with the parent firm or HQ may result directly in poor performance by the expatriate. Many international management specialists complain that too many executives go to foreign countries ill prepared, because their firms often fail to develop human resource policies to match their global strategies (Ioannou, 1994). There are four general beliefs about the way international managers adjust to conditions abroad (Dunbar and Katcher, 1990):

1 The 'our person in Havana' myth describes the well-connected firm employee abroad who experiences little difficulty in adjusting to or performing in a foreign country. Firms that view foreign assignment in this way do relatively little for their staff.
2 The 'lost employee' myth holds that the person who is out of sight is also out of mind. Such employees are isolated from the domestic realities of the firm and are uncertain as to when or whether they are to repatriate – or whether there will be a position for them on their return.

3 The 'ugly American myth' describes the expatriate who is unfamiliar with the cultural realities of the host country. They are not just unhappy living abroad, they are also a liability to their firms.
4 The 'cultural relativist' finds relocation challenging, both personally and professionally. These people are good at working with others, and firms assume that they will adapt to the foreign nation easily.

Box 9.2   What are the Goals of a Cross-cultural Training Programme?

The source of information: the trainee needs observation and interview skills.
Learning settings: the trainee needs to attend to all aspects of the environment, including each human encounter, as a source of information.
Problem solving: the trainee needs to define problems independently and gather information in real time.
The role of emotions and value: because problems are usually value- and emotion-laden, the trainee needs to recognize the relevant values, perceptions, attitudes and emotions, and their implications for action.
Criteria for successful learning: the trainee needs to assess effectiveness in terms of the attitudes of parties in the work setting and the duration of relationships.

Western firms who do not wish to see their expatriates in any of the above four situations will have to develop a systematic strategy for relocating employees in emerging economies. A strategy to manage relationships with expatriates may include training programmes, as illustrated in Box 9.2 and in the following examples:

- cultural training for expatriates and their families
- training in international business negotiations
- a tracking mechanism to follow (and suitably reward) the contributions made by the expatriate to the firm's business while abroad
- a communication mechanism between the expatriate and HQ of the firm – it is wise to keep the expatriate informed of any organizational or strategy changes that the firm may make during his or her absence
- incorporating the complex information gathered by the expatriate in future decision making at HQ

- a mechanism to tap into contacts and leads developed by the expatriate during a foreign assignment
- reintegration and repatriation training of expatriates into the domestic firm at suitable points on their return.

In international management, expatriate failure is considered one of the major problems. One researcher concludes that the reasons for this failure, in order of importance, are the inability of the spouse or manager to adjust, other family issues, the manager's level of maturity, and an inability to cope with larger overseas responsibilities (Hill, 2011). It is worthwhile to note here that a spouse's inability to adjust is considered the number one problem. The selection and training of an expatriate is thus a critical issue in the success of international operations. Moreover, the manager, along with their spouse and family, should be included in training programmes.

Managing relationships with foreign communities

It is always a good corporate communications strategy to invest time and resources in building a good image in the foreign communities in which a firm operates. A firm's participation in community activities improves its image, and this in turn attracts a better and more experienced workforce. Also, a community presence minimizes the negative stereotyping of 'foreign multinational imperialism', thus increasing customer confidence in the firm's products and services. Crisis management can be easier if the firm has a positive relationship with community leaders and has demonstrated that it is a good 'corporate citizen'.

A strategy to manage relationships with foreign communities may include the following:

- sponsoring sports, cultural events and festivals in the community
- reaching out a helping hand in times of natural disaster and other crises
- institutionalizing good human resource policies in the organization
- helping maintain a clean environment
- maintaining a complete regard and respect for the cultural norms and traditions of the community
- participating in social welfare programmes, such as healthcare, a clean water supply, and education.

Chapter Questions

1 Discuss common traits which can influence the negotiation process in emerging markets.
2 Suggest strategies for foreign firms to handle issues in the negotiation process in EMs.
3 Why are relationships emphasized in discussing business in EMs?
4 Discuss the criteria involved in selecting partners in EMs.
5 How can foreign firms manage relations with foreign partners and governments in EMs?

TEN   Assessing Risks and Opportunities in Emerging Economies

Managers from developed markets may hesitate to do business in emerging markets as these are so very different from developed markets. Managers can assume that differences between emerging and developed markets will decline and emerging markets will resemble developed markets. However both of these assumptions are inaccurate. Emerging markets can indeed provide enormous opportunities for firms from developed economies, but like all opportunities, they can also entail some risks. If these markets are not handled properly, firms can lose considerable amounts of money, along with their reputations. Multinational companies have to develop capabilities that allow them to anticipate and respond to upcoming opportunities, while handing disruptions and risks in emerging markets.

On one hand, multinationals have no choice but to compete in big emerging markets, because of the presence of growth in these markets. On the other hand, they cannot just sell standardized products with standardized marketing strategies in such markets, due to their differences as well as the presence of local competition. Considering the existence of numerous cultures, with their own institutional framework, political/legal forces and economic landscape, it would also be erroneous to assume that emerging markets will resemble developed markets in the future. Throughout this book, the message has been that MNCs and smaller companies planning to reap the benefits of emerging markets must rethink and adapt their strategies to these markets. In this book, the business environment is analysed and two of the most difficult aspects of doing business in these markets – entry and negotiation strategies – have been outlined.

In thinking about doing business in emerging markets and strategizing, firms need to consider the consumers and business models that can serve their needs, the characteristics of the market and the value chain, the availability of local partners, and the presence of competitors. While planning to enter and negotiate in a specific emerging market, firms also need to evaluate the potential of a particular market, have some knowledge of the infrastructure and distribution channels, decide on those who will negotiate and run the business, formulate their strategy on a country-by-country basis (and not a regional basis), and decide which entry strategy – export, joint venture, licensing, direct investment – can help them reap the maximum benefit from a particular market.

Strategic Alignment for Internationalization

All companies, large and small, need to have a well-thought-out strategy for going international. This strategy should be aligned with a company's own organizational capabilities and environment, and the capabilities of the other organization or company with whom it is building a partnership for entering a specific market. A company can complement its own capabilities by working with other organizations, such as banks, freight forwarders, different government offices, trade associations, and market-research companies. A good alignment between capability sources facilitates the process of going international and formulating an efficient marketing strategy. This is further explained in Figure 10.1.

Company capabilities: finding a fit

It is a well-documented fact in management literature that poor performance results when a company fails to align its capabilities with its business strategy. Whenever a company decides to internationalize its business, it should reassess its capabilities or strengths and weaknesses and try to find a fit between its capabilities and the internationalization process. This may involve an evaluation of the company's resources, technology, business processes, and the products or services that it wishes to sell from the target market perspective. We would recommend five key areas that a company must investigate before committing resources to export or other forms of internationalization. These five areas and the appropriate questions to be asked are as follows:

1 *Business background*

    a. How long has your firm been in business?
    b. How many full-time employees does your company have?

Figure 10.1 Key processes and decisions in going international

c. What were your gross sales last year?

d. What was the growth rate of your company over the past three years?

e. Which of the following best describes your sales and distribution activity: manufacturers' representatives only, direct sales force only, or a combination of sales force, representatives and distributors?

f. Which of the following best describes your scope of marketing: few local customers, few regional and national customers, a large base of local customers, a large base of regional customers, or a large base of national customers?

g. What is the current strategic emphasis of your company: maximum profitability and return on investment (ROI), equal emphasis on profitability and market share, strong emphasis on growth in domestic market share, or strong market share in key global markets?

h. What percentage of your total company sales should be represented by foreign market sales within the next 3–5 years?

i. Which of the following best describes your firm: currently not exporting, exporting by selling to middlemen in your home country, exporting directly to foreign agents, distributors and customers, exporting through a company-owned sales organization, or exporting through subsidiary(ies) in foreign markets?

j. Do you have access to external funds for expansion or working capital purposes?

k. Does your staff have adequate knowledge of foreign cultures and business customs?

l. How extensive is your staff's previous international business experience?

m. How familiar is your management with the language and culture of the target market?

2 *Motivation for going international*

a. Do you wish to export because you have excess production?

b. Do you wish to export to fill unsolicited orders only?

c. Do you wish to export to benefit solely by stabilizing seasonal market fluctuations?

d. Do you wish to internationalize to expand into key world markets?

e. Do you wish to internationalize to enhance your firm's competitiveness by acquiring market knowledge?

f. Do you wish to export to extend the life cycle of existing products in foreign markets?

g. Do you wish to internationalize to supplement domestic sales with occasional export sales?

h. Do you wish to internationalize to reduce risks by selling in diverse foreign markets?

i. Do you wish to internationalize to exploit the firm's unique technology and know-how?

j. Do you wish to internationalize to improve ROI for the entire company?

k. Is internationalization a part of your long-term expansion strategy?

3 *Top management commitment*

a. What view does the top management take concerning risk factors involved in getting into foreign markets: not willing to jeopardize current profits and ROI, will sacrifice current profits and ROI moderately, will sacrifice current profits and ROI significantly, or will sacrifice more than 20% ROI and profits?

a. How does your management intend to sell overseas in the next 3–5 years: selling through middlemen located in the USA, selling to or through agents or trading companies in foreign markets, selling directly to distributors in foreign markets, selling through at least one marketing subsidiary in key markets, or selling through marketing subsidiaries in major foreign markets?

b. What will be the size of funds that will be set aside to develop foreign markets in each of the three years on average: less than

$5,000 per year, between $5,000 and $25,000 per year, between $26,000 and $50,000 per year, between $51,000 and $100,000 per year, or more than $100,000 per year?

c. How much time is senior management willing to allocate to international expansion efforts: occasional or sporadic as required, up to a quarter of one person's time, up to a half of one person's time, one full-time person, or more than one full-time person?

d. How will you develop your management plan for foreign markets: no formal planning, at most through an annual budget, through marketing plans developed for specific needs or projects, by periodic marketing plans developed for total international operations, through periodic marketing plans developed for the total and for each market, or through regular marketing plans for the total, each market and each product?

e. What will be the size of funds that will be allocated in each of the first three years for market research, market analysis, and competitive analysis?

f. At what level will international personnel in your company be compensated: the most affordable level we can pay with our resources, a level compatible with third-level management in the company, competitively with the rate for equivalent positions in the industry, or higher than the rate for equivalent positions in the industry?

g. How long is top management willing to wait before achieving a break-even point on their foreign market investment? Is the commitment of top management long term?

h. What attitude does the management take toward long-term contractual relationships with overseas partners?

i. How does the top management envisage exporting: occasional activity, regular activity with no targeted export sales, regular activity with moderate levels of targeted exports, or regular activity with aggressive levels of targeted exports?

4 *Product strengths*

a. Does your product require extensive training to operate or use?
b. Does your product require considerable support following the sale?
c. Is your product versatile? Does it fulfill different needs?
d. Is your product bulky? Are the shipping costs for your product high?
e. Is your product category enjoying increased market demand in the domestic country?
f. Is your product unique, easily differentiated, or technologically advanced?
g. Is the production process exclusive to your firm?
h. Do your company R&D levels exceed the industry average?
i. Is your product competitively priced in the domestic market?

    j. Does your product have significant advantages over competing products?

    k. Does your product require extensive inventory investment by distributors?

    l. Does your product require a special domestic licence to export?

    m. Does your product require special storage?

5 *Market-specific strengths*

    a. Do you think your product will be well accepted in the foreign market?

    b. Will the climate in the target country restrict the life or use of your product?

    c. Are tariff levels low for your product?

    d. Can your product be shipped or disassembled to obtain lower duties?

    e. Will patent or trademark protection provide any advantage in the target market?

    f. Does your product face significant obstacles and high costs in complying with the standards and regulations of the target market?

    g. Are there any existing substitutes for your product in the target market?

    h. Will you be able to price your product competitively in the target market?

    i. Are there any serious nontariff barriers to importing your product by foreign market?

    j. Can the product and/or packaging be made suitable for foreign customers?

    k. Can manufacturing make any adaptations to enhance product appeal?

    l. Are product category sales in a growth stage in the target market?

    m. Is it difficult or easy to locate qualified distributors to promote and distribute your product?

    n. Can the credit terms and delivery requirements of the target market be met?

    o. Are there a number of strong, entrenched competitors in the target market, each having a significant market share?

    p. Is there a favourable attitude in the target country toward products made in your country?

Sometimes, just finding a fit between company capabilities and internationalization may not be enough; some key capabilities will have to be leveraged by adapting these to the foreign culture. Figure 10.2 represents the strategic intent of a firm that wants to grow and become more profitable and the capabilities it needs to align in order to become successful. To develop new customers and businesses, the firm decides to explore foreign markets. Though many academics would agree that most firms go through the evolutionary process of internationalization (i.e. exporting to foreign direct investment), the pace of global change has made it necessary for firms to skip some stages in the internationalization process, depending on their strategic intent.

Company competitiveness

Regardless of size, a firm's survival will depend on its managerial ability in setting new directions and achieving goals based on the requirements for competing in a global community. Continuous improvement is critical in the search for world-class status, but before a company can think about an improvement programme, it must develop a profile of its current status, analysing its strengths and weaknesses and formulating strategies for addressing any identified weaknesses.

A manager may take three steps to measure business performance:

1 Determining current performance levels in all areas of the corporation and then benchmarking these with competitor's will help managers in determining how their businesses are performing vis-à-vis the competition. The importance of measuring business performance can be emphasized with the popular management saying 'If you cannot measure it, you cannot manage it!'
2 Identifying, developing, and implementing both long- and short-term strategies to address areas requiring attention.
3 Implementing a continuous improvement programme that cuts across all aspects of the enterprise is necessary to increase productivity and place the company in a much improved competitive position.

A competitive analysis can follow either a horizontal or vertical approach to diffuse through the whole organization. Thus, it can analyse the company using its functional areas or processes. Another approach could be matching processes with functions to get a cross-functional matrix. The essence of this approach lies in its adoption with companies in the transition phase from a function-driven organization to a process-driven organization. Analysis through the coupling of vertical functions against horizontal processes provides the company with feedback on its transformation process. Competitive assessments may include the functions and processes illustrated in Box 10.1.

A company's global competitiveness is not only dependent on how well the functions and processes appearing in Box 10.1 are managed, but also on the specific capabilities it uses for gaining a competitive

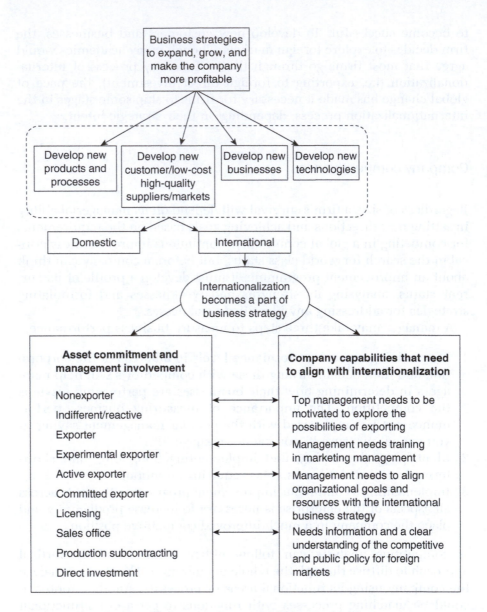

Figure 10.2   How to align company capabilities and make internationalization a business strategy

advantage abroad. These capabilities can include one or more of the following:

- product or process technology that is unique to the company
- logistics and distribution capabilities to meet high customer service levels

- smaller or compressed new-product development and introduction cycle times.

Managers may find some other areas not discussed above in which their firms can gain competitive advantage. However, we would assert that it is extremely important to perform a competitive analysis of the company and that this should be done internationally, not domestically.

Box 10.1 Functions and Processes that can be Used in a Competitive Assessment

Vertical functions

- Human resources
- Accounting
- Finance
- Technology
- Product design
- Manufacturing
- Marketing and sales
- Logistics
- Customer service

Cross-functional or horizontal processes

- New-product management
- Inventory management
- Quality Management
- Labor/management relationships
- Relationship management
- Information management
- Budgeting
- Financing
- Cost reduction
- Management of structure
- Safety processes
- Management of customer payment

Support functions

- Image
- Customer franchise
- Networks and alliances
- Global configuration

The use of multimedia technology and information technology has become widespread in business, and such technology enables the integration of a firm's value chain and global sharing of expertise. Today, many businesses operate in a similar structure to the example in Figure 10.3, and many firms will restructure and adopt processes resembling this example in the near future as they take advantage of opportunities in emerging markets and the technology which enables them to do so.

Evaluating the Potential of Emerging Markets

In developing strategies to enter emerging markets, firms need to (a) assess market potential and look at opportunities to access the market; and (b) create a strategy in terms of market entry and establishment. Although each of these steps is critical, the initial assessment of opportunities is especially important in emerging markets. In assessing opportunities, firms can use various techniques, such as gathering background information (desk research), evaluating unsolicited enquiries from foreign customers, and monitoring competitor activity.

Often, managers will complain about the limited availability of information when analysing the risks of doing business in another country. They can make use of two types of information available about emerging markets – primary and secondary. Primary data, which are more industry-specific and focused, can be obtained by contacting international business consulting companies, commercial attachés of embassies in foreign countries, and subsidiaries, agents or distributors in foreign markets. Associations, governments, trade organizations, and market information agencies can prove to be invaluable sources. A company may also benefit from its knowledge of existing customers and suppliers. In some cases, these sources can also help companies understand the inner workings of a market. For instance, if new regulations are passed, lawyers within the country or trade associations can better provide information about the background and incentives in passing the new law, as well as providing insight into how the new regulations will be applied. Building networks in potential markets can enable a company to access information and knowledge first hand and learn about the details of the operation within the market. Considering that the emerging market structure is more relationship-based when compared to developed markets, the importance of networking needs to be emphasized.

In emerging markets there are multiple sources of secondary data – data which has been collected and prepared by external organizations.

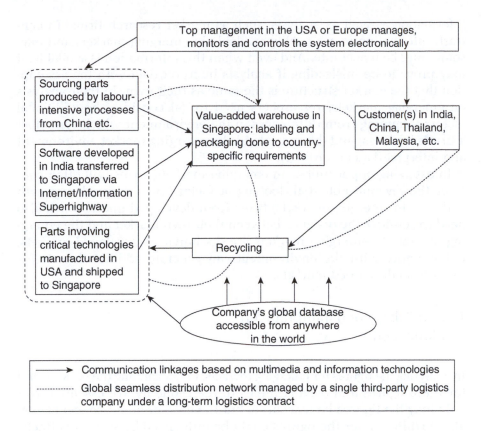

Figure 10.3   An example of a company doing business in emerging markets

The main resources that have been used throughout this book are outlined in the Appendix at the end of this chapter. Secondary data can be helpful in understanding emerging markets, however researchers need to be aware of the challenges associated with collecting and interpreting such data.

Analysing Data in Emerging Markets

In emerging markets, the limited availability of information and its reliability poses challenges in analysing the markets. Multinationals from developed markets are accustomed to operating in environments where reliable information related to the consumer, the competition, suppliers and distributors, is easy to access. Moreover, in their home economies they are able to benefit from the expertise of intermediaries that provide information as well as analysis, such as market research firms. In contrast, information is not readily available in emerging markets and may sometimes be inaccurate. And even when this information is available, it may prove to be misleading if analysts interpret data with the assumption that the market structure is the same as their own. In their analysis on emerging markets, researchers need to: (a) consider the additional factors stemming from differences in the environment which can affect a firm's business; and (b) understand the emerging market environment and interpret data accordingly.

In assessing opportunities in emerging markets, firms will often consider the revenue potential, looking at factors such as market growth and size. In emerging markets, firms from developed markets will also need to consider the distance between their own market and the emerging market. As emerging markets are dissimilar to developed markets, unfamiliarity with the environment can generate additional costs for firms from developed markets.

The availability and interpretation of information

In analysing the figures for emerging markets, understanding the background for these figures and driving forces in the economy are essential. Not only may the figures be inaccurate but the measurement concepts may also be different, or the figures might be influenced by seasonal effects. Thus, looking at the numbers without considering the market, its structure and the forces that affect it, may lead to erroneous conclusions (Pacek and Thorniley, 2007).

Information obtained in emerging markets may be misleading for multiple reasons. First of all, the informal economy is not included in information databases. The informal economy is a global phenomenon and therefore affects all countries. However, in many emerging markets, the size of the informal economy is bigger. Thus, in analysing a country where a significant portion of the economy is unrecorded, an analyst may conclude that the per capita income or growth rates are smaller than they are. In another example, many outlets may not be registered businesses. An analyst trying to formulate a distribution strategy might then be misled by data on registered outlets.

Many individuals and businesses will report lower incomes or not report at all, thereby leading to misconceptions about the size of the market as well as the business structure. Data may also be misleading due to differences in definitions and concepts between developed countries and emerging markets. For instance, a company may consider distribution, or infrastructure, looking at the figures on road availability in an emerging market. Such figures, though accurate, would be very misleading if that company does not recognize the difference between paved and non-paved roads. If a country's economy is highly dependent on a single industry, changes in that industry may lead the country to have unusually high or low growth figures in a given year. Alternatively, if the population growth of a country is exceptionally high, increased growth rates in GDP may be meaningless and the average income or consumption in the country may actually be decreasing.

Understanding emerging markets can help firms to estimate the potential of these markets, even in the presence of limited information. Firms able to understand the structure of emerging markets can analyse and interpret existing data accurately. For instance, the availability and reliability of information regarding the market can be observed by looking at the length of time that governments are able to borrow at a fixed interest rate. This indicates the period of time investors are willing to commit to, as well as their confidence in the overall reliability of the institutions in a given country. High yields on fixed rate debt also indicate the risks associated with an economy (Bruner et al., 2003).

Analysing inward and outward investment flows can help in understanding the market. For instance, if a current account deficit is large but foreign investment flows are significant, the deficit may not indicate a serious risk, as foreign income can enable the country to reduce that deficit. Alternatively, if the government is able to borrow at acceptable rates, then the budget deficit may not be a significant risk. In contrast, if the country has a history of dealing with budget deficits by printing money or the country has no source of funds, such as access to international loans or export capability, rising budget deficits can lead to high inflation. Foreign investment flows can also signal the structure of the economy and its vulnerability in the face of external shocks. An economy that is heavily dependent on a few export or import items is more likely to be affected by external volatility. Similarly, if foreign flows are dependent on a single country, then the market is bound to be affected by any change in that country (Pacek and Thorniley, 2007).

Factors such as the skills and flexibility of the population or available infrastructure and level of technology will influence business activities. However, before looking at the data, it is necessary to determine which characteristic of the economic environment is relevant for a given business. For instance, a producer of fine food products may define the economic system as population size and age structure, disposable household income, level of urbanization, climate, transportation, and communication.

The size and growth of a population can create opportunities for the marketer. The age distribution (whether a maturing or young population), how that population lives (urban or rural), and its capabilities are all factors which can either create market growth opportunities or affect the level of adaptation. Some indicators of economic wealth are gross domestic product, purchasing power, GDP per capita, the balance of payments, financial institutions, and the stock market. Estimating the size of the middle class also presents a major challenge in emerging market analysis. While per capita income may not reveal the size of the middle income, ratios showing the percentage of income held by the middle class can be enlightening in identifying opportunities in emerging markets.

The market potential in an EM can be measured by per capita income adjusted for differences in price. In this way, the purchasing power of the consumer can be better identified. Moreover, the increase in the per capita GDP, as well as the ratios related to income distribution and the changes in income distribution in an emerging market, can help identify growth patterns within the market. However, even when using per capita income figures, managers need to consider the unreported informal economy, as well as income distribution. Thus, such ratios need to be complemented by further research on rates of urbanization, income distribution, commercial infrastructure, and consumer spending data.

Indices on emerging markets

Differences between markets in terms of multiple factors, such as the economic environment, growth rates, political stability, openness to foreign investment, consumption potential and patterns, will affect the market's attractiveness for foreign investment (Cavusgil et al., 2004). Firms can identify potential markets by ranking them according to suitable indicators. However, a problem with this approach is that it does not account for product specificity or non-business related factors such as high cultural or institutional distance. Still, a preliminary analysis can be conducted by looking at difference indicators of market potential to generate a broad list of possible target markets (Cavusgil et al., 2004).

In analysing the attractiveness of emerging markets for entry and formulating entry strategies, openness to trade and investment, as well as the efficiency of the business environment in facilitating investment and trade transactions, are critical. There are many reliable sources for secondary data, such as Euromoney, Institutional Investor, The Economist Intelligence Unit, and World Bank, which publish country risk ratings semi-annually or annually. Also, following leads given by major finance and investment houses or banks and tapping into the resources of local universities may be helpful in risk analysis.

Table 10.1 shows the economic freedom scores prepared by *The Wall Street Journal*, which assess the ease at which business activities can be carried out in different economies. The Economic Freedom Index is created by looking at countries by different components and calculating their freedom on a scale of 1–100, with 100 representing the maximum level of freedom. Each country has different restrictions for foreign investment, such as various regulations, restricted access to foreign exchange, restrictions on capital transfers and payments, and the closing of certain industries to foreign investment (Heritage, 2011). The economic freedom scores of emerging markets are lower than the sources of advanced economies. However, when specific items are considered one can see that monetary freedom, government spending, and fiscal freedom figures for emerging markets and the developed economies are comparable, and the government spending figures for emerging markets are higher. This observation shows the positive effects of reforms in emerging markets focused on boosting the economy through increased trade, as well as their efforts to reduce macroeconomic instability.

Box 10.2   Economic Freedom Scores, 2011

Economic freedom scores are calculated by the *The Wall Street Journal* and the Heritage Foundation, in order to determine the ease of producing, trading, and consuming goods, and thus pursuing economic interests. Within this framework, business freedom measures the ease at which a business can be started, operated and closed in a given country, thereby assessing the regulations regarding the efficiency of the government. Trade freedom is the measure of barriers to trade. Monetary freedom measures factors such as inflation, price controls, and price stability. Government spending is a measure of the level of government expenditure. Fiscal freedom measures the tax burden. Property rights measure whether individuals can acquire property safely within a legal composition endorsed by the state. Investment freedom measures the level of constraints on the flow of investment capital. Financial freedom refers to banking efficiency and the level of involvement of the government in the financial sector. Corruption values examine the level of corruption in a country, and labour freedom measures indicate the level of legal framework governing the labour market. As seen in Table 10.1, developed countries mostly rank above emerging economies.

   Businesses need to consider the different implications of the business landscape in emerging economies, regulatory bodies governing the economy and their approach before considering entry into an economy. The scores also draw attention to the difference between developed economies and emerging markets, as well as the diversity in regulatory practices within EM countries.

(Continued)

(Continued)

Table 10.1 Economic freedom scores, 2011

2011	Overall score	Business freedom	Trade freedom	Fiscal freedom	Government spending	Monetary freedom	Investment freedom	Financial freedom	Property rights	Freedom from corruption	Labour freedom
UK	74.5	94.6	87.6	52	32.9	74.9	90	80	85	77	71.2
USA	**77.8**	91	86.4	68.3	54.6	77.4	75	70	85	75	95.7
Brazil	**56.3**	54.3	69.8	69	49.6	75.9	50	50	50	37	57.8
Russia	**50.5**	50.7	68.2	82.7	65.1	63.1	25	40	25	22	62.9
India	**54.6**	36.9	64.2	75.4	77.8	65.1	35	40	50	34	67.2
China	**52**	49.8	71.6	70.3	87	75.3	25	30	20	36	54.9
Chile	**77.4**	67.2	88	77.7	86.6	77.9	80	70	85	67	74.5
Colombia	**68**	86.1	73.2	74.5	78.9	75.8	65	60	50	37	79.3
Egypt	**59.1**	64.5	74	89.6	65.3	60.8	65	50	40	28	53.6
Pakistan	**55.1**	70.9	67	80.5	88.8	63.6	40	40	30	24	46.3
Malaysia	**66.3**	69.7	78.7	84.6	79.2	81.3	45	50	50	45	79.2
Mexico	**67.8**	87.3	81.2	81.3	83.1	75.7	65	60	50	33	60.9
South Africa	**62.7**	72.3	77.2	69.6	77.5	71.9	45	60	50	47	56.7
Turkey	**64.2**	68.7	85.4	78.2	83.6	72.7	70	50	50	44	39.6
Thailand	**64.7**	69.9	75.9	74.8	90.6	70.8	40	70	45	34	76.3
Indonesia	**56**	54.9	73.8	83	88.9	74.3	35	40	30	28	51.8
Peru	**68.6**	71.9	86	79.4	91	83.1	70	60	40	37	67.7

Source: Heritage Foundation, *Wall Street Journal.*

Table 10.2 shows the investment freedom analysis prepared by the Heritage organization. Investment freedom scores are calculated by looking at national treatment of foreign investment, the efficiency of investment laws and practices, restrictions on land ownership, sectorial investment restrictions, expropriation and foreign exchange controls. National treatment in international investment refers to the level of preferential treatment or equal treatment for domestic investors and foreign investors. Trade freedom scores are calculated by adding up the weighted averages of the tariff rates according to the share of each product in total imports and then adjusting the score according to the level of non-tariff barriers (Heritage, 2011). Fiscal freedom measures the tax burden imposed by the government. Business freedom is about the ease of starting a business.

Trade can be restricted by high tariffs or non-tariff barriers, such as quantity restrictions, price restrictions, regulatory restrictions (licensing, domestic content requirements, etc.), investment restrictions, customs restrictions, and direct government intervention (Heritage, 2011). In order to have a general idea of how different countries compare in terms of trade restrictions, looking at trade restrictiveness indices may be helpful. The Overall Trade Restrictiveness Index (OTRI) is generated by looking at a country's tariff schedule and non-tariff measures, and creating a uniform tariff rate, which corresponds to the rate that would be needed to maintain the country's import levels. The Tariff Trade Restrictiveness Index (TTRI) is similar in calculation, however it does not include non-tariff barriers (WTI, 2010). Some non-tariff barriers are hard to measure and are not always implemented as a restriction to trade. Hence, tariff trade restrictiveness may be a better indicator of a country's receptiveness to trade (World Bank, 2010b).

Table 10.3 shows the Overall Trade Restrictiveness and Tariff Trade Restrictiveness Indices for selected emerging markets. As agriculture is traditionally protected more than manufacturing industries, separate scores are calculated for each country. From the index, comparable tariff rates are observed in Turkey, Chile and Mexico to those of advanced countries in manufacturing industries. Of the countries within the table, Brazil, India and Egypt are associated with higher tariffs in manufacturing, as well as relatively higher scores for overall trade restrictiveness.

A country's position in the global supply chain is effected by the efficiency of trade transactions within that country which augments to competitiveness in trade. Ease of Doing Business Indices (Table 10.4), created by the World Bank, analyse the level of efficiency and bureaucracy in trade processes in terms of time and cost. Business activities in emerging markets can be hindered by excessive bureaucracy, which can be observed through burdensome administrative rules and the excessive requirements of paperwork, which cost both time and money.

Table 10.2 Investment freedom scores, 2011

	Overall Score	Business Freedom	Trade Freedom	Fiscal Freedom	Gov. Spending Freedom	Monetary Freedom	Investment Freedom	Financial Freedom	Property Rights	Freedom From Corruption	Labor Freedom
Chile	77	67	88	78	87	78	80	70	85	67	75
Peru	69	72	86	79	91	83	70	60	40	37	68
Mexico	68	87	81	81	83	76	65	60	50	33	61
Malaysia	66	70	79	85	79	81	45	50	50	45	79
Thailand	65	70	76	75	91	71	40	70	45	34	76
Turkey	64	69	85	78	84	73	70	50	50	44	40
South Africa	63	72	77	70	78	72	45	60	50	47	57
Egypt	59	65	74	90	65	61	65	50	40	28	54
Brazil	56	54	70	69	50	76	50	50	50	37	58
Philippines	56	43	78	79	91	76	40	50	30	24	51
Indonesia	56	55	74	83	89	74	35	40	30	28	52
Pakistan	55	71	67	81	89	64	40	40	30	24	46
India	55	37	64	75	78	65	35	40	50	34	67
China	52	50	72	70	87	75	25	30	20	36	55
Russia	51	51	68	83	65	63	25	40	25	22	63

Source: Heritage, 2011.

Table 10.3 The Trade Restrictiveness Index, 2008

	Overall Trade Restrictiveness Index (OTRI)			Tariff Trade Restrictiveness Index		
	Total	Agriculture	Manufacture	Total	Agriculture	Manufacture
USA	5.6%	18.1%	4.5%	1.3%	1.8%	1.2%
EU	5.1%	36.8%	3.0%	1.5%	8.2%	1.0%
Brazil	20.3%	22.3%	20.1%	8.1%	3.7%	8.3%
Russia	16.0%	25.2%	14.8%	4.8%	5.2%	4.8%
India	15.2%	47.7%	14.3%	9.0%	31.2%	8.4%
China	9.4%	15.0%	9.0%	4.6%	7.4%	4.4%
Chile	4.2%	21.7%	2.5%	0.9%	1.7%	0.9%
Mexico	16.6%	29.4%	15.3%	1.7%	2.0%	1.7%
Peru	17.2%	55.0%	15.7%	3.8%	14.1%	3.4%
Egypt	35.0%	46.6%	32.9%	8.5%	11.7%	7.9%
South Africa	4.3%	11.4%	4.0%	3.8%	5.5%	3.7%
Turkey	6.4%	24.1%	5.5%	1.7%	16.8%	0.9%

Source: (WTI, 2010).

The Ease of Doing Business Index evaluates countries in terms of difficulties in starting and operating a business. The factors considered within this index include items such as the ease of starting a business or dealing with permits, which also provide insight into bureaucracy levels in a given country.

Transparency, corruption, and competitiveness are often highlighted as potential risks in emerging markets. The Transparency Index, prepared by PricewaterhouseCoopers, measures transparency along five dimensions which are corruption, legal, economics, accounting and regulatory factors, and creates an opacity index. The index values indicate that the cost of doing business with countries that have higher opacity factors may be greater. Another valuable source in assessing risk is created by the International Institute for Management Development (IMD) and is called the World Competitiveness Index, which measures the overall competitiveness of a country. Transparency International has created the Corruption Perception Index (CPI), in order to show the influences of corruption on a given economy.

A comprehensive index for emerging markets: the Market Potential Index

A formal and systematic analysis of aggregate can be particularly fruitful. Michigan State University's (MSU) International Business Center (IBC)

Table 10.4 The Ease of Doing Business Index, 2009

Economy	Ease of Doing Business rank	Starting a business	Dealing with construction permits	Registering property	Getting credit	Protecting investors	Paying taxes	Trading across borders	Enforcing contracts	Closing a business
UK	4	17	16	22	2	10	16	15	23	7
USA	5	9	27	12	6	5	62	20	8	14
Thailand	19	95	12	19	72	12	91	12	25	46
Malaysia	21	113	108	60	1	4	23	37	59	55
South Africa	34	75	52	91	2	10	24	149	85	74
Mexico	35	67	22	105	46	44	107	58	81	23
Peru	36	54	97	24	15	20	86	53	110	96
Colombia	39	73	32	55	65	5	118	99	150	29
Chile	43	62	68	45	72	28	46	68	68	91
Turkey	65	63	137	38	72	59	75	76	26	115
Vietnam	78	100	62	43	15	173	124	63	31	124
China	79	151	181	38	65	93	114	50	15	68
Pakistan	83	85	98	126	65	28	145	81	155	67
Egypt	94	18	154	93	72	74	136	21	143	131
Argentina	115	142	168	118	65	109	143	115	45	77
Indonesia	121	155	60	98	116	44	130	47	154	142
Russia	123	108	182	51	89	93	105	162	18	103
Brazil	127	128	112	122	89	74	152	114	98	132
India	134	165	177	94	32	44	164	100	182	134
Philippines	148	156	156	102	128	132	124	61	118	153
Venezuela	172	144	96	101	176	179	178	167	74	152

Source: The World Bank Group, Doing Business, www. doingbusiness.org.

has developed an index which assesses the potential of emerging markets identified by *The Economist*. In order to create this index, eight economic, political and social variables were selected to characterize a market's attractiveness. The index was created to obtain the raw values of these variables by standardizing the items and putting them on a scale of 1 to 100 by using a formula (standardization is a statistical procedure enabling us to directly compare variables with very different distributions). The relative importance of each dimension was determined by interviewing a small number of international business professionals and educators (adelphi process). The dimensions that constitute the Market Opportunity Index (MOI) and data sources used in creating the index are shown in Table 10.5.

With state limitations in mind, the MOI can provide managers with valuable insights into the nature of EMs. Although EMs do share certain features, the index shows that considerable diversity remains. The rankings for each dimension (shown in Table 10.6) reveal significant variation. China, for example, is first in market size, but next to last in market intensity, low in commercial infrastructure, and last in economic freedom. Nevertheless, because of weighting, China's MOI is high.

Managers need to take some care in applying the index presented in Table 10.6. First, the MOI is an aggregate measure of an emerging market's attractiveness and is useful only in the initial stage of qualifying and ranking countries. For the market entry and market establishment stages, much more detailed and in-depth analysis is required. Second, although the seven dimensions provide a comprehensive characterization, additional aspects and alternative measures can be considered. For example, a more explicit representation of risk (commercial, monetary and political) can be accommodated. In the MOI, risk is embedded in the market receptivity dimension, because it reflects the openness of a country to imports. Third, the index is designed primarily for exporting companies. Businesses considering other forms of entry, such as direct investments and equity ventures, will need to examine additional variables. A final caveat about the reliability of the statistics used: the most credible sources and most recent available data were used, but as with any data set, there is always room for improvement.

It is important for managers to focus particularly on the dimensions and measures that are most relevant to their own products or services, such as the target market, distribution channels, and intensity of competition. For example, marketers of soft drinks will concentrate on surrogate indicators of product demand that are very different from those examined by medical-equipment marketers. It is also reasonable to expect that the weight of each dimension may have to be revised for different companies and circumstances.

Table 10.5 Dimensions of the Market Opportunity Index (MOI) and data sources

Dimension	Weight	Measures used	Data source
Market size	10/50	Urban population (million) – 2009	World Bank, World Development Indicators – 2009
		Electricity consumption (billion kwh) – 2007	US Energy Information Administration, International Energy Annual – 2007
Market growth rate	6/50	Average annual growth rate of primary energy use (%) 2003–2007	US Energy Information Administration, International Energy Annual – 2007
		Real GDP growth rate (%) – 2009	World Bank, World Development Indicators – 2009
Market intensity	7/50	GNI per capita estimates using PPP (US$) – 2009	World Bank, World Development Indicators – 2009
		Private consumption as a percentage of GDP (%) – 2008	World Bank, World Development Indicators – 2009
Market consumption capacity	5/50	Percentage share of middle class in consumption/income (2009)	World Bank, World Development Indicators – 2009
Commercial infrastructure	7/50	Main telephone lines (per 100 habitants) – 2009	International Telecommunication Union, ICT Indicators – 2009
		Cellular mobile subscribers (per 100 habitants) – 2009	International Telecommunication Union, ICT Indicators – 2009
		Number of PCs (per 1000 habitants) – 2009	Euromonitor International, Global Market Information Database
		Paved road density (km per million people) – 2009	Euromonitor International, Global Market Information Database
		Internet users (per 100 habitants) – 2009	International Telecommunication Union, ICT Indicators – 2009
		Population per retail outlet – 2009	Euromonitor International, Global Market Information Database
		Percentage of households with TV – 2009	Euromonitor International, Global Market Information Database
Economic freedom	5/50	Economic Freedom Index – 2010	Heritage Foundation, The Index of Economic Freedom – 2010
		Political Freedom Index – 2010	Freedom House, Survey of Freedom in the World – 2010
Market receptivity	6/50	Per capita imports from the USA (US$) – 2009	US Census Bureau Foreign Trade Division, Country Trade Data – 2009
		Trade as a percentage of GDP (%) – 2009	World Bank, World Development Indicators – 2009
Country risk	4/50	Country risk rating – 2010	Euromoney, Country Risk Survey – March 2010

Source: globalEDGE, 2011.

Table 10.6 The Market Potential Index (MPI) for Emerging Markets, 2010

Country	Market size	Market growth rate	Market intensity	Market consumption capacity	Commercial infrastructure	Economic freedom	Market receptivity	Country risk	Overall score
China	100	100	1	60	33	2	2	64	92
India	38	78	26	60	9	47	3	50	48
Turkey	6	36	67	65	48	58	10	40	36
Brazil	21	36	47	20	52	55	1	50	28
Indonesia	11	53	41	63	33	50	1	33	27
Mexico	10	18	61	27	46	70	17	51	27
Malaysia	3	19	29	73	59	49	28	37	26
Chile	2	13	50	24	50	100	11	71	26
Egypt	4	45	58	75	39	25	4	34	25
Thailand	4	33	36	52	54	43	16	38	21
Peru	2	41	50	36	33	69	3	41	17
Russia	24	1	40	49	65	11	2	44	17
Pakistan	6	58	61	79	1	29	1	1	14
Philippines	5	24	62	48	31	41	5	26	12
South Africa	6	24	46	1	12	67	29	48	8

Source: globalEDGE, 2011.

The MOI rankings are perhaps most useful for gaining insight into individual markets in a comparative sense. The index helps reduce the complexity of evaluating the relative attractiveness of EMs. With this knowledge of the trade-offs involved in choosing between EMs, managers can be more objective and systematic in selecting candidate markets. Once the number to be investigated is reduced to a manageable few, managers can then proceed to an in-depth analysis of the most promising EMs on offer.

Chapter Questions

1 Discuss the factors that need to be considered in aligning company capabilities with company strategy.
2 What are some of the key processes in going international? Discuss such processes in the context of internationalizing to EMs.
3 Discuss the factors that firms need to consider in researching EMs.

APPENDIX

Information Sources in Emerging Markets

Sources for General Information and Analysis		
Global EDGE	www.globaledge.msu.edu	Provides specialized knowledge on a wide range of topics on a country basis.
The US Department of Commerce	www.export.gov	Publishes comprehensive guides on doing business in different countries.
The CIA World Factbook	www.cia.gov/factbook/	Provides information on the background, economy, population, communication and infrastructure for different countries. Also gives country rankings for a wide array of indicators.
FDI profiles	www.vcc.columbia.edu	Provides information and analysis on multiple topics, such as foreign direct investment, policy changes, and multinationals in emerging markets.
Living abroad	www.livingabroad.com/	Provides data on different countries in a broad range of cultural dimensions.

(Continued)

(Continued)

Executive Planet	www.executiveplanet.com/	Provides country-based information on culture and etiquette.
Geert Hofstede's cultural dimensions	www.geert-hofstede.com/	Country-based analysis and scores based on Hofstede's cultural dimensions.
Nation Master	www.nationmaster.com	Provides country-based information and rankings on a wide array of topics such as crime, the economy, taxation, democracy, health, sports, etc.

Sources for Different Indices

Global EDGE	www.globaledge.msu.edu	Publishes the Market Potential Index.
A.T. Kearney	www.atkearney.com	Publishes indices such as the Global Retail Development Index, the globalization index, and the global services location index.
The Heritage Foundation	www.heritage.org/	Publishes the Index of Economic Freedom which compares countries according to measures such as business, trade, investment, property rights, and freedom.
Institute for Management Development	www.imd.org/	Publishes the World Competitiveness Yearbook which analyses and compares countries on their ability to create a business environment which can facilitate growth and the competitiveness of firms.
Transparency International	www.transparency.org	Publishes the Corruption Perception Index which ranks countries according to perceived levels of corruption.
Freedom House	www.freedomhouse.org/	Provides background on countries focusing on political rights civil liberties, and publishes an annual survey on the Progress of Freedom of the world.

Legatum Institute	www.li.com/	Provides country-based information on a range of topics, such as the economy, entrepreneurship, governance, health, safety, etc. Publishes the Legatum Prosperity Index which compares countries according to their wealth and quality of life.
Euromoney Country Risk	www.euromoneycountryrisk.com/	Provides country-based reports on economic, political and structural characteristics and publishes annual country risk ratings.
Global Competitiveness Report	www.weforum.org/en/initiatives	Provides a set of reports on a broad range of issues, such as the gender gap, global competitiveness, and global information technology.
Global Production Location Scoreboard	www.global-production.com	Benchmarks emerging markets and developing markets as locations for global production, and provides country comparisons based on various indicators such as industrial capability, export specialization, wage costs, etc.
The International Intellectual Property Alliance	www.iipa.com/	Provides country-based information on copyright enforcement and protection, and publishes the International Intellectual Property Rights Index.

Providers of Databases

Gapminder	www.gapminder.org/	An interactive database which combines data from multiple sources, such as the International Labour Organization, World Health Organization, World Bank, etc.
OECD	www.oecd.org	Provides data on international trade and investment.
The World Bank	www.worldbank.org	Provides comprehensive data on many topics such as millennium development goals, country governance indicators, gender, education statistics, and world development indicators.

(Continued)

(Continued)

The Economist Intelligence Unit	www.eiu.com	Provides country analysis reports and forecasts.
The United Nations	http://data.un.org/	Provides comprehensive data on a range of topics, such as crime, education, energy, finance, tourism, and information and communication technology.
The International Labour Organization	http://laborsta.ilo.org/	Provides labour statistics such as employment statistics, labour costs, wages, and hours of work.
The International Monetary Fund	www.imf.org	Provides a data series on indicators related to IMF lending, national accounts, the balance of payments, imports and exports.
The United Nations Conference on Trade and Development (UNCTAD)	http://unctadstat.unctad.org	An interactive database which provides data on various topics related to trade and foreign investment.
GE Health of Nations	www.healthofnations.com/	Provides data and information on healthcare issues on a country basis.

References

Abramson, N. & Merchant, H. 2008. Red Star China: discovering the essence of Guanxi. *Competing in Emerging Markets,* Chapter 5. Abingdon: Routledge.

Accenture 2008. Multi-Polar World 2: The Rise of the Emerging-Market Multinational. *Understanding the Multi-Polar World.* Accenture Policy & Corporate Affairs, http://www.accenture.com/SiteCollectionDocuments/PDF/MPW2.pdf. Accessed 30/5/2012.

Accenture 2012. *Fast Forward to Growth: Seizing Opportunities in High-growth Markets.* The Accenture Institute for High Performance. http://www.accenture.com/us-en/Pages/insight-fast-forward-growth-seizing-opportunities-high-growth-markets.aspx. Accessed 30/05/2012.

Acuff, F. 1993. *How to Negotiate Anything with Anyone Anywhere in the World.* New York: American Management Association.

Acuff, F. 2008. *How to Negotiate Anything with Anyone Anywhere Around the World.* New York: American Management Association (AMACOM).

Adair, W. L. & Brett, J. M. 2005. The negotiation dance: time, culture, and behavioral sequences in negotiation. *Organization Science*, vol. 16, issue 1, 33–51.

Adair, W., Brett, J., Lempereur, A., Okumura, T., Shikhirev, P., Tinsley, C. & Lytle, A. 2004. Culture and negotiation strategy. *Negotiation Journal*, vol. 20, 87–111.

ADB, 2011. *The Informal Sector and Informal Employment in Indonesia.* Asian Development Bank, BPS Statistics Indonesia. Metro Manila, the Phillipines.

Aggarwal, R. 1989. International business through barter and counter-trade. *Long Range Planning*, vol. 22, issue 3, 75–81.

Aggarwal, R. 2009. Economic development, business strategy, and corporate restructuring in India. *Journal of Indian Business Research*, vol. 1, issue 1, 14–25.

Aguilar, M., Becerra, J., Juan, J. D., Leon, E., Nieponice, G., Pena, I., Pikman, M. & Ukon, M. 2009. The 2009 BCG multilatinas. *The Boston Consulting Group*, 1–15. http://www.bcg.com/expertise_impact/publications/publicationdetails.aspx?id=tcm:12-26556. Accessed on 30/05/2012.

Aguilar, M., Boutenko, V., Michael, D., Rastogi, V., Subramanian, A. & Zhou, Y. 2010. The internet's new billion. *The Boston Consulting Group*, 4–28.

Ahmed, V. & Wahab, M. A. 2011. Foreign assistance and economic growth: evidence from Pakistan 1972–2010. http://www.bcg.com/documents/file58645.pdf. Accessed on 31/05/2012.

Ahrend, R. 2005. Can Russia break the 'resource curse'? *Eurasian Geography and Economics*, vol. 46, 584–609.

Aidis, R. & Adachi, Y. 2007. Russia: firm entry and survival barriers. *Economic Systems*, vol. 6, issue 8, 391–411.

Airoldi, M., Biscarini, L. & Saracino, V. 2010. *The Global Infrastructure Challenge*. The Boston Consulting Group. http://www.bcg.com/expertise_impact/industries/public_sector/publicationdetails.aspx?id=tcm:12-55995&mid=tcm:12-53912. Accessed on 30/05/2012.

Aitken, B., Hanson, G. H. & Harrison, A. E. 1997. Spillovers, foreign investment and export behavior. *Journal of International Economics*, vol. 43, issues 1–2, 103–132.

Al-Khalifa, A. K. & Peterson, S. E. 1999. The partner selection process in international joint ventures. *European Journal of Marketing*, vol. 33, issue 11/12, 1064–1081.

Albaum, G. & Duerr, E. 2008. *International Marketing and Export Management*. Essex: Prentice-Hall.

Alcácer, J. & Chung, W. 2011. Benefiting from location: knowledge retrieval. *Global Strategy Journal*, vol.1, issue 3–4, 233–236.

Ambler, T., Xi, C. & Witzel, M. 2008. *Doing Business in China*. London: Taylor & Francis.

Amsden, A. H. 1989. *Asia's Next Giant: Late Industrialization in South Korea*. Oxford, UK: OUP.

Anand, J., Brenes, E. R., Karnani, A. & Rodriquez, A. 2006. Strategic responses to economic liberalization in emerging economies: lessons from experience. *Journal of Business Research*, vol. 59, issue 3, 365–371.

Anderson, E. & Gatignon, H. 1986. Modes of foreign entry: a transaction cost analysis and propositions. *Journal of International Business Studies*, vol. 17, issue 3, 1–26.

Anderson, J. & Billou, N. 2007. Serving the world's poor: innovation at the base of the economic pyramid. *Journal of Business Strategy*, vol. 28, issue 2, 14–21.

Anderson, J. & Markides, C. 2007. Strategic innovation at the base of the economic pyramid. *Harvard Business Online*. http://hbr.org/product/strategic-innovation-at-the-base-of-the-pyramid/an/SMR267-PDF-ENG. Accessed on 30/05/2012

Ang, J. B. 2008. Determinants of foreign direct investment in Malaysia. *Journal of Policy Modeling*, vol. 30, issue 1, 185–189.

Aninat, C., Benavente, J. M., Briones, I., Eyzaguirre, N., Navia, P. & Olivari, J. 2010. The political economy of productivity: the case of Chile (April 2010). IDB Working Paper No.22. Available at SSRN:http://ssrn.com/abstract=1807607.]

Arellano-Yanguas, J. 2008. *A Thoroughly Modern Resource Curse?: The New Natural Resource Policy Agenda and the Mining Revival in Peru.* Institute of Development Studies, University of Sussex, UK.

Arellano-Yanguas, J. 2011. Aggravating the resource curse: decentralisation, Mining and conflict in Peru. *Journal of Development Studies*, vol. 47, issue 4, 617–638.

Arias, J., Azuara, O., Bernal, P., Heckman, J. J. & Villarreal, C. 2010. Policies to promote growth and economic efficiency in Mexico, NBER Working Papers 16554, National Bureau of Economic Research, Inc.

Arora, A., Fosfuri, A. & Gambardella, A. 2001. Markets for technology and their implications for corporate strategy. *Industrial and Corporate Change*, vol. 10, issue 2, 419.

Arroyo, F. & Edmunds, J. C. 2010. The macro dimensions of Chile's export dilemma. *Global Economy Journal*, vol. 9, issue 4, ISSN (Online) 1525-5861, DOI: 10.2202/1524-5861.1546, January.

Åslund, A., Guriev, S. & Kuchins, A. 2010. *Russia After the Global Economic Crisis.* Washington, DC: Peterson Institute.

Åslund, A. & Kuchins, A. 2009. *The Russia Balance Sheet.* Washington, DC: Peterson Institute.

Aswathappa, A. 2005. *International Business.* Tata McGraw-Hill Education, India.

Athreye, S. & Godley, A. 2009. Internationalization and technological leap-frogging in the pharmaceutical industry. *Industrial and Corporate Change*, vol. 18, issue 2, 295–323.

Athreye, S. & Kapur, S. 2009. Introduction: the internationalization of Chinese and Indian firms – Trends, motivations and strategy. *Industrial and Corporate Change*, vol. 18, issue 2, 209–221.

Athukorala, P. 2011. Trade policy in Malaysia: liberalization process, structure of protection, and reform agenda. *ASEAN Economic Bulletin*, vol. 22, issue 1, 19–34.

Atsmon, Y., Kertesz, A. & Vittal, I. 2011. Is your emerging market strategy local enough? *McKinsey Quarterly*, April, 50–61.

Aulakh, P. S. & Kotabe, M. 2008. Institutional changes and organizational transformation in developing economies. *Journal of International Management*, vol. 14, issue 3, 209–216.

Austin, J. E. 2002. *Managing in Developing Countries: Strategic Analysis and Operating Techniques.* New York: Free.

Aykut, D. & Goldstein, A. 2007. Developing country multinationals: South–South investment comes of age. *Industrial Development for the 21st Century: Sustainable Development Perspectives.* New York: United Nations Department of Economic, Social Affairs. 85–116.

Bach, D., Newman, A. L. & Weber, S. 2006. The international implications of China's fledgling regulatory state: from product maker to rule maker. *New Political Economy*, vol. 11, issue 4, 499–518.

Bahadir, S. C., Bharadwaj, S. & Parzen, M. 2009. A meta-analysis of the determinants of organic sales growth. *International Journal of Research in Marketing*, vol. 26, issue 1, 263–275.

Banerjee, S. G., Oetzel, J. M. & Ranganathan, R. 2006. Private provision of infrastructure in emerging markets: do institutions matter? *Development Policy Review*, vol. 24, issue 2, 175–202.

Bartlett, C. & Goshal, S. 2000. Going global: lessons from latemovers. *Harvard Business Review*, March-April, 132–142.

Basri, M. C. & Rahardja, S. 2010. The Indonesian economy amidst the global crisis: good policy and good luck. *ASEAN Economic Bulletin*, vol. 27, issue 1, 77–97.

Bausch, A., Fritz, T. & Boesecke, K. 2007. Performance effects of internationalization strategies: a meta-analysis. *Research in Global Strategic Management*, issue 13, 143–176.

BCG 2011. *Special Report: Rethinking Operations for a Two-Speed World*. Available at: https://www.bcgperspectives.com/content/articles/innovation_supply_chain_management_rethinking_operations_for_two_speed_world_knowledge_at_wharton/. Accessed on 30/05/2012.

Beamish, P. W. & Lupton, N. C. 2009. Managing joint ventures. *The Academy of Management Perspectives* (formerly *The Academy of Management Executive*) (*AMP*), vol. 23, issue 2, 75–94.

Beardsley, S. C. & Evans, A. L. 1998. Who will connect you? *McKinsey Quarterly*. Available at http://www.mckinseyquarterly.com/Who_will_connect_you_317. Accessed on 30/05/2012.

Beittel, J. S. & Margesson, R. 2010. Chile Earthquake: US and International Response. Available at http://assets.opencrs.com/rpts/R41112_20100311.pdf. Accessed on 30/05/2012.

Bell, M. & Pavitt, K. 1993. Technological accumulation and industrial growth: contrasts between developed and developing countries. *Industrial and Corporate Change*, vol. 2, issue 1, 157–210.

Bello, D. C. & Gilliland, D. I. 1997. The effect of output controls, process controls, and flexibility on export channel performance. *Journal of Marketing*, vol. 61, issue 1, 22–38.

Bensidoun, I., Lemoine, F. & Ünal, D. 2009. The integration of China and India into the world economy: a comparison. *European Journal of Comparative Economics*, vol. 6, issue 1, 131–155.

Bernanke, B. S. 2010. Rebalancing the global recovery. Available at http://www.federalreserve.gov/newsevents/speech/bernanke20101119a.htm. Accessed on 30/05/2012.

Bhat, J. M., Gupta, M. & Murthy, S. N. 2006. Overcoming requirements engineering challenges: lessons from offshore outsourcing. *Software: IEEE*, vol. 23, issue 5, 38–44.

Bhattacharya, A. K. & Michael, D. C. 2011. How local companies keep multinationals at bay. *Harvard Business Review on Thriving in Emerging Markets*. Boston, MA: Harvard Business School Publishing Corporation, 65–99

Bhaumik, S. K., Driffield, N. & Pal, S. 2009. Does ownership structure of emerging market firms affect their outward FDI? The case of the Indian automative and pharmaceutical sectors. *Journal of International Business Studies*, vol. 41, issue 3, 437–450.

Bianchi, C. 2009. Retail internationalization from emerging markets: case study evidence from Chile. *International Marketing Review*, vol. 26, issue 2, 221–243.

Bianchi, C. & Ostale, E. 2006. Lessons learned from unsuccesful internationalization attempts: examples of multinational retailers in Chile. *Journal of Business Research*, vol. 59, issue 1, 140–147.

Black, J. S. & Morrison, A. J. 2010. A cautionary tale for emerging market giants. *Harvard Business Review*, vol. 88, issue 9, 99–106.

Bonaglia, F., Goldstein, A. & Matthews, J. 2007. Accelerated internationalization by emerging multinationals: the case of the white goods sector. *Journal of World Business*, vol. 42, issue 4, 369–383.

Bose, R. 2009. *India Business Checklists: An Essential Guide to Doing Business*. Singapore: Wiley.

BrandFinance 2011. Brand Finance Global 500. *Global 500*. London, UK: Brand Finance.

Bremmer, I. 2009. State capitalism and the crisis. *McKinsey Quarterly*, July. Available at http://www.mckinseyquarterly.com/State_capitalism_and_the_crisis_2403. Accessed on 30/05/2012.

Bremmer, I. 2010. The end of the free market: who wins the war between states and corporations? *European View*, 1–4.

Brett, J. M. & Gelfand, M. J. 2005. Lessons from abroad: when culture affects negotiating style. *Harvard Business Review*, vol. 9, issue 2, 1–5.

Brouthers, L. E., Nakos, G., Hadjimarcou, J. & Brouthers, K. D. 2009. Key factors for successful export performance for small firms. *Journal of International Marketing*, vol. 17, issue 3, 21–38.

Bruner, R. F., Conroy, R. M., Li, W., O'Halloran, E. F. & Lleras, M. P. 2003. *Investing in Emerging Markets*. VA: The Research Foundation of AIMR (The Association for Investment Management and Research).

Buckley, P. J. & Casson, M. C. 1998. Analyzing foreign market entry strategies: extending the internationalization approach. *Journal of International Business Studies*, vol. 29, issue 3, 539–561.

Buckley, P. J., Clegg, J. L., Cross, A. R., Voss, H., Rhodes, M. & Zheng, P. 2008. Explaining China's Outward FDI: An Institutional Perspective. In Sauvant, K. P. (ed.) *The Rise of Transnational Corporations from Emerging Markets: Threat of Opportunity?* Cheltenham: Edward Elgar.

Buckley, P. J. & Ghauri, P. N. 1999. *The Internationalization of the Firm*. Andover: Cengage Learning EMEA.

Buckley, P. J. & Ghauri, P. N. 2004. Globalization, economic geography and the strategy of multinational enterprises. *Journal of International Business Studies*, vol. 35, 81–98.

Buckley, P. J., Clegg, L. J., Cross, A. R., Liu, X., Voss, H. & Zheng, P. 2007. The determinants of Chinese outward foreign direct investment. *Journal of International Business Studies*, vol. 38, issue 4, 499–518.

Budhwar, P. S. & Varma, A. 2011. *Doing Business in India: Building Research-Based Practice.* New York: Routledge.

Busse, M. 2009. Tariffs, transport costs and the WTO Doha Round: the case of developing countries. *Ester Centre Journal of International Law and Trade Policy*, vol. 4, issue 1.

Busse, M., Königer, J. & Nunnenkamp, P. 2010. FDI promotion through bilateral investment treaties: more than a bit? *Review of World Economics*, vol. 146, issue 1, 147–177.

Butt, M. S. & Bandara, J. S. 2009. *Trade Liberalization and Regional Disparity in Pakistan.* Oxon, UK: Routledge.

Bytyci, M. 2009. *Phatic Communication.* Munich, Germany: GRIN Verlag.

Caballero, R. & Dornbusch, R. 2002. Argentina: *A Rescue Plan that Works.* Available at http://cdi.mecon.gov.ar/biblio/docelec/mit/rudig200202.pdf (accessed 17 December 2011).

Calof, J. L. & Beamish, P. W. 1995. Adapting to foreign markets: explaining internationalization. *International Business Review*, vol. 4, issue 2, 115–131.

Cantwell, J. & Barnard, H. 2008. Do firms from emerging markets have to invest abroad? Outward FDI and the competitiveness of firms. In Sauvant, K. P. (ed.) *The Rise of Transnational Corporations from Emerging Markets: Threat of Opportunity?* Cheltenham: Edward Elgar.

Caprio, G. 2005. *The Future of State-owned Financial Institutions.* Washington, DC: Brookings Institute.

Carvalho, F. & Goldstein, A. 2009. The 'making of' national giants: the international expansion for oil companies from Brazil and China. In Dolfsma, W., Duysters, G. & Costa, I. (eds) *Multinationals and Emerging Economies: The Quest for Innovation and Sustainability.* Cheltenham: Edward Elgar.

Casanova, L. 2009. *Global Latinas: Latin America's Emerging Multinationals.* New York: Palgrave Macmillan.

Cateora, P. R., Gilly, M. C. & Graham, J. L. 2009. *International Marketing.* New York: McGraw-Hill Irwin.

Cavusgil, S. T., Kiyak, T. & Yeniyurt, S. 2004. Complementary approaches to preliminary foreign market opportunity assessment: country clustering and country ranking. *Industrial Marketing Management*, vol. 33, issue 7, 607–617.

Cavusgil, S. T., Yaprak, A. & Yeoh, P. L. 1993. A decision-making framework for global sourcing. *International Business Review*, vol. 2, issue 2, 143–156.

Cavusgil, T., Knight, G. & Riesenberger, J. R. 2008. *International Business: Strategy, Management and the New Realities.* Harlow: Pearson Education, Alibris UK.

Chalamish, E. 2009. Protectionism and sovereign investment post global recession. OECD Global Forum on International Investment VIII, December. Available at: www. oecd. org/investment/gfi-8

Chamon, M. & Prasad, E. S. 2008. Why are saving rates of urban households in China rising?, *American Economic Journal: Macroeconomics*, American Economic Association, vol. 2, issue 1, 93–130.

Chan, C. M., Isobe, T. & Makino, S. 2008. Which country matters? Institutional development and foreign affiliate performance. *Strategic Management Journal*, vol. 29, issue 11, 1179–1205.

Chandra, M. & Nelankavil, J. P. 2008. Product development and innovation for developing countries: potential and challenges. *Journal of Management Development*, vol. 27, issue 10, 1017–1025.

Chao, M. C. H. & Kumar, V. 2010. The impact of institutional distance on the international diversity performance relationship. *Journal of World Business*, vol. 45, issue 1, 93–103.

Chavan, A. L., Gorney, D., Prabhu, B. & Arora, S. 2009. The washing machine that ate my sari – mistakes in cross-cultural design. *Interactions*, vol. 16, issue 1, 26–31.

Chen, R. 2004. Corporate reputation: pricing and competing in Chinese markets – strategies for multinationals. *Journal of Business Strategy*, vol. 25, issue 6, 45–50.

Chen, S. H., Lee, H. T. & Wu, Y. F. 2008. Applying an ANP approach to partner selection for strategic alliance. *Management Decision*, vol. 46, issue 3, 449–465.

Chiao, Y. C., Lo, F. Y. & Yu, C. M. 2010. Choosing between wholly-owned subsidiaries and joint ventures of MNCs from an emerging market. *International Marketing Review*, vol. 27, issue 5, 338–365.

Child, J. & Rodrigues, S. B. 2005. The internationalization of Chinese firms: a case for theoretical extension? *Management and Organization Review*, vol. 1, issue 3, 381–410.

Ching, M. K. 2008. *CFO Guide to Doing Business in China*. New York: Wiley.

Cho, D. S., Kim, D. J. & Rhee, D. K. 1998. Latecomer strategies: evidence from the semiconductor industry in Japan and Korea. *Organization Science*, vol. 9, issue 4, 489–505.

Choi, H. 2011. Building a presence in today's growth markets: the experience of privately held companies. Pricewaterhousecoopers LLP. Available at http://www.pwc.com/ca/en/private-company/publications/2011-05-indonesia-en.pdf. Accessed on 30/05/2012.

Chu-Weininger, M. Y. L. & Weininger, M. A. 2009. Cross-cultural markets and consumer behaviors: the case of China and Turkey. *Journal of Euromarketing*, vol. 18, issue 1-2, 189–198.

Claessens, S., Dell'ariccia, G., Igan, D. & Laeven, L. 2010. Cross-country experiences and policy implications from the global financial crisis. *Economic Policy*, vol. 25, issue 62, 267–293.

Clausen, A. 2010. Economic globalization and regional disparities in the Philippines. *Singapore Journal of Tropical Geography*, vol. 31, issue 3, 299–316.

Colburn, F. D. 2009. Latin America: captive to commodities. *Dissent*, vol. 56, 29–32.

Colphan, A. M., Hikino, T. & Lincoln, J. R. 2010. *The Oxford Handbook of Business Groups*. Oxford: Oxford University Press.

Compeau, D., Fanf, Y. & Yin, M. 2010. Google in China. *Richard Ivey School of Business*, 1–11.

Constantinou, D. & Ashta, A. 2011. Financial crisis: lessons from microfinance. *Strategic Change*, vol. 20, issue 5–6, 187–203.

Constanza, C. 2009. Retail internationalization from emerging markets: case study evidence from Chile. *International Marketing Review*, vol. 26, issue 2, 221–243.

Contractor, F. J. 2007. The evolutionary or multi-stage theory of internationalization and its relationship to the regionalisation of firms. *Research in Global Strategic Management*, vol. 13, issue 4, 11–29.

Conway, T. & Swift, J. S. 2000. International relationship marketing: the importance of psychic distance. *European Journal of Marketing*, vol. 34, issue 11/12, 1391–1414.

Court, D. & Narasimhan, L. 2010. Capturing the world's emerging middle class. *McKinsey Quarterly*. Available at http://www.mckinseyquarterly.com/Capturing_the_worlds_emerging_middle_class_2639. Accessed on 30/05/2012.

Cuervo-Cazurra, A. 2006. Business groups and their types. *Asia Pacific Journal of Management*, vol. 23, issue 4, 419–437.

Cuerva-Cazurra, A. 2007. Sequence of Value Added Activities in the Multinationalization of Developing Country Firms. *Journal of International Management*, vol. 13, 258–277.

Cuervo-Cazurra, A. & Dau, L. A. 2008. Structural reform and firm profitability in developing countries. *Emerging Multinationals: Outward Foreign Direct Investment from Emerging and Developing Economies*. Copenhagen: Copenhagen Business School.

Cuervo-Cazurra, A. & Genc, M. 2008. Transforming disadvantages into advantages: developing country MNEs in the least developed countries. *Journal of International Business Studies*, vol. 39, issue 6, 957–979.

Culpan, R. 2009. A fresh look at strategic alliances: research issues and future directions. *International Journal of Strategic Business Alliances*, vol. 1, issue 1, 4–23.

Currie, W. L., Michell, V. & Abanishe, O. 2008. Knowledge process outsourcing in financial services: the vendor perspective. *European Management Journal*, vol. 26, issue 2, 94–104.

Da Rocha, A., Dept, I.-A. D. B. R. & Network, L. A. R. 2008. *The Emergence of New and Successful Export Activities in Brazil: Four Case Studies from the Manufacturing and the Agricultural Sector*. Inter-American Development Bank, USA.

Damijan, J. P., Knell, M., Majcen, B. & Rojec, M. 2003. The role of FDI, R&D accumulation and trade in transferring technology to transition countries: evidence from firm panel data for eight transition countries. *Economic Systems*, vol. 27, issue 2, 189–204.

D'Andrea, G., Marcotte, D. & Morrison, G. D. 2010. The globe: let emerging market customers be your teachers. *Harvard Business Review*, December, 2010, available at http://hbr.org/2010/12/the-globe-let-emerging-market-customers-be-your-teachers/ar/1. Accessed on 30/05/2012.

Daniels, J. D., Radebaugh, L. H. & Sullivan, D. P. 1995. *International Business*. London: Addison-Wesley.

Danis, W. M., De Clercq, D. & Petricevic, O. 2010. Are social networks more important for new business activity in emerging than developed economies? An empirical extension. *International Business Review*, vol. 20, issue 4, 394–408.

Das, T. & Kumar, R. 2011. Interpartner negotiations in alliances: a strategic framework. *Management Decision*, vol. 49, issue 8, 1235–1256.

David, R. J. & Han, S. K. 2004. A systematic assessment of the empirical support for transaction cost economics. *Strategic Management Journal*, vol. 25, issue 1, 39–58.

Davidson, K. 2009. Ethical concerns at the bottom of the pyramid: where CSR meets BOP. *Journal of International Business Ethics*, vol. 2, issue 1, 22–32.

Dawar, N. & Chattopadhyay, A. 2002. Rethinking marketing programmes for emerging markets. *Long Range Planning*, vol. 35, issue 5, 457–474.

Dawar, N. & Frost, T. 1999. Competing with giants: survival strategies for local companies in emerging markets. *Harvard Business Review*, March–April, vol. 77, issue 2, 119–129.

De Gregorio, J. 2011. *Chile: Policy Responses to the Global Crisis*. Citeseer, Available at http://www.bis.org/review/r110119a.pdf. Accessed on 30/05/2012.

De Mooij, M. K. 2009. *Global Marketing and Advertising: Understanding Cultural Paradoxes*. Thousand Oaks, CA: Sage.

De Souza, A. 2011. The politics of personality in Brazil. *Journal of Democracy*, vol. 22, issue 2, 75–88.

Declercq, D., Danis, W. M. & Dakhil, M. 2009. The moderating effect of institutional context on the relationship between associational activity and new business activity in emerging economies. *International Business Review*, vol. 19, issue 1, 85–101.

Deitz, G. D., Tokman, M., Richey, R. G. & Morgan, R. M. 2010. Joint venture stability and cooperation: direct, indirect and contingent effects of resource complementarity and trust. *Industrial Marketing Management*, vol. 39, issue 5, 862–873.

Denekamp, J. G. 1995. Intangible assets, internalization, and foreign direct investment in manufacturing. *Journal of International Business Studies*, vol. 25, issue 4, 493–504.

Deng, P. 2009. Why do Chinese firms tend to acquire strategic assets in international expansion? *Journal of World Business*, vol. 44, issue 1, 74–84.

Devinney, T. M. 2010. Living in a Global Monitory Democracy: Social Responsibility, Global Strategy and the Multinational Enterprise (June 2010). Available at SSRN: http:ssrn.com/abstract = 1633971.

Dhanaraj, C. & Beamish, P. W. 2003. A resource based approach to the study of export performance. *Journal of Small Business Management*, vol. 41, issue 3, 242–261.

Dieckmann, R., Speyer, B. & Walter, N. 2007. Microfinance: an emerging investment opportunity. *Deutsche Bank Research: Current Issues – Frankfurt*. Available at http://www.dbresearch.com/PROD/DBR_INTERNET_EN-PROD/PROD0000000000219174.pdf. Accessed on 30/05/2012.

Djankov, S., Glaeser, E., La Porta, R., Lopez-De-Silanes, F. & Shleifer, A. 2003. The new comparative economics. *Journal of Comparative Economics*, vol. 31, 595–619.

Dobbs, R., Remes, J. & Smit, S. 2011. The world's new growth frontier: midsize cities in emerging markets. *McKinsey Quarterly*, 46–50. Available at http://www.mckinseyquarterly.com/The_worlds_new_growth_frontier_Midsize_cities_in_emerging_markets_2775. Accessed on 30/05/2012.

Doctor, M. 2009. Furthering industrial development in Brazil: globalization and the national innovation system. Rio de Janeiro: Latin American Studies Association. http://lasa.international.pitt.edu/members/congress-papers/lasa2009/files/DoctorMahrukh.pdf

Doh, J. P., Bunyaratavej, K. & Hahn, E. D. 2009. Separable but not equal: the location determinants of discrete services offshoring activities. *Journal of International Business Studies*, vol. 40, issue 6, 926–943.

Domingues, L. V. & Brenes, E. R. 1997. The internationalization of Latin American enterprises and market liberalization in the Americas: a vital linkage. *Journal of Business Research*, vol. 38, issue 1, 3–16.

Donaldson, R. H. & Nogee, J. L. 2009. *The Foreign Policy of Russia: Changing Systems, Enduring Interests*. Armonk, NY: ME Sharpe Inc.

Doney, P. M., Barry, J. M. & Abratt, R. 2007. Trust determinants and outcomes in global B2B services. *European Journal of Marketing*, vol. 41, issue 9/10, 1096–1116.

Dong, M. C., Tse, D. K. & Cavusgil, S. T. 2008. Efficiency of governance mechanisms in China's distribution channels. *International Business Review*, vol. 17, issue 5, 509–519.

Duisters, D., Duysters, G. & De Man, A. P. 2011. The partner selection process: steps, effectiveness, governance. *International Journal of Strategic Business Alliances*, vol. 2, issue 1–2, 7–25.

Dunbar, E. & Katcher, A. 1990. Preparing managers for foreign assignments. *Training and Development Journal*, vol. 44, issue 9, 45–47.

Dunning, J. H. 1994. *Reevaluating the Benefits of Foreign Direct Investment*. Reading: University of Reading, Department of Economics, UK.

Dunning, J. H. 2004. Determinants of foreign direct investment: globalization-induced changes and the role of policies. *Toward Pro-poor Policies: Aid, Institutions, and Globalization*. 5th Annual World Bank Conference on Development Economics Europe, Paris, France.

Dunning, J. H. 2009. Location and the multinational enterprise: a neglected factor. *Journal of International Business Studies*, vol. 40, issue 1, 5–19.

Dunning, J. H., Kim, C. & Park, D. 2008. Old wine in new bottles: a comparison of emerging market TNCs today and developed country TNCs thirty years ago. In Sauvant, K. P. (ed.) *The Rise of Transnational*

Corporations from Emerging Markets: Threat or Opportunity. Cheltenham: Edward Elgar.

Economist 2009. Sharia calling: a political row about Muslim law, *The Economist.* Available at: www.economist.com/node/14859353. Accessed on 15/11/2011.

Economist 2011a. Beyond economics: businesspeople need to think harder about political risk. *The Economist,* 10 February. Avaialable at http://www.economist.com/node/18112117. Accessed on 30/05/2012.

Economist 2011b. *Pocket World in Figures.* London: Profile Books.

Economist Intelligence Unit (EIU) 2011. Global intelligence and analysis. *The Economist.* Available at: www.eiu.com/Default.aspx. Accessed on 17/12/2011.

Egan, H. & Ovanessoff, A. 2011. Gearing up for growth. Available at: www.accenture.com/SiteCollectionDocuments/PDF/Gearing_Up_For_Growth_Five_Imperatives_For_Success_In_Emerging_Markets.pdf. Accessed 19/12/2011.

Elango, B. & Pattnaik, C. 2007. Building capabilities for international operations through networks: a study of Indian firms. *Journal of International Business Studies,* vol. 38, issue 4, 541–555.

Elg, U. 2008. Inter-firm market orientation and the influence of network and relational factors. *Scandinavian Journal of Management,* vol. 24, issue 1, 55–68.

Elg, U., Ghauri, P. N. & Tarnovskaya, V. 2008. The role of networks and matching in market entry to emerging retail markets. *International Marketing Review,* vol. 25, issue 6, 674–699.

Enderwick, P. 2007. *Understanding Emerging Markets: China and India.* London: Routledge.

Enderwick, P. 2009. Large emerging markets (LEMs) and international strategy. *International Marketing Review,* vol. 26, issue 1, 7–16.

Estrin, S., Pouliakova, S. & Shapiro, D. 2009. The performance effects of business groups in Russia. *Journal of Management Studies,* vol. 46, issue 3, 393–420.

Eurasia. 2011. *Top Risks 2011* [Online]. Eurasia Group. Accessed on 31/05/2012.

Euromonitor. 2012. Euromonitor International. http://www.euromonitor.com/.

Evans, P. B. 1995. *Embedded Autonomy: States and Industrial Transformation,* New York: Princeton University Press.

Eyring, M. J., Johnson, M. W. & Nair, H. 2011. New business models in emerging markets. *Harvard Business Review of Thriving in Emerging Markets.* Boston, MA: Harvard Business School Publishing Corporation.

Fan, Q., Reis, J. G., Jarvis, M., Beath, A. & Frauscher, K. 2008. *The Investment Climate in Brazil, India, and South Africa.* Available at http://info.worldbank.org/etools/docs/library/242750/Brazil-India-South%20Africa%20Investment%20Climate%20Comparison%20Final.pdf

Fang, E. E. & Zou, S. 2009. Antecedents and consequences of marketing dynamic capabilities in international joint ventures. *Journal of International Business Studies*, vol. 40, pp, 742–761.

Farrell, D. 2004. The hidden dangers of the informal economy. *McKinsey Quarterly*, 3. , available at http://www.mckinseyquarterly.com/The_hidden_dangers_of_the_informal_economy_1448. Accessed on 30/05/2012.

Farrell, D. 2007. *Offshoring: Understanding the Emerging Global Labor Market*. Boston, MA: Harvard Business Press, MA, US.

Farrell, D., Kaka, N. & Sturze, S. 2005. Ensuring India's offshoring future. *McKinsey Quarterly*, available at http://www.mckinseyquarterly.com/Ensuring_Indias_offshoring_future_1660. Accessed on 30/05/2012.

Fdimarkets 2012. fDIMarkets.com Crossborder Investment Monitor. http://www.fdimarkets.com/index.cfm?page_name=markets. The Financial Times Limited.

Fernandez, Z. & Nieto, M. J. 2006. Impact of ownership on the international involvement of SMEs. *Journal of International Business Studies*, vol. 37, issue 3, 340–351.

Ferraro, G. P. 2002. *The Cultural Dimension of International Business*. Englewood Cliffs, NJ: Prentice Hall.

Fidrmuc, J. & Korhonen, I. 2010. The impact of the global financial crisis on business cycles in Asian emerging economies. *Journal of Asian Economics*, vol. 21, issue 3, 293–303.

Filatotchev, I., Strange, R., Piesse, J. & Lien, Y. C. 2007. FDI by firms from newly industrialized economies in emerging markets: corporate governance, entry mode and location. *Journal of International Business Studies*, vol. 38, issue 4, 556–572.

Fletcher, R. 2009. Countertrade and international outsourcing: a relationship and network perspective. *IUG Business Review*, vol. 2, issue 1, 25.

Fleury, A. & Fleury, M. T. L. 2011. *Brazilian Multinationals: Competences for Internationalization*. Cambridge: Cambridge University Press.

Forsans, N. & Nelson, D. 2008. *Doing Business in India. DK Essential Managers.* New York: Dorling Kindersley.

Fosfuri, A. & Motta, M. 1999. Multinationals without advantages. *Scandinavian Journal of Economics*, vol. 101, issue 4, 617–630.

Franco, E., Ray, S. & Ray, P. K. 2011. Patterns of innovation practices of multinational-affiliates in emerging economies: evidences from Brazil and India. *World Development*, vol. 39, issue 7,1249–1260.

Franke, J. & Nicholson, N. 2002. Who shall we send? *International Journal of Cross Cultural Management*, vol. 2, issue 1, 21–36.

Freeman, S. & Sandwell, M. 2008. Professional service firms entering emerging markets: the role of network relationships. *Journal of Services Marketing*, vol. 22, issue 3, 198–212.

FTSE. 2012. FTSE Emerging Markets [Online]. Available at www.ftse.com/Indices/FTSE_Emerging_Markets/index.jsp. Accessed on 24/02/2012.

Gadiesh, O., Leung, P. & Vestring, T. 2008. The battle for China's good-enough market. *Harvard Business Review on Emerging Markets*. Boston, MA: Harvard Business School Publishing Corporation.

Galinsky, A. D., Maddux, W. W., Gilin, D. & White, J. B. 2008. Why it pays to get inside the head of your opponent. *Psychological Science*, vol. 19, issue 4, 378–384.

Gallo, M. A. & Sveen, J. 1991. Internationalizing the family business: facilitating and restraining factors. *Family Business Review*, vol. 4, issue 2, 181–190.

Geiger, R. 2008. Corporate governance of emerging-market TNCs: why does it matter? In Sauvant, K. P. (ed.) *The Rise of Transnational Corporations from Emerging Markets: Threat of Opportunity?* Cheltenham: Edward Elgar.

Ghauri, P. & Fang, T. 2001. Negotiating with the Chinese: a socio-cultural analysis. *Journal of World Business*, vol. 36, issue 3, 303–325.

Ghauri, P. 2001. Negotiating international industrial projects: MNCS versus emerging markets, in Arch G. Woodside (ed.) *Getting Better at Sensemaking (Advances in Business Marketing and Purchasing, Vol. 9)*. Bradford: Emerald Group Publishing Limited, 187–201.

Ghauri, P. 2003. A framework for international business negotiations. *International Business Negotiations*. Oxford: Pergamon press.

Ghauri, P. & Cateora, P. 2010. *International Marketing*. London: McGraw-Hill Education.

Ghauri, P. & Holstius, K. 1996. The role of matching in the foreign market entry process in the Baltic States. *European Journal of Marketing*, vol. 30, issue 2, 75–88.

Ghauri, P. & Usunier, J. C. 2003. *International Business Negotiations*. Bradford: Emerald.

Ghauri, P. & Yamin, M. 2009. Revisiting the impact of multinational enterprises on economic development. *Journal of World Business*, vol. 44, issue 2, 105–107.

Ghemawat, P. 2007. *Redefining Global Strategy: Crossing Borders in a World Where Differences Still Matter*. Boston, MA: Harvard Business School Publishing.

Ghemawat, P. 2010. Finding your strategy in the new landscape. *Harvard Business Review*, vol. 88, issue 3, 55–60.

Gifford, M. & Montemayor, R. 2008. *An Overview Assessment of the Revised Draft WTO Modalities for Agriculture*. Geneva: International Centre for Trade and Sustainable Development (ICTSD).

Gillespie, K., Jeannet, J. P. & Hennessey, H. D. 2010. *Global Marketing*. Oklahoma City, OK: South-Western Publishing.

Glaeser, E. L., La Porta, R., Lopez-De-Silanes, F. & Shleifer, A. 2004. Do institutions cause growth? *Journal of Economic Growth*, vol. 9, issue 3, 271–303.

Glick, R., Moreno, R. & Spiegel, M. 2001. *Financial Crises in Emerging Markets*. Cambridge: Cambridge University Press.

Globaledge 2011. *globalEDGE 1994–2011*. Michigan State University [online]. Available at: http://globaledge.msu.edu/. Accessed on 17/12/2011.

Globerman, S. & Shapiro, D. M. 2008. Outward FDI and the economic performance of emerging markets. In Sauvant, K. P. (ed.) *The Rise of*

Transnational Corporations from Emerging Markets: Threat or Opportunity? Cheltenham: Edward Elgar.

GMCI 2010. 2010 Global Manufacturing Competitiveness Index. In DELOITTE (ed.). Available at http://www.deloitte.com/view/en_GX/global/industries/manufacturing/a1a52c646d069210VgnVCM200000bb-42f00aRCRD.htm. Accessed on 30/05/2012.

Goerzen, A. & Asmussen, C. G. 2007. The geographic orientation of multinational enterprises and its implications for performance. In A. M. Rugman (ed.), Regional Aspects of Multinationality and Performance Research in Global Strategic Management, vol. 13, 65–83.

Goldman Sachs 2003. Dreaming with BRICs: the path to 2050. *Global Economics Paper* [online]. Available at www2.goldmansachs.com/our-thinking/brics/brics-reports-pdfs/brics-/dream.pdf. Accessed on 17/12/2011.

Goman, C. K. 2008. *The Nonverbal Advantage: Secrets and Science of Body Language at Work.* San Francisco, CA: Berrett-Koehler Publishers.

Gomes-Casseres, B. 1994. Group versus group: how alliance networks compete. *Harvard Business Review,* 62–74.

Gorodnichenko, Y., Svejnar, J. & Terrell, K. 2008. *Globalization and Innovation in Emerging Markets.* Cambridge, MA: National Bureau of Economic Research.

Gottschalk, P. & Solli-sæther, H. 2006a. Maturity model for IT outsourcing relationships. *Industrial Management & Data Systems,* vol. 106, issue 2, 200–212.

Govindarajan, V. & Ramamurti, R. 2011. Reverse innovation, emerging markets, and global strategy. *Global Strategy Journal,* vol. 1, issue 3–4, 191–205.

Graham, J. L. & Lam, N. M. 2003. The Chinese negotiation. *Harvard Business Review,* vol. 81, 82–91.

Grant Thornton. 2010. Emerging markets: leading the way to recovery [online]. Grant Thornton International Ltd. Available at www.internationalbusinessreport.com. Accessed on 24/02/2011.

Green, F. & Dickerson Jorge, A. 2001. A picture of wage inequality and the allocation of labor through a period of trade liberalization: the case of Brazil. *World Development,* vol. 29, issue 11, 1923–1939.

Griffith-Jones, S., Ocampo, J. A. & Stiglitz, J. E. 2010. *Time for a Visible Hand: Lessons from the 2008 World Financial Crisis.* Oxford: Oxford University Press.

Grueber, M. & Studt, T. 2010. Global R&D funding forecast. *R&D Magazine.* vol. 52, 31–64.

Gubbi, S. R., Aulakh, P. S., Ray, S., Sarkar, M. & Chittoor, R. 2009. Do international acquisitions by emerging-economy firms create shareholder value? The case of Indian firms. *Journal of International Business Studies,* vol. 41, 397–418.

Guérin, I., Roesch, M., Venkatasubramanian, G. & D'Espallier, B. 2011. Credit from whom and for what? The diversity of borrowing sources and uses in rural Southern India. *Journal of International Development*, vol. 24, Issue Supplement S1, 122–137.

Guillen, M. F. 2010. Capability building in business groups. In *The Oxford Handbook of Business Groups*. New York: Oxford University Press.

Gupta, N. 2011. Globalization does lead to change in consumer behavior: An empirical evidence of impact of globalization on changing materialistic values in Indian consumers and its aftereffects. *Asia Pacific Journal of Marketing and Logistics*, vol. 23, issue 3, 251–269.

Gupta, R., Jambunathan, S. & Netzer, T. 2010. Building India: transforming the nation's logistics infrastructure. *McKinsey-India*. Available at http://www.mckinsey.com/locations/india/mckinseyonindia/pdf/Logistics_Infrastructure_by2020_fullreport.pdf. Accessed on 30/05/2012.

Hacklin, F., Marxt, C. & Fahrni, F. 2006. Strategic venture partner selection for collaborative innovation in production systems: a decision support system-based approach. *International Journal of Production Economics*, vol. 104, issue 1, 100–112.

Hadjikhani, A., Lee, J. W. & Ghauri, P. N. 2008. Network view of MNCs' socio-political behavior. *Journal of Business Research*, vol. 61, issue 9, 912–924.

Hägele, K. C. 2010. *International Management*. Munich: GRIN Verlag.

Hall, E. 2000. Monochronic and polychronic time. *Intercultural communication: A reader,* vol. 9, 280–286.

Hall, E. & Hall, M. 2001. Key concepts: underlying structures of culture. In *International HRM: Managing Diversity in the Workplace*. Oxford: Blackwell, 24–41.

Hall, E. T. & Hall, M. R. 1990. *Understanding Cultural Differences*. Maine, USA: Intercultural.

Hamann, R., Reddy, C. & Kapfudzaruwa, F. 2010. *An Investigation into the Antecedents of Corporate Strategic Change with Regard to Black Economic Empowerment and Corporate Social Responsibility in South Africa*. Available at http://www.giz.de/Themen/de/dokumente/2010-en-uct-report-bee-csr.pdf. Accessed on 30/05/2012.

Hammond, A., Kramer, W. J., Tran, J., Katz, R. & Walker, C. 2007. *The Next 4 Billion: Market Size and Business Strategy at the Bottom of the Pyramid*. Washington, USA.

Hang, C. C., Chen, J. & Subramian, A. M. 2010. Developing disruptive products for emerging economies: lessons from Asian cases. *Research-Technology Management*, vol. 53, issue 4, 21–26.

Hanson, P. 2009. Russia to 2020. *Finmeccanica Occasional Paper.* Rome: Finmeccanica.

Harris, J. 2009. Statist globalization in China, Russia and the Gulf states. *Perspectives on Global Development and Technology*, vol. 8, issue 2, 139–163.

Hassan, K. & Lewis, M. 2007. *Handbook of Islamic Banking*. Cheltenham, UK: Edward Elgar Publishing.

Hatani, F. 2009. The logic of spillover interception: the impact of global supply chains in China. *Journal of World Business*, vol. 44, issue 2, 158–166.

Hausmann, R., Klinger, B. & Development, H. U. C. F. I. 2008. *Growth Diagnostics in Peru*. Cambridge, MA: Center for International Development at Harvard University, MA, US.

HBR 2003. *Negotiation*. Boston, MA: Harvard Business School Publishing Corporation.

HBR 2005. *The Essentials of Negotiation*. Boston, MA: Harvard Business Press.

Headifen, R. 2011. Building a presence in today's growth markets: the experience of privately held companies. Price Waterhouse Coopers LLP. Available at http://www.pwc.com/ca/en/private-company/publications/2011-05-indonesia-en.pdf. Accessed on 30/05/2012.

Heleniak, T. 2009. Population perils in Russia at the beginning of the 21st century. In *After Putin's Russia: Past Imperfect, Future Unknown*. Lanham, MD: Rowman and Littlefield Publishers. 133–158.

Henisz, W. J. & Zelner, B. A. 2010. The hidden risks in emerging markets. *Harvard Business Review*, vol. 88, issue 4, 88–95.

Hennart, J. F. 2009. Down with the MNE-centric theories! Market entry and expansion as the bundling of MNE and local assets. *Journal of International Business Studies*, vol. 40, issue 9, 1432–1454.

Heritage 2011. 2011 Index of Economic Freedom. In: JOURNAL, T. H. F. A. T. W. S. (ed.). http://www.heritage.org/index/about

Hermes, N. & Lensink, R. 2007. The empirics of microfinance: what do we know? *The Economic Journal*, vol. 117, issue 517, F1–F10.

Hess, A. M. & Rothaermel, F. T. 2011. When are assets complementary? Star scientists, strategic alliances, and innovation in the pharmaceutical industry. *Strategic Management Journal*, vol. 32, issue 8, 895–909.

Hesse, H., Jobst, A. & Solé, J. 2008. Trends and challenges in Islamic finance. *World Economics*, vol. 9, number 2, 175–193.

Hewlett, S. A. & Rashid, R. 2011. The battle for female tralen in emerging markets. In *Thriving in Emerging Markets*. Boston, MA: Harvard Business School Publishing Corporation.

Hexter, J. & Woetzel, J. R. 2007. *Operation China: From Strategy to Execution*. Massachusetts: Harvard Business Press.

Hill, C. W. L. 2006. *Global Business Today*. New York: McGraw-Hill Irwin.

Hill, C. W. L. 2011. *International Business: Competing in the Global Marketplace*. New York: McGraw-Hill Irwin.

Hill, C. W. L., Mckaig, T. & Richardson, T. 2009. *Global Business Today*. New York: McGraw-Hill Irwin.

Hite, J. M. & Hesterly, W. S. 2001. The evolution of firm networks: from emergence to early growth of the firm. *Strategic Management Journal*, vol. 22, issue 3, 275–286.

Hitt, M. A., Dacin, M. T., Levitas, E., Arregle, J. L. & Borza, A. 2000. Partner selection in emerging and developed market contexts: resource-based and organizational learning perspectives. *Academy of Management Journal*, vol. 49, issue 3, 449–467.

Hitt, M. A., Harrison, J., Ireland, R. D. & Best, A. 2002. Attributes of successful and unsuccessful acquisitions of US firms. *British Journal of Management*, vol. 9, issue 2, 91–114.

Hobday, M. & Colpan, A. M. 2010. Technological innovation and business groups. In *The Oxford Handbook of Business Groups*. New York: Oxford University Press.

Hofstede, G. 1994. The business of international business is culture. *International Business Review*, vol. 3, issue 1, 1–14.

Hofstede, G 2001. *Culture's Consequences: Comparing Values, Behaviors, Institutions and Organizations Across Nations*, Second Edition. Thousand Oaks, CA: SAGE Publications.

Hofstede, G. 2006. What did GLOBE really measure? Researchers' minds versus respondents' minds. *Journal of International Business Studies*, vol. 37, issue 6, 882–896.

Hofstede, G. 2009. *Geert Hofstede Cultural Dimensions*. Available at www.geert-hofstede.com/index.shtml. Accessed on 16/11/2011.

Hofstede, G. & Bond, M. H. 1984. Hofstede's culture dimensions. *Journal of Cross-cultural Psychology*, vol. 15, 417–433.

Hofstede, G. & Hofstede, G. J. 2005. Cultures in organizations. *Cultures Consequences*, 373–421. Available at: http://www.mendeley.com/research/sensemaking-in-organizations-foundations-for-organizational-science.

Hofstede, G. H., Hofstede, G. J. & Minkov, M. 2010. *Cultures and Organizations: Software for the Mind*. New York: McGraw-Hill Professional.

Holden, N. 2002. Cross-cultural Management: *A Knowledge Management Perspective*. Harlow: Pearson Education

Hoskisson, R. E., Johnson, R. A., Tihanyi, L. & White, R. E. 2005. Diversified business groups and corporate refocusing in emerging economies. *Journal of Management*, vol. 31, issue 6, 941–965.

Hout, T. M. & Ghemawat, P. 2011. China vs the world. *Harvard Business Review of Thriving in Emerging Markets*. Boston, MA: Harvard Business School Publishing Corporation.

HSBC 2010. Doing Business in Mexico. HSBC Mexico [online]. Available at: www.bwob.ca/wp-content/uploads/2011/10/110317_hsbc_doing_business_in_mexico.pdf. Accessed on 17/12/2011.

Hsu, C. C. & Pereira, A. 2008. Internationalization and performance: the moderating effects of organizational learning. *Omega: The International Journal of Management Science*, vol. 36, issue 2, 188–205.

Huggins, R. & Izushi, H. 2009. Regional benchmarking in a global context: knowledge, competitiveness, and economic development. *Economic Development Quarterly*, vol. 23, issue 4, 275–293.

Hughes, B. 2010. An Analysis of the Population, Economic and Socioeconomic Dynamics of Chile through 2040. Available at http://www.iccwbo.biz/uploadedFiles/BASCAP/Pages/Chile%202040.pdf. Accessed on 30/05/2012.

Hult, G. T. M., Cavusgil, S. T., Deligonul, S., Kiyak, T. & Lagerstrom, K. 2006. What drives performance in globally focused marketing organizations? A three country study. *Journal of International Marketing*, vol. 15, issue 2, 58–85.

IKLE, F. C. 1964. *How Nations Negotiate*. New York: Praeger.

IMF 2009. *Coordinated Direct Investment Survey* [online]. Available at http://cdis.imf.org/. Accessed on 19/12/2011.

IMF 2011a. *World Economic Outlook Database*, September. Available at: http://www.imf.org/external/pubs/ft/weo/2011/02/weodata/index.aspx.

IMF 2011b. *World Economic Outlook: Tensions from the Two-speed Recovery – Unemployment, Commodities and Capital Flows*. Washington, DC: International Monetary Fund.

INSEAD. 2011. *Insead Knowledge* [online]. Available at http://knowledge.insead.edu/Bottompyramid.cfm. Accessed on 16/12/2011.

Intarakumnerd, P. & Lecler, Y. 2010. Sustainability of Thailand's competitiveness: the policy challenges. *Asian-Pacific Economic Literature*, vol. 25, issue 1, 169–170.

Ioannou, L. 1994. Cultivating the new expatriate executive. *International Business*, vol. 7, 40–46.

IPR 2010. *The International Property Rights Index: 2010 Report*. Washington, DC: The Americans for Tax Reform Foundation/Property Rights Alliance.

Iqbal, M. S., Shaikh, F. M. & Shar, A. H. 2010. Causality relationship between foreign direct investment, trade and economic growth in Pakistan. *Asian Social Science*, vol. 6, issue 9, 82–95.

Jain, S. C. 2003. *Handbook of Research in International Marketing*. Cheltenham, UK: Edward Elgar Publishing.

Jansson, H. 2008. *International Business Strategy in Emerging Country Markets: The Institutional Network Approach*. Cheltenham, UK: Edward Elgar Publishing.

Jenkins, R. 2005. Globalization, corporate social responsibility and poverty. *International Affairs*, vol. 81, issue 3, 525–540.

Jensen, N. M. 2009. Firm-level Responses to Politics: Political Institutions and the Operations of US Multinationals. Unpublished, available at http://nathanjensen.wustl.edu/research.html

Jin, D., Michael, D. C., Foo, P., Guevara, J., Pena, I., Tratz, A. & Verma, S. 2010. Winning in emerging-market cities: a guide to the world's largest growth opportunity. *The Boston Consulting Group*, 1–25.

Johanson, J. & Vahlne, J. E. 1977. The internationalization process of the firm: a model of knowledge development and increasing foreign market commitments. *Journal of International Business Studies*, available at http://www.bcg.com/documents/file60078.pdf. Accessed on 30/05/2012.

Johanson, J. & Vahlne, J. E. 1990. The mechanism of internationalization. *International Marketing Review*, vol. 7, issue 4, 11–24.

Johanson, J. & Vahlne, J. E. 1993. Management of internationalization. In Zan, L., Zambpon, S. and Pettigrew, A.M. (eds.), *Perspectives on Strategic Change*. Boston, MA: Kluver, 43–78.

Johanson, J. & Wiedersheim-Paul, F. 1975. The internationalization of the firm: four Swedish cases. *Journal of Management Studies*, vol. 12, issue 3, 305–323.

Johnson, B. 2011. The CEO of Heinz on powering growth in emerging markets. *Harvard Business Review*, October. Available at http://hbr.org/2011/10/the-ceo-of-heinz-on-powering-growth-in-emerging-markets/ar/1. Accessed on 30/05/2012.

Kacou, E. 2010. *Entrepreneurial Solutions for Prosperity in BoP Markets*. Englewood Cliffs, NJ: Pearson, Prentice-Hall.

Kahn, J. 2002. *Federalism, Democratization, and the Rule of Law in Russia*, Oxford University Press, UK.

Kamminga, P. E. & Van Der Meer-Kooistra, J. 2007. Management control patterns in joint venture relationships: a model and an exploratory study. *Accounting, Organizations and Society*, vol. 32, issue 1–2, 131–154.

Kamran, Q. 2011. Complexity of negotiation and negotiation of complexity: getting to trust. *Current Issues in Economic and Management Sciences*, International Conference for Doctoral Students, November 10–12, Riga, Latvia.

Kant, R. 2008. The rise of TNCs from emerging markets: challenges faced by firms from India. In Sauvant, K. P. (ed.) *The Rise of Transnational Corporations from Emerging Markets: Threat or Opportunity?* Cheltenham: Edward Elgar Publishing.

Karamchandani, A., Kubzansky, M. & Lalwani, N. 2011. Is the bottom of the pyramid really for you? *Harvard Business Review*, vol. 89, 107–111.

Karnani, A. 2006. Mirage at the bottom of the pyramid: how the private sector can help alleviate poverty. *California Management Review*, vol. 49, issue 4, 90–112.

Katz, L. 2006. *Negotiating International Business*. Charleston, SC: Booksurge.

Khanna, T. & Palepu, K. 2000. The future of business groups in emerging markets: long-run evidence from Chile. *Academy of Management Journal*, vol. 43, issue 3, 268–285.

Khanna, T. & Palepu, K. 2004. Emerging giants: building world class companies from emerging markets. *Harvard Business Review*, 1–43.

Khanna, T. & Palepu, K. 2008. Emerging giants: building world-class companies in developing countries. *Harvard Business Review on Emerging Markets*. Boston, MA: Harvard Business School Publishing Corporation.

Khanna, T. & Palepu, K. 2010. *Winning in Emerging Markets: A Road Map for Strategy and Execution*. Boston, MA: Harvard Business Press.

Khanna, T., Palepu, K. & Sinha, J. 2005. Strategies that fit emerging markets. *Harvard Business Review*, vol. 84, issue 10, 63–76.

Khanna, T., Palepu, K. & Sinha, J. 2011. Strategies that fit emerging markets. *Thriving in Emerging Markets*. Boston, MA: Harvard Business School Publishing Corporation.

Khanna, T. & Yafeh, Y. 2007. Business groups in emerging markets: paragons or parasites? *Journal of Economic Literature*, vol. 45, issue 2, 331–372.

Kharas, H. 2010. *The Emerging Middle Class in Developing Countries*. Washington, DC: Wolfensohn Center for Development, The Brookings Institution.

Khemani, R. S. & Carrasco-Martin, A. 2008. Investment climate, competition policy, and economic development in Latin America, *Chicago Kent Law Review*, vol. 83, 67–79.

Kim, D., Kandemir, D. & Cavusgil, T. S. 2008. The role of family conglomerates in emerging markets: what Western companies should know. *Competing in Emerging Markets*. Abingdon, Oxford: Routledge. Chapter 14.

Kirkpatrick, D. D. & Afify, H. 2011. Steel tycoon with links to Mubarak is sentenced. *The New York Times*, 15 October. Available at http://www.nytimes.com/2011/09/16/world/middleeast/egypt-sentences-mubarak-era-tycoon-ahmed-ezz-to-prison.html. Accessed on 30/05/2012.

Kleijnen, M., Lee, N. & Wetzels, M. 2009. An exploration of consumer resistance to innovation and its antecedents. *Journal of Economic Psychology*, vol. 30, issue 3, 344–357.

Kolk, A. & Van Tulder, R. 2006. Poverty alleviation as business strategy? Evaluating commitments of frontrunner multinational corporations. *World Development*, vol. 34, issue 5, 789–801.

Kołodko, G. W. 2003. *Emerging Market Economies: Globalization and Development*. Aldershot: Ashgate.

Kretzberg, A. 2008. *Market Entry Strategies for Emerging Economies*. Frankfurt am Main: Peter Lang.

Krishna, R. 2011. Building a presence in today's growth markets: the experience of privately held companies. Washington, DC: Pricewaterhouse Coopers.

Kuijs, L. 2005. Investment and saving in China. World Bank Policy Research Paper Series No. 3633. NewYork: World Bank.

Kumar, R. 2009. Global financial and economic crisis: impact on India and policy response. *UNDP Global Financial Crisis: Impact on India's Poor – Some Initial Perspectives*. New Delhi: UNDP India.

Kumar, R. 2010. Do remittances matter for economic growth of the Philippines? An investigation using bound test analysis. Available at http://papers.ssrn.com/sol3/papers.cfm. Draft paper. Available at http://papers.ssrn.com/sol3/papers.cfm?abstract_id = 1565903.

Kumar, V. & Annushkina, O. 2010. Entry modes and dynamics. In *Doing Business in India: Building research-based practice*, edited by P. Budhawar and A. Verma, London: Routledge. 103–21.

Lall, S. 2001. FDI and development: research issues in the emerging context. *Studies in International Business and the World Economy*. Adelaide: University of Adelaide, Centre for International Economic Studies.

Landrum, N. E. 2007. Advancing the 'base of the pyramid' debate. *Strategic Management Review*, vol. 1, issue 1, 1–12.

Langfield-Smith, K. 2008. The relations between transactional characteristics, trust and risk in the start-up phase of a collaborative alliance. *Management Accounting Research*, vol. 19, issue 4, 344–364.

Laudicina, P. A. 2010. Globalization enters a new era: what course will it take? *Corporate Finance Review*, vol. 14, issue 5, 5–12.

Lawn, P. A. 2008. *Sustainable Welfare in the Asia-Pacific: Studies using the Genuine Progress Indicator*. Cheltenham: Edward Elgar Publishing, UK.

Lawson, S. & Gilman, D. B. 2009. The power of the purse: gender equality and middle class spending. *Global Markets Institute*, Goldman Sachs, Available at http://www.goldmansachs.com/our-thinking/women-and-economics/power-of-purse.pdf. Accessed on 30/05/2012.

Lee, K. & Peng, M. W. 2008. From diversification premium to diversification discount during institutional transitions. *Journal of World Business*, vol. 43, issue 1, 47–65.

Lee, S. H. & Makhija, M. 2009. Flexibility in internationalization: is it valuable during an economic crisis? *Strategic Management Journal*, vol. 30, issue 5, 537–555.

Lerpold, L. 2012. The contextualization of a microfinance model: from India to South Africa. *Thunderbird International Business Review*, vol. 54, issue 1,117–129.

Leung, T., Chan, R. Y. K., Lai, K. & Ngai, E. W. T. 2011. An examination of the influence of guanxi and xinyong (utilization of personal trust) on negotiation outcome in China: an old friend approach. *Industrial Marketing Management*, vol. 40, issue 7,1193–1205.

Lewicki, R. J., Litterer, J., Minton, J. & Saunders, D. 1994. *Negotiation*. Boston, MA: Irwin.

Li, J., Zhou, C. & Zajac, E. J. 2009. Control, collaboration, and productivity in international joint ventures: theory and evidence. *Strategic Management Journal*, vol. 30, issue 8, 865–884.

Li, P. P. 2007. Toward an integrated theory of multinational evolution: the evidence of Chinese multinational enterprises as latecomers. *Journal of International Management*, vol. 13, issue 3, 296–318.

Liao, T. S. & Rice, J. 2009. Innovation investments, market engagement and financial performance: a study among Australian manufacturing SMEs. *Research Policy*, vol. 39, issue 1, 117–125.

Lipuma, J. A., Newbert, S. L. & Doh, J. P. 2011. The effect of institutional quality on firm export performance in emerging economies: a contingency model of firm age and size. *Small Business Economics*, DOI: 10.1007/s11187-011-9395-7. Online First™.

Llaudes, R., Salman, F., Chivakul, M. & Fund, I. M. 2010. *The Impact of the Great Recession on Emerging Markets*. Geneva: International Monetary Fund. Available at http://www.imf.org/external/pubs/ft/wp/2010/wp10237.pdf

Lodhi, M. 2011. *Pakistan: Beyond the 'Crisis State'*. New York: Columbia University Press.

London, T. 2008. The base-of-the-pyramid perspective: a new approach to poverty alleviation. In G.T. Solomon (Ed.), *Academy of Management Best Paper Proceedings*.

London, T., Anupindi, R. & Sheth, S. 2010. Creating mutual value: lessons learned from ventures serving base of the pyramid producers. *Journal of Business Research*, vol. 63, issue 6, 582–594.

London, T. & Hart, S. L. 2004. Reinventing strategies for emerging markets: beyond the transnational model. *Journal of International Business Studies*, vol. 35, issue 5, 350–370.

London, T. & Hart, S. L. 2011. *Next Generation Business Strategies for the Base of the Pyramid*. Harlow: Pearson Education.

Lorenzoni, G. & Lipparini, A. 1999. The leveraging of inter-firm relationships as a distinctive organizational capability: a longitudinal study. *Strategic Management Journal*, vol. 20, issue 4, 317–338.

Lu, J. W. & Ma, X. 2008. The contingent value of local partners' business group affiliations. *Academy of Management Journal (AMJ)*, vol. 51, issue 2, 295–314.

Lunnan, R. & Haugland, S. A. 2008. Predicting and measuring alliance performance: a multidimensional analysis. *Strategic Management Journal*, vol. 29, issue 5, 545–556.

Luo, Y. 2001. Toward a cooperative view of MNC-host government relations: building blocks and performance implications. *Journal of International Business Studies*, vol. 32, issue 3, 401–419.

Luo, Y. 2002. *Multinational Enterprises in Emerging Markets*. Copenhagen: Copenhagen Business School Press.

Luo, Y. & Tung, R. L. 2007. International expansion of emerging market enterprises: a springboard perspective. *Journal of International Business Studies*, vol. 38, issue 4, 481–498.

Luthans, F., Doh, J. P. & Hodgetts, R. M. 2009. *International Management: Culture, Strategy, and Behavior*. New York: McGraw-Hill Irwin.

Luthra, S., Mangaleswaran, R. & Padhi, A. 2005. When to make India a manufacturing base. *McKinsey Quarterly*. Available at http://www.mckinseyquarterly.com/Energy_Resources_Materials/Chemicals/When_to_make_India_a_manufacturing_base_1650. Accessed on 30/05/2012.

Lymbersky, C. 2008. *Market Entry Strategies: Text, Cases and Readings in Market Entry Management*. Christoph Lymbersky.

Macotela, A. 2011. Building a presence in today's growth markets: the experience of privately held companies. PricewaterhouseCoopers LLP. Available at http://www.pwc.com/ca/en/private-company/publications/2011-05-indonesia-en.pdf. Accessed on 30/05/2012.

Magnus, G. 2008. *The Age of Aging: How Demographics are Changing the Global Economy and our World*. Singapore: John Wiley & Sons (Asia).

Magnus, G. 2010. *Uprising: Will Emerging Markets Shape or Shake the World Economy?* Chichester, West Sussex: Wiley.

Magstadt, T. M. 2010. *Understanding Politics: Ideas, Institutions, and Issues*. California: Wadsworth.

Mahmood, I. P. & Mitchell, W. 2004. Two faces: effects of business groups on innovation in emerging econimies. *Management Science*, vol. 50, issue 10, 1348–1365.

Mair, J. & Marti, I. 2009. Entrepreneurship in and around institutional voids: a case study from Bangladesh. *Journal of Business Venturing*, vol. 24, issue 5, 419–435.

Makino, S., Lau, C. M. & Yeh, R. S. 2002. Asset-exploitation versus asset-seeking: implications for location choice of foreign direct investment from newly industrialised economies. *Journal of International Business Studies*, vol. 33, issue 3, 403–421.

Mankoff, J. 2009. *Russian Foreign Policy: The Return of Great Power Politics*. Lanham, MD: Rowman & Littlefield.

Marchick, D. M. & Slaughter, M. J. 2008. *Global FDI Policy: Correcting a Protectionist Drift*. New York: Council on Foreign Relations Press.

Marin, A. & Bell, M. 2003. Technology Spillovers from Foreign Direct Investment: An Exploration of the Active Role of MNC Subsidiaries in the Case of Argentina in the 1990s. Druid Summer Conference on Creating Sharing and Transferring Knowledge, Copenhagen, 12 May.

Marinov, M. A. & Marinova, S. T. 2000. Foreign direct investment in the emerging markets of Central and Eastern Europe: motives and marketing strategies. In Yaprak, A. and Tutek, H. (ed.) *Globalization, the Multinational Firm, and Emerging Economies (Advances in International Marketing, Vol. 10)*.Bradford: Emerald Group Publishing Limited, 21–52.

Marr, J. & Reynard, C. 2010. *Investing in Emerging Markets: The BRIC Economies and Beyond*. Chichester: Wiley.

Marriot, I. 2008. *Global Sourcing Scenario: Heading to the Next Stage of Maturity*. London: Gartner Research.

Mascarenhas, B. 1982. Coping with uncertainty in international business. *Journal of International Studies*, vol. 13, issue 2, 87–98.

Masud, M. R., Yusoff, Z. M., Hamid, H. A. & Yahaya, N. 2008. Foreign direct investment in Malaysia: findings of the quarterly survey of international investment and services. *Journal of the Department of Statistics, Malaysia*, vol. 1, 1–9.

Mathews, J. A. 2002. *Dragon Multinationals: A New Model for Global Growth*. New York: Oxford University Press.

Mathews, J. A. 2006. Dragon multinationals: new players in the 21st century globalization. *Asia Pacific Journal of Management*, vol. 23, issue 2, 5–27.

Matusitz, J. & Reyers, A. 2010. A behemoth in India. *South Asia Research*, vol. 30, issue 3, 233–252.

McCutchen, W., Swamidass, P. M. & Teng, B. S. 2007. Strategic alliance termination and performance: the role of task complexity, nationality and experience. *Journal of High Technology Management Research*, vol. 18, issue 2,191–202.

McKinsey 2010. McKinsey Global Survey Results: Economic Conditions Snapshot. Available at http://www.mckinseyquarterly.com/Economic_Conditions_Snapshot_December_2010_McKinsey_Global_Survey_results_2720, accessed on 30/05/2012.

Megginson, W. L. & Netter, J. M. 2001. From state to market: a survey of empirical studies on privatization. *Journal of Economic Literature*, vol. 39, issue 2, 321–389.

Mendonca, C. 2011. Building a presence in today's growth markets: the experience of privately held companies. PricewaterhouseCoopers, LLP. Available at http://www.pwc.com/ca/en/private-company/publications/2011-05-brazil-en.pdf. Accessed on 30/05/2012.

Meyer, K. E., Estrin, S., Bhaumik, S. K. & Peng, M. W. 2009. Institutions, resources, and entry strategies in emerging economies. *Strategic Management Journal*, vol. 30, issue 1, 61–80.

Meyer, P. J. 2010. *Chile: Political and Economic Conditions and US Relations.* Darby, PA, US: DIANE Publishing.

Miller, D., LEE, J., Chang, S. & Lebreton-Miller, I. 2009a. Filling the institutional void: the social behavior and performance of family vs non family technology firms in emerging markets. *Journal of International Business Studies*, vol. 40, issue 5, 802–817.

Miller, S. R., Thomas, D. E., Eden, L. & Hitt, M. 2009b. Knee deep in the big muddy: the survival of emerging market firms in developed markets. *Management International Review*, vol. 48, issue 6, 645–666.

Miroshnikov, M. 2009. Russia: the knight on the crossroad. Europe-Asia Studies, 10, 1760.

Moe, N. B. & Šmite, D. 2008. Understanding a lack of trust in global software teams: a multiple-case study. *Software Process: Improvement and Practice*, vol. 13, issue 3, 217–231.

Montiel, P. J. 2003. *Macroeconomics in Emerging Markets.* New York: Cambridge University Press.

Montiel, P. J. 2011. *Macroeconomics in Emerging Markets*, 2nd edition. New York: Cambridge University Press.

Moore, C. W. & Woodrow, P. J. 2010. *Handbook of Global and Multicultural Negotiation.* San Fransisco, CA: Jossey-Bass.

Moran, R. T. & Stripp, W. G. 1991. *Dynamics of Successful International Business Negotiations.* Houston, TX: Gulf Publishing Co.

Morck, R., Yeung, B. & Zhao, M. 2008. Perspectives on China's outward foreing direct investment. *Journal of International Business Studies*, vol. 39, issue 3, 337–350.

Morduch, J., Cull, R. & Demirguc-Kunt, A. 2009. Microfinance meets the market. *Journal of Economic Perspectives*, vol. 23, issue 1, 167–192.

Morrison, T. & Conaway, W. A. 2006. *Kiss, Bow or Shake Hands.* Avon, MA: Adams Media.

MSCI 2012. MSCI, Index definitions [Online]. Available at www.msci.com/products/indices/tools/index.html#EM. Accessed on 24/02/2012.

Mühlbacher, H., Leihs, H. & Dahringer, L. 2006. *International Marketing: A Global Perspective.* Andover: Cengage Learning EMEA.

Münch, R. & Smelser, N. J. 1992. *Theory of Culture.* Berkeley, CA: University of California Press.

Murphy, A. M. 2009. Indonesia returns to the international stage: good news for the USA. *Orbis*, vol. 53, issue 1, 65–79.

Narula, R. 2009. Do multinationals matter for emerging markets or vice versa? In: Dolfsma, W., Duysters, G. & Costa, I. (eds) *Multinationals and*

Emerging Economies: The Quest for Innovation and Sustainability. Cheltenham: Edward Elgar.

Naughton, B. 2009. Understanding the Chinese stimulus package. *China Leadership Monitor*, vol. 28, issue 2, 1–12.

Nelson, D. & Forsans, N. 2008. *Doing Business in India.* New York: Dorling Kindersley.

Nevins, J. L. & Money, R. B. 2008. Performance implications of distributor effectiveness, trust, and culture in import channels of distribution. *Industrial Marketing Management*, vol. 37, issue 1, 46–58.

Newberry, D. 2008. The role of small-and medium-sized enterprises in the futures of emerging economies. Earth Trends: Environmental Invormation (World Resources Institute).

Nielsen, B. B. 2003. An empirical investigation of the drivers of international strategic alliance formation. *European Management Journal*, vol. 21, issue 3, 301–322.

Nunes, P. F. & Purdy, M. 2008. Brave New World. *Outlook* [online]. Available at www.accenture.com/SiteCollectionDocuments/PDF/OutlookPDF_MultiPolarWorld_03.pdf. Accessed on 14/10/2011.

O'Connell, A. 2009. Using gifts and trees to make recyclers of Indian consumers. *Harvard Business Review,* September. Available at http://hbr.org/2009/09/using-gifts-and-trees-to-make-recyclers-of-indian-consumers/ar/1. Accessed on 31/05/2012.

O'Neill, J. 2001. Dreaming with BRICs: the path to 2050. A Goldman Sachs, *global economics paper no 99.*

O'Neill, J. & Stupnytska, A. 2009, The long-term outlook for the BRICs and N-11 post crisis. Global Economics Paper No. 192. *Goldman Sachs Global Economics, Commodities and Strategy Research*, available at http://www.goldmansachs.com/our-thinking/brics/brics-reports-pdfs/long-term-outlook.pdf. Accessed on 30/05/2012.

O'Neill, J. & Stupnytska, A. 2009. Global Economics Paper No: 192, The Long-Term Outlook for the BRICs and N-11 Post Crisis. *Goldman Sachs Global Economics, Commodities and Strategy Research*, 3–27.

O'Neill, J. 2011. *The Growth Map: Economic Opportunity in the BRICs and Beyond.* London: Penguin Group.

OECD 2007. *OECD Investment Policy Reviews: Egypt.* Paris: OECD.

OECD 2008a. *Globalization and Emerging Economies: Brazil, Russia, India, Indonesia, China and South Africa.* Paris: OECD.

OECD 2008b. *OECD Investment Policy Reviews: Peru.* Paris: OECD.

OECD 2008c. *OECD Investment Policy Reviews: Russian Federation – Strengthening the Policy Framework for Investment.* Paris: OECD.

Olekalns, M. & Brett, J. M. 2008. Beyond the deal: next generation negotiation skills. Introduction to Special Issue. *Negotiation and Conflict Management Research*, vol. 1, issue 4, 309–314.

Ones, D. S. & Viswesvaran, C. 1999. Relative importance of personality dimensions for expatriate selection: a policy capturing study. *Human Performance*, vol. 12, issue 3/4 275–294.

Onkvisit, S. & Shaw, J. J. 2008. *International Marketing: Strategy and Theory*. Oxford: Taylor & Francis Group.

Oshri, I., Kotlarsky, J., Willcocks, L. P. & Willcocks, L. 2009. *The Handbook of Global Outsourcing and Offshoring*. Basingstoke: Palgrave Macmillan.

Osterwalder, A., Pigneur, Y. & Tucci, C. L. 2005. Clarifying business models: origins, present, and future of the concept. *Communications of the Association for Information Systems,* vol. 16, issue 1, 1–25.

Ozorhon, B., Arditi, D., Dikmen, I. & Birgonul, M. T. 2008. Effect of partner fit in international construction joint ventures. *Journal of Management in Engineering*, vol. 24, issue 1, 12–20.

Pacek, N. & Thorniley, D. 2007. *Emerging Markets: Lessons for Business Success and the Outlook for Different Markets*. New York: Bloomberg.

Park, S. H., Li, S. & Tse, D. K. 2006. Market liberalization and firm performance during China's economic transition. *Journal of International Business Studies*, vol. 37, issue 1, 127–147.

Parker, R. S., Haytko, D. & Hermans, C. 2009. Individualism and collectivism: reconsidering old assumptions. *Journal of International Business Research*, vol. 8, issue 1, 127–139.

Parnell, J. A. 2008. Strategy execution in emerging economies: assessing strategic diffusion in Mexico and Peru. *Management Decision*, vol. 46, issue 9, 1277–1298.

Peng, M. W. 2003. Institutional transitions and strategic choices. *Academy of Management Review*, vol. 28, issue 2, 275–296.

Peng, M. W., Lee, S. H. & Wang, D. Y. L. 2005. What determines the scope of the firm over time? A focus on institutional relatedness. *Academy of Management Review*, vol. 33, issue 3, 622–633.

Peng, M. W. & Zhou, J. Q. 2005. How network strategies and institutional transitions evolve in Asia. *Asia Pacific Journal of Management*, vol. 22, issue 4, 321–336.

Persinger, E. S., Civi, E. & Vostina, S. W. 2011. The born global entrepreneur in emerging economies. *International Business & Economics Research Journal (IBER)*, vol. 6, issue 3, 73–82.

Pietroni, D., Van Kleef, G. A. & De Dreu, C. K. W. 2008. Response modes in negotiation. *Group Decision and Negotiation*, vol. 17, 31–49.

Plester, B. A. 2008. Laugh out loud: how organizational culture influences workplace humour. A thesis presented in partial fulfilment for the degree of PhD in Management at Massey University, Albany, New Zealand.

Poulis, K. & Yamin, M. 2009. Tourism as a leverage of internationalization for consumer goods firms: a case study approach. *Advances in International Marketing*, vol. 20, 69–85.

Prahalad, C. 2010. *The Fortune at the Bottom of the Pyramid: Eradicating Poverty through Profits*. Harlow: Pearson Education.

Prahalad, C. 2011. Bottom of the pyramid as a source of breakthrough innovations. *Journal of Product Innovation Management*, vol. 29, issue 1, 21–32.

Prahalad, C. & Hammond, A. 2002. Serving the world's poor, profitably. *Harvard Business Review*, vol. 80, issue 9, 48–59.

Prahalad, C. & Lieberthal, K. 2003. The end of corporate imperialism. *Harvard Business Review*, 26–35.

Pueyo, A., García, R., Mendiluce, M. & Morales, D. 2011. The role of technology transfer for the development of a local wind component industry in Chile. *Energy Policy*, vol. 39, issue 7, 4274–4283.

Puffer, S. M., McCarthy, D. J. & Boisot, M. 2010. Entrepreneurship in Russia and China: the impact of formal institutional voids. *Entrepreneurship Theory and Practice*, vol. 34, issue 3, 441–467.

Qiang, C. Z. W. 2010. Broadband infrastructure investment in stimulus packages: relevance for developing countries. World Bank, available at http://siteresources.worldbank.org/EXTINFORMATIONANDCOMMUNICATIONANDTECHNOLOGIES/Resources/282822-1208273252769/Broadband_Investment_in_Stimulus_Packages.pdf. Accessed on 30/05/2012.

Rahman, Z. & Bhattacharyya, S. K. 2003. Sources of first mover advantages in emerging markets – an Indian perspective. *European Business Review*, vol. 15, issue 6, 361–371.

Rajan, R. 2010. *Fault Lines: How Hidden Fractures Still Threaten the World Economy*. Princeton, NJ: Princeton University Press.

Raju, S. & Mukherjee, J. 2010. Fiscal deficit, crowding out and the sustainability of economic growth. *Asia Visions*, vol 31, 1–31.

Ralston, D. A., Terpstra-Tong, J., Terpstra, R. H., Wang, X. & Egri, C. 2006. Today's state-owned enterprises of China: are they dying dinosaurs or dynamic dynamos? *Strategic Management Journal*, vol. 27, issue 9, 825–843.

Ramachandran, I., Clark, K., Mciver, D. & Miller, S. R. 2011. Selecting state or private joint venture partners in emerging markets: impact of liability of foreignness and rule of law. In Christian Geisler Asmussen, Torben Pedersen, Timothy M. Devinney and Laszlo Tihanyi (eds) *Dynamics of Globalization: Location-Specific Advantages or Liabilities of Foreignness?* (*Advances in International Management*, vol. 24), Bradford: Emerald, 153–179

Ramamurti, R. 2008. What have we learned about emerging market MNEs? *Emerging Multinationals in Emerging Markets*. Cambridge: Cambridge University Press.

Ramamurti, R., Singh, J. V. & Netlibrary, I. 2009. *Emerging Multinationals in Emerging Markets*. Cambridge: Cambridge University Press.

Read, B. 2008. Emerging market strategy: managing in a flux. *Logistics Management*, vol. 47, issue 6, 41–44.

Rivera-Santos, M. & Rufín, C. 2010. Global village vs. small town: understanding networks at the base of the pyramid. *International Business Review*, vol. 19, issue 2, 126–139.

Rodrik, D. 2006. Good-bye Washington consensus, hello Washington confusion? A review of the World Bank's economic growth in the 1990s: learning from a decade of reform. *Journal of Economic Literature*, vol. 44, issue 4, 973–987.

Roe, M. J. & Siegel, J. 2008. Political instability's impact on financial development. *Harvard Law and Economics Discussion Paper*. Available at http://www.law.harvard.edu/faculty/workshops/open/papers0708/roe.paper.pdf. Accessed on 31/05/2012.

Rosinski, P. 2003. *Coaching across Cultures: New Tools for Leveraging National, Corporate, and Professional Differences*. London: Nicholas Brearley Publishing.

Rothaermel, F. T. & Boeker, W. 2008. Old technology meets new technology: complementarities, similarities, and alliance formation. *Strategic Management Journal*, vol. 29, issue 1, 47–77.

Roy, J. P. & Oliver, C. 2009. International joint venture partner selection: the role of the host-country legal environment. *Journal of International Business Studies*, vol. 40, issue 5, 779–801.

Rudd, J. E. & Lawson, D. R. 2007. *Communicating in Global Business Negotiations: A Geocentric Approach*. Thousand Oaks, CA: Sage Publications.

Rugman, A. M. 2008. How global are TNCs from emerging markets? In Sauvant, K. P. (ed.), *The Rise of Transnational Corporations from Emerging Markets: Threat or Opportunity*, Cheltenham? UK: Edward Elgar Publishing.

Rugman, A. M. & Oh, C. H. 2010. Does the regional nature of multinationals affect the multinationality and performance relationship? *International Business Review*, vol. 19, issue 5, 479–488.

Rui, H. & Yip, G. S. 2007. Foreign acquisitions by Chinese firms: a strategic intent perspective. *Journal of World Business*, vol. 43, issue 2, 213–226.

Sachdeva, A. 2007. International investment: a developing country perspective. *Journal of World Investment and Trade*, vol. 8, issue 4, 533–548.

Sachs, G. 2003. Dreaming with BRICs: the path to 2050. Global Economics Paper No. 99, 1 October.

Sachs, J. D. 2008. The rise of TNCs from emerging markets: the global context. In: Sauvant, K. P. (ed.), *The Rise of Transnational Corporations from Emerging Markets: Threat or Opportunity*? Cheltenham, UK: Edward Elgar Publishing.

Saebi, T. & Dong, Q. 2009. Strategic motivations for international alliances: the Chinese perspective. In Dolfsma, W., Duysters, G. & Costa, I. (eds), *Multinationals and Emerging Economies: The Quest for Innovation and Sustainability*. Cheltenham, UK: Edward Elgar Publishing.

Saee, J. 2008. Best practice in global negotiation strategies for leaders and managers in the 21st century. *Journal of Business Economics and Management*, vol. 9, issue 4, 309–318.

Saleh, H. 2011. Egyptian steel magnate jailed for corruption. *Financial Times,* 15 September.

Samovar, L. A., Porter, R. E. & Mcdaniel, E. R. 2009. *Communication between Cultures*. Ohio: Wadsworth.

Samovar, L. A., Porter, R. E. & Mcdaniel, E. R. 2011. *Intercultural Communication: A Reader*. Ohio: Wadsworth.

Santiso, J. 2003. *The Political Economy of Emerging Markets*. Basingstoke: Palgrave Macmillan.

Saorín-Iborra, M. C. 2008. Time pressure in acquisition negotiations: its determinants and effects on parties' negotiation behaviour choice. *International Business Review*, vol. 17, issue 3, 285–309.

Sathe, D. & Aradhana, A. 2007. Knowledge process outsourcing: the big game. Sourcingmag.com. Available at http://www.sourcingmag.com/content/c060503a.asp. Accessed on 31/05/2012.

Sauvant, K. P. 2008. The rise of TNCs from emerging markets: the issues. In: Sauvant, K. P. (ed.), *The Rise of Transnational Corporations from Emerging Markets: Threat or Opportunity?* Cheltenham, UK: Edward Elgar Publishing.

Sauvant, K. P., Sachs, L., Davies, K. & Zandvliet, R. 2011. *FDI Perspectives: Issues in International Investment*. New York: Vale Columbia Center on Sustainable International Investment.

Schaffer, R., Agusti, F. & Earle, B. 2008. *International Business Law and its Environment*. Charleston, SC: South-Western Publishing.

Schein, E. H. 2009. *The Corporate Culture Survival Guide*. San Francisco, CA: Jossey-Bass.

Schneider, B. R. 2010. Business groups and the state: the politics of expansion, restructuring, and collapse. In *The Oxford Handbook of Business Groups*. New York: Oxford University Press.

Schreiner, M., Kale, P. & Corsten, D. 2009. What really is alliance mangement capability and how does it impact alliance outcomes and success? *Strategic Management Journal*, vol. 30, issue 1, 1395–1419.

Schwab, S. C. 2011. After Doha. *Foreign Affairs*, May–June, 90.

Sebenius, J. K. 2002. The hidden challenge of cross-border negotiations. *Harvard Business Review*, March, 4–11.

Semnani-Azad, Z. & Adair, W. 2011. *Nonverbal Cues Associated with Negotiation 'Styles' Across Cultures*. IACM 24th Annual Conference Paper. Available at SSRN: http://ssrn.com/abstract=1872173

Sen, S. 2010. Sovereign wealth funds: an examination of the rationale. *American Review of Political Economy*, vol. 8, issue 1, 44–57.

Shaffer, G., Sanchez, M. R., Rosenberg, B. & De Relaciones Internacionales, A. 2008. Winning at the WTO: the development of a trade policy community within Brazil. *Dispute Settlement at the WTO*. Cambridge: Cambridge University Press.

Sharma, P. 2010. Country of origin effects in developed and emerging markets: exploring the contrasting roles of materialism and value consciousness. *Journal of International Business Studies*, vol. 42, 285–306.

Sheth, J. N. & Parvatiyar, A. 1992. Towards a theory of business alliance formation. *Scandinavian International Business Review*, vol. 1, issue 3, 71–87.

Simonin, B. L. 1997. The importance of collaborative know-how: an empirical test of the learning organization. *Academy of Management Journal*, vol. 40, issue 5, 1150–1174.

Singer, A. E. 2006. Business strategy and poverty alleviation. *Journal of Business Ethics*, vol. 66, 225–231.

Singh, M., Nejadmalayeri, A. & Matur, I. 2007. Performance impact of business group affiliation: an analysis of the diversification-performance link in a developing economy. *Journal of Business Research*, vol. 60, issue 4, 339–347.

Skinner, G. 2011. The neoclassical counterrevolution and developing economies: a case study of political and economic changes in the Philippines. *Social Sciences Journal*, vol. 7, issue 1, 12–22.

Slangen, A. H. L. & Hennart, J. F. 2008. Do multinationals really prefer to enter culturally distant countries through greenfields rather than through acquisitions? The role of parent experience and subsidiary autonomy. *Journal of International Business Studies*, vol. 39, issue 3, 472–490.

Spence, M. M., Manning, L. M. & Crick, D. 2008. An investigation into the use of collaborative ventures in the internationalization of high performing Canadian SMEs. *European Management Journal*, vol. 26, issue 6, 412–428.

Stanley, W. B. 2005. Social studies and the social order: transmission or transformation? *Social Education*, vol. 69, issue 5, 282–286.

Stolt, R. 2010. *Sourcing in Emerging Markets: Particularities and Challenges*. Berlin: GRIN Verlag.

Stuart, T. E. 2000. Interorganizational alliances and the performance of firms: a study of growth and innovation rates in a high-technology industry. *Strategic Management Journal*, vol. 21, issue 8, 791–811.

Subbarao, D. 2009. Impact of the global financial crisis on India: collateral damage and response. Speech delivered at the Symposium on 'The Global Economic Crisis and Challenges for the Asian Economy in a Changing World', Institute for International Monetary Affairs, 18 February.

SWF 2011. *SWF Institute* [online]. Sovereign Wealth Funds Institute. Available at www.swfinstitute.org/. Accessed on 14/12/2011.

Taft-Morales, M. 2009. Peru: Current Conditions and US Relations. DTIC document.

Talay, M. B., Seggie, S. H. & Cavusgil, E. 2009. Exploring correlates of product launch in collaborative ventures: an empirical investigation of pharmaceutical alliances. *Journal of Product Innovation Management*, vol. 26, issue 4, 360–370.

Tanggapan, D., Geetha, C., Mohidin, R. & Vincent, V. 2011. The relationship between economic growth and foreign direct investment in Malaysia: analysis based on location advantage theory. *Management*, vol. 1, no 2, 24–31.

Tatoglu, E. 2000. Western joint ventures in Turkey: strategic motives and partner selection criteria. *European Business Review*, vol. 12, issue 3, 137–147.

Teagarden, M. B. & Cai, D. H. 2009. Learning from dragons who are learning from us: developmental lessons from Chinese global companies. *Organizational Dynamics*, vol. 38, issue 1, 73–81.

Thomas, K. L. & Chen, M.-J. 2003. *Cultural Foundations in Communication: Relationship-building in the Chinese Context*. Charlottesville, VA: University of Virginia, Darden School Foundation.

Thomson One Banker 2011. Thomson One Banker, Thomson Financial.

Tiwana, A. & Bush, A. A. 2007. A comparison of transaction cost, agency, and knowledge-based predictors of IT outsourcing decisions: a US–Japan cross-cultural field study. *Journal of Management Information Systems*, vol. 24, issue 1, 259–300.

Tracey, P. & Phillips, N. 2011. Entrepreneurship in emerging markets. *Management International Review*, vol. 49, issue 4, 1–17.

Tsai, K. H. & Wang, J. C. 2007. External technology acquisition and firm performance: a longitudinal study. *Journal of Business Venturing*, vol. 23, issue 1, 91–112.

Tse, E. 2011. Is it too late to enter China? *Harvard Business Review on Thriving in Emerging Markets*. Boston, MA: Harvard Business School Publishing Corporation.

UKTI 2010a. *China Business Guide*. UK Trade & Investment and China–Britain Business Council. Available at http://ols.cbbc.org/downloads/China_Business_Guide%202010.pdf. Accessed on 31/05/2012.

UKTI 2010b. *Doing Business in Chile* [online]. UK Trade & Investment. Available at www.ukti.gov.uk/export/countries.html. Accessed on 19/12/2011.

UKTI 2010c. *Doing Business In Egypt* [online]. UK Trade & Investment. Available at www.ukti.gov.uk/export/countries.html. Accessed on 19/12/2011.

UKTI 2010d. *Doing Business in Indonesia* [online]. UK Trade & Investment. Available at www.ukti.gov.uk/export/countries.html. Accessed on 19/12/2011.

UKTI 2010e. *Doing Business in Pakistan* [online]. UK Trade & Investment. Available at http://www.ukti.gov.uk/export/countries/asiapacific/southasia/pakistan/doingbusiness.html. Accessed on 31/05/2012.

UKTI 2010f. *Doing Business in Peru* [online]. UK Trade & Investment. Available at www.ukti.gov.uk/export/countries.html. Accessed on 19/12/2011.

UKTI 2010g. *Malaysia Business Guide* [online]. UK Trade & Investment. Available at www.ukti.gov.uk/export/countries.html. Accessed on 19/12/2011.

UKTI 2010h. *Mexico Business Guide* [online]. UK Trade & Investment. Available at www.ukti.gov.uk/export/countries.html. Accessed on 19/12/2011.

UKTI 2010i. *Phillipines Business Guide* [online]. UK Trade & Investment. Available at www.ukti.gov.uk/export/countries.html. Accessed on 19/12/2011.

UKTI 2010j. *South Africa Business Guide* [online]. UK Trade & Investment. Available at www.ukti.gov.uk/export/countries.html Accessed on 19/12/2011.

UNCTAD 2000. *Tax Incentives and Foreign Direct Investment: A Global Survey*. Available at www.unctad.org/en/docs/iteipcmisc3_en/pdf.

UNCTAD 2011. *World Investment Report 2011: Non Equity Modes of International Production and Development*. Geneva: United Nations.

UNESCO 2011. *UNESCO Science Report 2010: The Current Status of Science Around the World*. Paris: UNESCO.

US COMMERCE 2010. *Doing Business in Egypt: Country Commercial Guide for US Companies.* Washington, DC: US Commercial Service.

US COMMERCE 2011a. *Doing Business Guides.* Washington, DC: US Commercial Service. Available at http://export.gov/. Accessed on 19/12/2011.

US COMMERCE 2011b. *Doing Business in Brazil: Country Commercial Guide for US Companies.* Washington, DC: US Commercial Service.

US COMMERCE 2011c. *Doing Business in China: Country Commercial Guide for US Companies.* Washington, DC: US Commercial Service.

US COMMERCE 2011d. *Doing Business in India: Country Commercial Guide for US Companies.* Washington, DC: US Commercial Service.

US COMMERCE 2011e. *Doing Business in Indonesia: Country Commercial Guide for US Companies.* Washington, DC: US Commercial Service.

US COMMERCE 2011f. *Doing Business in Malaysia: Country Commercial Guide for US Companies.* Washington, DC: US Commercial Service.

US COMMERCE 2011g. *Doing Business in Mexico: Country Commercial Guide for US Companies.* Washington, DC: US Commercial Service.

US COMMERCE 2011h. *Doing Business in Pakistan: Country Commercial Guide for US Companies.* Washington, DC: US Commercial Service.

US COMMERCE 2011i. *Doing Business in Peru: Country Commercial Guide for US Companies.* Washington, DC: US Commercial Service.

US COMMERCE 2011j. *Doing Business in the Phillipines: Country Commercial Guide for US Companies.* Washington, DC: US Commercial Service.

US COMMERCE 2011k. *Doing Business in Russia: Country Commercial Guide for US Companies.* Washington, DC: US Commercial Service.

US COMMERCE 2011l. *Doing Business in South Africa: Country Commercial Guide for US Companies.* Washington, DC: US Commercial Service.

Usdiken, B. 2010. The kin and the professional. In *The Oxford Handbook of Business Groups.* New York: Oxford University Press.

Usunier, J.-C. 2003a. The role of time in international business negotiations. In: *International Business Negotiations.* Oxford: Elsevier, 171, 192.

Usunier, J. C. 2003b. Cultural aspects of international business negotiations. In: *International Business Negotiations.* Oxford: Elsevier, 97–135.

Van Aardt, C. J. 2011. The changing income demographics of South Africa. *Southern African Journal of Demography*, vol. 12, issue 1, 5–37.

Van Agtmael, A. W. 2007. *The Emerging Markets Century: How a New Breed of World-class Companies is Overtaking the World.* London: Simon & Schuster.

Van Der Berg, S. 2010. Current poverty and income distribution in the context of South African history. No 22/2010, Working Papers, Stellenbosch University, Department of Economics.

Van Weele, A. J. 2009. *Purchasing and Supply Chain Management: Analysis, Strategy, Planning and Practice.* Andover: Cengage Learning EMEA.

Vega-Jurado, J., Gutierrez-Gracia, A. & Fernandez-De-Lucio, I. 2008. Analysing the determinants of firms' absorptive capacity: beyond R&D. *R&D Management*, vol. 38, issue 4, 392–405.

Verma, S., Sanghi, K., Michaelis, H., Dupoux, P., Khanna, D. & Peters, P. 2011a. Companies on the move: rising standards from rapidly developing economies are reshaping global industries. *BCG Global Challengers*. The Boston Consulting Group. Available at http://www.bcg.com.cn/export/ sites/default/en/files/publications/reports_pdf/BCG_Companies_on_the_ Move_Jan_2011_ENG.pdf. Accessed on 31/05/2012.

Verma, S., Sanghi, K., Michaelis, H., Dupoux, P., Khanna, D. & Peters, P. 2011b. The success of challengers: companies on the move. The Boston Consulting Group. Available at https://www.bcgperspectives.com/content/ articles/globalization_companies_on_the_move_2011_global_challengers/. Accessed on 31/05/2012.

Vetere, F., Smith, J. & Gibbs, M. 2009. Phatic interactions: being aware and feeling connected. *Awareness Systems*, Human-Computer Interaction Series, 173–186.

Villarreal, M. A. 2010. Mexico's Free Trade Agreements. Congressional Research Service. Available at http://www.fas.org/sgp/crs/row/R40784. pdf. Accessed on 31/05/2012.

Walters, J., Hsu, H., Jap, W., Jin, D., Kluz, D., Liao, C. & Lui, V. 2010. Unlocking China's consumer power: the keys to the kingdom. In Group, T. B. C. (ed.) *BCG Perspectives*. Available at http://www.bcg.com/ documents/file39807.pdf. Accessed on 31/05/2012.

Wan, W. P. 2005. Country resource environments, firm capabilities, and corporate diversification strategies. *Journal of Management Studies*, vol. 42, issue 1, 161–182.

Warr, P. G. 2007. Long-term economic performance in Thailand. *ASEAN Economic Bulletin*, vol. 24, issue 1, 138–163.

Weigelt, C. 2009. The impact of outsourcing new technologies on integrative capabilities and performance. *Strategic Management Journal*, vol. 30, issue 6, 595–616.

Wells, L. T. 2009. Third world multinationals: a look back. In: Ramamurti, R. & Singh, J. V. (eds) *Emerging Multinationals in Emerging Markets*. Cambridge: Cambridge University Press.

Welzel, C. 2009. Political culture. In *The SAGE Handbook of Comparative Politics*, 299–318. London: Sage Publications.

WEO 2010. Recovery, risk and rebalancing. *World Economic Outlook*. Washington, DC: International Monetary Fund. Available at http://www.imf. org/external/pubs/ft/weo/2010/02/pdf/front.pdf. Accessed on 31/05/2012.

Wilkinson, I. & Young, L. 2002. On cooperating firms, relations and networks. *Journal of Business Research*, vol. 55, issue 2, 123–132.

Willcocks, L., Hindle, J., Feeny, D. & Lacity, M. 2004. IT and business process outsourcing: the knowledge potential. *Information Systems Management*, vol. 21, issue 3, 7–15.

Wilson, D., Kelston, A. L. & Swarnali, A. 2010. *Goldman Sachs Global Economics, Commodities and Strategy Research, BRICs Monthly*, issue 11/06, 1–4.

Wilson, D., Burgi, C. & Carlson, S. 2011a. The BRICs remain in the fast lane. *BRICs Monthly*, Goldman Sachs, issue 11/06, 1–4.

Wilson, D., Burgi, C. & Carlson, S. 2011b. Population growth and ageing in the BRICs. *BRICs Monthly*, vol. 11, issue 5, 31

Wilson, D., Kelston, A. L. & Swarnali, A. 2010. *Goldman Sachs Global Economics, Commodities and Strategy Research,* BRICs Monthly, issue 11/06, 1–4.

Wilson, D. & Stupnytska, A. 2007. *The N-11: More than an Acronym.* Goldman Sachs, Global Economics Paper, 153.

WIR 2010. *World Investment Report 2010: Investing in a Low Carbon Economy.* United Nations Conference on Trade and Development. Geneva: UN.

WIR 2011. *World Investment Report 2011: Non-Equity Modes of International Production and Development.* Geneva: United Nations Conference on Trade and Development (UNCTAD).

Wisse, D. 2011. *Sustainability of Microfinance and Bottom of the Pyramid.* Rotterdam: Erasmus University.

World Bank 2009. *Information and Communications for Development: Extending Reach and Increasing Impact.* Washington, DC: World Bank Publications.

World Bank 2010a. *Global Monitoring Report 2010: The MDGs After the Crisis.* Washington, DC: World Bank Publications.

World Bank 2010b. *Logistics Performance Index.* World Bank International Trade and Transport Department. Washington, DC: World Bank Publications.

World Bank 2011a. *Doing Business in 2012: Doing Business in a More Transparent World.* Washington, DC: World Bank Publications.

World Bank 2011b. *Global Development Horizons 2011 – Multipolarity: The New Global Economy.* Washington, DC: World Bank Publications.

World Bank 2011c. *Global Economic Prospects: Navigating Strong Currents.* Washington, DC: World Bank Publications.

World Data Bank 2011. *World Development Indicators (WDI) and Global Development Finance (GDF).* Washington, DC: World Bank Publications.

WTI 2010. *World Trade Indicators 2009/10.* Washington, DC: World Bank Publications. Available at http://info.worldbank.org/etools/wti/docs/userguide.pdf. Accessed on 31/05/2012.

WTO 2011b. *Trade Profiles: Mexico.* Geneva: World Trade Organization.

WTO 2011c. WTO and Preferential Trade Agreements: From Co-Existence to Coherence. *World Trade Report.* Geneva: World Trade Organization.

Wu, J. & Pangarkar, N. 2006. Rising to the global challenge: strategies for firms in emerging markets. *Long Range Planning,* vol. 39, issue 3, 295–313.

Xie, W. & Wu, G. 2003. Differences between learning processes in small tigers and large dragons: learning processes of two color TV (CTV) firms within China. *Research Policy,* vol. 32, issue 8, 1463–1479.

Yang, Y., Singhal, S. & Xu, Y. C. 2009. *Offer with Choices and Accept with Delay: A Win–Win Strategy Model for Agent Based Automated Negotiation.* Indiana: ICIS.

Yeniyurt, S. & Townsend, J. D. 2003. Does culture explain acceptance of new products in a country? An empirical investigation. *International Marketing Review,* vol. 20, issue 4, 377–396.

Yiu, D. W., Lau, C. M. & Bruton, G. D. 2007. International venturing by emerging economy firms: the effects of firm capabilities, home country networks, and corporate entrepreneurship. *Journal of International Business Studies*, vol. 38, issue 4, 519–540.

Yunus, M., Moingeon, B. & Lehmann-Ortega, L. 2010. Building social business models: lessons from the Grameen experience. *Long Range Planning*, vol. 43, issues 2–3, 308–325.

Zaheer, S. 1995. Overcoming the liability of foreignness. *The Academy of Management Journal*, vol. 38, issue 2, 341–363.

Zhai, E., Shi, Y. & Gregory, M. 2007. The growth and capability development of electronics manufacturing service (EMS) companies. *International Journal of Production Economics*, vol. 107, issue 1, 1–19.

Zhang, T. & Zhou, H. 2009. The significance of cross-cultural communication in international business negotiation. *International Journal of Business and Management*, vol. 3, issue 2, 103–132.

Zhang, X., Lesser, V. & Wagner, T. 2006. Integrative negotiation among agents situated in organizations. *Systems, Man, and Cybernetics, Part C: Applications and Reviews, IEEE Transactions on Systems*, vol. 36, issue 6, 19–30.

Zhang, Y., Li, H., Hitt, M. A. & Cui, G. 2007. R&D intensity and international joint venture performance in an emerging market: moderating effects of market focus and ownership structure. *Journal of International Business Studies*, vol. 38, 944–960.

Zou, Z., Tseng, T. L. B., Sohn, H., Song, G. & Gutierrez, R. 2011. A rough set based approach to distributor selection in supply chain management. *Expert Systems with Applications*, vol. 38, issue 1, 106–115.

Index

Page numbers in *italics* refer to boxes, figures and tables.

account clearing 234
acquisitions 242-3
  mergers and (M&A) 134, 138,
    140-4, 146
Acuff, F. 257, 264, 292, 293, 294, 297-8,
    299-300, 301, 302, 304
Africa 194-5, 304
  see also Egypt; South Africa
Asia 178-82
  financial crises 12, 178
  negotiation process 298-302
  see also named countries
assets/asset-seeking motives of EM firms
    121-2, 135-6

bargaining position of negotiators 284-5
barter transactions 234
Bharracharya, A.K. and Michael, D.C.
    117-18, 121, 126, 127, 129
bidding for global tenders 214-22
body language 278
bottom of the pyramid (BoP) segment
    111-16
Brazil 153-8
  and China, state-owned oil/gas
    sector *78-9*
  doing business in 157-8
  economic outlook 155-7
  negotiation process 292-3
bribes 39-40
BRIC economies
  brands in Global 500 *119*
  car penetration 91, *92*
  change in economic output 152-3

BRIC economies *cont.*
  consumer expenditure *96*
  cultural dimensions *52-3*
  economic growth 150-2
  education levels 17
  employment *156*
  major strengths and weaknesses *154*
  negotiation process 292-8
  and New Frontier Economies 5-7
  old-age dependency ratio 16
  share of exports *155*
  technology and telecommunications 100-1
  see also named countries
business alliances, typology of 307
business environment, knowledge of 123-5
business groups 71-4
  MNC partnerships 147-8
  ownership in 74-81
  as response to institutional inefficiencies
    81-3
business model adaptation 110-11
  China *106*
business process outsourcing (BPO) 224
buyback 235

Cateora, P.
  et al. 280
  see also Ghauri, P.
Cavusgil, S.T. et al. 30, 34, 44, 58, 59, 73,
    134-5, 213, 222, 234, 244, 338
Chile 176-8
  doing business in 177-8
  economic outlook 176-7
  negotiation process 303-4

China 164–7
  and Brazil, state-owned oil/gas
    sector *78–9*
  Danfoss: business model adaptation *106*
  differences between consumers *108*, 109
  doing business in 166–7
  economic outlook 165–6
  negotiation process 295–8
  rising protectionism *36–7*
  state and business groups *80*
  trade reforms 46–7
civil law and common law, distinction
    between 32–3
clearing 234
co-worker negotiations 255
collaboration
  MNCs and business groups 73, 74
  see also partners
collectivism and individualism 30–1, 51,
    55, 58–9
command economies 32
commitment 309, 314–15, 328–9
common law and civil law, distinction
    between 32–3
communication
  high and low context cultures 53–4, *55*
  negotiations 263–4, 276–80, 296–7
  verbal and non-verbal 56, 277–8
  see also language
companies/firms (EMs)
  challenges 127–31
  characteristics 121–7
  internationalization 131–44
  strategies *120*, 121
company capabilities 326–31, *332*
company competitiveness 331–4
competition: EM firms and MNCs 25
competitive bidding 219–20
conflict and cooperation in negotiation
    process 268
Confucian societies 58–9
  and Guanxi 59, 296–7
consortia 237
consumption 21–2
  bottom of the pyramid (BoP) segment
    111–16
  car penetration, BRICs 91, *92*
  see also middle class
contract laws 32–3
contract manufacturing 232
contract-based (non-equity) entry strategies
    207, 227–38, *252*
control: entry modes 249–50
corporate governance 129
Corruption Perception Index (CPI) 343

cost factors influencing entry strategies 246,
    248–9
counter purchase 235
countertrade 233–4
cross-licensing agreements 237–8
culture(s)
  contemporary changes affecting 57–61
  cross-cultural training programme
    goals *322*
  definition, characteristics and dimensions
    50–3
  elements 54–7
  high and low context 53–4, *55*
  material 56–7
  and negotiations 258, 261–4,
    288–91, 296–7
  understanding and management of
    differences 50, 59–61, 248
customer relations 319
customer services 313

data sources and analysis 334–6, 349–52
    appendix
  availability and interpretation 336–8
  indices 338–48, 350–1 *appendix*
decisions/decision-making
  factors affecting FDI location *241–2*
  negotiation process 264
  outsourcing 225–6
demographics *see* population
dependency
  on advanced economies 85–90
  power relations in negotiation 268–9,
    283–4
distribution and infrastructure gaps 66–7,
    123–4
distributor selection 313, *314*
  commitment 314–15
  facilitating factors 318
  financial strengths and performance
    315–16
  marketing skills 316–17
  product factors 317–18
Dunbar, E. and Katcher, A. 321–2

Ease of Doing Business Index 341–3, *344*
economic environment
  challenges 84–90
  differences 62–83
economic freedom scores 338–9, *340*
economic and political characteristics
    17–20, 27
economic and political systems 32
education 17, 56
  see also training

efficiency *see* infrastructure; institutional
    voids
efficiency-seeking motives 134–5, 205–6
Egypt *196*, *197*, 199–201
    doing business in 200–1
    economic outlook 199–200
    government influence on business *42*
    negotiation process 305
emerging markets
    classification *3–5*
    common features 14–20
    definition 3–7
    key factors 2–3
    outlook 7–10
    trends *2*
employee training 81, 82, 322–3
employment
    BRIC economies *156*
    integrating population into 84
    stability 313
Enderwick, P. 19, 21, 65, 107, 110, 249, 250
English language 279–80
entry modes and strategies 206–8
    advantages and disadvantages *245*
    contract-based (non-equity) 207,
        227–38, *252*
    dissimilarities in EM environment 204
    factors influencing 244–53
    investment (FDI) 208, 238–44, *252*
    motives 205–6
    trade-based 207, 208–27
environmental responsibility 104–5
ethical issues 38–40
evaluation *see* data sources and analysis
expatriate employees 321–3
expectations in negotiation process 269
export growth 12–13
export management companies (EMCs) and
        export trading companies, distinction
        between 210
exporting 208–9
    direct 211–14
    indirect 209–10

family-owned business groups 74–6
family-owned small and medium sized
        enterprises (SMEs) 83
feasibility reports 216–18
financial crises 12, 18
    Asia 12, 178
    global (2008) 13, 19, 21–2, 148–50
    and reforms 47–50
financial institutions
    Islamic 33
    state-owned *77–8*, 79–81

financial services sector 99, 103
    government involvement in 45–6
financial status
    distributor selection 315–16
    partner selection 310–11
first-mover advantage 250–1
Fleury, A. and Fleury, M.T.L. 59
flexibility in negotiations 265
foreign communities, relationship
        management in 323
Foreign Corrupt Practices Act (FCPA), US 39
foreign distributors *see* distributor
        selection
foreign governments *see* government(s)
foreign investment/foreign direct investment
        (FDI) 13–14, 145–7
    from EMs 131, *132*
    entry modes 208, 238–44, *252*
    financial crises and reforms 47–50, 148–50
    and third parties 65
franchising 229–30

Gadiesh, O. et al. 130
GDP 7–8, *9*, *10*, 17
    BRIC economies 150–2
    Latin America 168, 170
gender inequality, decrease in 101–2
Ghauri, P. 256, 263, 264, 265, 278, 280, 281,
        282, 284, 306
    and Cateora, P. 12, 26, 27, 29, 34, 37, 50,
        55–6, 57, 169, 208, 237, 248, 261,
        262, 263, 286
    and Fang, T. 295–6
    and Holstius, K. 204, 320
    and Usunier, J.C. 54, 257, 276, 306
Ghemawat, P. 62, 110
GINI index 71
global financial crisis *see under* financial
        crises
global sourcing 222–3
global strategy of MNCs 21–5
global tenders, bidding for 214–22
globalization and culture 58
governance, corporate 129
government(s)
    and business groups 74
    ethical issues 38–40
    and MNCs 148
    promotion of industries/companies 118
    protectionism 34–7
    relationship management 320–1
    structural reforms 44–50
greenfield investments 138–9, 146, 243–4
    BRIC economies *151*
growing markets 21–3

Guanxi 59, 296–7
Guillen, M.F. 73

Hall, E. 54, 262–3
and Hall, M. 50, 53–4
hierarchies
business groups 71
and negotiationsq 291
Hill, C.W.L. 31, 32, 33, 37, 55, 56,
234, 240, 243, 246, 323
et al. 232
Hofstede, G. 51–3, 291
Holden, N. 51

Ikle, F.C. 254, 285
IMF *see* International Monetary Fund
income distribution 68–71, 84
BRICs 93–4
India 161–4
consumer research 109–10
culture *60–1*
doing business in 163–4
e-Choupals *115*
economic outlook 161–3
GE Healthcare *65–6*
negotiation process 294–5
Tata Group *75–6*, 81, 82, 111
indices 338–48
individualism 31
and collectivism 30–1, 51,
55, 58–9
Indonesia 184–7
doing business in 186–7
economic outlook 185–6
negotiation process 299–300
informal economy 40–1
informal meetings 270–1
information
evaluation *see* data sources and analysis
role of intermediaries 64, 65
information technology outsourcing (ITO)
224
infrastructure
gaps 66–8
investment 102–3, 148
projects 233
and urbanization 168, *169*, 180
innovation 85–6
institutional voids 63–6
business groups as response to 81–3
and development 84–5
EM firms' experience of 125–6
integrative ('win-win') negotiations 256–7
intellectual property (IP) rights 37–8, 44, 46,
309, 318

intermediaries 64, 65, 125
and exporters 212–13
international business
challenges *247*
key factors affecting 2–3, 25–7
International Monetary Fund (IMF) 7–8, 18,
21, 166, 168–9, 172, 194
financial crises and rescue funds 48
Statistics Database 12–13
international negotiations 255–6
internationalization
EM companies 131–44
strategic alignment for 326–34
internet 57–8, 100–1
investment
infrastructure 102–3, 148
technology 85–90, 104–5
see also foreign investment/foreign direct
investment (FDI)
investment entry modes 208, 238–44, *252*
investment freedom scores 341, *342*
Islamic law 33

joint ventures 238–40
Brazil 157–8
see also partners

Khanna, T.
and Palepu, K. 20, 63, 64, 65,
66, 74, 81, 117, 122–3, 125–6,
128, 140
and Yafeh, Y. 71, 128
Kim, D. et al. 75
knowledge
EM firms 122–5
self-knowledge in negotiations 259
knowledge process outsourcing
(KPO) 224

language 56, 279–80, *283–4*
body 278
see also communication
latecomer advantages 127, 251–2
Latin America 167–70
major strengths and
weaknesses *171*
negotiation process 302–4
see also Chile; Mexico; Peru
legal and political systems 32–44, 260
liability of foreigness (LoF) 248–9
licensing 228, *229*
cross-licensing agreements 237–8
logistics performance index 68, *69*
London, T. and Hart, S.L. 112, 118
low-carbon investments 104–5

Magnus, G. 7, 12, 19, 24, 25, 47, 131, 133,
   134, 139
Malaysia 187–9
   doing business in 188–9
   economic outlook 187–8
   negotiation process 299
management contracts 231–2
managerial capabilities 128–30
manufacturing bases (MNEs) 23–5
manufacturing-related joint ventures 312
market
   characteristics 20
   entry *see* entry modes and strategies
   knowledge 122–3
Market Opportunities Index (MOI)
   345, *346*, 348
Market Potential Index (MPI) *347*
market-seeking motives 133, 205
market-specific strengths 330
marketing capabilities/skills 130–1, 311–12,
   316–17
marketing subsidiaries 238
material culture 56–7
Mercosur 169
mergers and acquisitions (M&A) 134, 139,
   140–4, 146
Mexico 170–4
   doing business in 173–4
   economic outlook 172–3
   negotiation process 302–3
microfinance 99
mid-sized cities, growth of 94–8
middle class 84
   consumption 92–105
   and opportunities 105–11
mixed economic systems 32
multinational enterprises/companies
   (MNEs/MNCs) 13, 20
global strategy 21–5
spill-over effects and technology
   transfer 86–7

national governments *see* government(s)
negotiation framework 265–76
negotiation process 254–8
   communication 263–4, 276–80, 296–7
   outcome 275–6
   preparing for success 258
   self-knowledge 259
   team members 280–1
   understanding partners 259–65
negotiation stages 269
   1: offer 270
   2: informal meetings 270–1
   3: strategy formulation 271–2

negotiation stages *cont.*
   4: face-to-face 272–4
   5: implementation 274–5
negotiations
   bidding for global tenders 220–1
   cultural issues 258, 261–4, 288–91, 296–7
   power relations 268–9, 283–4
   relationship building and management
      276–81, 286–7, 318–23
      Africa 304–5
      Asia 298–302
      BRIC economies 292–8
      Turkey 305–6
negotiators 267–8
   characteristics 285–7
   strategies 281–5
networks 58–9
   business groups 71
   EM firms 126
New Frontier Economies
   brands in Global 500 *119*
   BRIC economies and 5–7
   consumptions expenditure *97*
   see also Africa; Asia; Latin America; *named
      countries*
non-equity collaborative ventures 235–6
non-equity (contract-based) entry strategies
   207, 227–38, *252*
non-verbal communication 56, 277–8

offset 235
offshore outsourcing 224–5
organizational learning 136
organizational resources 312–13
outsourcing 23–5, 223–5
   decision 225–6
   global sourcing and 222–3
   relationship management 226–7
ownership in business groups 74–81

Pakistan 191–4
   doing business in 193–4
   economic outlook 192–3
   negotiation process 300–1
   privatization of state-owned financial
      institutions *77–8*
partners
   negotiation process 259–65
   relationship management 318–19
   selection 308
      partner-related criteria 308–10
      task-related criteria 310–13
Peru 174–6
   doing business in 176
   economic outlook 174–5

Peru *cont.*
  negotiation process 303
Philippines 189–91
  doing business in 190–1
  economic outlook 190
  negotiation process 301–2
political and economic characteristics
    17–20, 27
political risk insurance (PRI) 43
political risks 33–4, 41–3
political and social factors in
    negotiations 260–1
political systems 29–32
  and economic systems 32
  and legal systems 32–44, 260
  types 30–1
population
  ageing 16, 160
  characteristics 14–17
  integration into employment 84
  younger 100–1
power relations in negotiations
    268–9, 283–4
privatization of state-owned enterprises
    (SOEs) 35, 76–8
problem-solving approach to
    negotiations 265
product factors
  company capabilities 329–30
  distributor selection 317–18
property rights *see* intellectual
    property (IP) rights
protectionism 34–7

R&D capabilities 135–6, 311
R&D investment 87–9
regional trade 147
relationship management
  outsourcing 226–7
  see also under negotiations
religion and value systems 55–6
resource-seeking motives
    133–4, 206
rural development 98
Russia 158–61
  doing business in 160–1
  economic outlook 159–60
  negotiation process 293–4

savings 84–5
  China 165–6
self-knowledge in
    negotiations 259
services sector 99
Sheth, J.N. and Parvatiyar, A. 307

social class
  and social mobility 55
  see also bottom of the pyramid (BoP)
    segment; middle class
social structure 54–5
socialism 30–1
South Africa 195–9
  doing business in 198–9
  economic outlook 195–8
  negotiation process 304–5
south-to-north FDI 140–4
south-to-south FDI 139–40, *141*
sovereign wealth funds (SWFs) 48–50
spill-over effects 86–7
state capitalism 48–9
  and sovereign wealth funds (SWFs) 48–50
state-owned enterprises (SOEs) 18, 19, 75,
    76–81
  competitive bidding 219
  internationalization of 136–7, *138*, 139,
    140–4
  privatization of 35, 76–8
strategic alliances 236–7
strategic factors in negotiations 264
structural reforms 44–50
subcontracting 232
subcultures 58
supply chains and infrastructure gaps 67–8

technology
  and agriculture, India *115*
  cross-licensing agreements 237–8
  and economic culture 56–7
  information and multimedia 334, *335*
  information technology outsourcing
    (ITO) 224
  internet 57–8, 100–1
  investment 85–90, 104–5
  latecomer advantages 127
  low-carbon 104–5
  and marketing capabilities 130–1
  and telecommunications 100–1
technology transfer 86–7, 231
Thailand 182–4
  doing business in 184
  economic outlook 183–4
  negotiation process 298–9
third parties
  foreign investors and 65
  negotiation framework 267
time
  monochromic and polychromic 54, 291
  negotiation process 262–3, 291
timing of entry 250
totalitarianism 31

trade agreements 10–12
trade and foreign investment 10–14
trade reforms 46–7
trade restrictiveness indices 341, *343*
trade volumes 145, *146*, 147
trade-based entry strategies 207, 208–27
training
    employees 81, 82, 322–3
    see also education
Transparency Index 343
Turkey *196*, *197*, 201–3
    doing business in 202–3
    economic outlook 202
    negotiation process 305–6
turnkey projects 232–3

UNCTAD 13, 24, 224, 227, 230, 232
United States (US)
    cultural borrowing 57
    Foreign Corrupt Practices Act (FCPA) 39
    and Mexico 171–2
    and Philippines 189–90

urbanization 15, 91, 102–3
    growth of mid-sized cities 94–8
    and infrastructure 168, *169*, 180

value systems 55–6

wholly-owned entry strategies 240–1
    factors affecting location decisions
        241–2
'win-win' (integrative) negotiations
        256–7
World Bank 8, 14, 40, 87, 125, 131, 139,
        165, 170, 174, 177
    Database *71*
    Ease of Doing Business Index
        341–3, *344*
    logistics performance index 68, *69*
World Competitiveness Index 343
World Trade Organization (WTO) 11–12, 13,
        18, 41, 161, 172, 183

younger populations 100–1